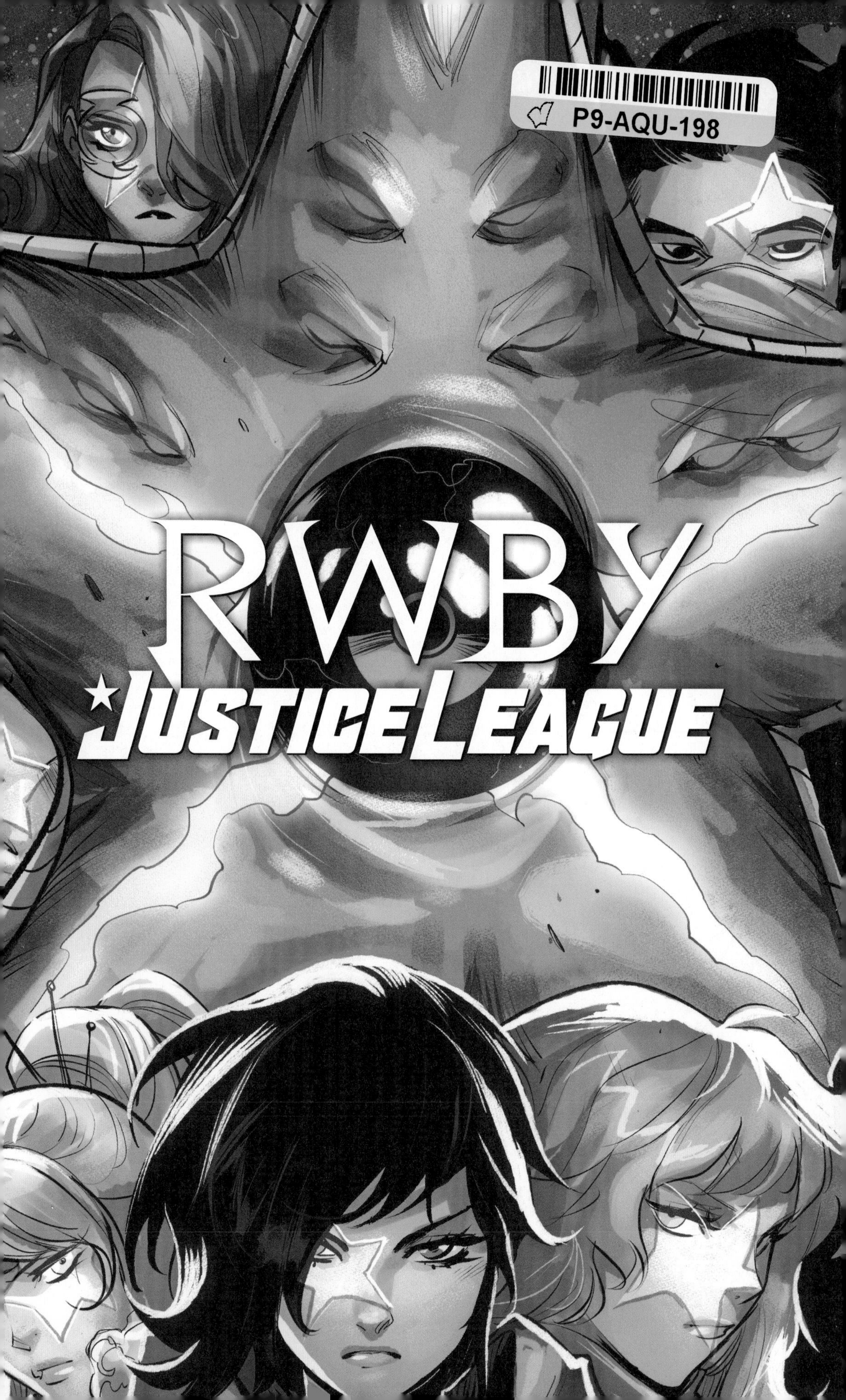
RWBY
JUSTICE LEAGUE

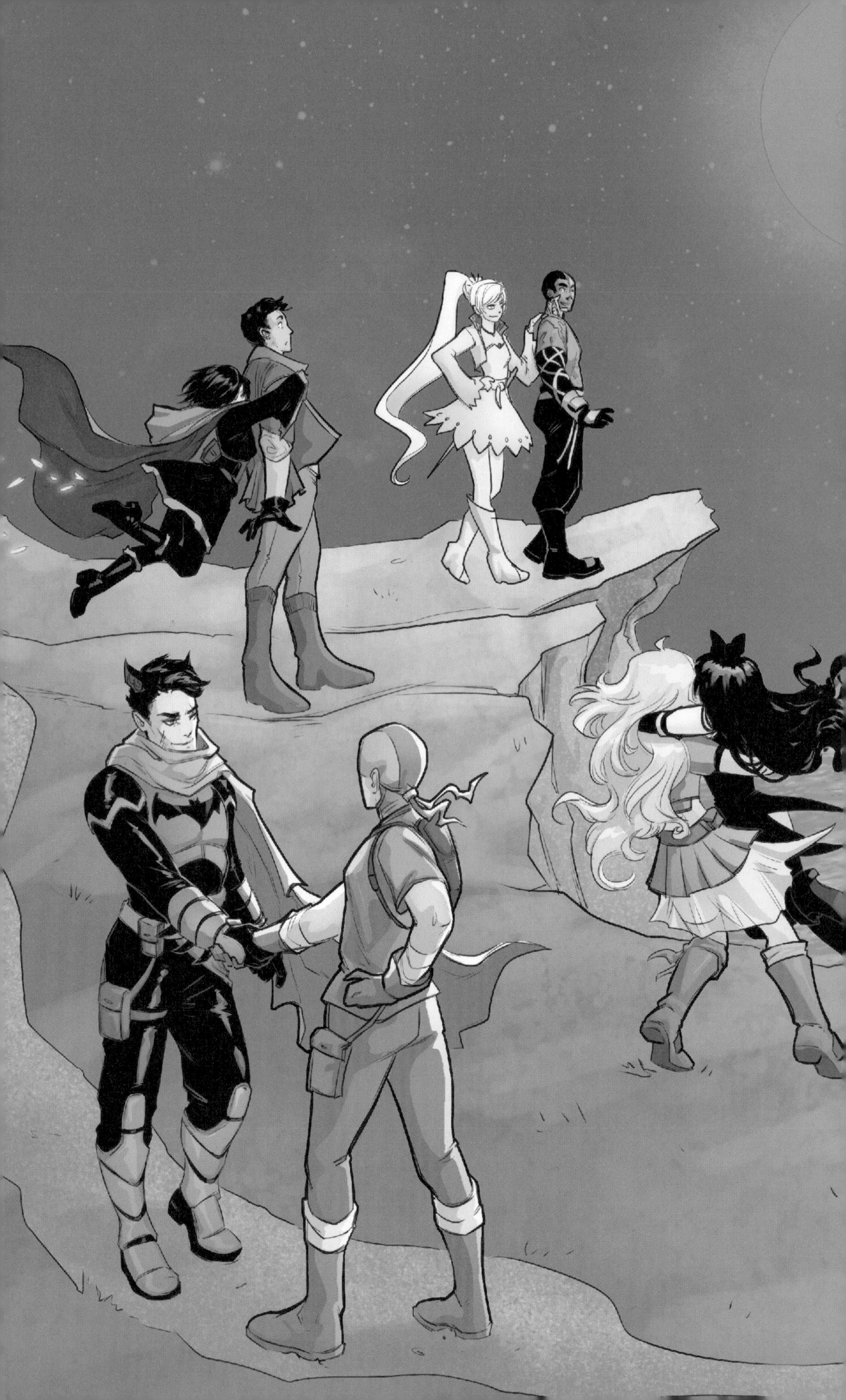

RWBY

Justice League

MARGUERITE **BENNETT**
writer

ANEKE
STEPHANIE **PEPPER**
EMANUELA **LUPACCHINO**
MEGHAN **HETRICK**
pencillers

ANEKE
STEPHANIE **PEPPER**
WADE **VON GRAWBADGER**
MEGHAN **HETRICK**
inkers

HI-FI
colorist

GABRIELA **DOWNIE**
BECCA **CAREY**
letterers

MIRKA **ANDOLFO**
collection cover artist

SUPERMAN created by
JERRY **SIEGEL** and JOE **SHUSTER**.
By special arrangement with
the Jerry Siegel Family.

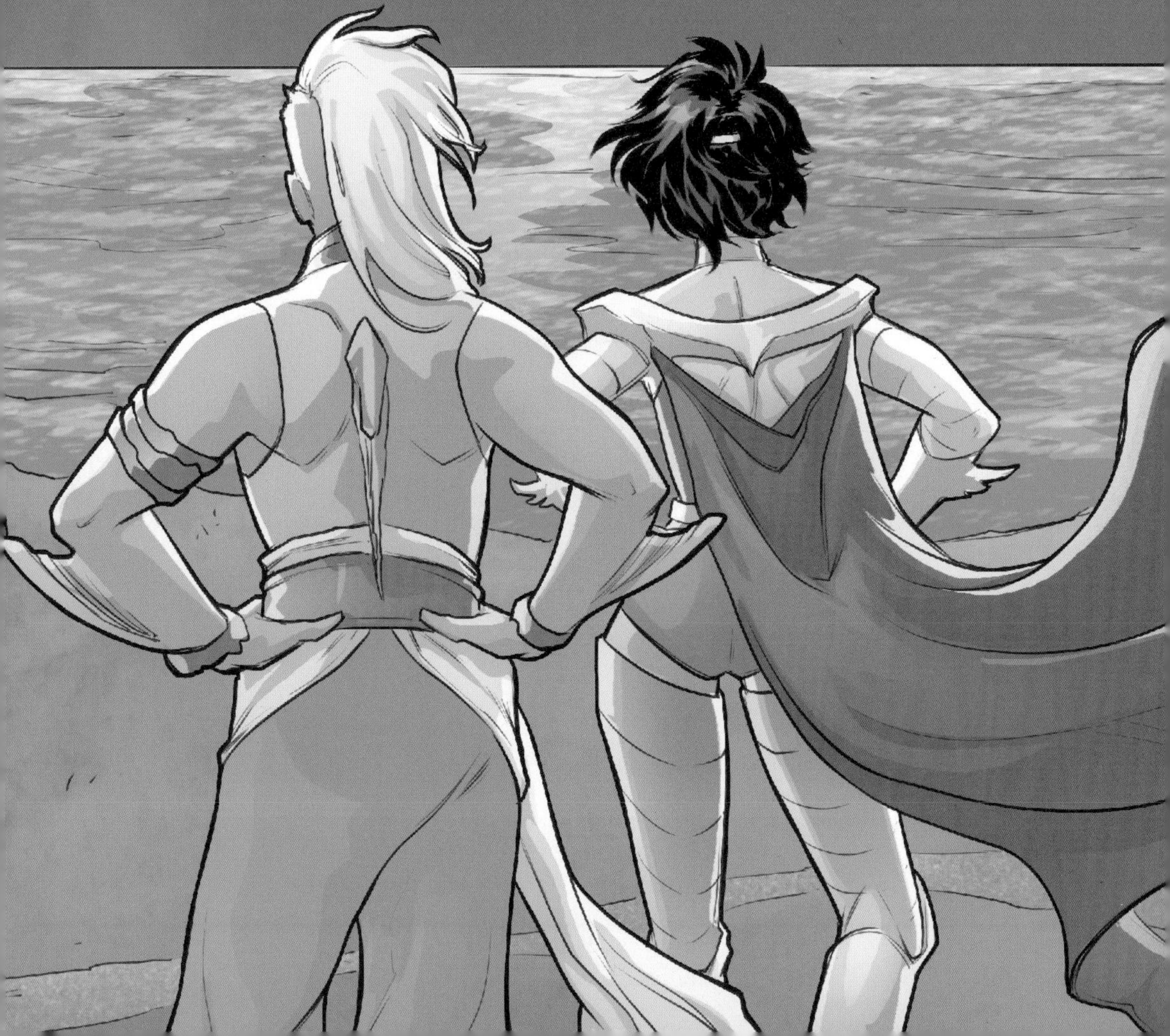

ANDREW MARINO Editor – Original Series & Collected Edition
STEVE COOK Design Director – Books
DAMIAN RYLAND Publication Design
DANIELLE RAMONDELLI Publication Production

MARIE JAVINS Editor-in-Chief, DC Comics

ANNE DePIES Senior VP – General Manager
JIM LEE Publisher & Chief Creative Officer
DON FALLETTI VP – Manufacturing Operations & Workflow Management
LAWRENCE GANEM VP – Talent Services
ALISON GILL Senior VP – Manufacturing & Operations
JEFFREY KAUFMAN VP – Editorial Strategy & Programming
NICK J. NAPOLITANO VP – Manufacturing Administration & Design
NANCY SPEARS VP – Revenue

RWBY/JUSTICE LEAGUE

DC Comics, 2900 West Alameda Ave., Burbank, CA 91505
Printed by Solisco Printers, Scott, QC, Canada. 4/8/22. First Printing. ISBN: 978-1-77951-530-8.

Library of Congress Cataloging-in-Publication Data is available.

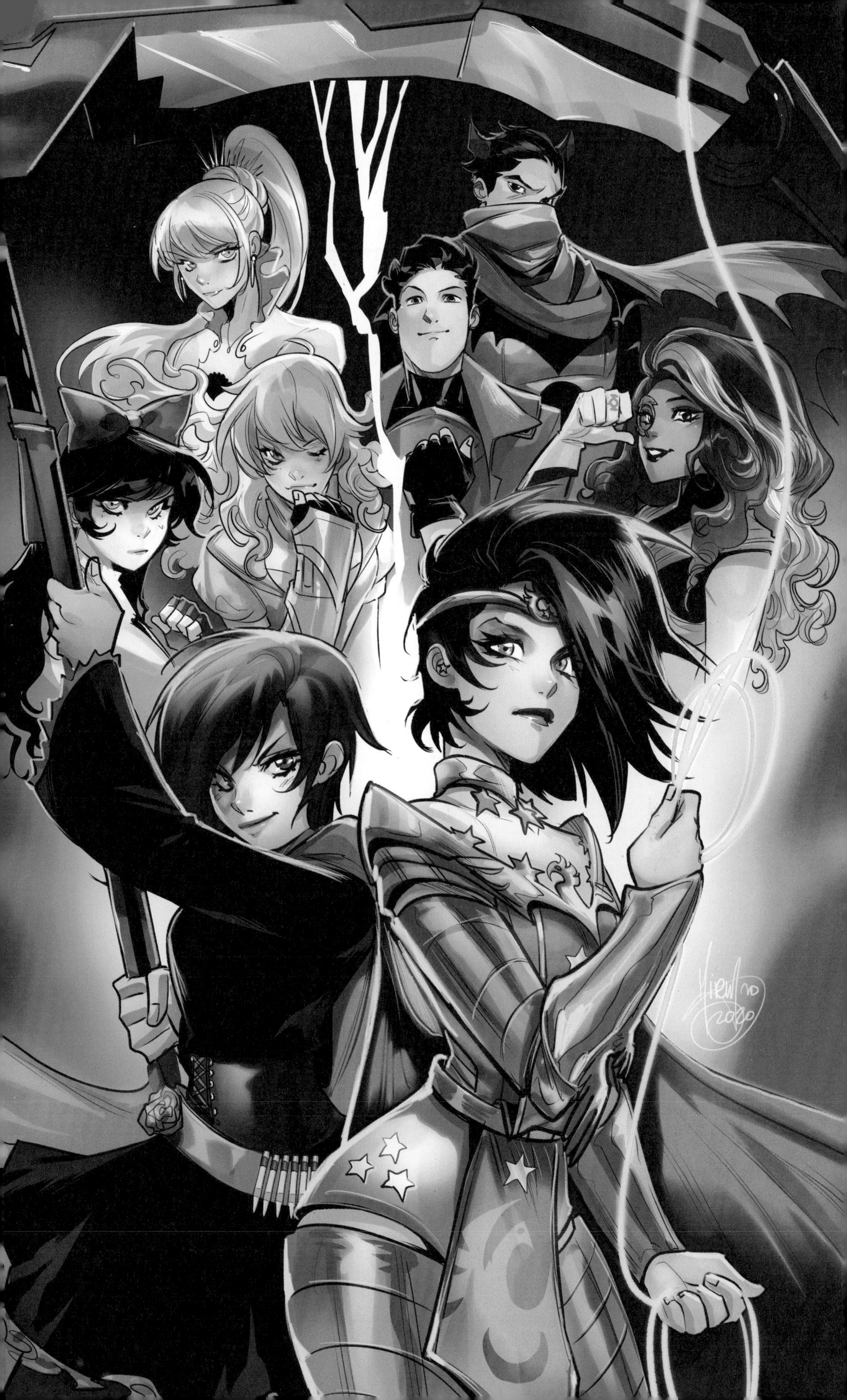

Variant cover by **SIMONE DI MEO**

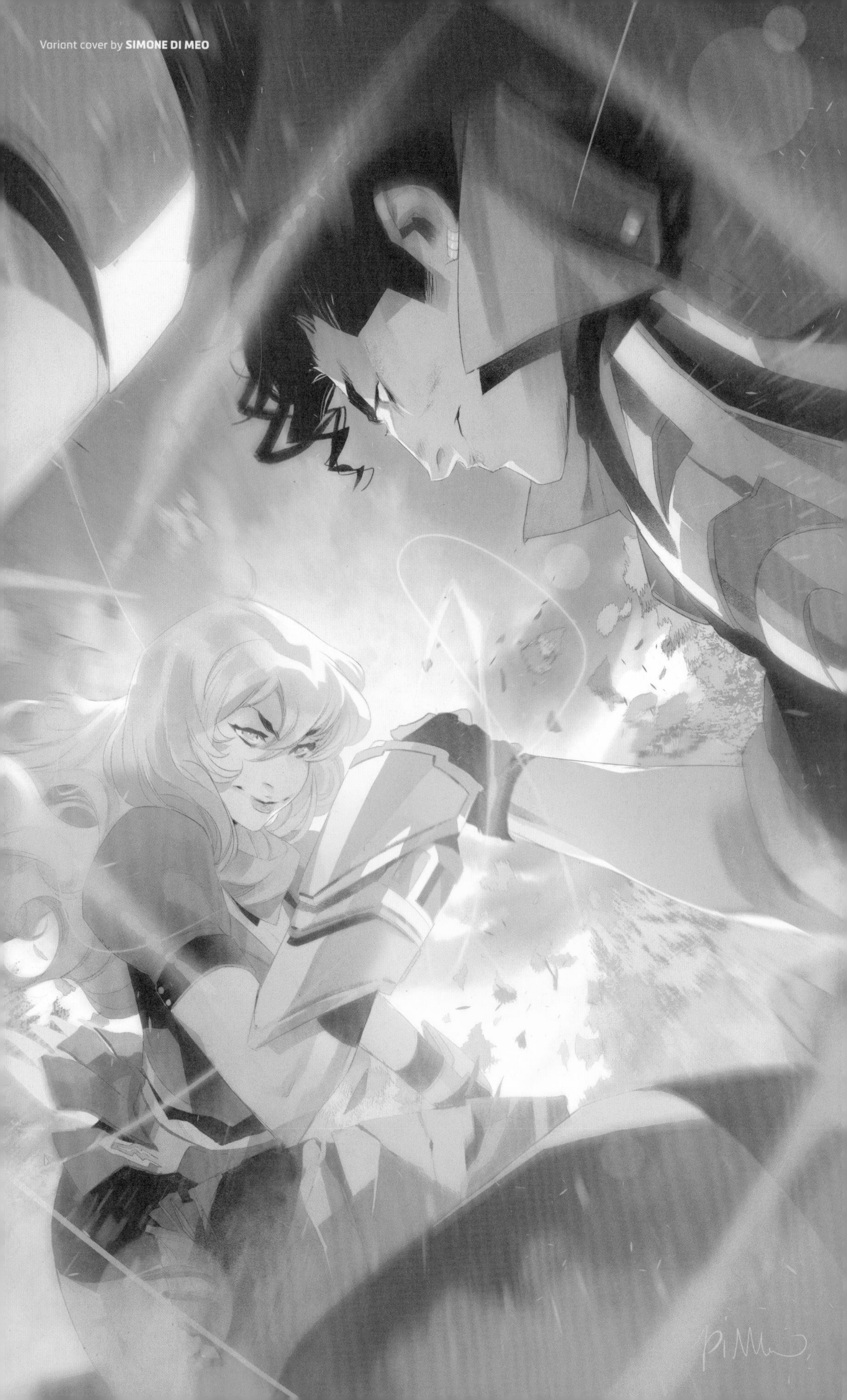

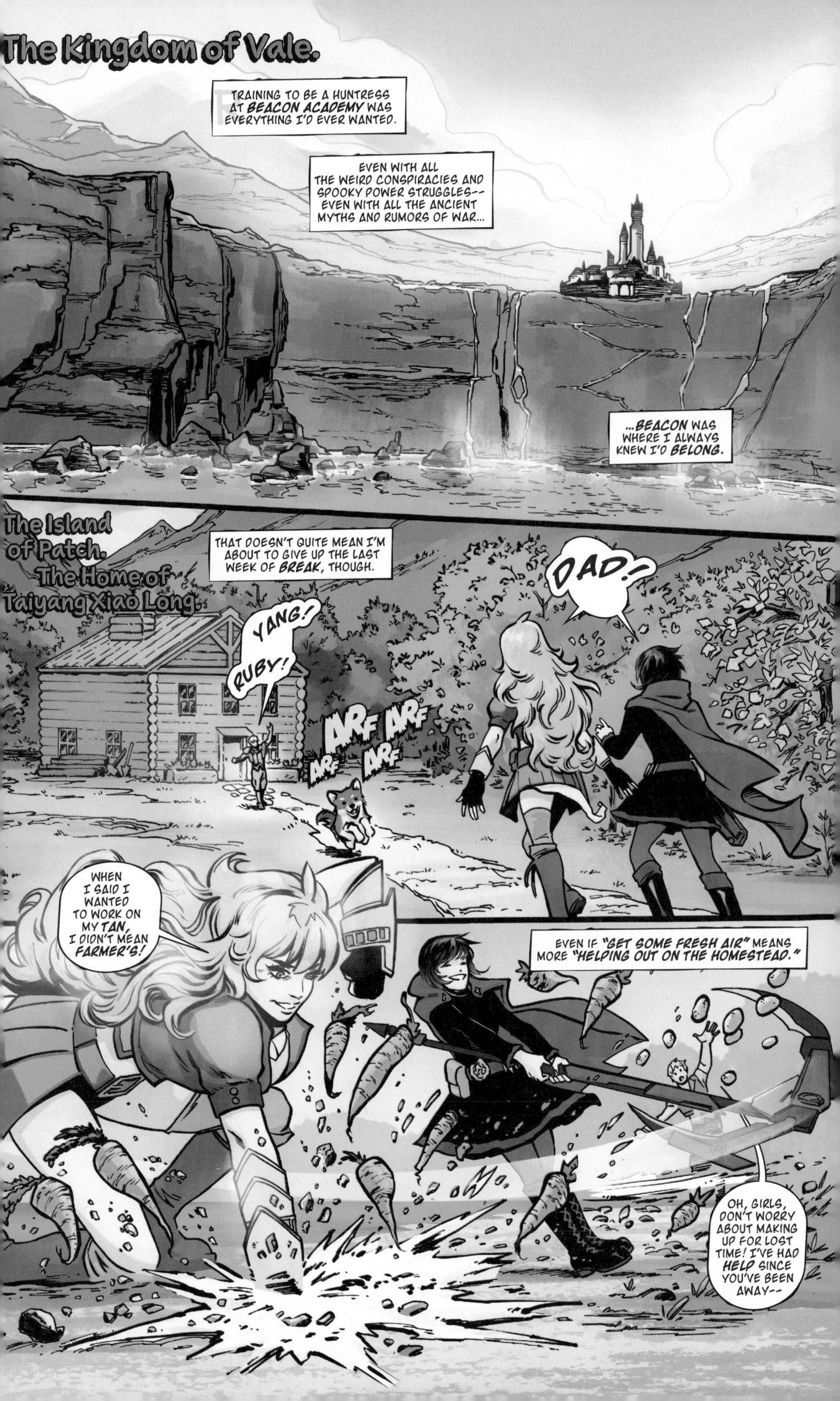
The Kingdom of Vale.
TRAINING TO BE A HUNTRESS AT BEACON ACADEMY WAS EVERYTHING I'D EVER WANTED.
EVEN WITH ALL THE WEIRD CONSPIRACIES AND SPOOKY POWER STRUGGLES-- EVEN WITH ALL THE ANCIENT MYTHS AND RUMORS OF WAR...
...BEACON WAS WHERE I ALWAYS KNEW I'D BELONG.
The Island of Patch. The Home of Taiyang Xiao Long.
THAT DOESN'T QUITE MEAN I'M ABOUT TO GIVE UP THE LAST WEEK OF BREAK, THOUGH.
DAD!
YANG!
RUBY!
ARF ARF
ARF ARF
WHEN I SAID I WANTED TO WORK ON MY TAN, I DIDN'T MEAN FARMER'S!
EVEN IF "GET SOME FRESH AIR" MEANS MORE "HELPING OUT ON THE HOMESTEAD."
OH, GIRLS, DON'T WORRY ABOUT MAKING UP FOR LOST TIME! I'VE HAD HELP SINCE YOU'VE BEEN AWAY--

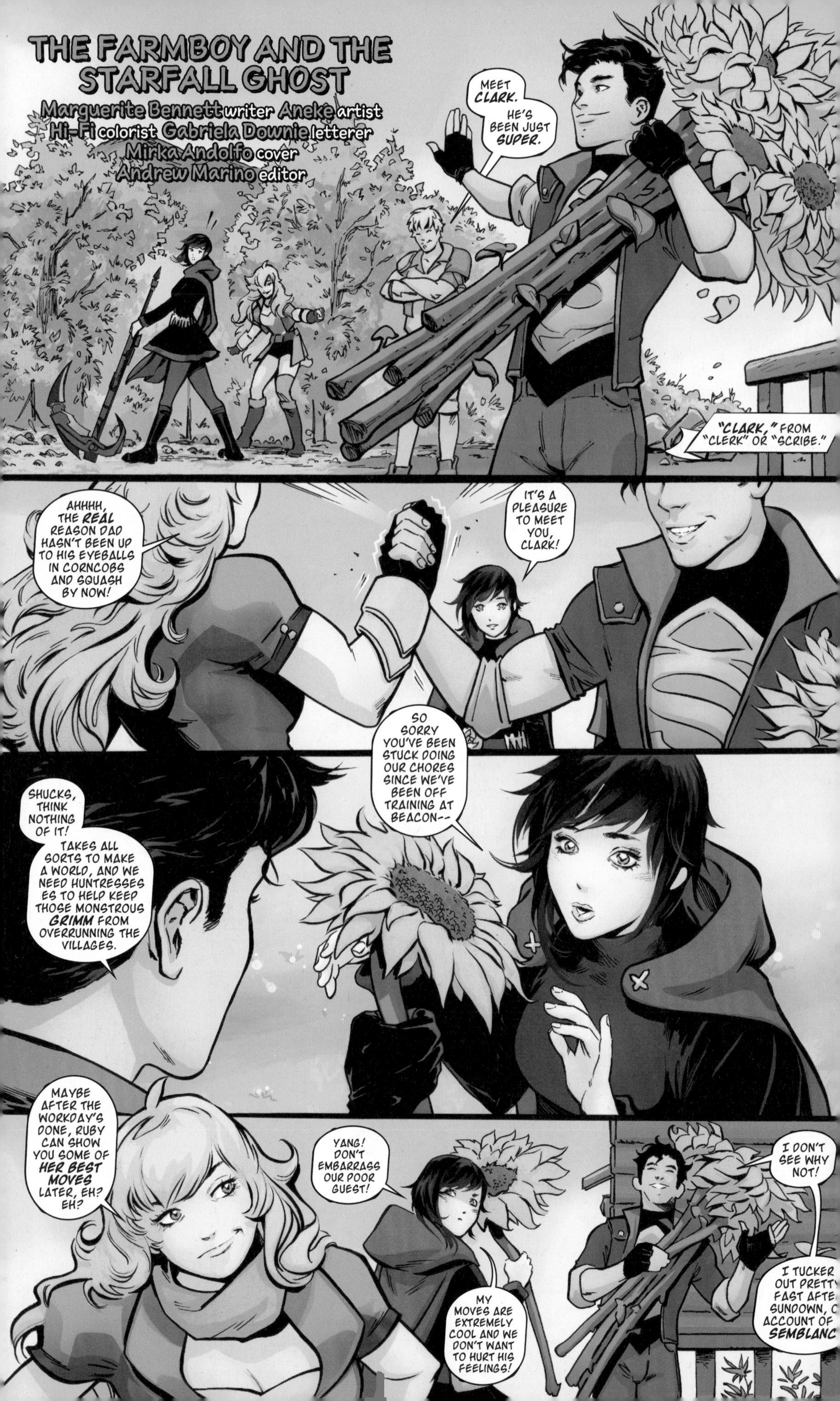
THE FARMBOY AND THE STARFALL GHOST
Marguerite Bennett writer Aneke artist
Hi-Fi colorist Gabriela Downie letterer
Mirka Andolfo cover
Andrew Marino editor
MEET CLARK.
HE'S BEEN JUST SUPER.
"CLARK," FROM "CLERK" OR "SCRIBE."
AHHHH, THE REAL REASON DAD HASN'T BEEN UP TO HIS EYEBALLS IN CORNCOBS AND SQUASH BY NOW!
IT'S A PLEASURE TO MEET YOU, CLARK!
SO SORRY YOU'VE BEEN STUCK DOING OUR CHORES SINCE WE'VE BEEN OFF TRAINING AT BEACON--
SHUCKS, THINK NOTHING OF IT!
TAKES ALL SORTS TO MAKE A WORLD, AND WE NEED HUNTRESSES ES TO HELP KEEP THOSE MONSTROUS GRIMM FROM OVERRUNNING THE VILLAGES.
MAYBE AFTER THE WORKDAY'S DONE, RUBY CAN SHOW YOU SOME OF HER BEST MOVES LATER, EH? EH?
YANG! DON'T EMBARRASS OUR POOR GUEST!
MY MOVES ARE EXTREMELY COOL AND WE DON'T WANT TO HURT HIS FEELINGS!
I DON'T SEE WHY NOT!
I TUCKER OUT PRETT FAST AFTE SUNDOWN, C ACCOUNT OF SEMBLANC

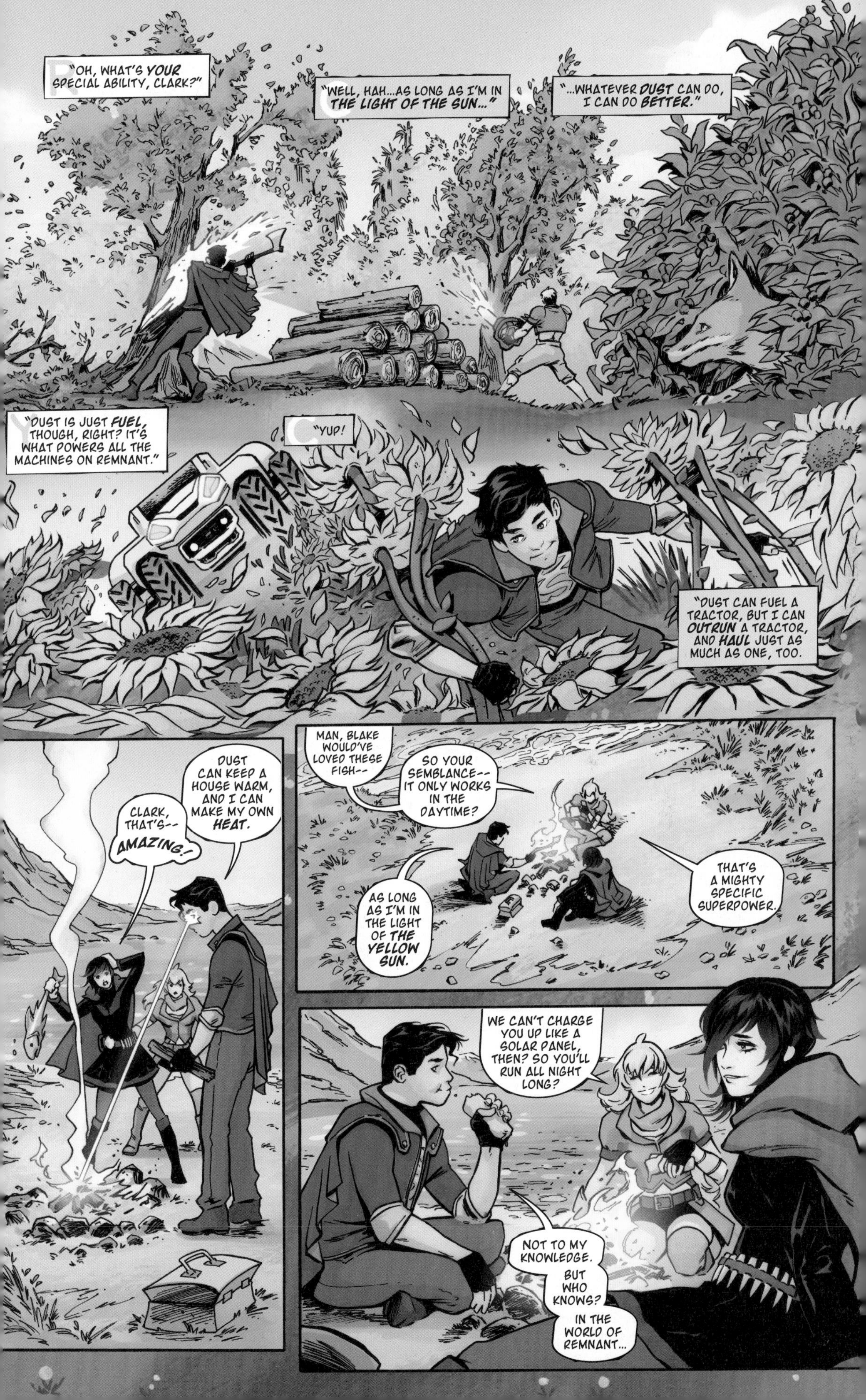
"OH, WHAT'S YOUR SPECIAL ABILITY, CLARK?"
"WELL, HAH...AS LONG AS I'M IN THE LIGHT OF THE SUN..."
"...WHATEVER DUST CAN DO, I CAN DO BETTER."
"DUST IS JUST FUEL, THOUGH, RIGHT? IT'S WHAT POWERS ALL THE MACHINES ON REMNANT."
"YUP!
"DUST CAN FUEL A TRACTOR, BUT I CAN OUTRUN A TRACTOR, AND HAUL JUST AS MUCH AS ONE, TOO.
DUST CAN KEEP A HOUSE WARM, AND I CAN MAKE MY OWN HEAT.
CLARK, THAT'S-- AMAZING!
MAN, BLAKE WOULD'VE LOVED THESE FISH--
SO YOUR SEMBLANCE-- IT ONLY WORKS IN THE DAYTIME?
AS LONG AS I'M IN THE LIGHT OF THE YELLOW SUN.
THAT'S A MIGHTY SPECIFIC SUPERPOWER.
WE CAN'T CHARGE YOU UP LIKE A SOLAR PANEL, THEN? SO YOU'LL RUN ALL NIGHT LONG?
NOT TO MY KNOWLEDGE.
BUT WHO KNOWS?
IN THE WORLD OF REMNANT...

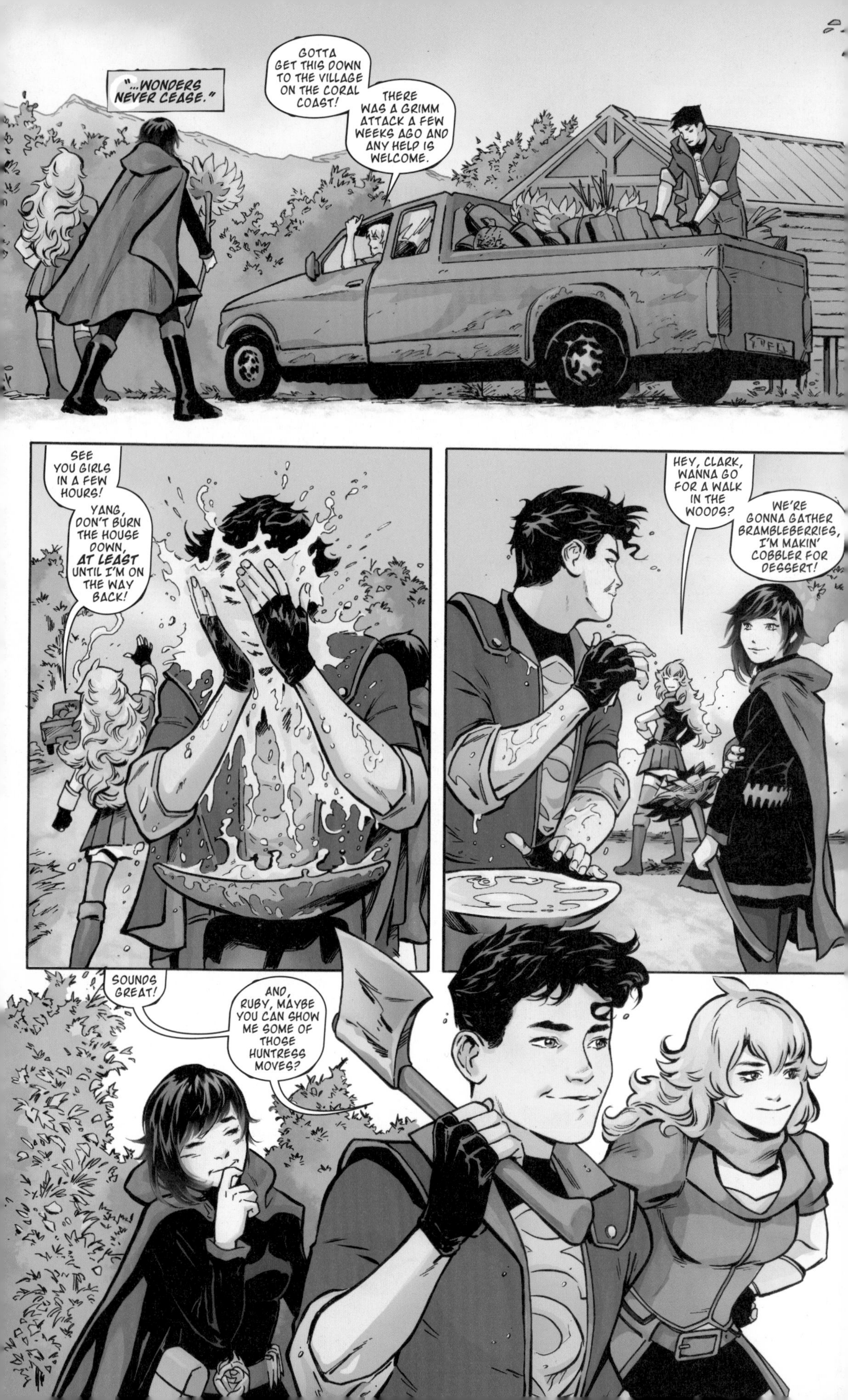
"...WONDERS NEVER CEASE."
GOTTA GET THIS DOWN TO THE VILLAGE ON THE CORAL COAST!
THERE WAS A GRIMM ATTACK A FEW WEEKS AGO AND ANY HELP IS WELCOME.
SEE YOU GIRLS IN A FEW HOURS!
YANG, DON'T BURN THE HOUSE DOWN, AT LEAST UNTIL I'M ON THE WAY BACK!
HEY, CLARK, WANNA GO FOR A WALK IN THE WOODS?
WE'RE GONNA GATHER BRAMBLEBERRIES, I'M MAKIN' COBBLER FOR DESSERT!
SOUNDS GREAT!
AND, RUBY, MAYBE YOU CAN SHOW ME SOME OF THOSE HUNTRESS MOVES?

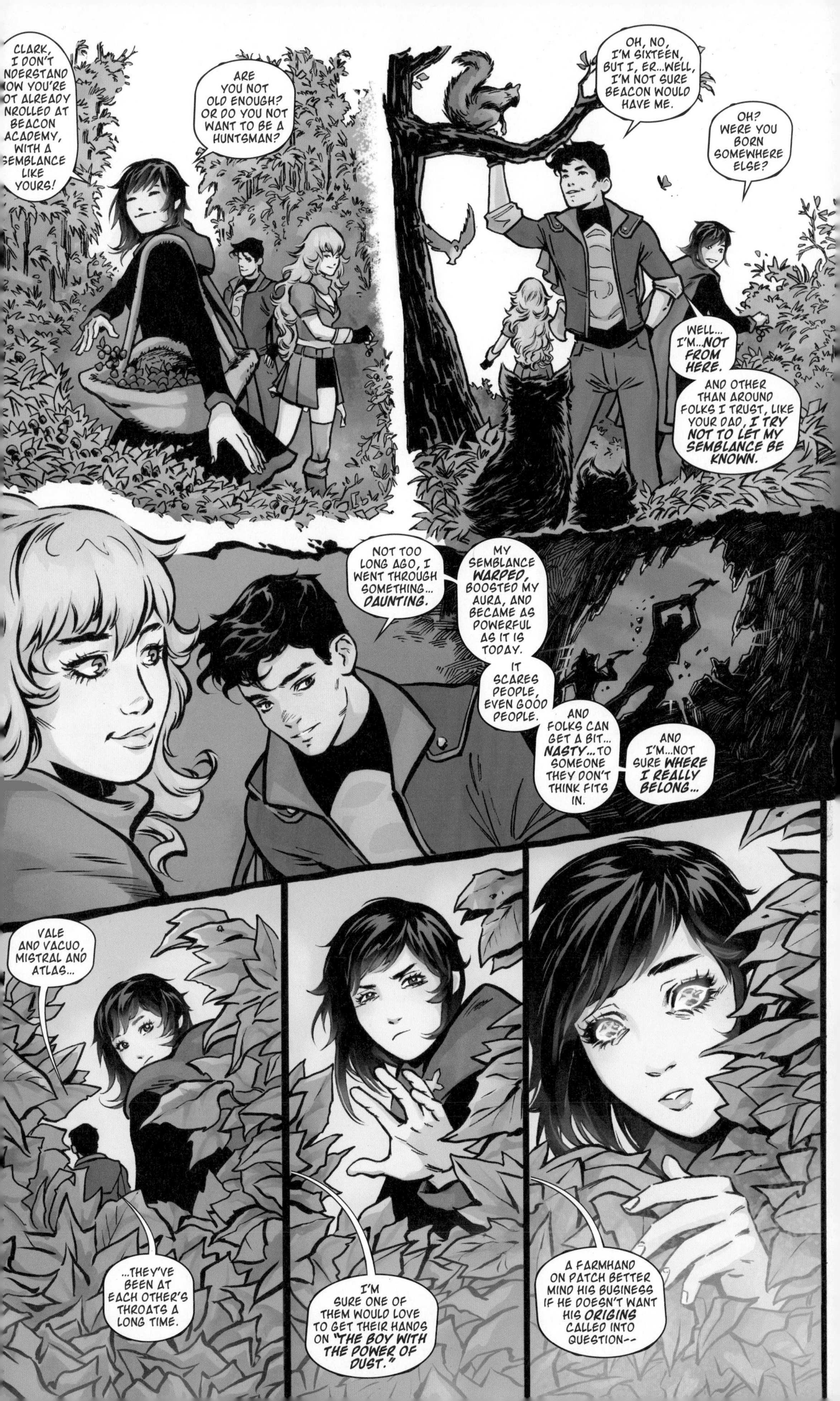
CLARK, I DON'T NDERSTAND OW YOU'RE OT ALREADY NROLLED AT BEACON ACADEMY, WITH A EMBLANCE LIKE YOURS!
ARE YOU NOT OLD ENOUGH? OR DO YOU NOT WANT TO BE A HUNTSMAN?
OH, NO, I'M SIXTEEN, BUT I, ER...WELL, I'M NOT SURE BEACON WOULD HAVE ME.
OH? WERE YOU BORN SOMEWHERE ELSE?
WELL... I'M...NOT FROM HERE.
AND OTHER THAN AROUND FOLKS I TRUST, LIKE YOUR DAD, I TRY NOT TO LET MY SEMBLANCE BE KNOWN.
NOT TOO LONG AGO, I WENT THROUGH SOMETHING... DAUNTING.
MY SEMBLANCE WARPED, BOOSTED MY AURA, AND BECAME AS POWERFUL AS IT IS TODAY.
IT SCARES PEOPLE, EVEN GOOD PEOPLE.
AND FOLKS CAN GET A BIT... NASTY...TO SOMEONE THEY DON'T THINK FITS IN.
AND I'M...NOT SURE WHERE I REALLY BELONG...
VALE AND VACUO, MISTRAL AND ATLAS...
...THEY'VE BEEN AT EACH OTHER'S THROATS A LONG TIME.
I'M SURE ONE OF THEM WOULD LOVE TO GET THEIR HANDS ON "THE BOY WITH THE POWER OF DUST."
A FARMHAND ON PATCH BETTER MIND HIS BUSINESS IF HE DOESN'T WANT HIS ORIGINS CALLED INTO QUESTION--

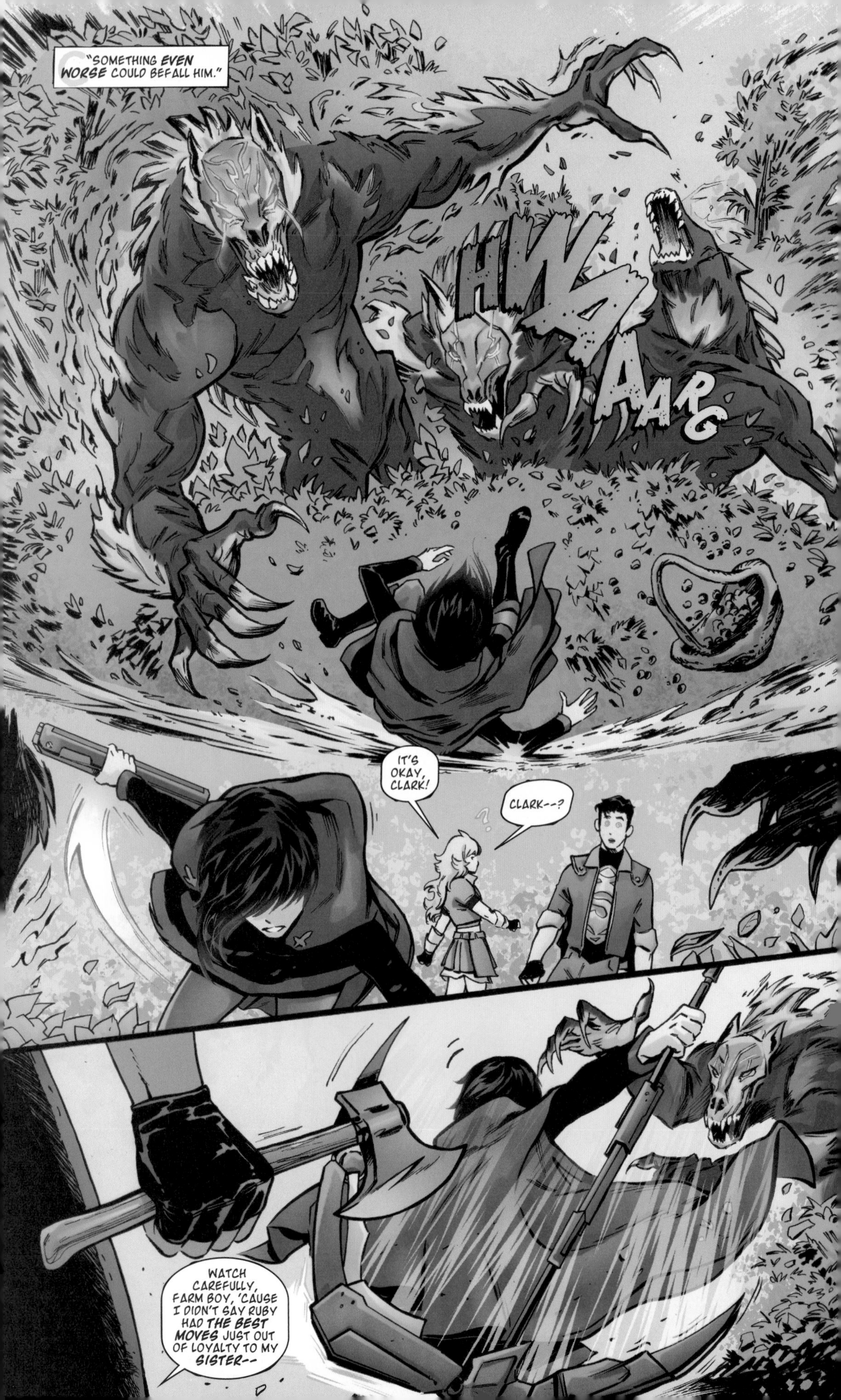
"SOMETHING EVEN WORSE COULD BEFALL HIM."
HWSAARG
IT'S OKAY, CLARK!
?
CLARK--?
WATCH CAREFULLY, FARM BOY, 'CAUSE I DIDN'T SAY RUBY HAD THE BEST MOVES JUST OUT OF LOYALTY TO MY SISTER--

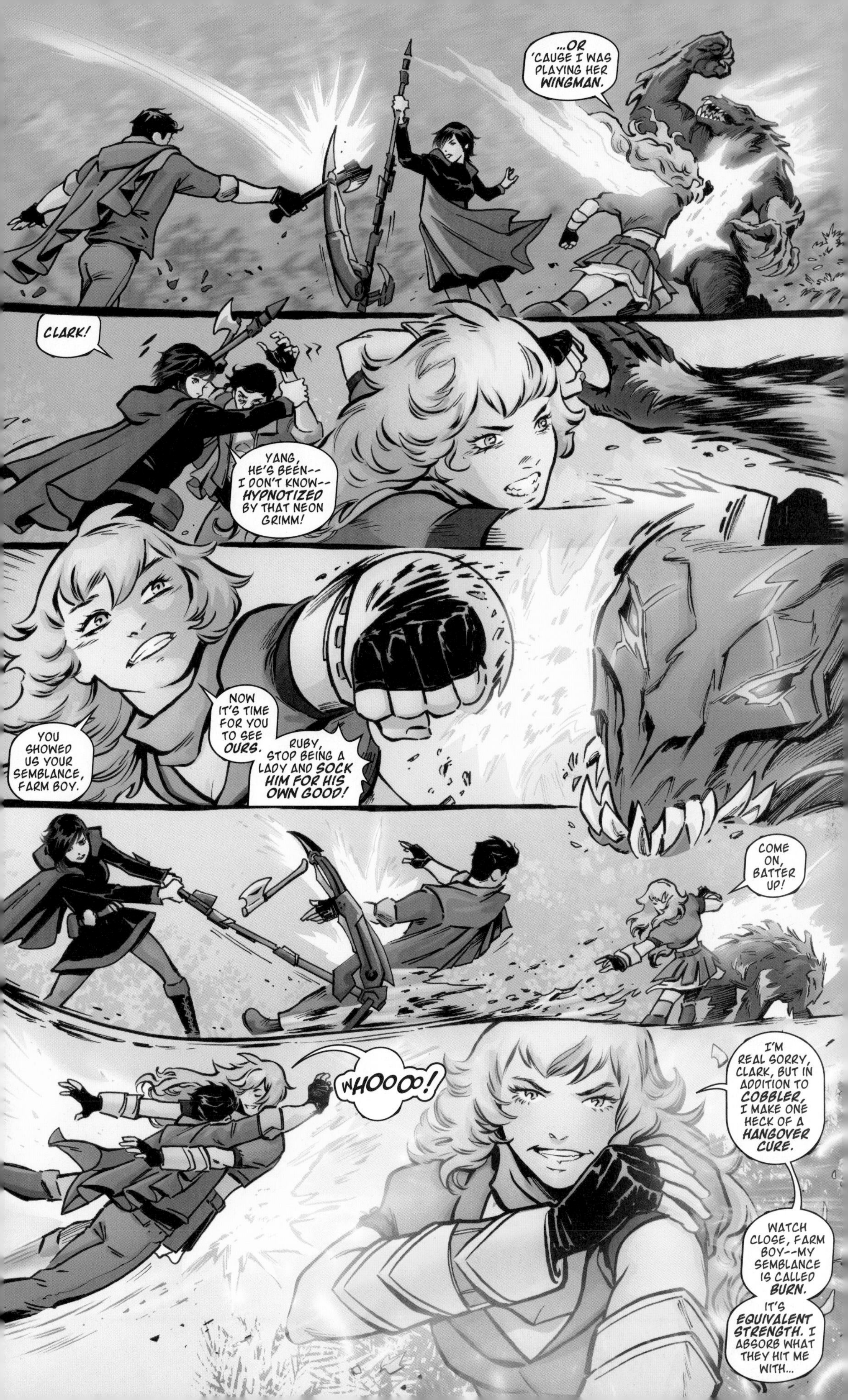

...OR 'CAUSE I WAS PLAYING HER WINGMAN.
CLARK!
YANG, HE'S BEEN-- I DON'T KNOW-- HYPNOTIZED BY THAT NEON GRIMM!
YOU SHOWED US YOUR SEMBLANCE, FARM BOY.
NOW IT'S TIME FOR YOU TO SEE OURS.
RUBY, STOP BEING A LADY AND SOCK HIM FOR HIS OWN GOOD!
COME ON, BATTER UP!
WHOOOO!
I'M REAL SORRY, CLARK, BUT IN ADDITION TO COBBLER, I MAKE ONE HECK OF A HANGOVER CURE.
WATCH CLOSE, FARM BOY--MY SEMBLANCE IS CALLED BURN.
IT'S EQUIVALENT STRENGTH. I ABSORB WHAT THEY HIT ME WITH...

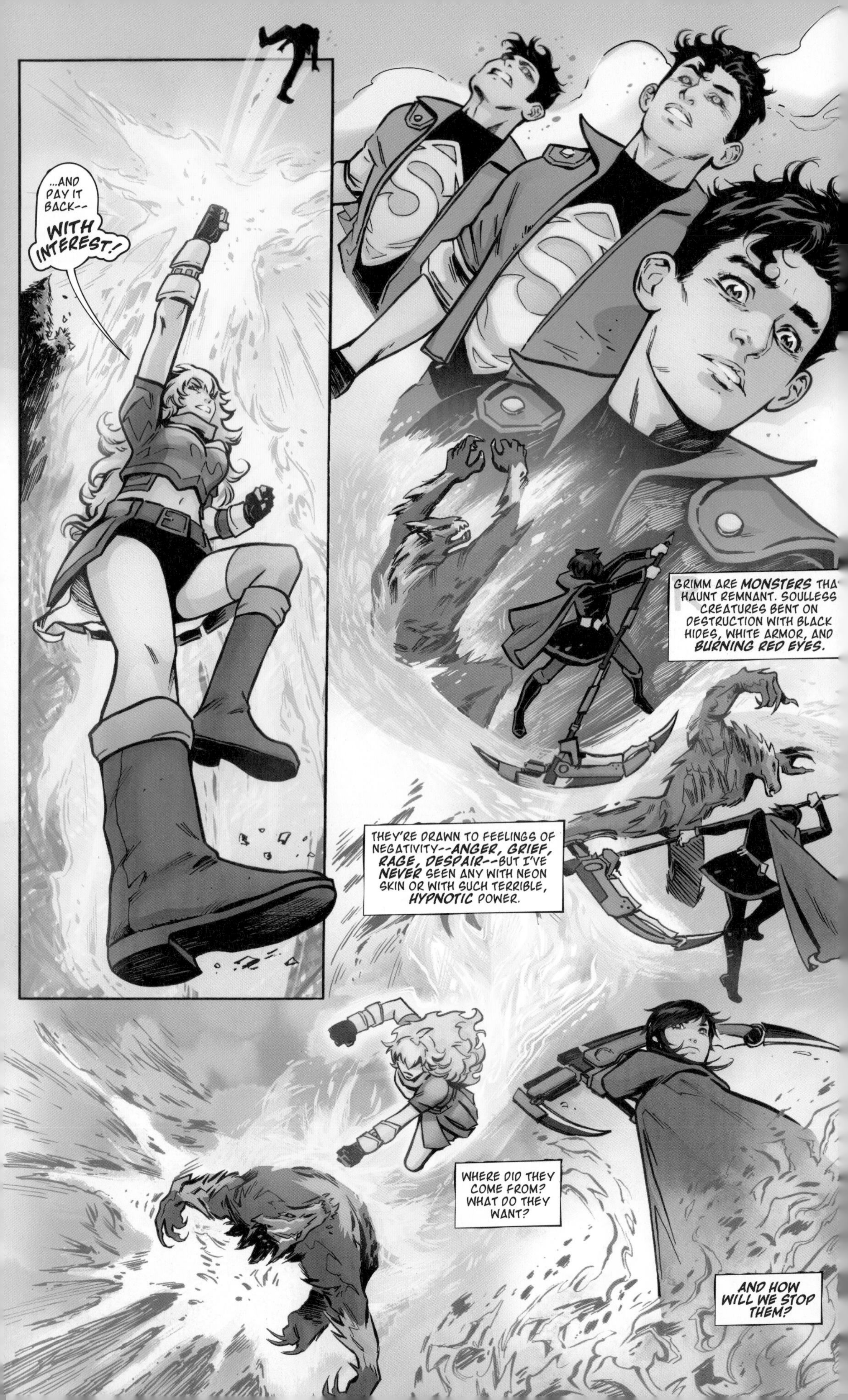
...AND PAY IT BACK-- WITH INTEREST!
GRIMM ARE MONSTERS THA HAUNT REMNANT. SOULLESS CREATURES BENT ON DESTRUCTION WITH BLACK HIDES, WHITE ARMOR, AND BURNING RED EYES.
THEY'RE DRAWN TO FEELINGS OF NEGATIVITY--ANGER, GRIEF, RAGE, DESPAIR--BUT I'VE NEVER SEEN ANY WITH NEON SKIN OR WITH SUCH TERRIBLE, HYPNOTIC POWER.
WHERE DID THEY COME FROM? WHAT DO THEY WANT?
AND HOW WILL WE STOP THEM?

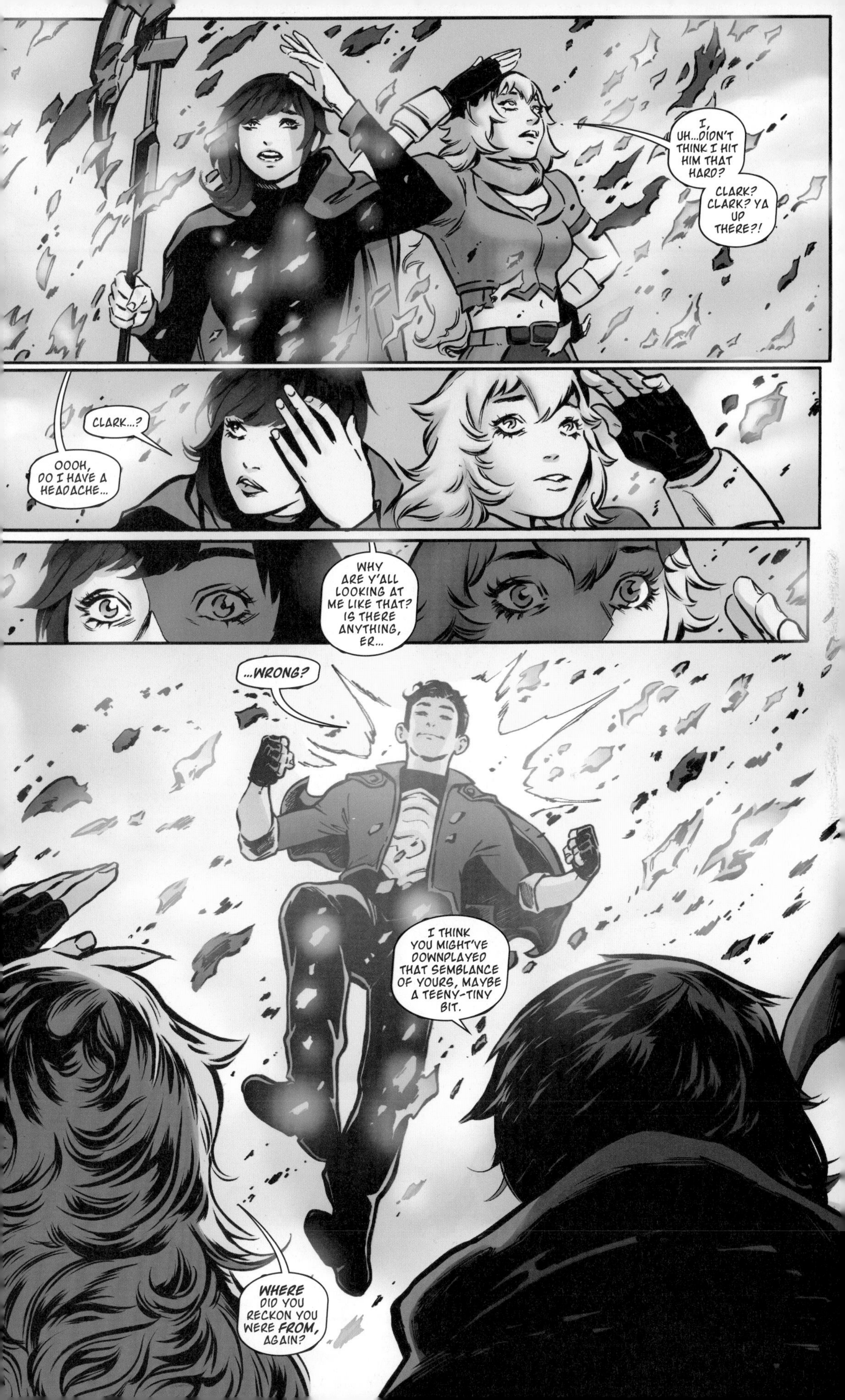
I, UH...DIDN'T THINK I HIT HIM THAT HARD?
CLARK? CLARK? YA UP THERE?!
CLARK...?
OOOH, DO I HAVE A HEADACHE...
WHY ARE Y'ALL LOOKING AT ME LIKE THAT? IS THERE ANYTHING, ER...
...WRONG?
I THINK YOU MIGHT'VE DOWNPLAYED THAT SEMBLANCE OF YOURS, MAYBE A TEENY-TINY BIT.
WHERE DID YOU RECKON YOU WERE FROM, AGAIN?

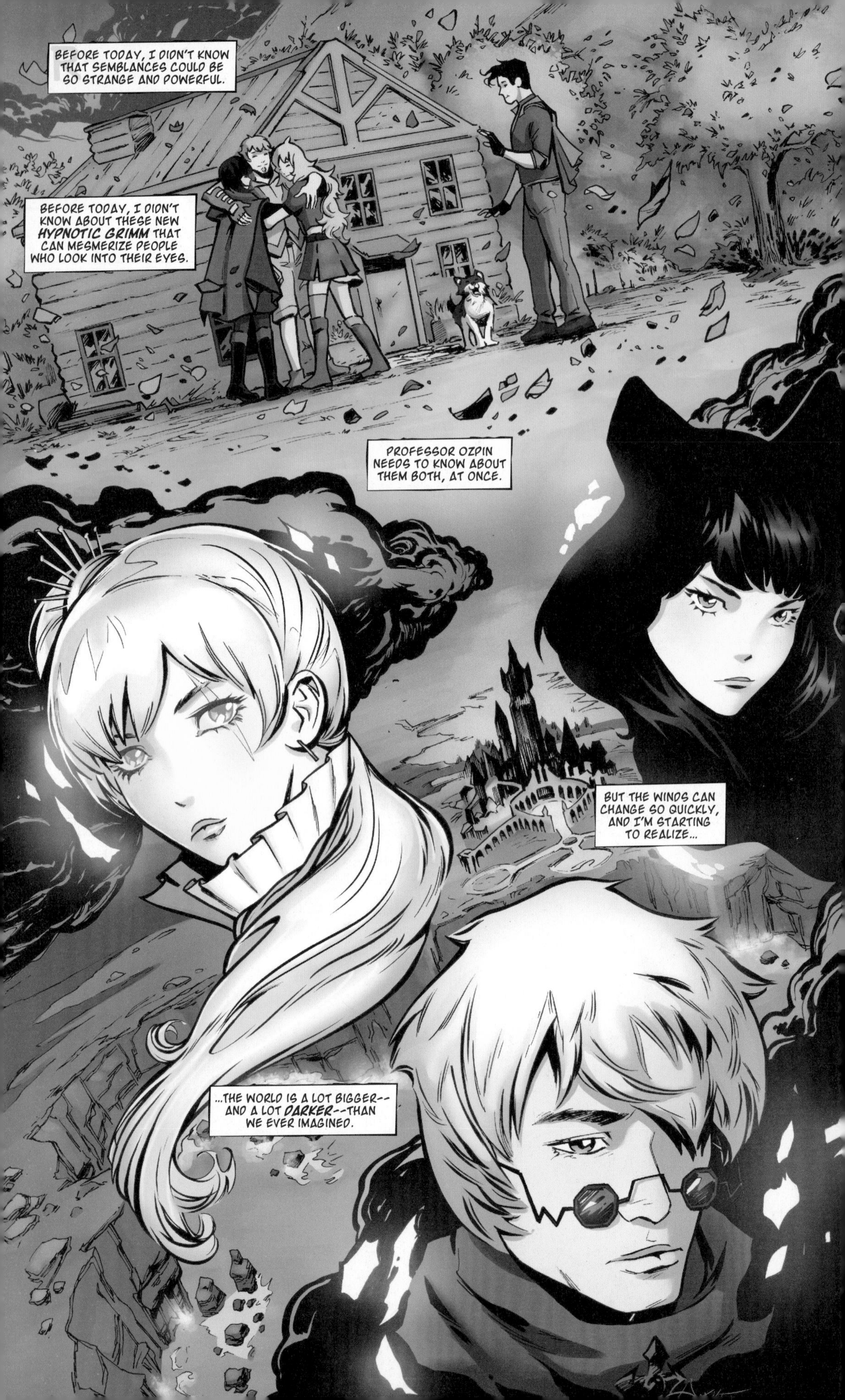
BEFORE TODAY, I DIDN'T KNOW THAT SEMBLANCES COULD BE SO STRANGE AND POWERFUL.
BEFORE TODAY, I DIDN'T KNOW ABOUT THESE NEW *HYPNOTIC GRIMM* THAT CAN MESMERIZE PEOPLE WHO LOOK INTO THEIR EYES.
PROFESSOR OZPIN NEEDS TO KNOW ABOUT THEM BOTH, AT ONCE.
BUT THE WINDS CAN CHANGE SO QUICKLY, AND I'M STARTING TO REALIZE...
...THE WORLD IS A LOT BIGGER--AND A LOT *DARKER*--THAN WE EVER IMAGINED.

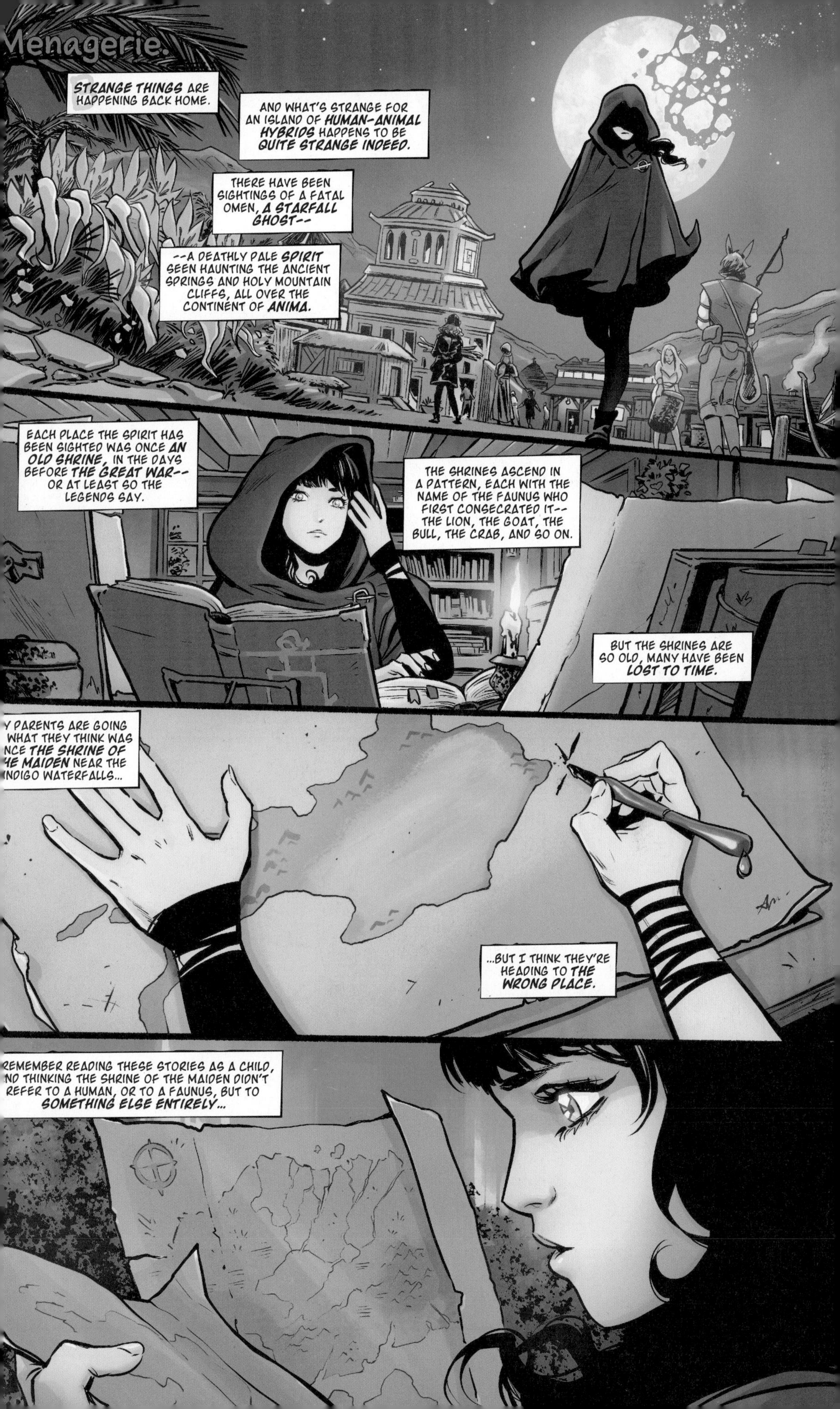

Menagerie.
STRANGE THINGS ARE HAPPENING BACK HOME.
AND WHAT'S STRANGE FOR AN ISLAND OF HUMAN-ANIMAL HYBRIDS HAPPENS TO BE QUITE STRANGE INDEED.
THERE HAVE BEEN SIGHTINGS OF A FATAL OMEN, A STARFALL GHOST--
--A DEATHLY PALE SPIRIT SEEN HAUNTING THE ANCIENT SPRINGS AND HOLY MOUNTAIN CLIFFS, ALL OVER THE CONTINENT OF ANIMA.
EACH PLACE THE SPIRIT HAS BEEN SIGHTED WAS ONCE AN OLD SHRINE, IN THE DAYS BEFORE THE GREAT WAR-- OR AT LEAST SO THE LEGENDS SAY.
THE SHRINES ASCEND IN A PATTERN, EACH WITH THE NAME OF THE FAUNUS WHO FIRST CONSECRATED IT-- THE LION, THE GOAT, THE BULL, THE CRAB, AND SO ON.
BUT THE SHRINES ARE SO OLD, MANY HAVE BEEN LOST TO TIME.
Y PARENTS ARE GOING WHAT THEY THINK WAS NCE THE SHRINE OF HE MAIDEN NEAR THE NDIGO WATERFALLS...
...BUT I THINK THEY'RE HEADING TO THE WRONG PLACE.
REMEMBER READING THESE STORIES AS A CHILD, ND THINKING THE SHRINE OF THE MAIDEN DIDN'T REFER TO A HUMAN, OR TO A FAUNUS, BUT TO SOMETHING ELSE ENTIRELY...

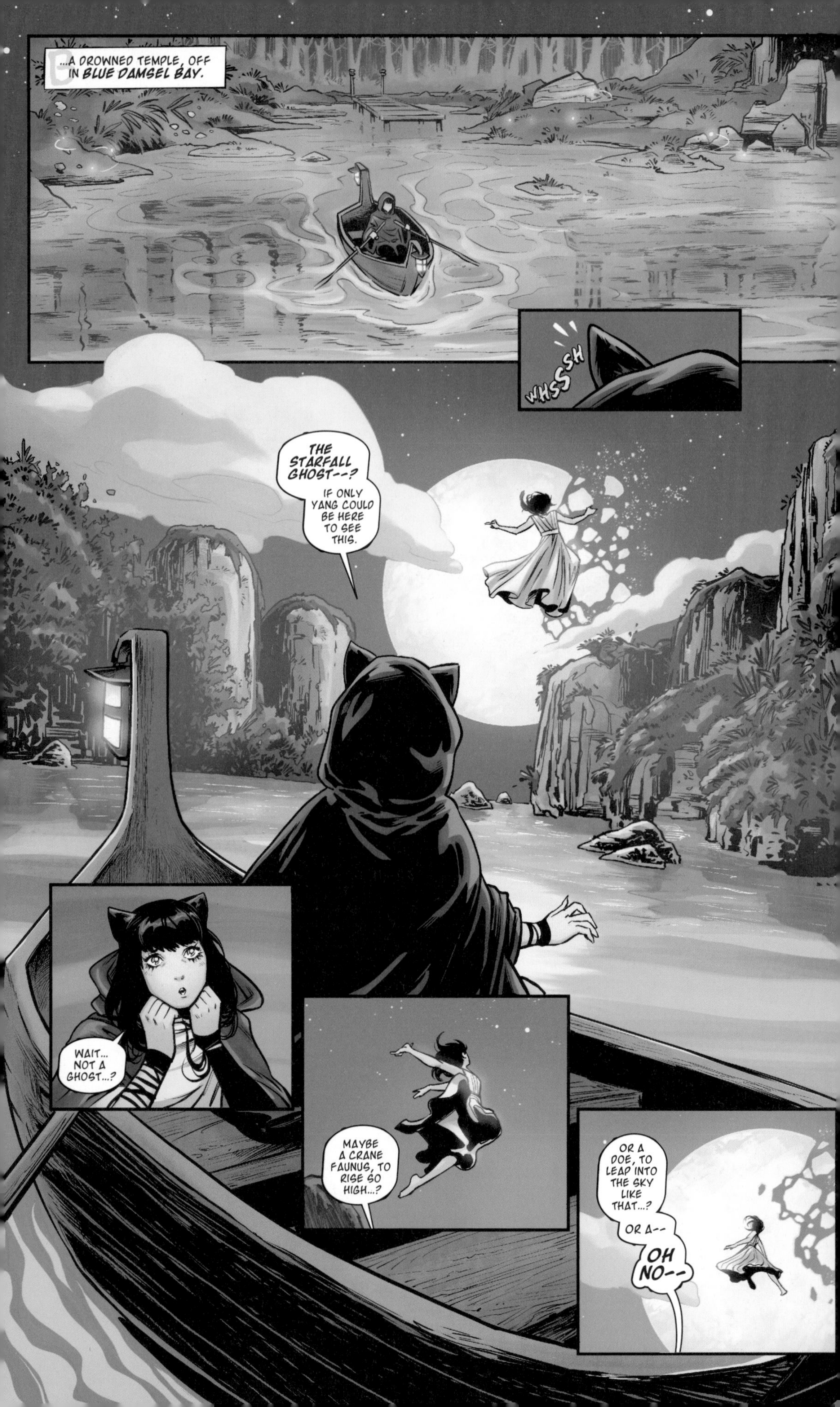
...A DROWNED TEMPLE, OFF IN BLUE DAMSEL BAY.
WHSSSH
THE STARFALL GHOST--?
IF ONLY YANG COULD BE HERE TO SEE THIS.
WAIT... NOT A GHOST...?
MAYBE A CRANE FAUNUS, TO RISE SO HIGH...?
OR A DOE, TO LEAP INTO THE SKY LIKE THAT...?
OR A--
OH NO--

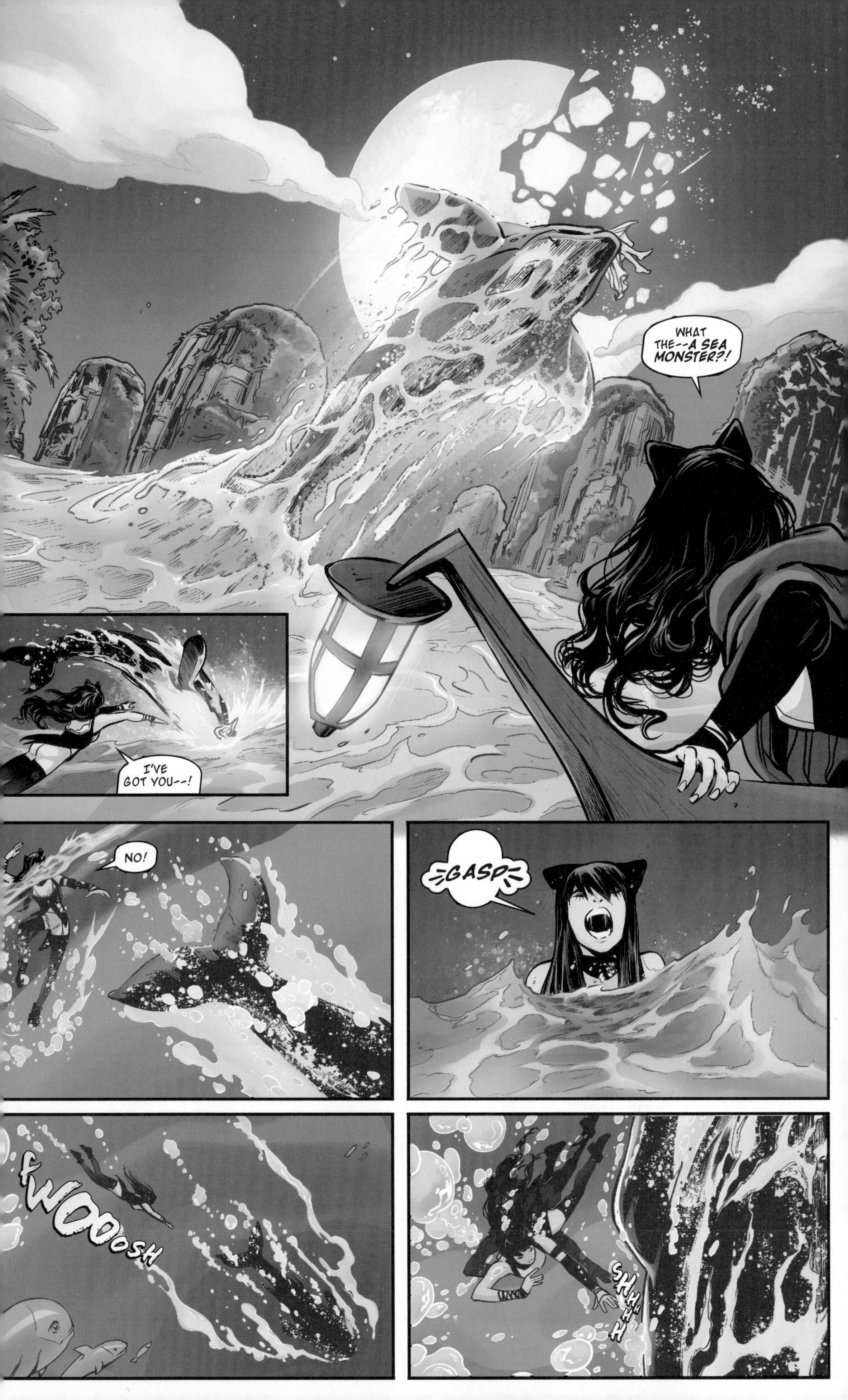
WHAT THE--A SEA MONSTER?!
I'VE GOT YOU--!
NO!
GASP
fWOOoSH
SHHHH

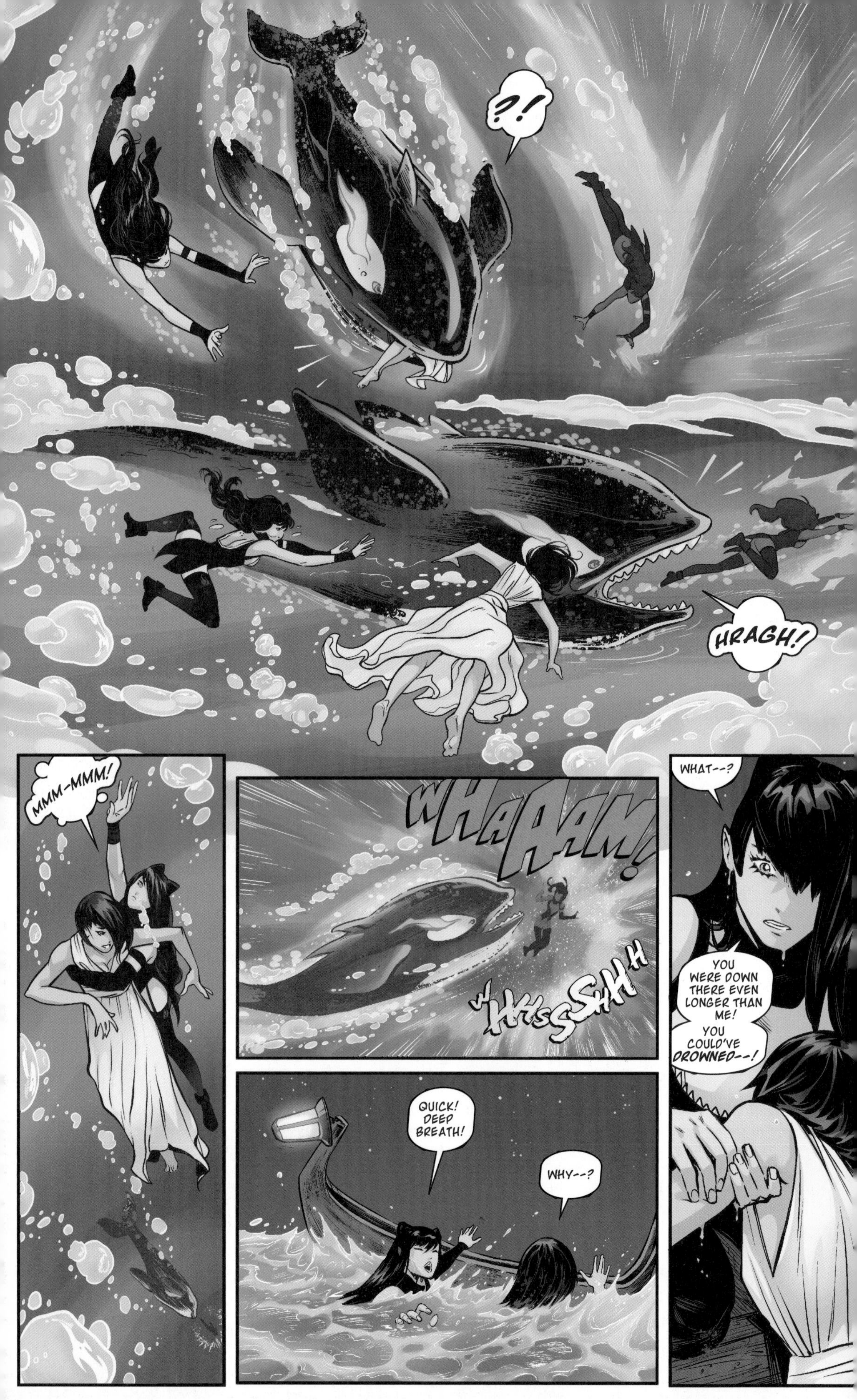
?!
HRAGH!
MMM-MMM!
WHAAAM!
WHISSSHH
QUICK! DEEP BREATH!
WHY--?
WHAT--?
YOU WERE DOWN THERE EVEN LONGER THAN ME!
YOU COULD'VE DROWNED--!

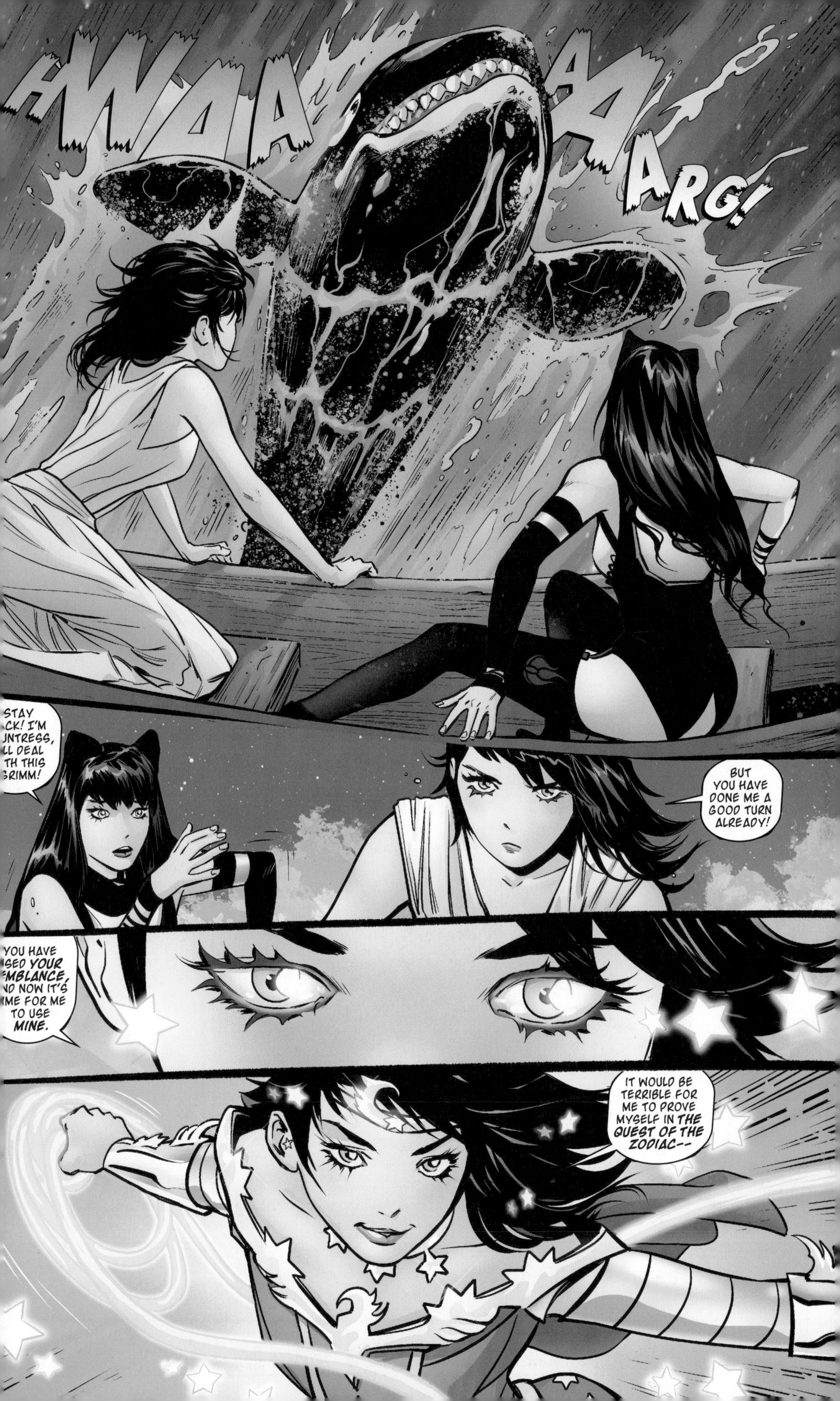

HWAA AARG!
STAY CK! I'M UNTRESS, LL DEAL TH THIS GRIMM!
BUT YOU HAVE DONE ME A GOOD TURN ALREADY!
YOU HAVE SED **YOUR** EMBLANCE, ND NOW IT'S ME FOR ME TO USE **MINE**.
IT WOULD BE TERRIBLE FOR ME TO PROVE MYSELF IN **THE QUEST OF THE ZODIAC--**

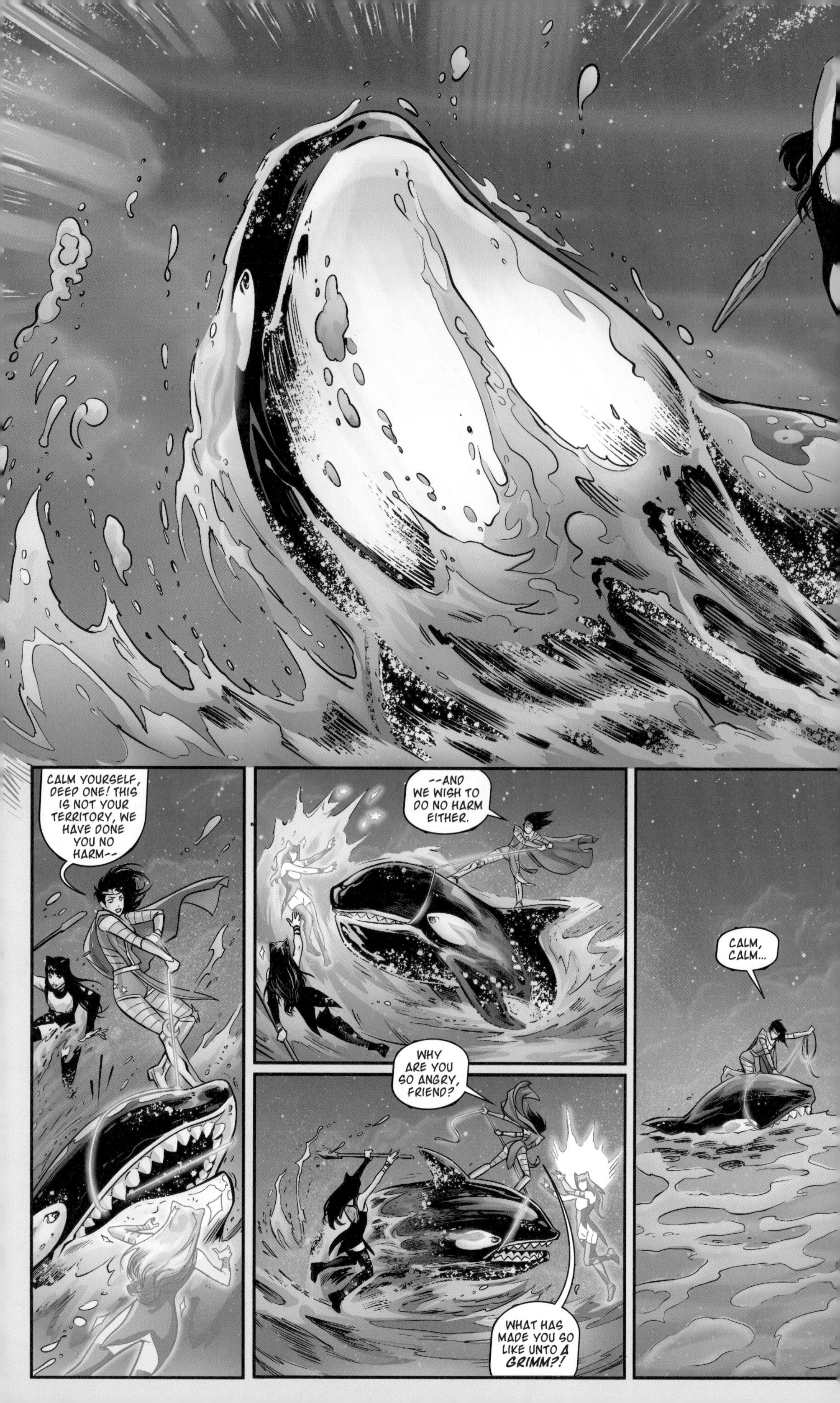
CALM YOURSELF, DEEP ONE! THIS IS NOT YOUR TERRITORY, WE HAVE DONE YOU NO HARM--
--AND WE WISH TO DO NO HARM EITHER.
WHY ARE YOU SO ANGRY, FRIEND?
WHAT HAS MADE YOU SO LIKE UNTO A GRIMM?!
CALM, CALM...

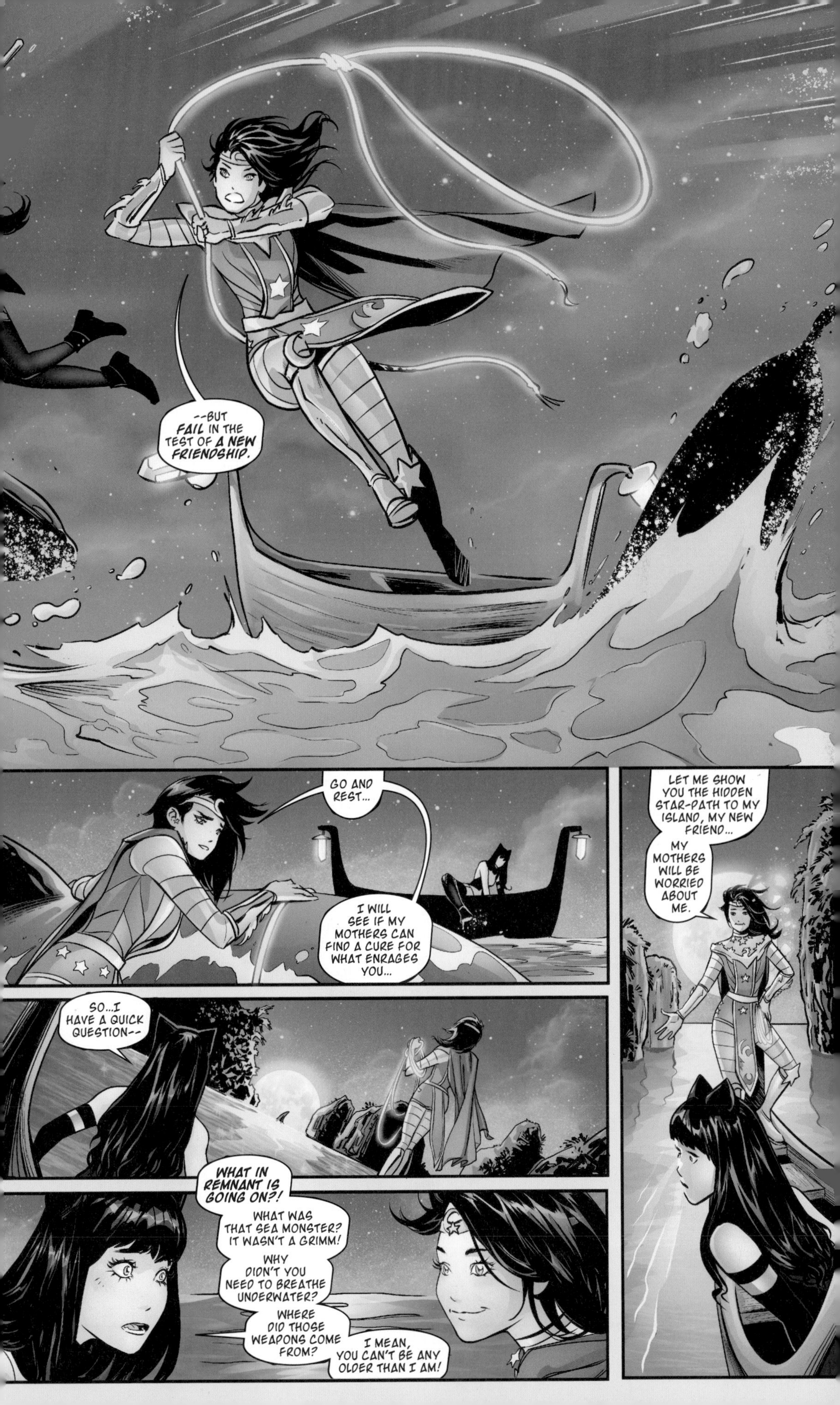
--BUT FAIL IN THE TEST OF A NEW FRIENDSHIP.
GO AND REST...
I WILL SEE IF MY MOTHERS CAN FIND A CURE FOR WHAT ENRAGES YOU...
LET ME SHOW YOU THE HIDDEN STAR-PATH TO MY ISLAND, MY NEW FRIEND...
MY MOTHERS WILL BE WORRIED ABOUT ME.
SO...I HAVE A QUICK QUESTION--
WHAT IN REMNANT IS GOING ON?!
WHAT WAS THAT SEA MONSTER? IT WASN'T A GRIMM!
WHY DIDN'T YOU NEED TO BREATHE UNDERWATER?
WHERE DID THOSE WEAPONS COME FROM?
I MEAN, YOU CAN'T BE ANY OLDER THAN I AM!

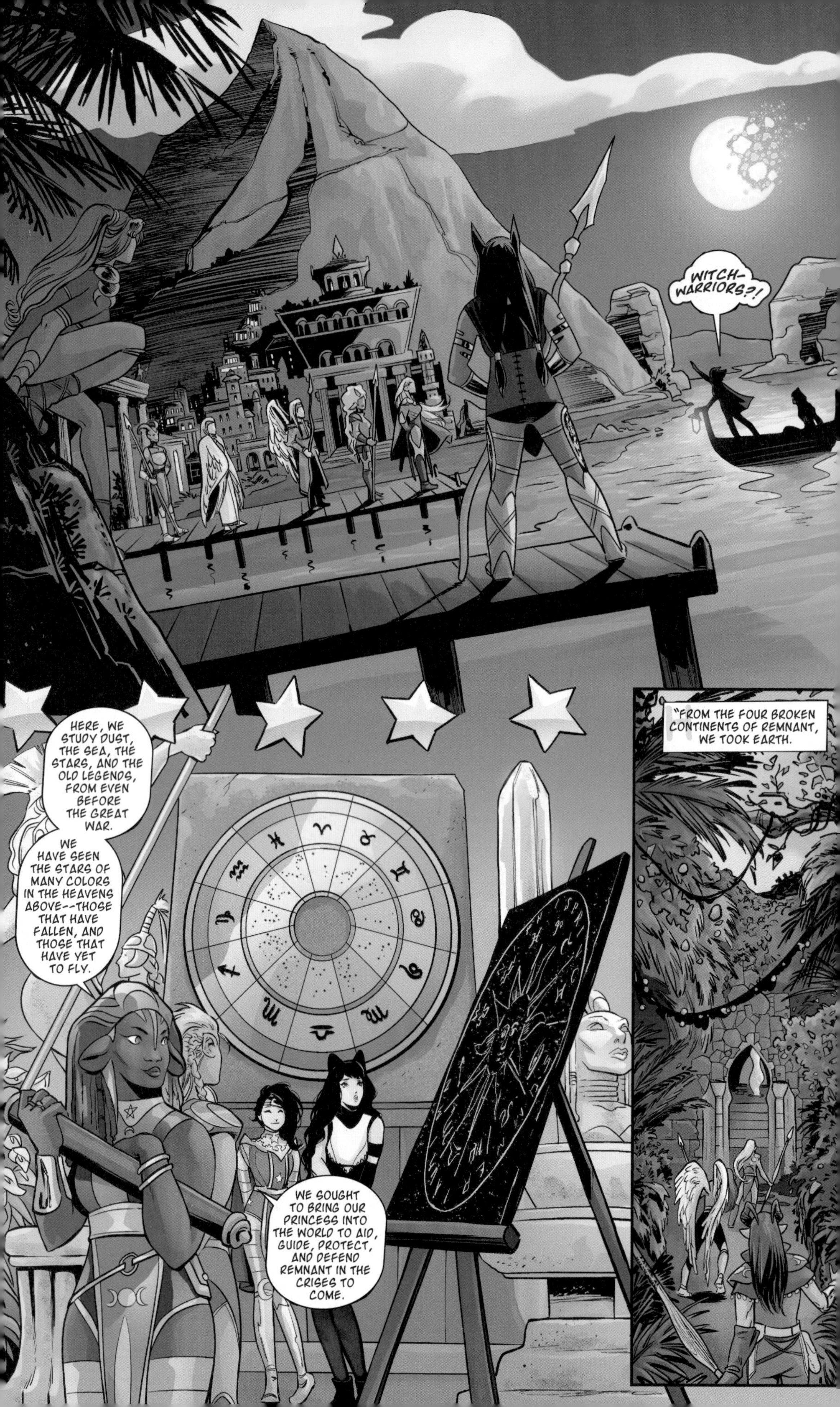
WITCH-WARRIORS?!
HERE, WE STUDY DUST, THE SEA, THE STARS, AND THE OLD LEGENDS, FROM EVEN BEFORE THE GREAT WAR.
WE HAVE SEEN THE STARS OF MANY COLORS IN THE HEAVENS ABOVE--THOSE THAT HAVE FALLEN, AND THOSE THAT HAVE YET TO FLY.
WE SOUGHT TO BRING OUR PRINCESS INTO THE WORLD TO AID, GUIDE, PROTECT, AND DEFEND REMNANT IN THE CRISES TO COME.
"FROM THE FOUR BROKEN CONTINENTS OF REMNANT, WE TOOK EARTH.

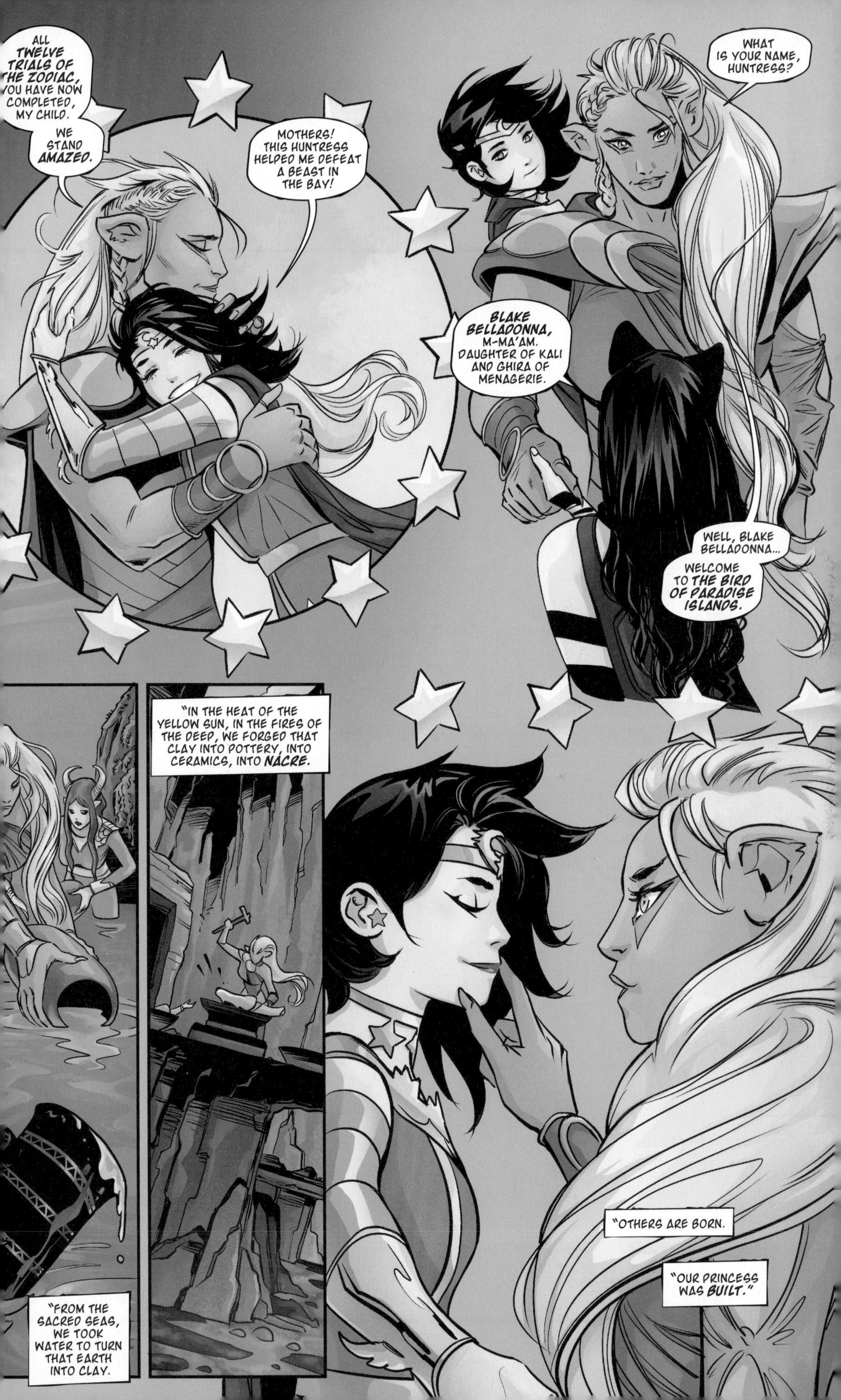
ALL TWELVE TRIALS OF THE ZODIAC, YOU HAVE NOW COMPLETED, MY CHILD.
WE STAND AMAZED.
MOTHERS! THIS HUNTRESS HELPED ME DEFEAT A BEAST IN THE BAY!
WHAT IS YOUR NAME, HUNTRESS?
BLAKE BELLADONNA, M-MA'AM. DAUGHTER OF KALI AND GHIRA OF MENAGERIE.
WELL, BLAKE BELLADONNA...
WELCOME TO THE BIRD OF PARADISE ISLANDS.
"FROM THE SACRED SEAS, WE TOOK WATER TO TURN THAT EARTH INTO CLAY.
"IN THE HEAT OF THE YELLOW SUN, IN THE FIRES OF THE DEEP, WE FORGED THAT CLAY INTO POTTERY, INTO CERAMICS, INTO NACRE.
"OTHERS ARE BORN.
"OUR PRINCESS WAS BUILT."

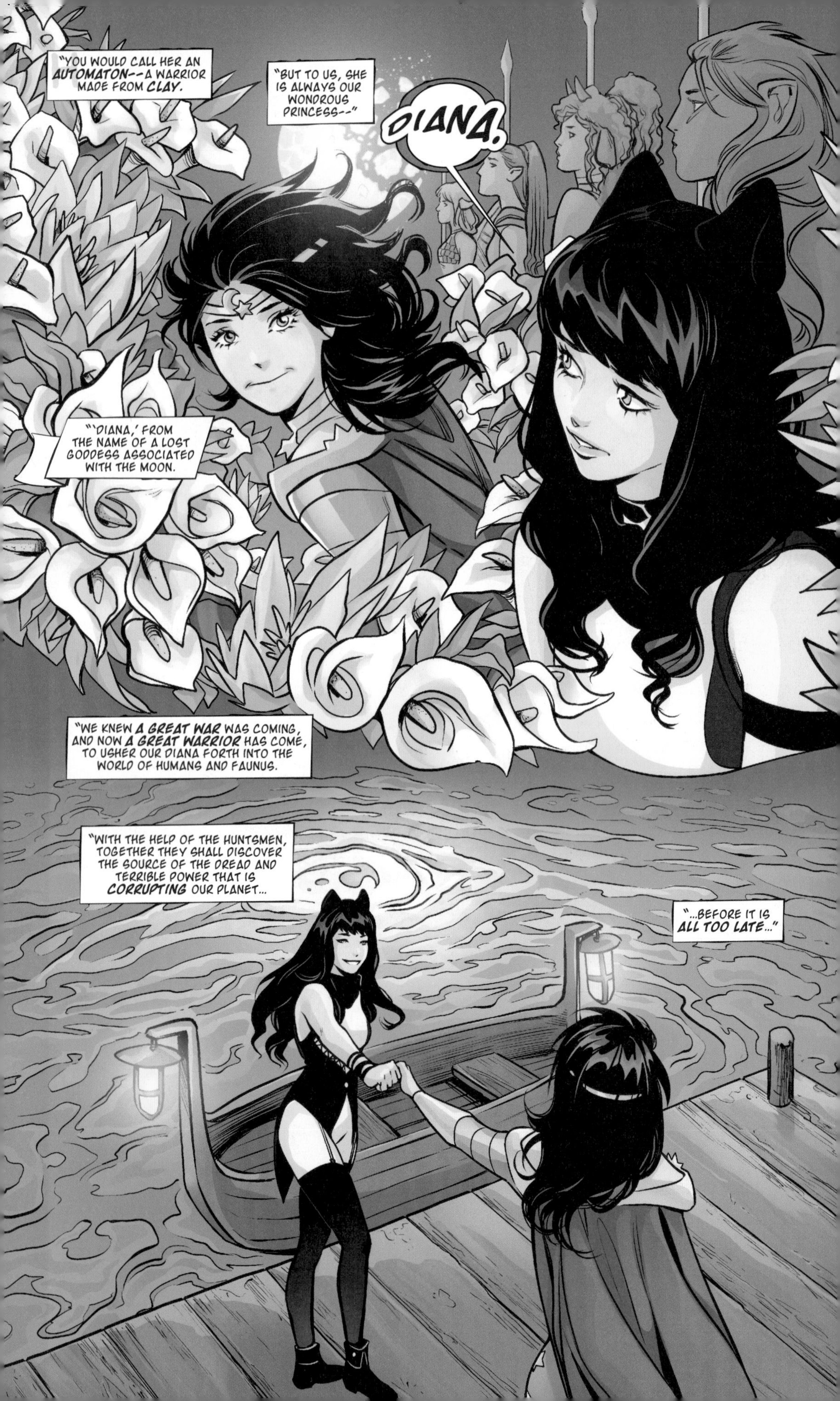
"YOU WOULD CALL HER AN AUTOMATON--A WARRIOR MADE FROM CLAY.
"BUT TO US, SHE IS ALWAYS OUR WONDROUS PRINCESS--"
DIANA.
"'DIANA,' FROM THE NAME OF A LOST GODDESS ASSOCIATED WITH THE MOON.
"WE KNEW A GREAT WAR WAS COMING, AND NOW A GREAT WARRIOR HAS COME, TO USHER OUR DIANA FORTH INTO THE WORLD OF HUMANS AND FAUNUS.
"WITH THE HELP OF THE HUNTSMEN, TOGETHER THEY SHALL DISCOVER THE SOURCE OF THE DREAD AND TERRIBLE POWER THAT IS CORRUPTING OUR PLANET...
"...BEFORE IT IS ALL TOO LATE..."

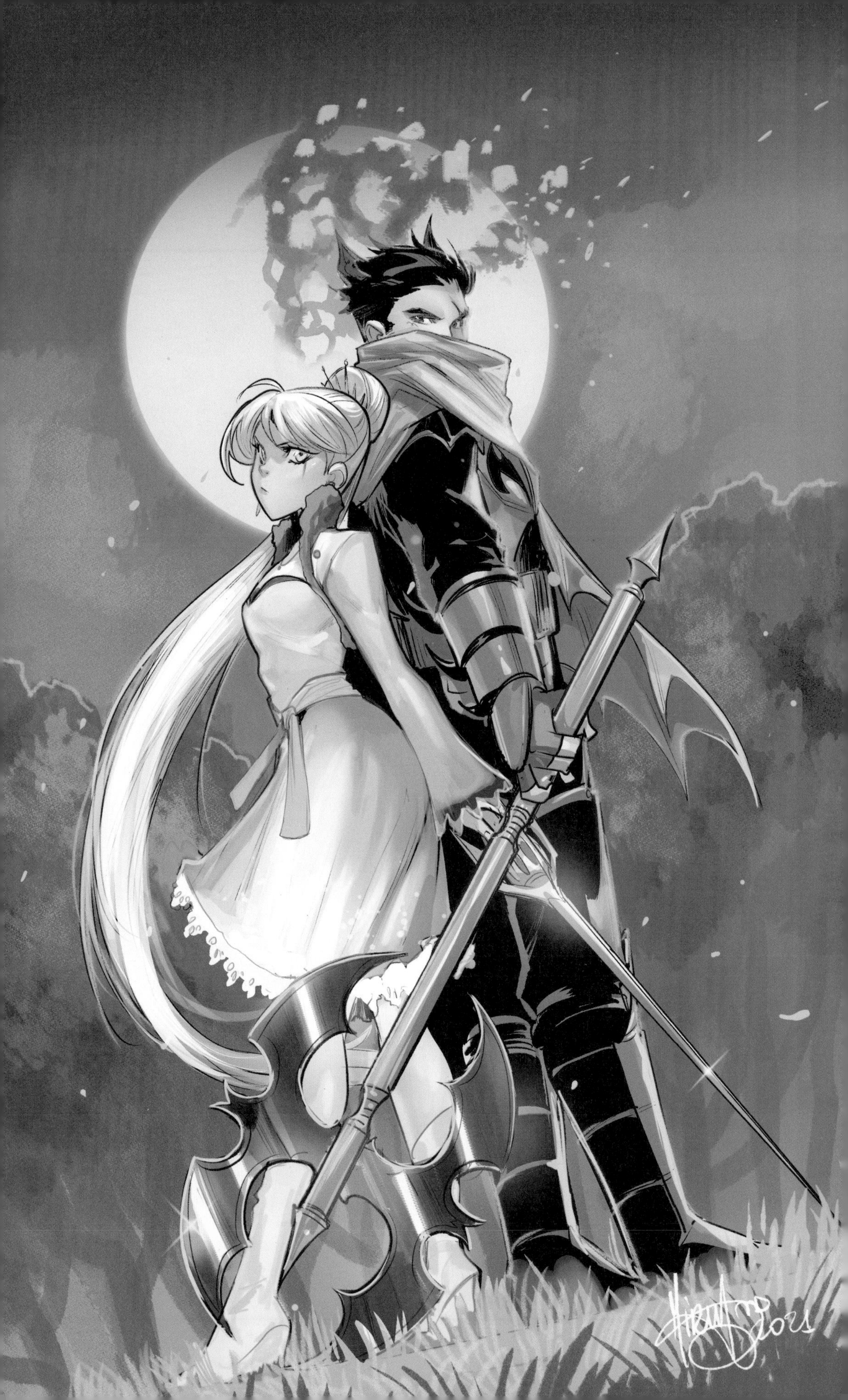

Variant cover by **SIMONE DI MEO**

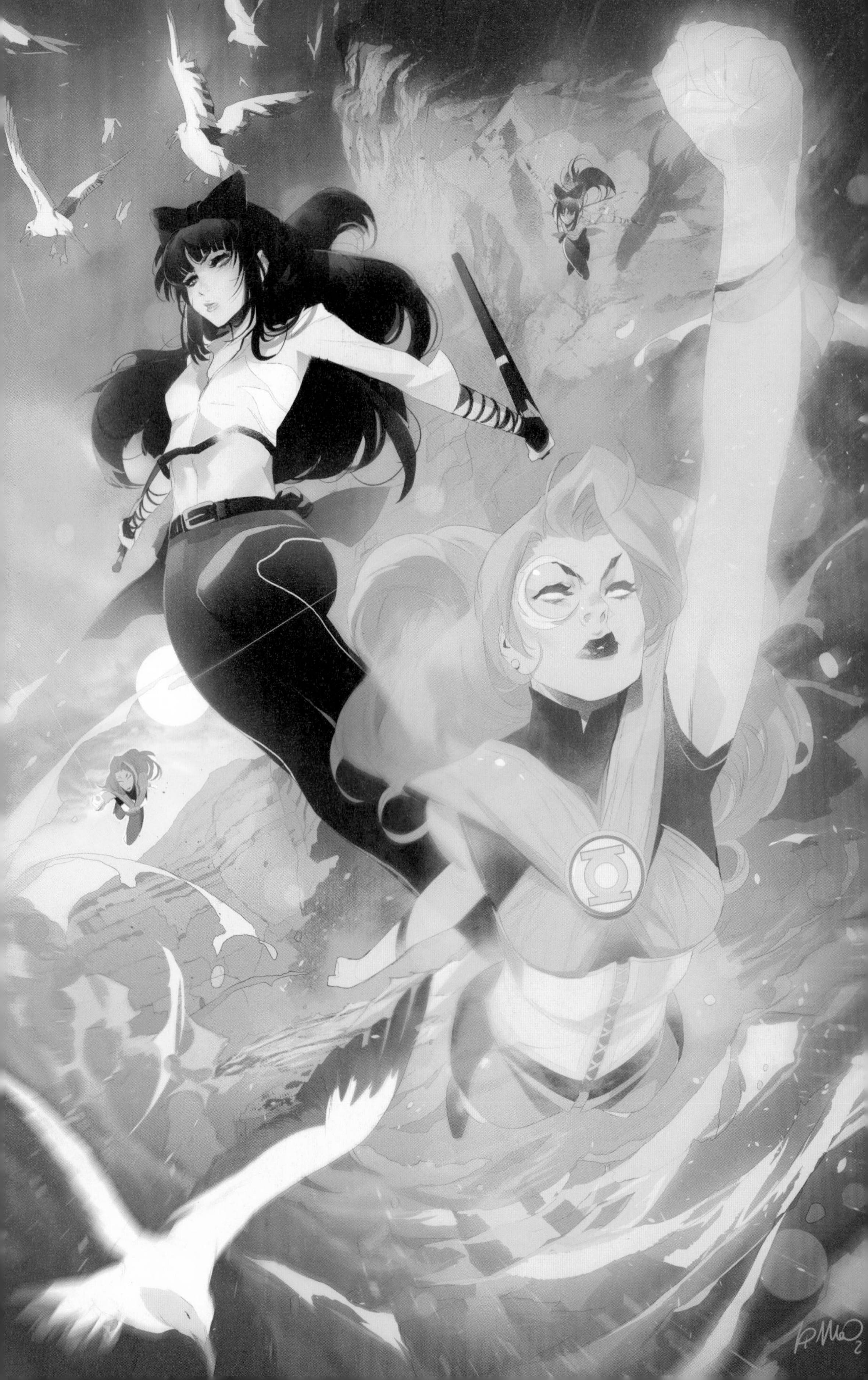

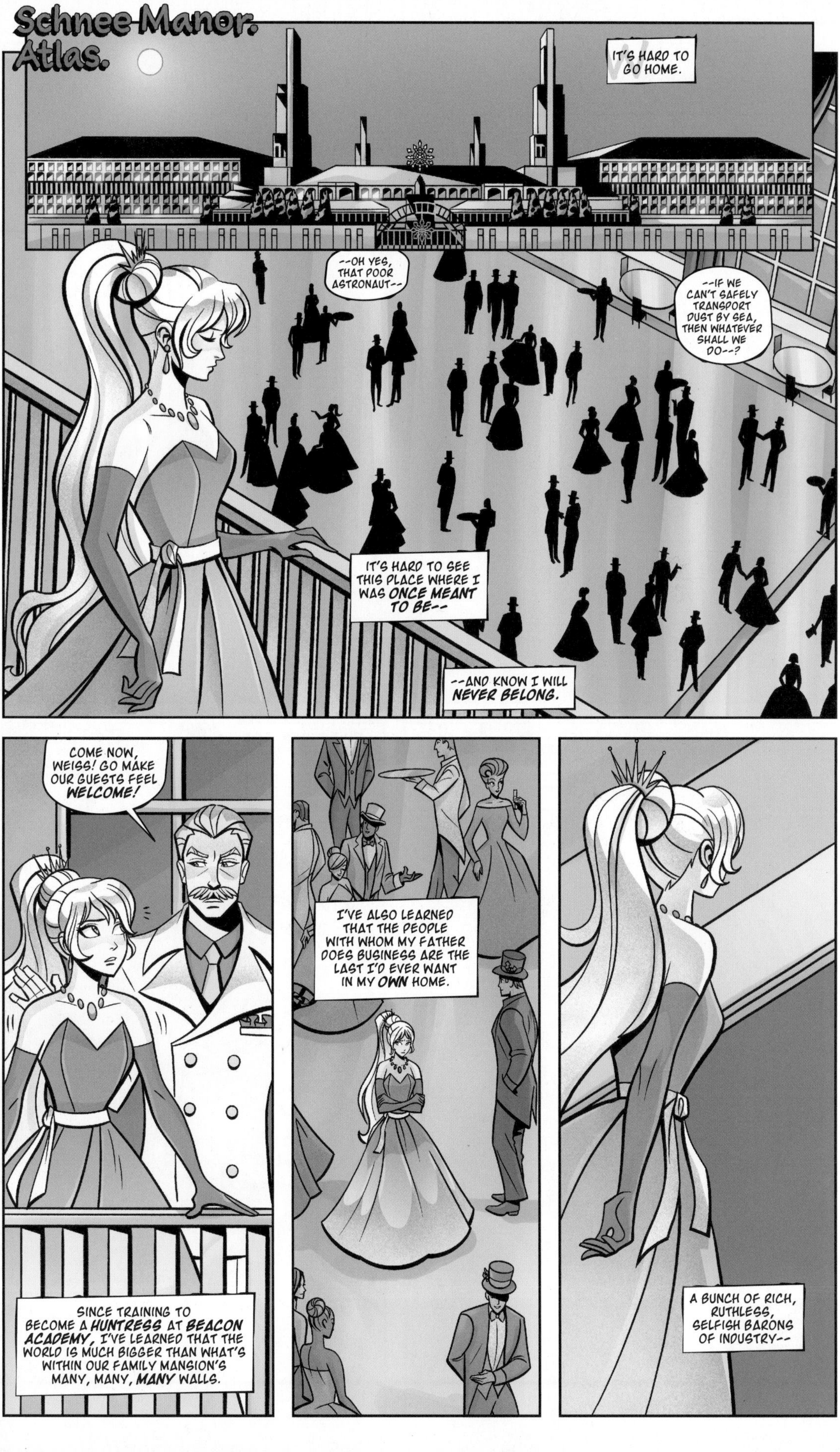
Schnee Manor. Atlas.
IT'S HARD TO GO HOME.
--OH YES, THAT POOR ASTRONAUT--
--IF WE CAN'T SAFELY TRANSPORT DUST BY SEA, THEN WHATEVER SHALL WE DO--?
IT'S HARD TO SEE THIS PLACE WHERE I WAS ONCE MEANT TO BE--
--AND KNOW I WILL NEVER BELONG.
COME NOW, WEISS! GO MAKE OUR GUESTS FEEL WELCOME!
SINCE TRAINING TO BECOME A HUNTRESS AT BEACON ACADEMY, I'VE LEARNED THAT THE WORLD IS MUCH BIGGER THAN WHAT'S WITHIN OUR FAMILY MANSION'S MANY, MANY, MANY WALLS.
I'VE ALSO LEARNED THAT THE PEOPLE WITH WHOM MY FATHER DOES BUSINESS ARE THE LAST I'D EVER WANT IN MY OWN HOME.
A BUNCH OF RICH, RUTHLESS, SELFISH BARONS OF INDUSTRY--

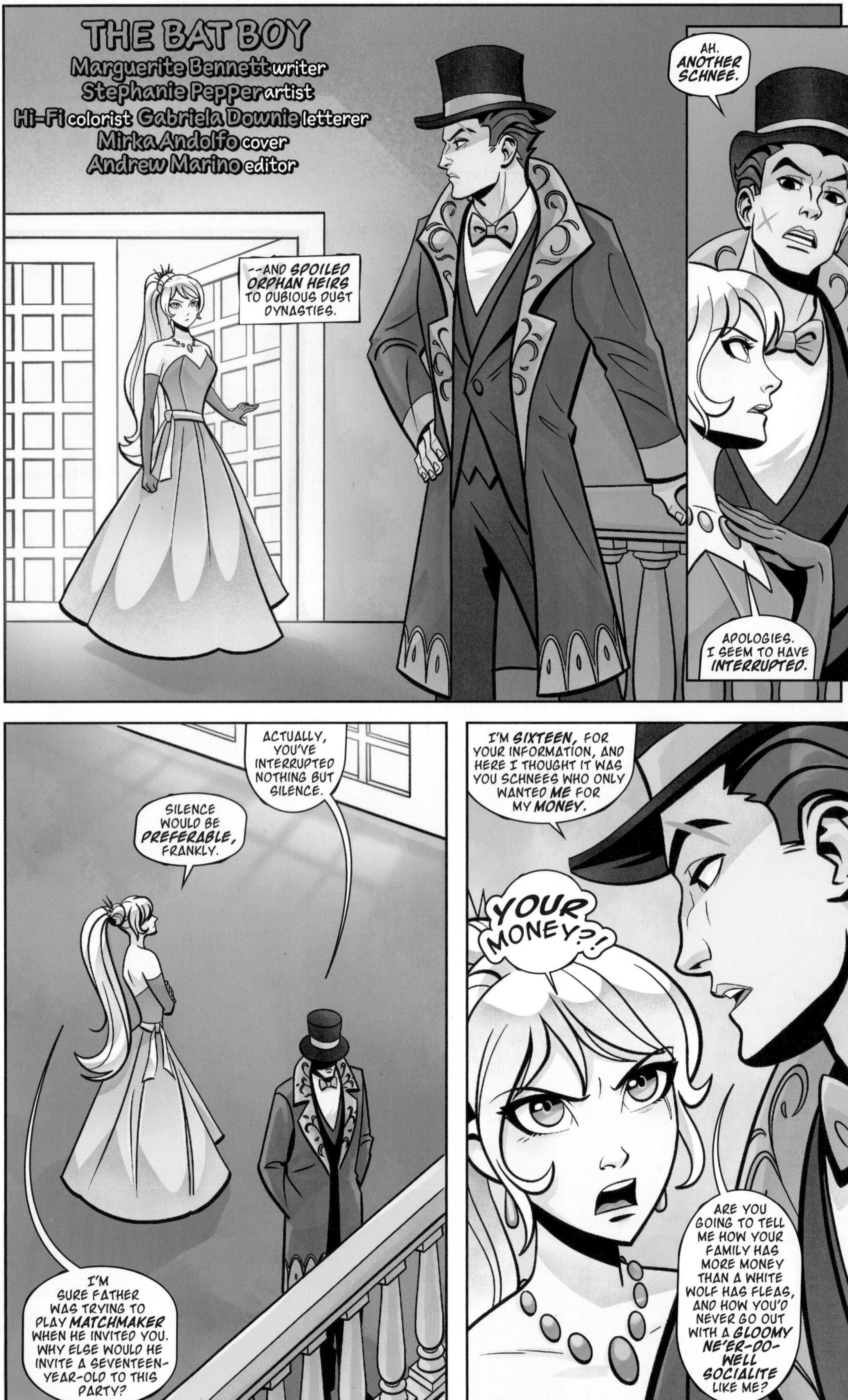
THE BAT BOY
Marguerite Bennett writer
Stephanie Pepper artist
Hi-Fi colorist Gabriela Downie letterer
Mirka Andolfo cover
Andrew Marino editor
--AND SPOILED ORPHAN HEIRS TO DUBIOUS DUST DYNASTIES.
AH. ANOTHER SCHNEE.
APOLOGIES. I SEEM TO HAVE INTERRUPTED.
ACTUALLY, YOU'VE INTERRUPTED NOTHING BUT SILENCE.
SILENCE WOULD BE PREFERABLE, FRANKLY.
I'M SURE FATHER WAS TRYING TO PLAY MATCHMAKER WHEN HE INVITED YOU. WHY ELSE WOULD HE INVITE A SEVENTEEN-YEAR-OLD TO THIS PARTY?
I'M SIXTEEN, FOR YOUR INFORMATION, AND HERE I THOUGHT IT WAS YOU SCHNEES WHO ONLY WANTED ME FOR MY MONEY.
YOUR MONEY?!
ARE YOU GOING TO TELL ME HOW YOUR FAMILY HAS MORE MONEY THAN A WHITE WOLF HAS FLEAS, AND HOW YOU'D NEVER GO OUT WITH A GLOOMY NE'ER-DO-WELL SOCIALITE LIKE ME?

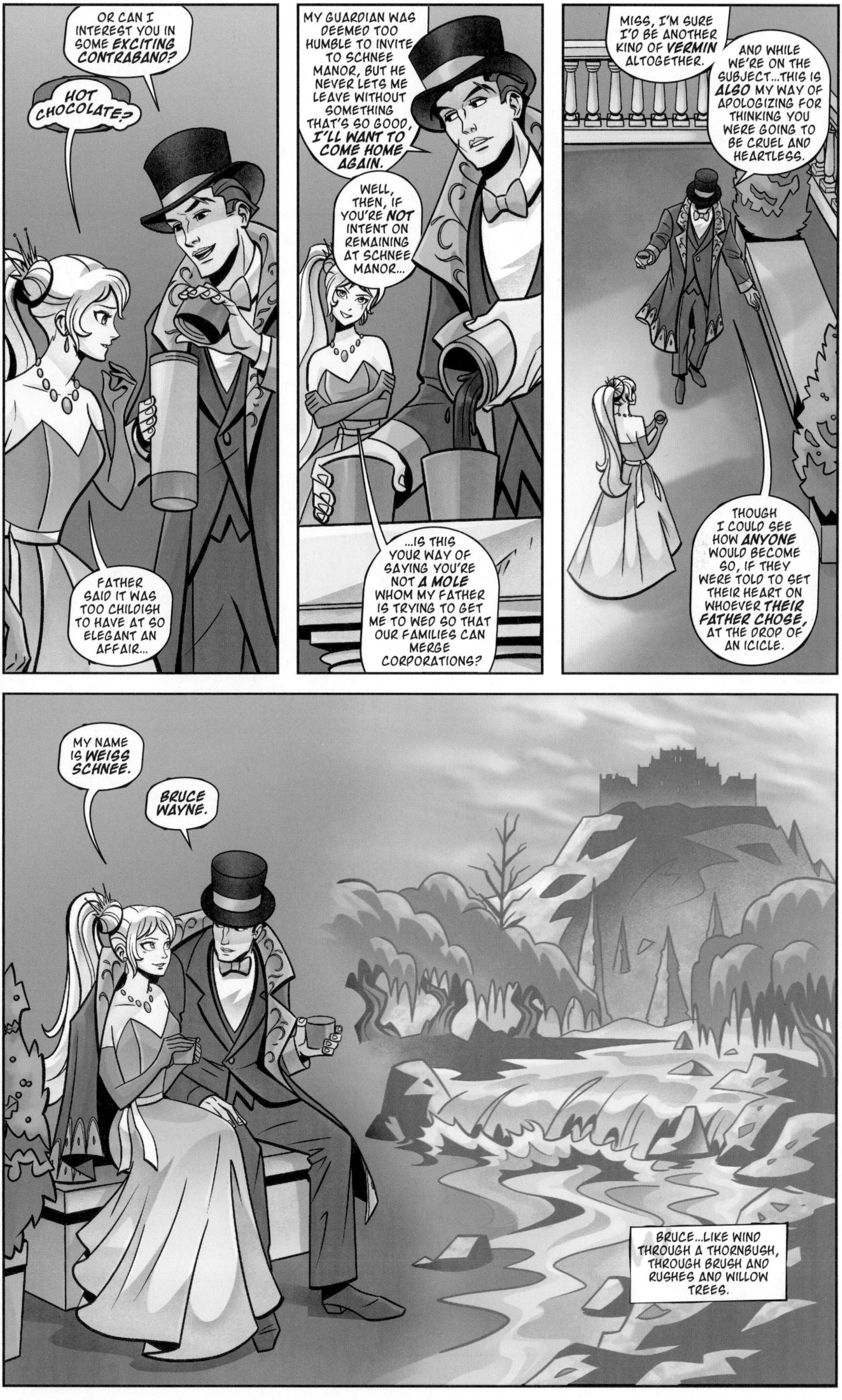
OR CAN I INTEREST YOU IN SOME EXCITING CONTRABAND?
HOT CHOCOLATE?
FATHER SAID IT WAS TOO CHILDISH TO HAVE AT SO ELEGANT AN AFFAIR...
MY GUARDIAN WAS DEEMED TOO HUMBLE TO INVITE TO SCHNEE MANOR, BUT HE NEVER LETS ME LEAVE WITHOUT SOMETHING THAT'S SO GOOD, I'LL WANT TO COME HOME AGAIN.
WELL, THEN, IF YOU'RE NOT INTENT ON REMAINING AT SCHNEE MANOR...
...IS THIS YOUR WAY OF SAYING YOU'RE NOT A MOLE WHOM MY FATHER IS TRYING TO GET ME TO WED SO THAT OUR FAMILIES CAN MERGE CORPORATIONS?
MISS, I'M SURE I'D BE ANOTHER KIND OF VERMIN ALTOGETHER.
AND WHILE WE'RE ON THE SUBJECT...THIS IS ALSO MY WAY OF APOLOGIZING FOR THINKING YOU WERE GOING TO BE CRUEL AND HEARTLESS.
THOUGH I COULD SEE HOW ANYONE WOULD BECOME SO, IF THEY WERE TOLD TO SET THEIR HEART ON WHOEVER THEIR FATHER CHOSE, AT THE DROP OF AN ICICLE.
MY NAME IS WEISS SCHNEE.
BRUCE WAYNE.
BRUCE...LIKE WIND THROUGH A THORNBUSH, THROUGH BRUSH AND RUSHES AND WILLOW TREES.

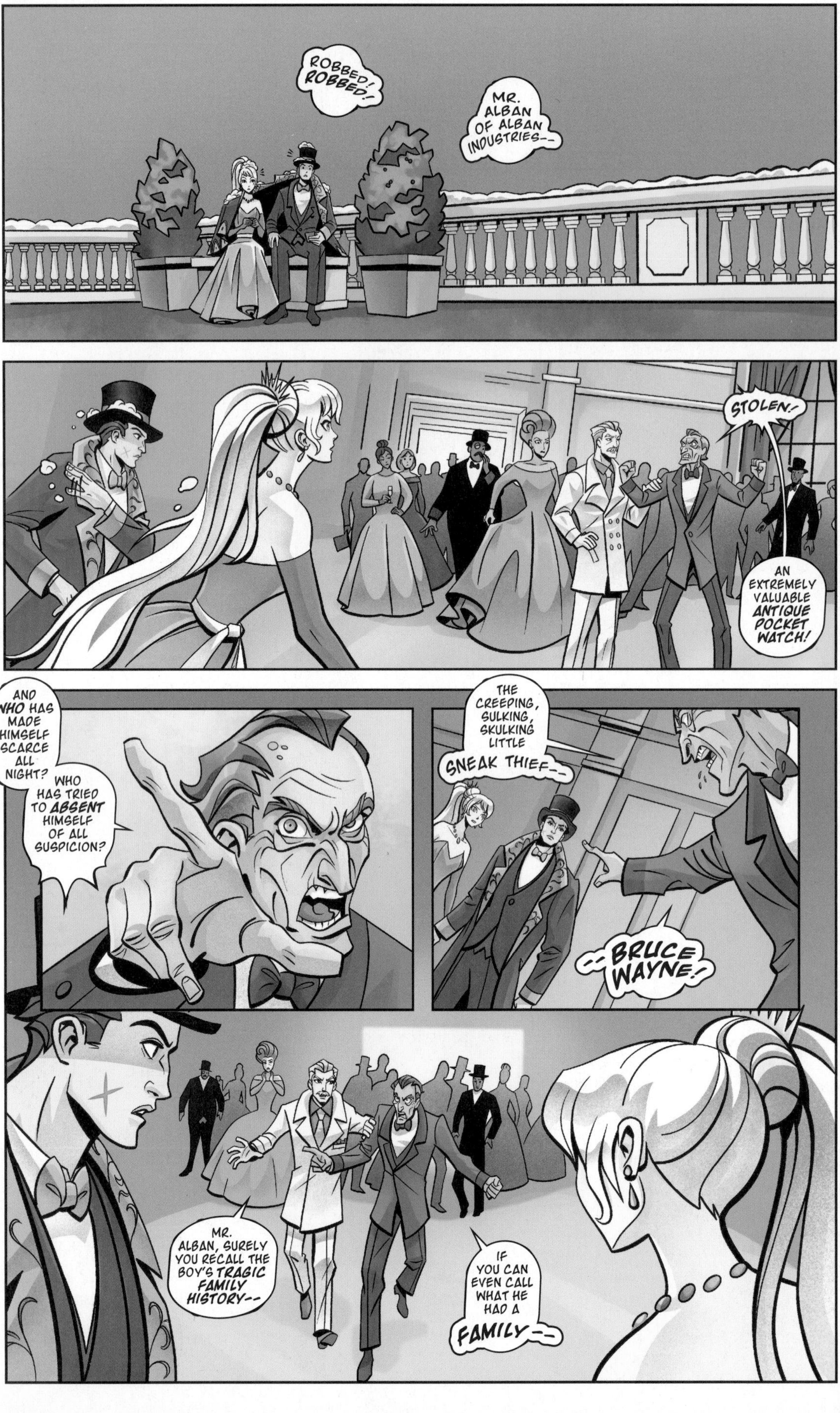
ROBBED! ROBBED!
MR. ALBAN OF ALBAN INDUSTRIES--
STOLEN!
AN EXTREMELY VALUABLE ANTIQUE POCKET WATCH!
AND WHO HAS MADE HIMSELF SCARCE ALL NIGHT?
WHO HAS TRIED TO ABSENT HIMSELF OF ALL SUSPICION?
THE CREEPING, SULKING, SKULKING LITTLE
SNEAK THIEF--
--BRUCE WAYNE!
MR. ALBAN, SURELY YOU RECALL THE BOY'S TRAGIC FAMILY HISTORY--
IF YOU CAN EVEN CALL WHAT HE HAD A FAMILY--

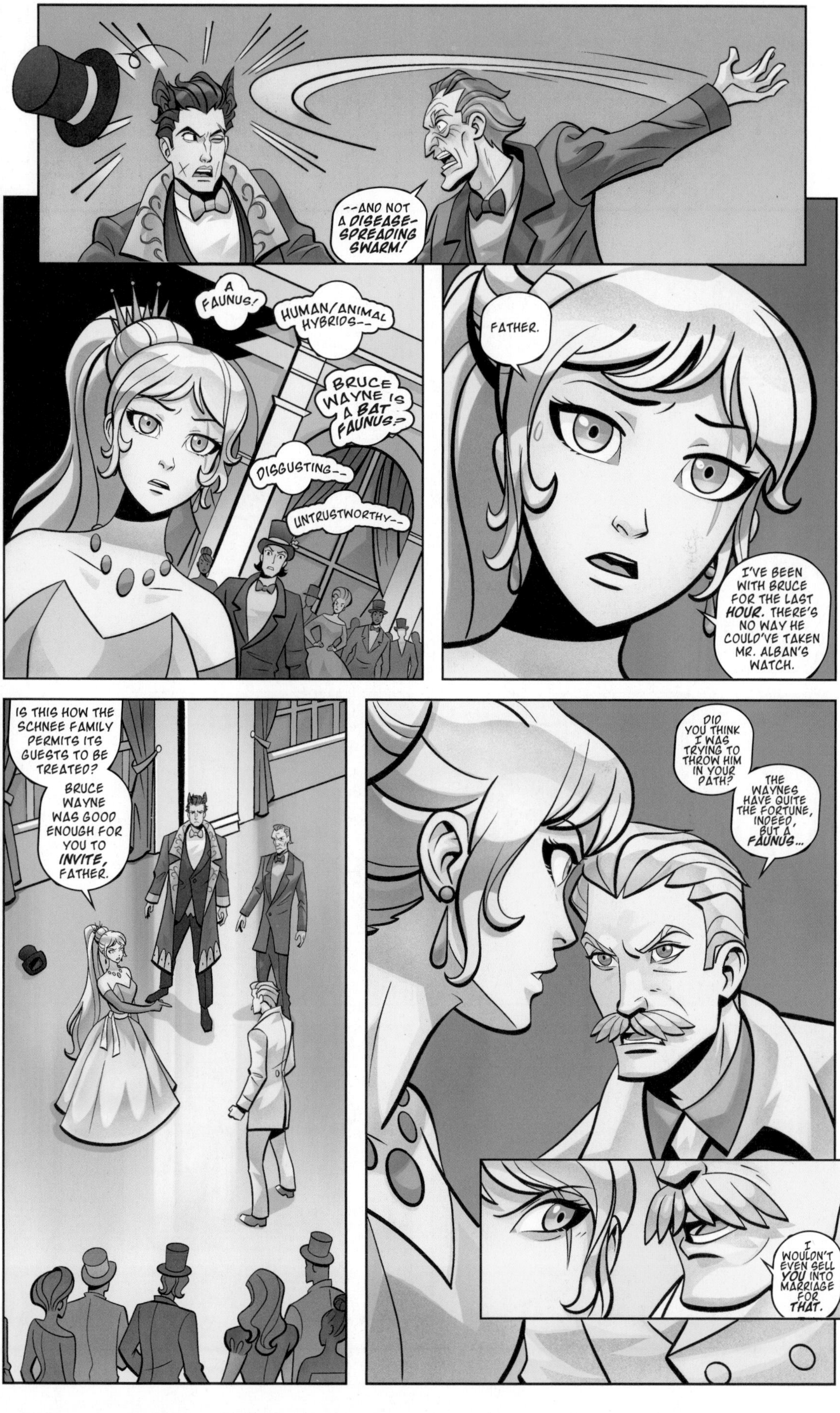
--AND NOT A DISEASE-SPREADING SWARM!
A FAUNUS!
HUMAN/ANIMAL HYBRIDS--
BRUCE WAYNE IS A BAT FAUNUS?
DISGUSTING--
UNTRUSTWORTHY--
FATHER.
I'VE BEEN WITH BRUCE FOR THE LAST HOUR. THERE'S NO WAY HE COULD'VE TAKEN MR. ALBAN'S WATCH.
IS THIS HOW THE SCHNEE FAMILY PERMITS ITS GUESTS TO BE TREATED?
BRUCE WAYNE WAS GOOD ENOUGH FOR YOU TO INVITE, FATHER.
DID YOU THINK I WAS TRYING TO THROW HIM IN YOUR PATH?
THE WAYNES HAVE QUITE THE FORTUNE, INDEED, BUT A FAUNUS...
I WOULDN'T EVEN SELL YOU INTO MARRIAGE FOR THAT.

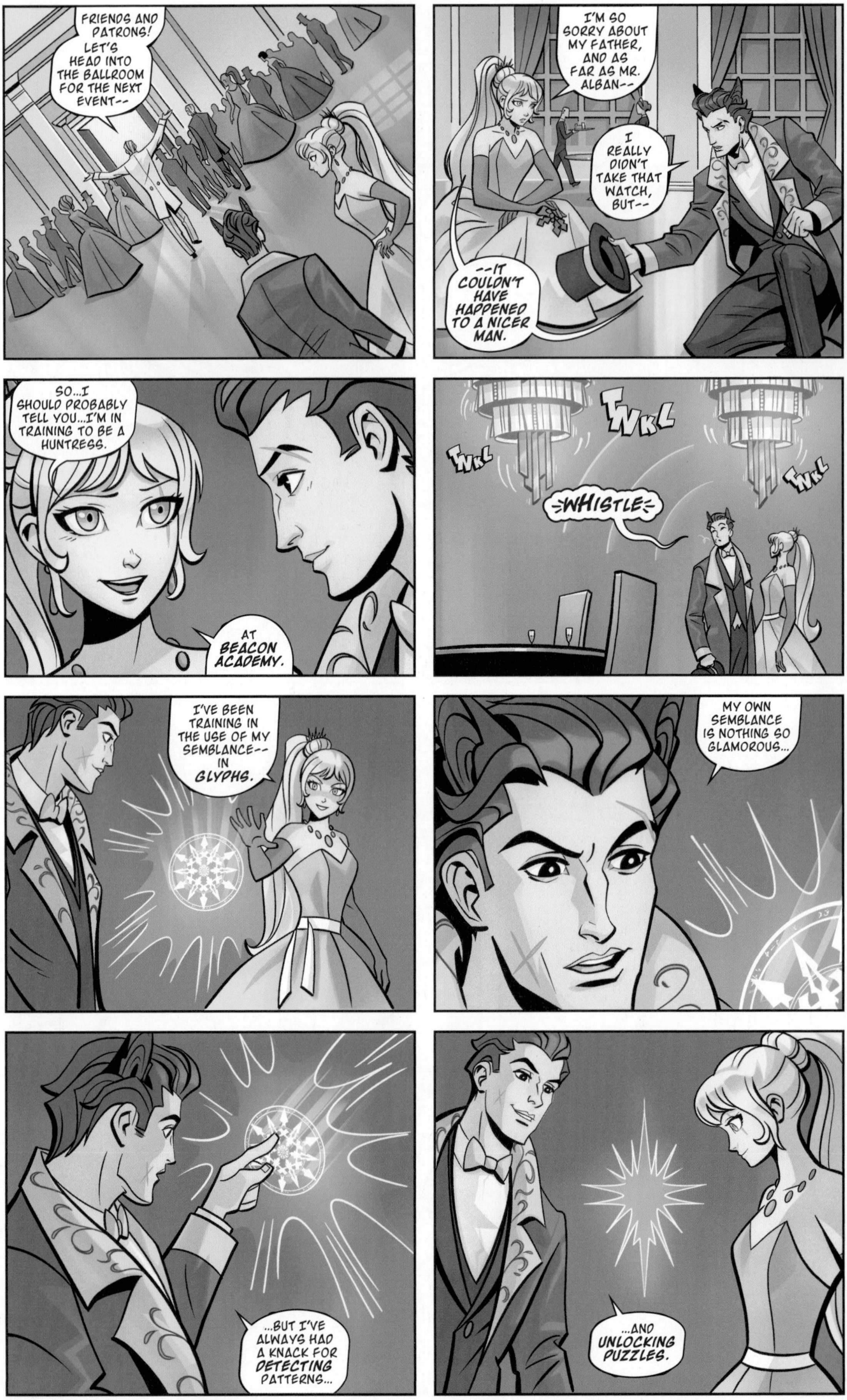
FRIENDS AND PATRONS! LET'S HEAD INTO THE BALLROOM FOR THE NEXT EVENT--
I'M SO SORRY ABOUT MY FATHER, AND AS FAR AS MR. ALBAN--
I REALLY DIDN'T TAKE THAT WATCH, BUT--
--IT COULDN'T HAVE HAPPENED TO A NICER MAN.
SO...I SHOULD PROBABLY TELL YOU...I'M IN TRAINING TO BE A HUNTRESS.
AT BEACON ACADEMY.
TNKL
TNKL
TNKL
WHISTLE
I'VE BEEN TRAINING IN THE USE OF MY SEMBLANCE--IN GLYPHS.
MY OWN SEMBLANCE IS NOTHING SO GLAMOROUS...
...BUT I'VE ALWAYS HAD A KNACK FOR DETECTING PATTERNS...
...AND UNLOCKING PUZZLES.

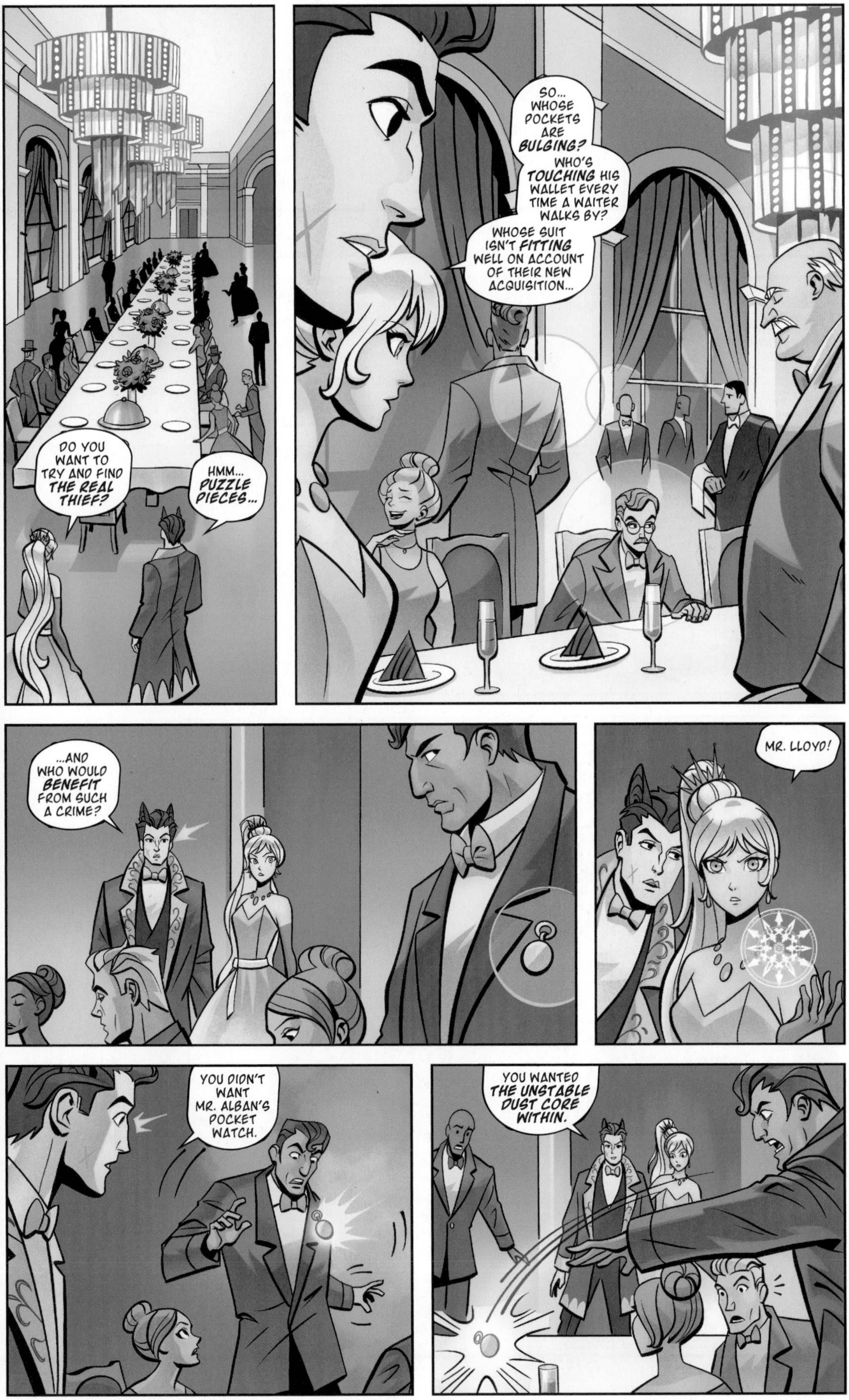
DO YOU WANT TO TRY AND FIND THE REAL THIEF?
HMM... PUZZLE PIECES...
SO... WHOSE POCKETS ARE BULGING?
WHO'S TOUCHING HIS WALLET EVERY TIME A WAITER WALKS BY?
WHOSE SUIT ISN'T FITTING WELL ON ACCOUNT OF THEIR NEW ACQUISITION...
...AND WHO WOULD BENEFIT FROM SUCH A CRIME?
MR. LLOYD!
YOU DIDN'T WANT MR. ALBAN'S POCKET WATCH.
YOU WANTED THE UNSTABLE DUST CORE WITHIN.

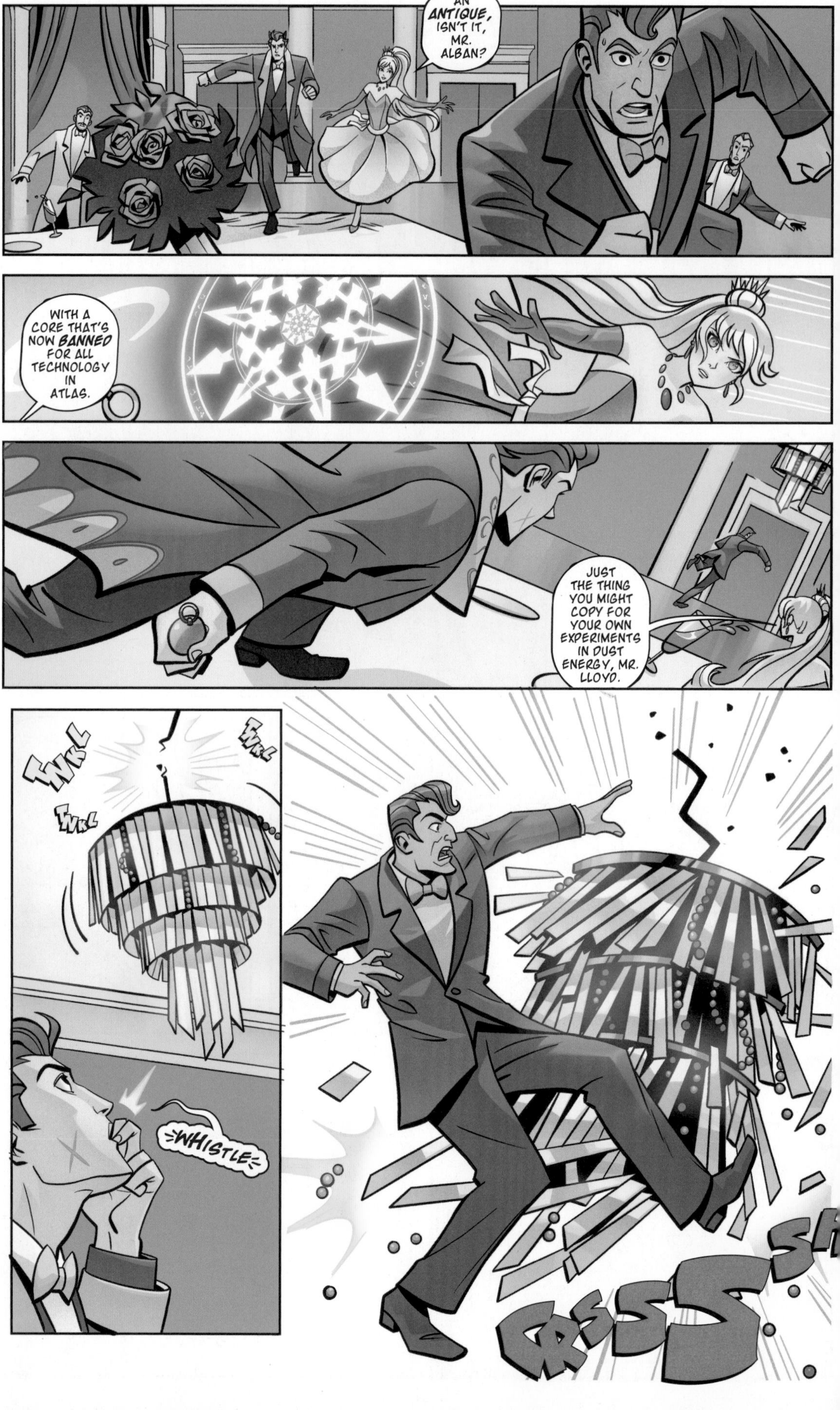
AN ANTIQUE, ISN'T IT, MR. ALBAN?
WITH A CORE THAT'S NOW BANNED FOR ALL TECHNOLOGY IN ATLAS.
JUST THE THING YOU MIGHT COPY FOR YOUR OWN EXPERIMENTS IN DUST ENERGY, MR. LLOYD.
TWKL
TWKL
TWKL
WHISTLE
CRSSSSH

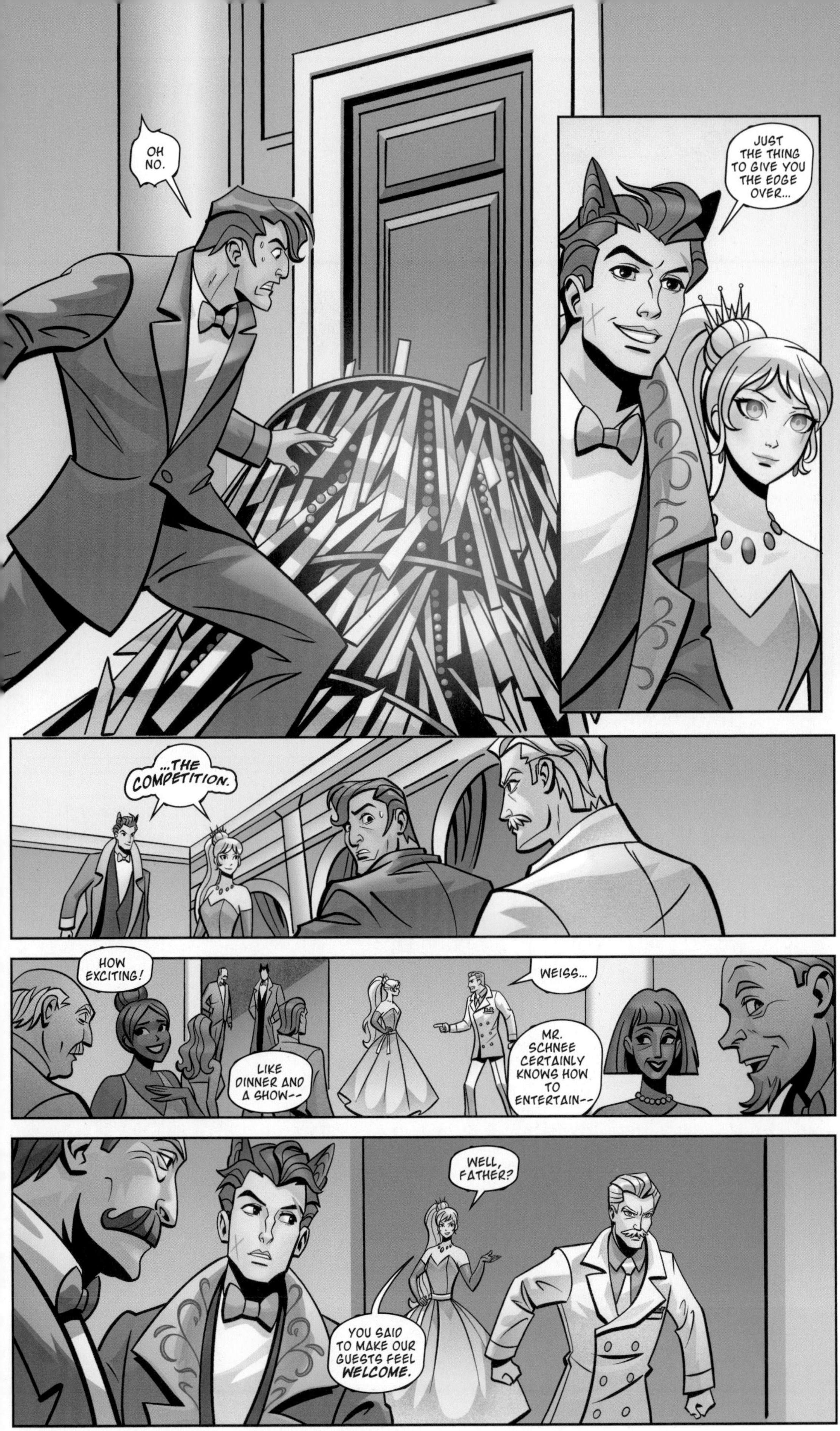
OH NO.
JUST THE THING TO GIVE YOU THE EDGE OVER...
...THE COMPETITION.
HOW EXCITING!
LIKE DINNER AND A SHOW--
WEISS...
MR. SCHNEE CERTAINLY KNOWS HOW TO ENTERTAIN--
WELL, FATHER?
YOU SAID TO MAKE OUR GUESTS FEEL WELCOME.

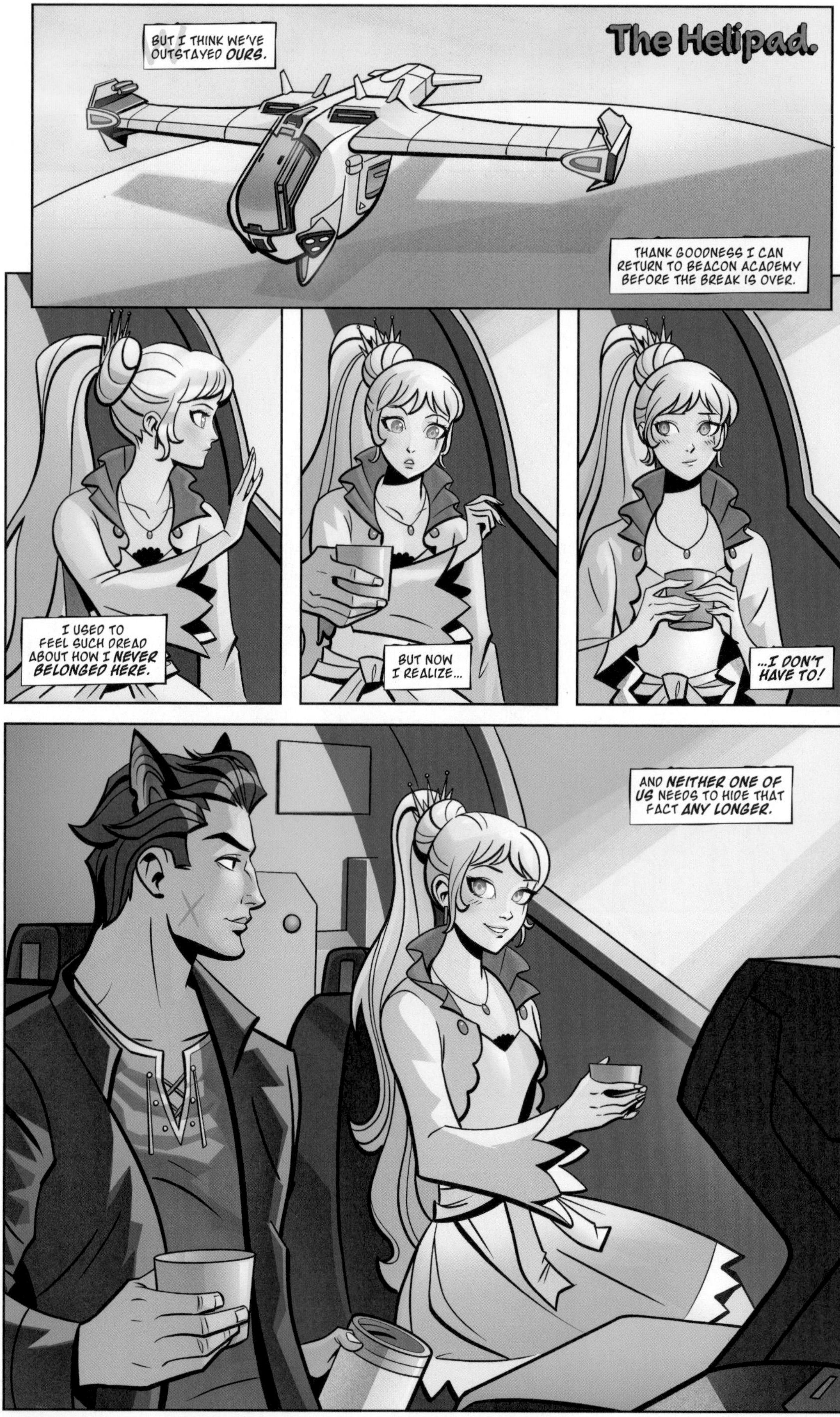

The Helipad.
BUT I THINK WE'VE OUTSTAYED OURS.
THANK GOODNESS I CAN RETURN TO BEACON ACADEMY BEFORE THE BREAK IS OVER.
I USED TO FEEL SUCH DREAD ABOUT HOW I NEVER BELONGED HERE.
BUT NOW I REALIZE...
...I DON'T HAVE TO!
AND NEITHER ONE OF US NEEDS TO HIDE THAT FACT ANY LONGER.

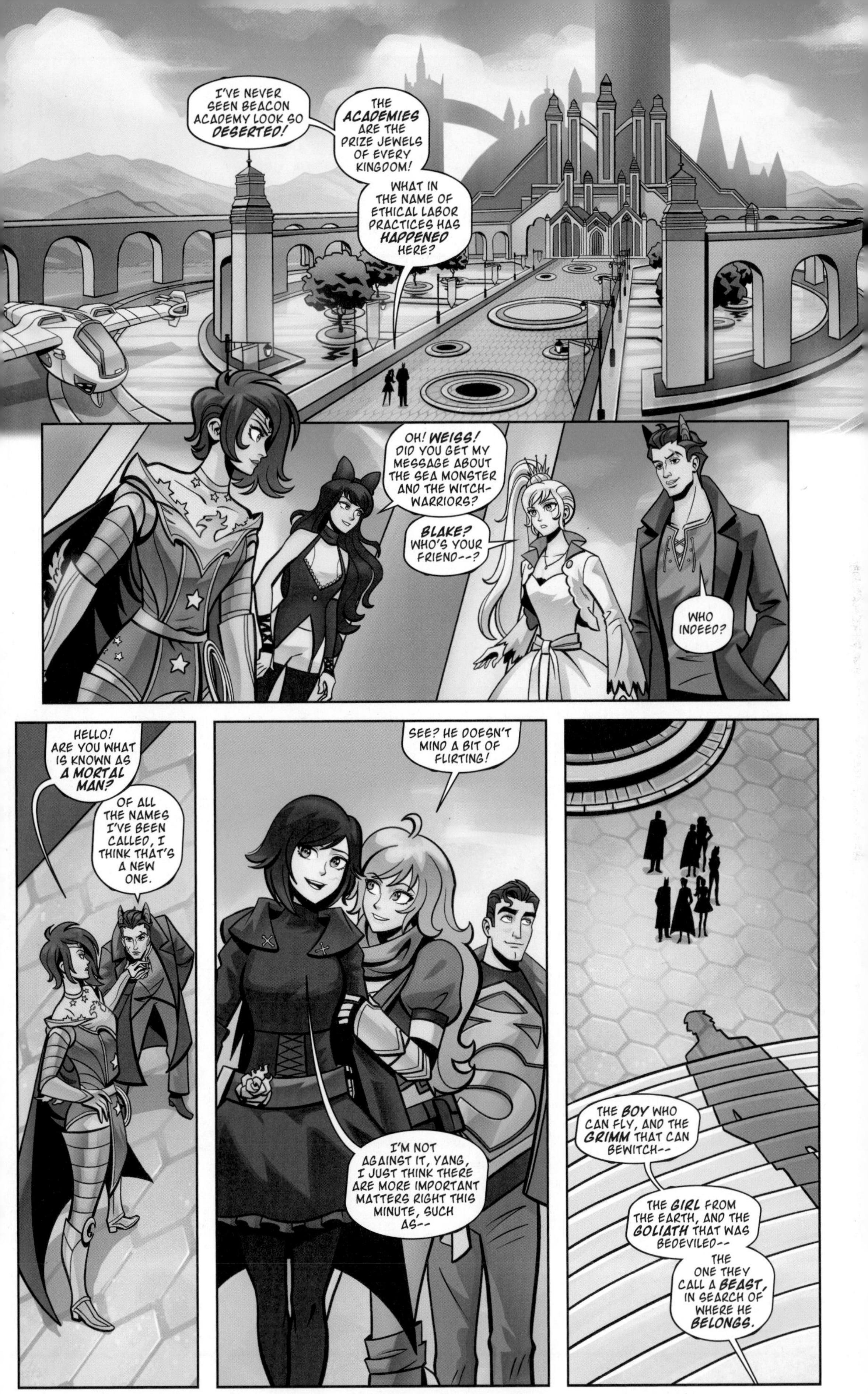
I'VE NEVER SEEN BEACON ACADEMY LOOK SO DESERTED!
THE ACADEMIES ARE THE PRIZE JEWELS OF EVERY KINGDOM!
WHAT IN THE NAME OF ETHICAL LABOR PRACTICES HAS HAPPENED HERE?
OH! WEISS! DID YOU GET MY MESSAGE ABOUT THE SEA MONSTER AND THE WITCH-WARRIORS?
BLAKE? WHO'S YOUR FRIEND--?
WHO INDEED?
HELLO! ARE YOU WHAT IS KNOWN AS A MORTAL MAN?
OF ALL THE NAMES I'VE BEEN CALLED, I THINK THAT'S A NEW ONE.
SEE? HE DOESN'T MIND A BIT OF FLIRTING!
I'M NOT AGAINST IT, YANG, I JUST THINK THERE ARE MORE IMPORTANT MATTERS RIGHT THIS MINUTE, SUCH AS--
THE BOY WHO CAN FLY, AND THE GRIMM THAT CAN BEWITCH--
THE GIRL FROM THE EARTH, AND THE GOLIATH THAT WAS BEDEVILED--
THE ONE THEY CALL A BEAST, IN SEARCH OF WHERE HE BELONGS.

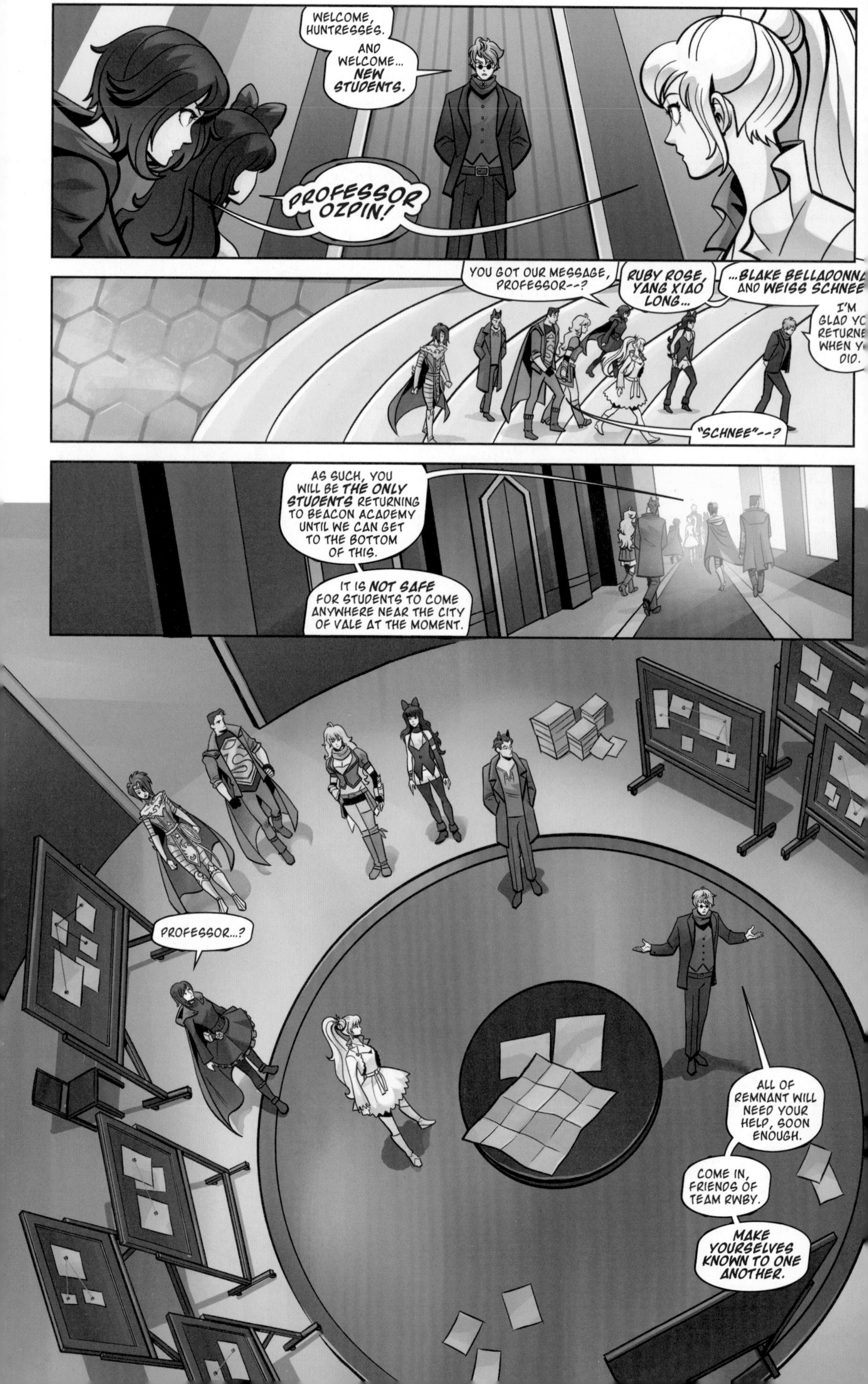
WELCOME, HUNTRESSES.
AND WELCOME... NEW STUDENTS.
PROFESSOR OZPIN!
YOU GOT OUR MESSAGE, PROFESSOR--?
RUBY ROSE, YANG XIAO LONG...
...BLAKE BELLADONNA AND WEISS SCHNEE
I'M GLAD YO RETURNE WHEN YO DID.
"SCHNEE"--?
AS SUCH, YOU WILL BE THE ONLY STUDENTS RETURNING TO BEACON ACADEMY UNTIL WE CAN GET TO THE BOTTOM OF THIS.
IT IS NOT SAFE FOR STUDENTS TO COME ANYWHERE NEAR THE CITY OF VALE AT THE MOMENT.
PROFESSOR...?
ALL OF REMNANT WILL NEED YOUR HELP, SOON ENOUGH.
COME IN, FRIENDS OF TEAM RWBY.
MAKE YOURSELVES KNOWN TO ONE ANOTHER.

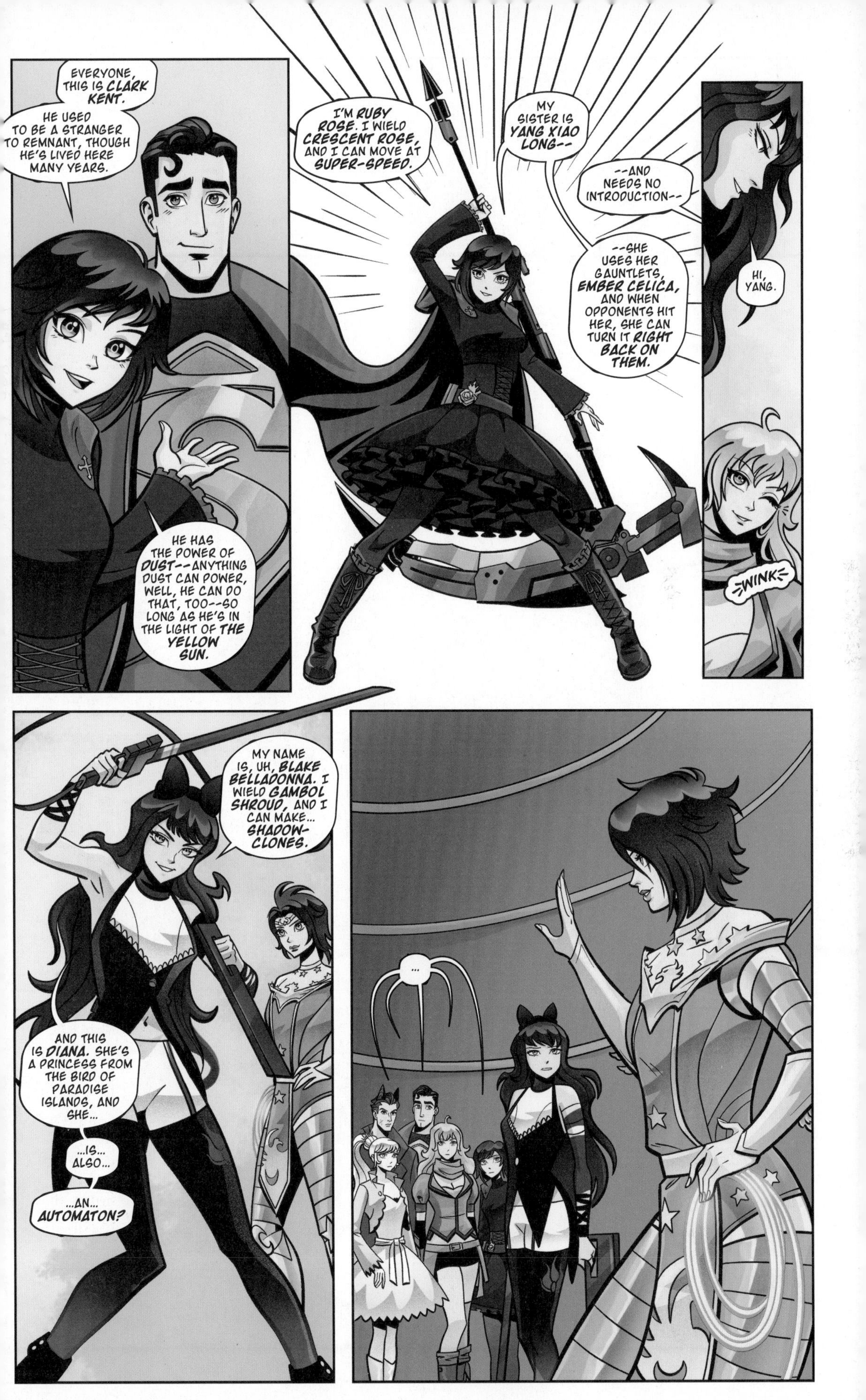
EVERYONE, THIS IS CLARK KENT.
HE USED TO BE A STRANGER TO REMNANT, THOUGH HE'S LIVED HERE MANY YEARS.
HE HAS THE POWER OF DUST--ANYTHING DUST CAN POWER, WELL, HE CAN DO THAT, TOO--SO LONG AS HE'S IN THE LIGHT OF THE YELLOW SUN.
I'M RUBY ROSE. I WIELD CRESCENT ROSE, AND I CAN MOVE AT SUPER-SPEED.
MY SISTER IS YANG XIAO LONG--
--AND NEEDS NO INTRODUCTION--
--SHE USES HER GAUNTLETS, EMBER CELICA, AND WHEN OPPONENTS HIT HER, SHE CAN TURN IT RIGHT BACK ON THEM.
HI, YANG.
WINK
MY NAME IS, UH, BLAKE BELLADONNA. I WIELD GAMBOL SHROUD, AND I CAN MAKE... SHADOW-CLONES.
AND THIS IS DIANA. SHE'S A PRINCESS FROM THE BIRD OF PARADISE ISLANDS, AND SHE...
...IS... ALSO...
...AN... AUTOMATON?
...

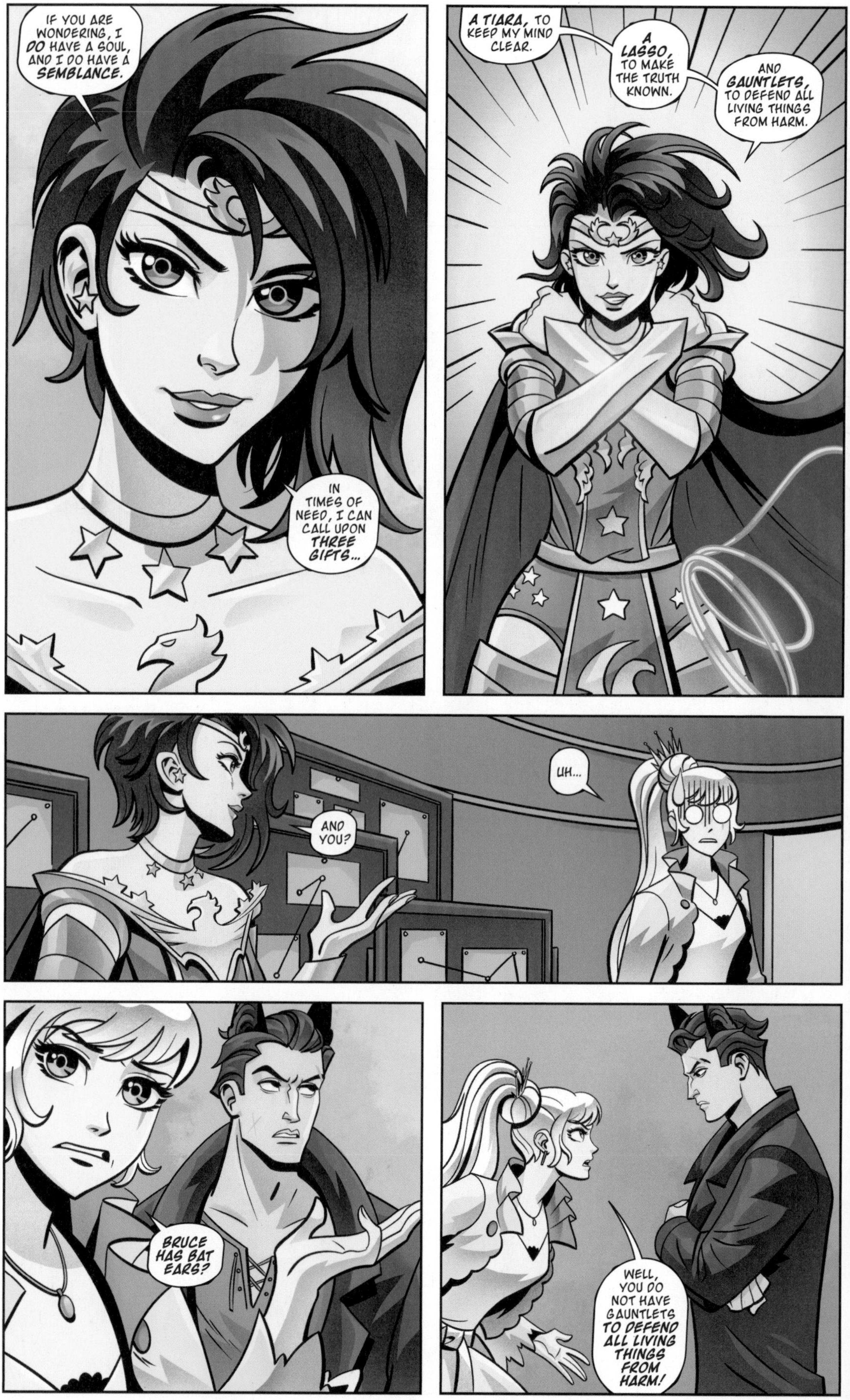
IF YOU ARE WONDERING, I DO HAVE A SOUL, AND I DO HAVE A SEMBLANCE.
IN TIMES OF NEED, I CAN CALL UPON THREE GIFTS...
A TIARA, TO KEEP MY MIND CLEAR.
A LASSO, TO MAKE THE TRUTH KNOWN.
AND GAUNTLETS, TO DEFEND ALL LIVING THINGS FROM HARM.
AND YOU?
UH...
BRUCE HAS BAT EARS?
WELL, YOU DO NOT HAVE GAUNTLETS TO DEFEND ALL LIVING THINGS FROM HARM!

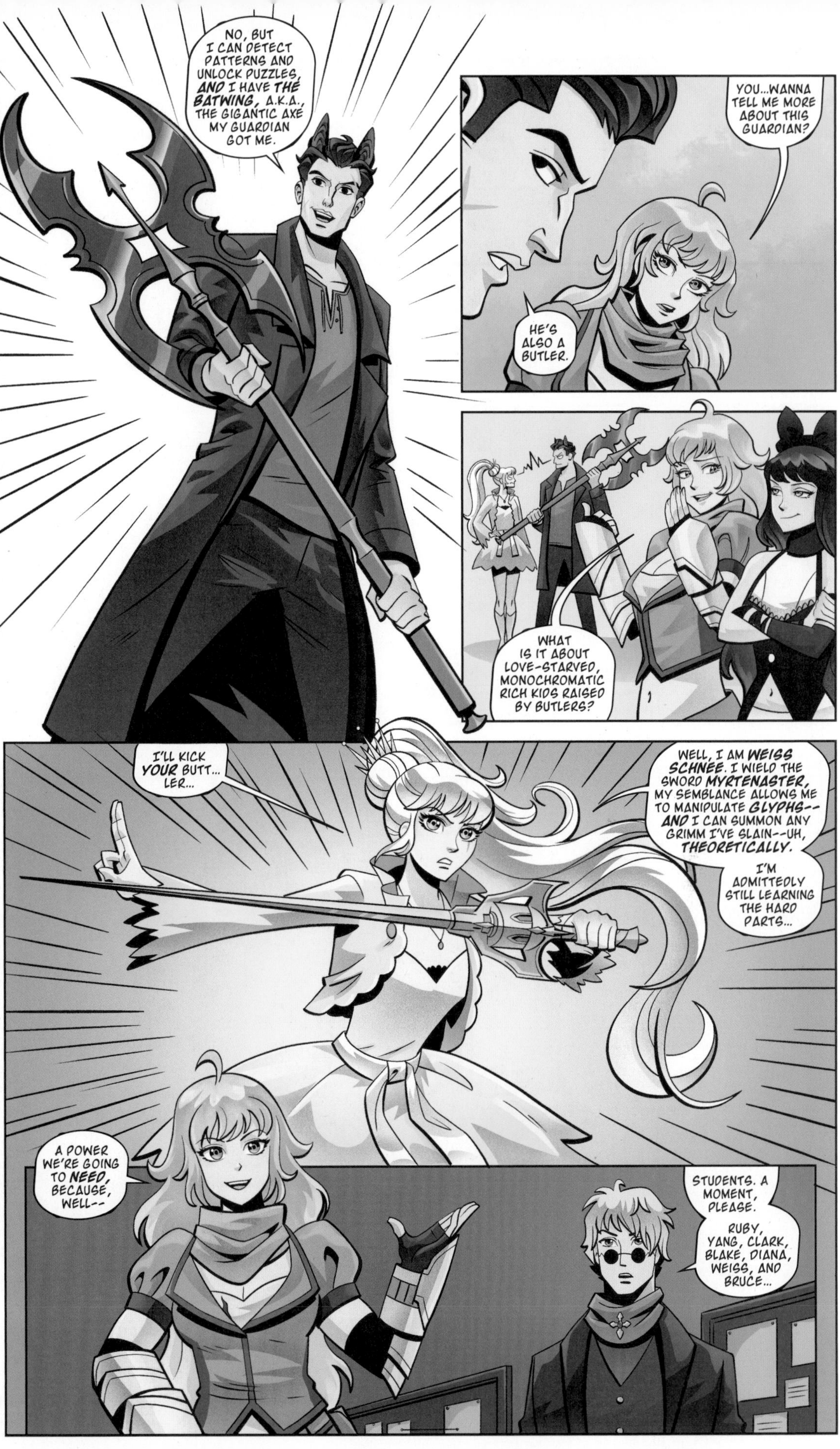
NO, BUT I CAN DETECT PATTERNS AND UNLOCK PUZZLES, AND I HAVE THE BATWING, A.K.A., THE GIGANTIC AXE MY GUARDIAN GOT ME.
YOU...WANNA TELL ME MORE ABOUT THIS GUARDIAN?
HE'S ALSO A BUTLER.
WHAT IS IT ABOUT LOVE-STARVED, MONOCHROMATIC RICH KIDS RAISED BY BUTLERS?
I'LL KICK YOUR BUTT... LER...
WELL, I AM WEISS SCHNEE. I WIELD THE SWORD MYRTENASTER, MY SEMBLANCE ALLOWS ME TO MANIPULATE GLYPHS--AND I CAN SUMMON ANY GRIMM I'VE SLAIN--UH, THEORETICALLY.
I'M ADMITTEDLY STILL LEARNING THE HARD PARTS...
A POWER WE'RE GOING TO NEED, BECAUSE, WELL--
STUDENTS. A MOMENT, PLEASE.
RUBY, YANG, CLARK, BLAKE, DIANA, WEISS, AND BRUCE...

AT THE MOMENT, YOU ARE *THE ONLY HUNTSMEN LEFT IN THE KINGDOM OF VALE.*

WHAT?!

WHERE IS EVERYONE ELSE?

THIS IS HIGHLY UNORTHODOX, AND WILL BE A MATTER OF STRICTEST SECRECY, AMONG THE KINGDOMS OF REMNANT AS WELL AS AMONG YOUR FELLOW HUNTSMEN-IN-TRAINING, SHOULD THEY RETURN.

"SHOULD THEY RETURN"--?!

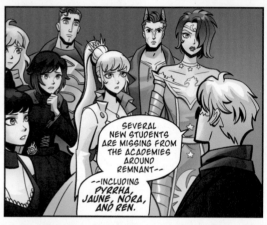

SEVERAL NEW STUDENTS ARE MISSING FROM THE ACADEMIES AROUND REMNANT--

--INCLUDING *PYRRHA, JAUNE, NORA, AND REN.*

STUDENTS HAVE BEEN TAKEN FROM ALL OVER REMNANT, IN BROAD DAYLIGHT AND DARKEST NIGHT, ON ISLANDS AND IN CITIES...

THOSE WITH *UNUSUALLY POWERFUL SEMBLANCES* WERE TARGETED AND DISAPPEARED.

I'VE PUT TOGETHER EVIDENCE OF *STRONG, STRANGE, OR RARE SEMBLANCES* PRESENT IN THE CITY, BUT THIS IS A VERY PERSONAL QUESTION, AS YOU UNDERSTAND, AND MY DATA IS *INCOMPLETE.*

QUARTER

SPEEDSTER

DISAPPEARANCES NEAR DUST SHOPS

ASTRONAUT GONE MISSING

MOREOVER, I FEARED ALLOWING THE STUDENTS TO RETURN...

...IF THEY ARE BEING TARGETED, THEN IT WOULD PUT *ALL OF OUR CHICKS IN ONLY ONE NEST,* SO TO SPEAK, AND MIGHT DRAW TROUBLE RIGHT HERE TO US.

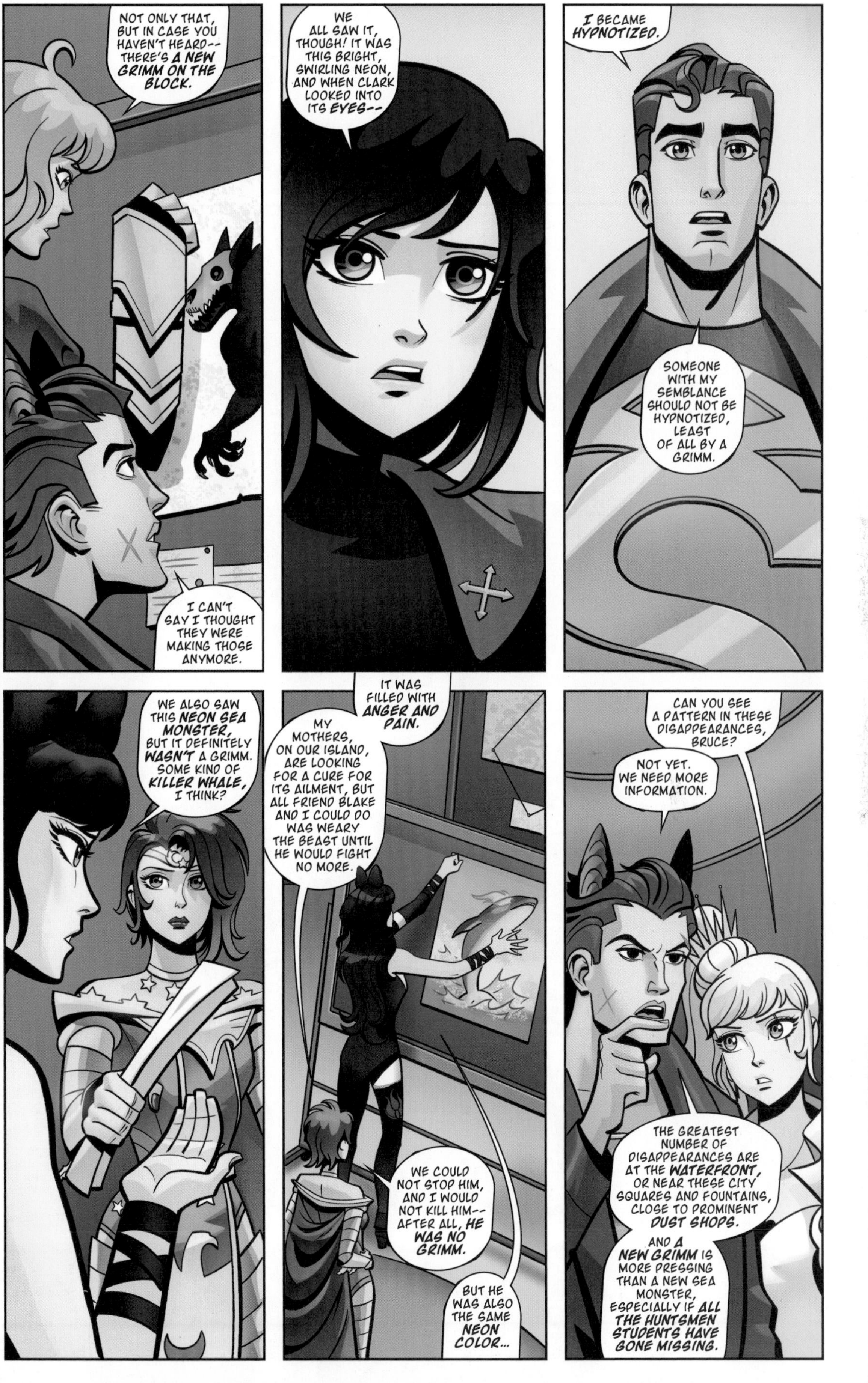
NOT ONLY THAT, BUT IN CASE YOU HAVEN'T HEARD-- THERE'S A NEW GRIMM ON THE BLOCK.
I CAN'T SAY I THOUGHT THEY WERE MAKING THOSE ANYMORE.
WE ALL SAW IT, THOUGH! IT WAS THIS BRIGHT, SWIRLING NEON, AND WHEN CLARK LOOKED INTO ITS EYES--
I BECAME HYPNOTIZED.
SOMEONE WITH MY SEMBLANCE SHOULD NOT BE HYPNOTIZED, LEAST OF ALL BY A GRIMM.
WE ALSO SAW THIS NEON SEA MONSTER, BUT IT DEFINITELY WASN'T A GRIMM. SOME KIND OF KILLER WHALE, I THINK?
IT WAS FILLED WITH ANGER AND PAIN.
MY MOTHERS, ON OUR ISLAND, ARE LOOKING FOR A CURE FOR ITS AILMENT, BUT ALL FRIEND BLAKE AND I COULD DO WAS WEARY THE BEAST UNTIL HE WOULD FIGHT NO MORE.
WE COULD NOT STOP HIM, AND I WOULD NOT KILL HIM-- AFTER ALL, HE WAS NO GRIMM.
BUT HE WAS ALSO THE SAME NEON COLOR...
CAN YOU SEE A PATTERN IN THESE DISAPPEARANCES, BRUCE?
NOT YET. WE NEED MORE INFORMATION.
THE GREATEST NUMBER OF DISAPPEARANCES ARE AT THE WATERFRONT, OR NEAR THESE CITY SQUARES AND FOUNTAINS, CLOSE TO PROMINENT DUST SHOPS.
AND A NEW GRIMM IS MORE PRESSING THAN A NEW SEA MONSTER, ESPECIALLY IF ALL THE HUNTSMEN STUDENTS HAVE GONE MISSING.

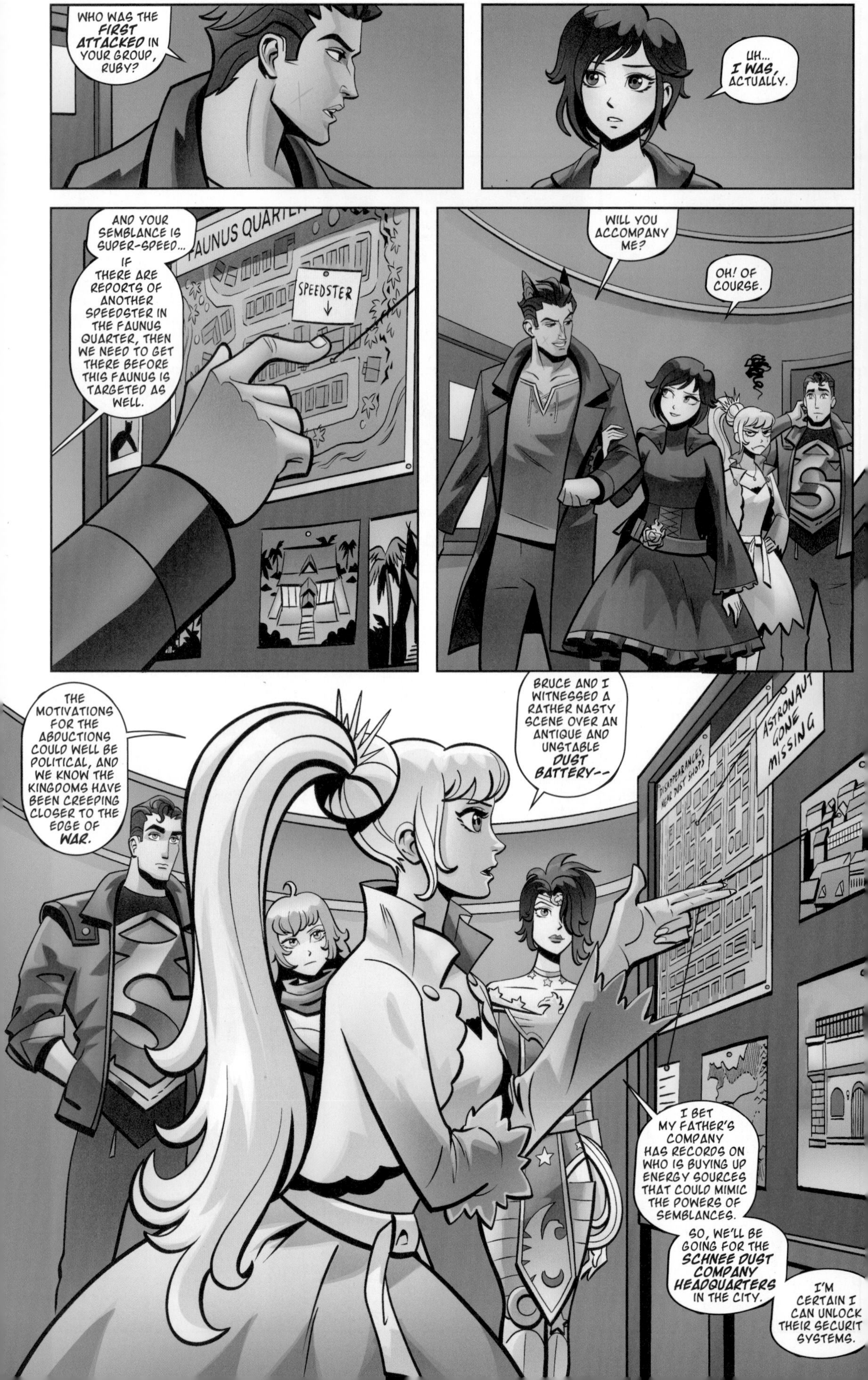

WHO WAS THE FIRST ATTACKED IN YOUR GROUP, RUBY?
UH... I WAS, ACTUALLY.
FAUNUS QUARTER
AND YOUR SEMBLANCE IS SUPER-SPEED...
IF THERE ARE REPORTS OF ANOTHER SPEEDSTER IN THE FAUNUS QUARTER, THEN WE NEED TO GET THERE BEFORE THIS FAUNUS IS TARGETED AS WELL.
SPEEDSTER
WILL YOU ACCOMPANY ME?
OH! OF COURSE.
THE MOTIVATIONS FOR THE ABDUCTIONS COULD WELL BE POLITICAL, AND WE KNOW THE KINGDOMS HAVE BEEN CREEPING CLOSER TO THE EDGE OF WAR.
BRUCE AND I WITNESSED A RATHER NASTY SCENE OVER AN ANTIQUE AND UNSTABLE DUST BATTERY--
DISAPPEARANCES NEAR DUST SHOPS
ASTRONAUT GONE MISSING
I BET MY FATHER'S COMPANY HAS RECORDS ON WHO IS BUYING UP ENERGY SOURCES THAT COULD MIMIC THE POWERS OF SEMBLANCES.
SO, WE'LL BE GOING FOR THE SCHNEE DUST COMPANY HEADQUARTERS IN THE CITY.
I'M CERTAIN I CAN UNLOCK THEIR SECURIT SYSTEMS.

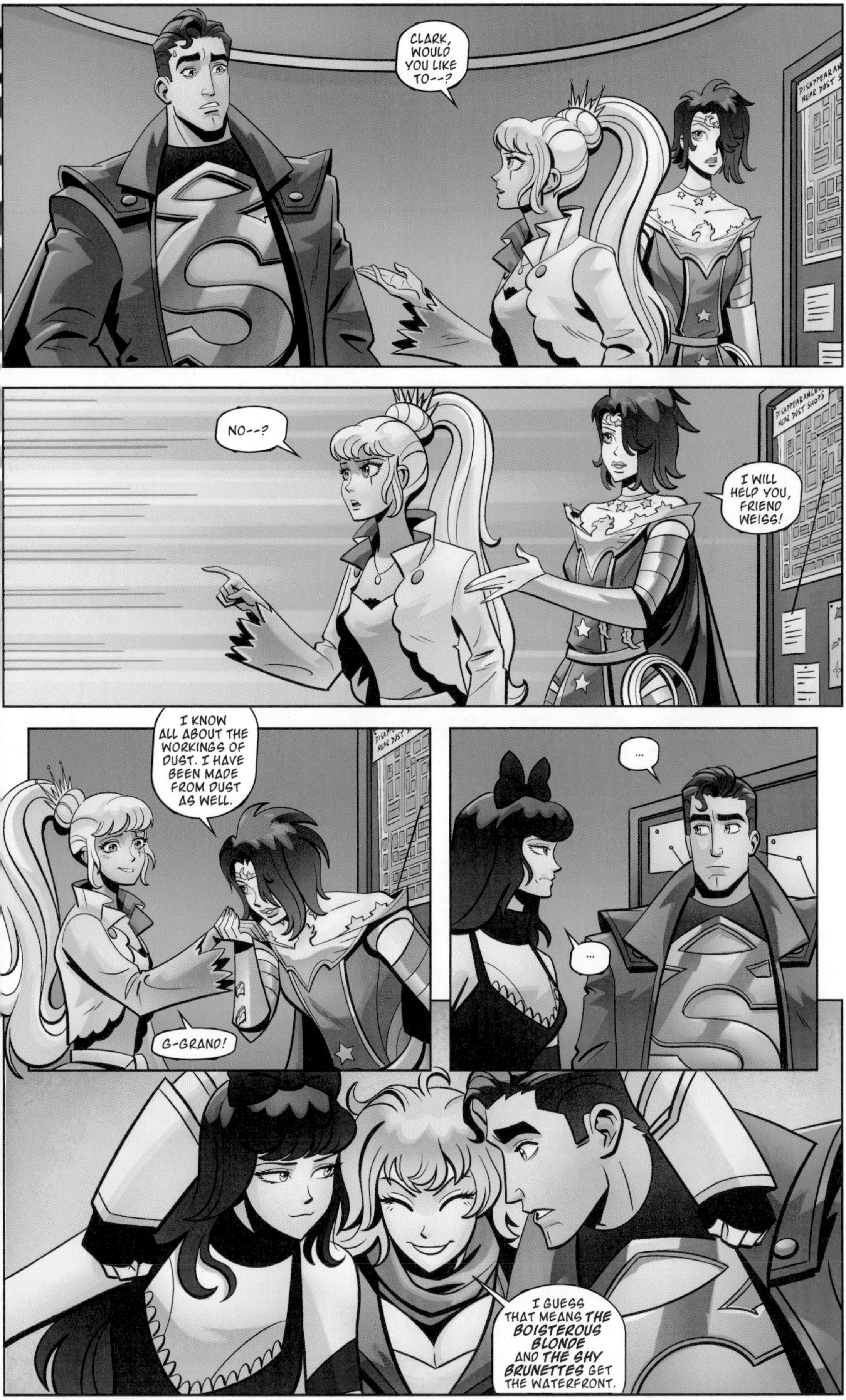
CLARK, WOULD YOU LIKE TO--?
NO--?
I WILL HELP YOU, FRIEND WEISS!
DISAPPEARANCES NEAR DUST SHOPS
I KNOW ALL ABOUT THE WORKINGS OF DUST. I HAVE BEEN MADE FROM DUST AS WELL.
G-GRAND!
...
...
I GUESS THAT MEANS THE BOISTEROUS BLONDE AND THE SHY BRUNETTES GET THE WATERFRONT.

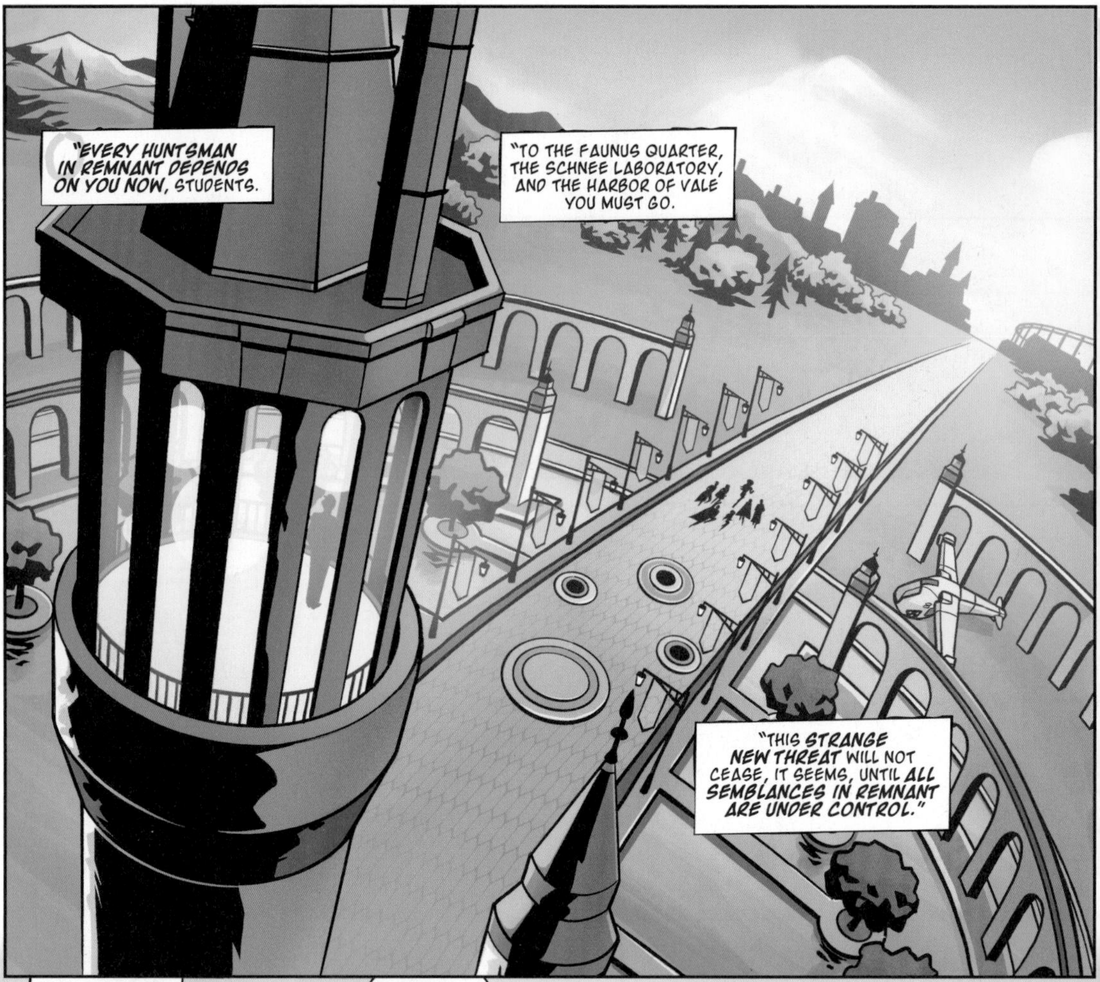
"EVERY HUNTSMAN IN REMNANT DEPENDS ON YOU NOW, STUDENTS.
"TO THE FAUNUS QUARTER, THE SCHNEE LABORATORY, AND THE HARBOR OF VALE YOU MUST GO.
"THIS STRANGE NEW THREAT WILL NOT CEASE, IT SEEMS, UNTIL ALL SEMBLANCES IN REMNANT ARE UNDER CONTROL."

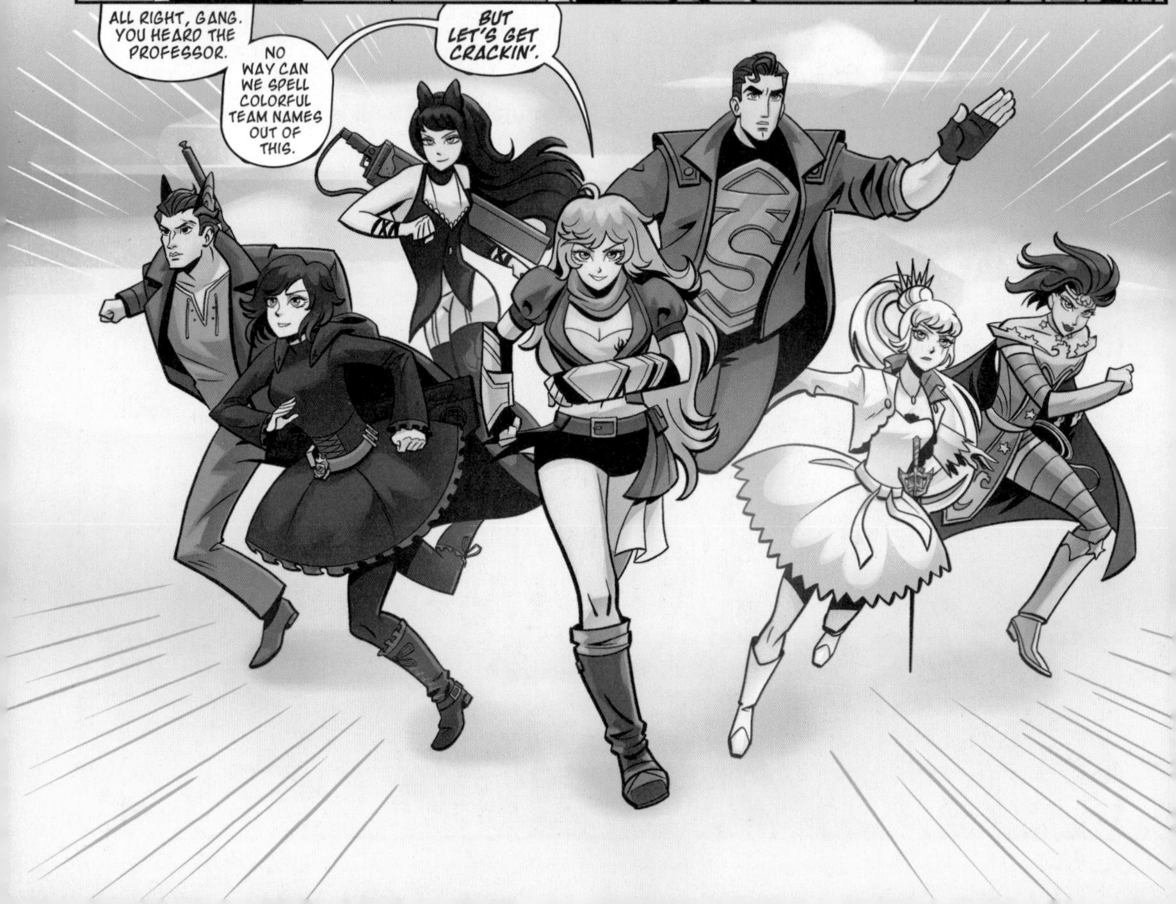
ALL RIGHT, GANG. YOU HEARD THE PROFESSOR.
NO WAY CAN WE SPELL COLORFUL TEAM NAMES OUT OF THIS.
BUT LET'S GET CRACKIN'.

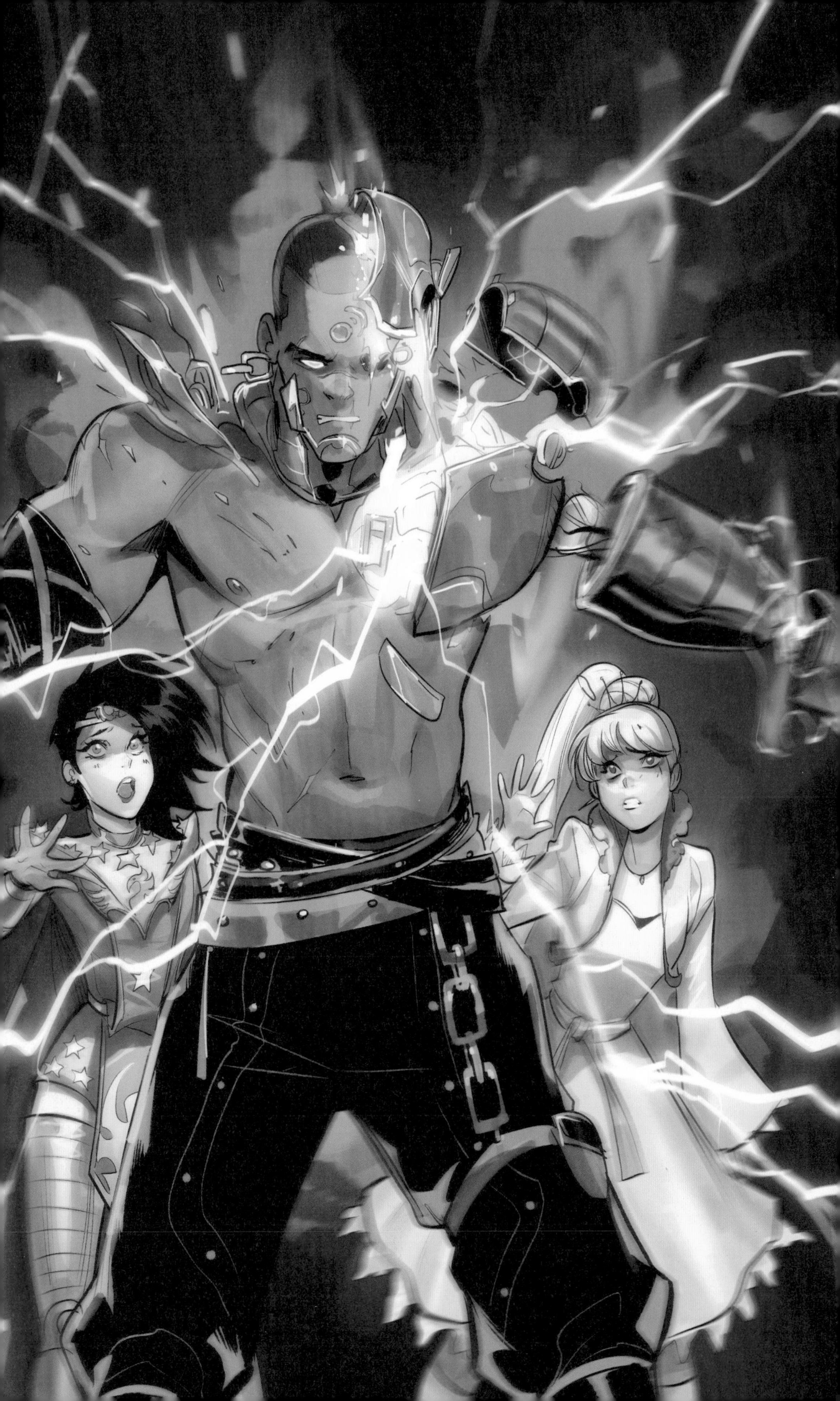

Variant cover by **SIMONE DI MEO**

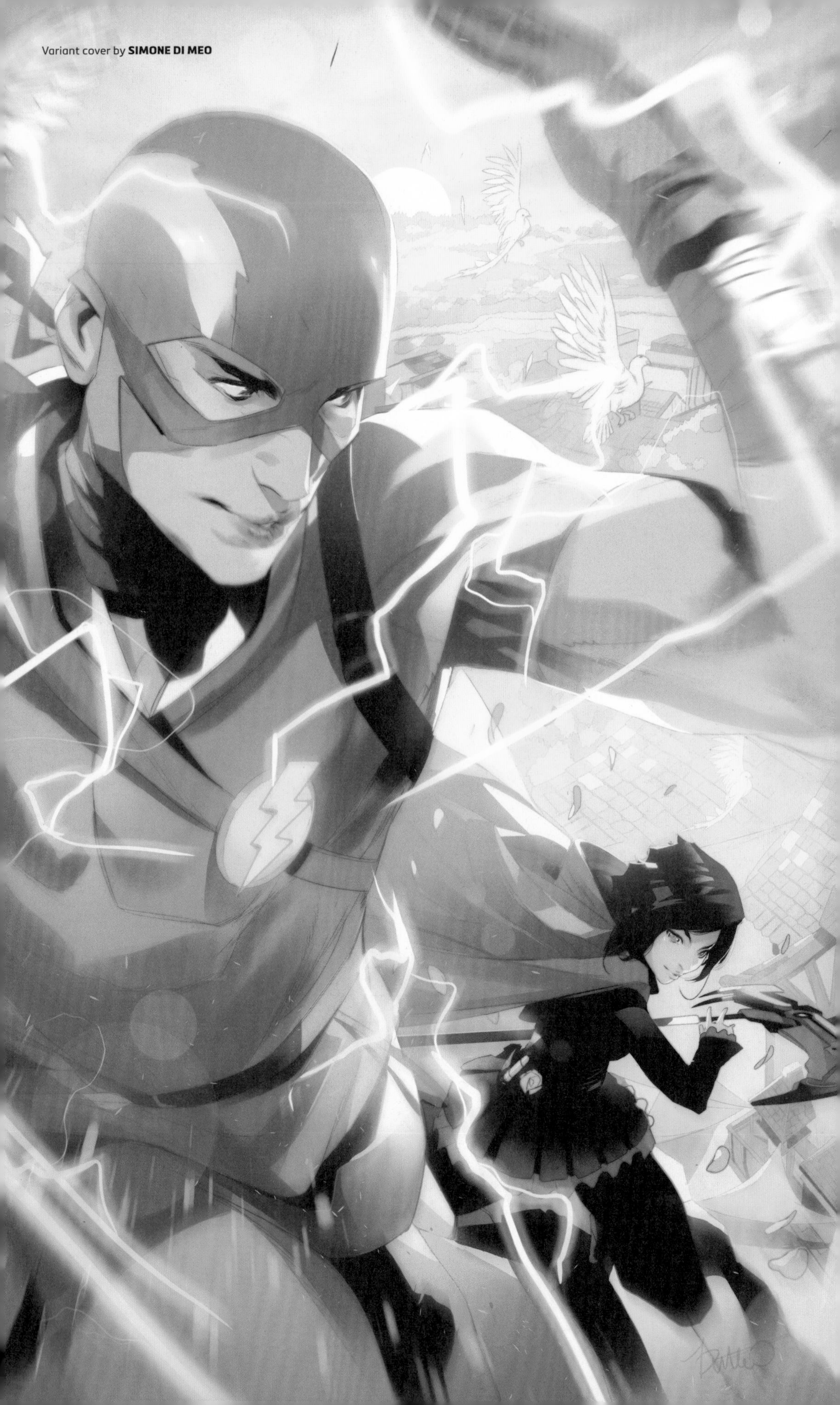

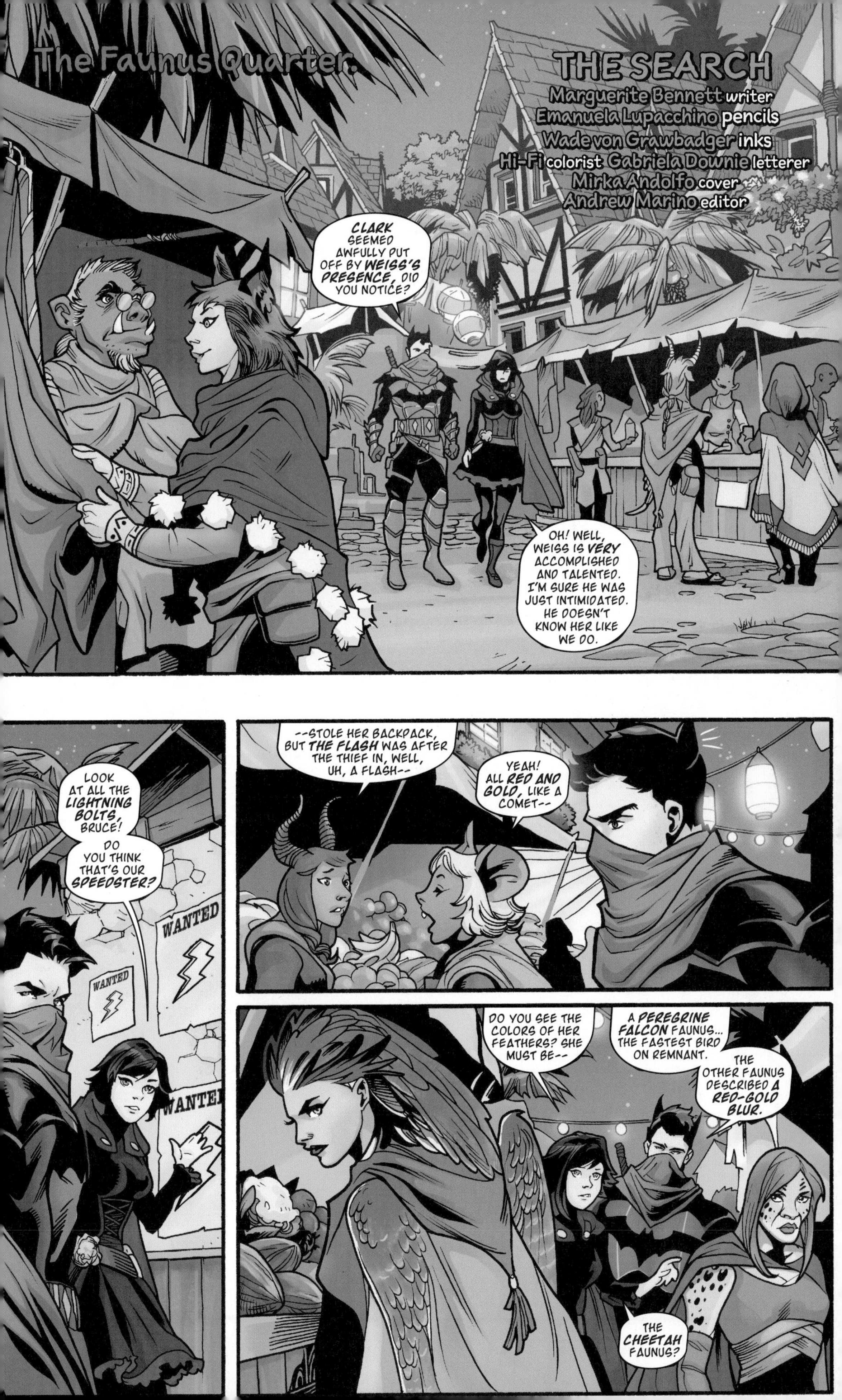
The Faunus Quarter.
THE SEARCH
Marguerite Bennett writer
Emanuela Lupacchino pencils
Wade von Grawbadger inks
Hi-Fi colorist Gabriela Downie letterer
Mirka Andolfo cover
Andrew Marino editor
CLARK SEEMED AWFULLY PUT OFF BY WEISS'S PRESENCE, DID YOU NOTICE?
OH! WELL, WEISS IS VERY ACCOMPLISHED AND TALENTED. I'M SURE HE WAS JUST INTIMIDATED. HE DOESN'T KNOW HER LIKE WE DO.
LOOK AT ALL THE LIGHTNING BOLTS, BRUCE!
DO YOU THINK THAT'S OUR SPEEDSTER?
WANTED
WANTED
WANTE
--STOLE HER BACKPACK, BUT THE FLASH WAS AFTER THE THIEF IN, WELL, UH, A FLASH--
YEAH! ALL RED AND GOLD, LIKE A COMET--
DO YOU SEE THE COLORS OF HER FEATHERS? SHE MUST BE--
A PEREGRINE FALCON FAUNUS... THE FASTEST BIRD ON REMNANT.
THE OTHER FAUNUS DESCRIBED A RED-GOLD BLUR.
THE CHEETAH FAUNUS?

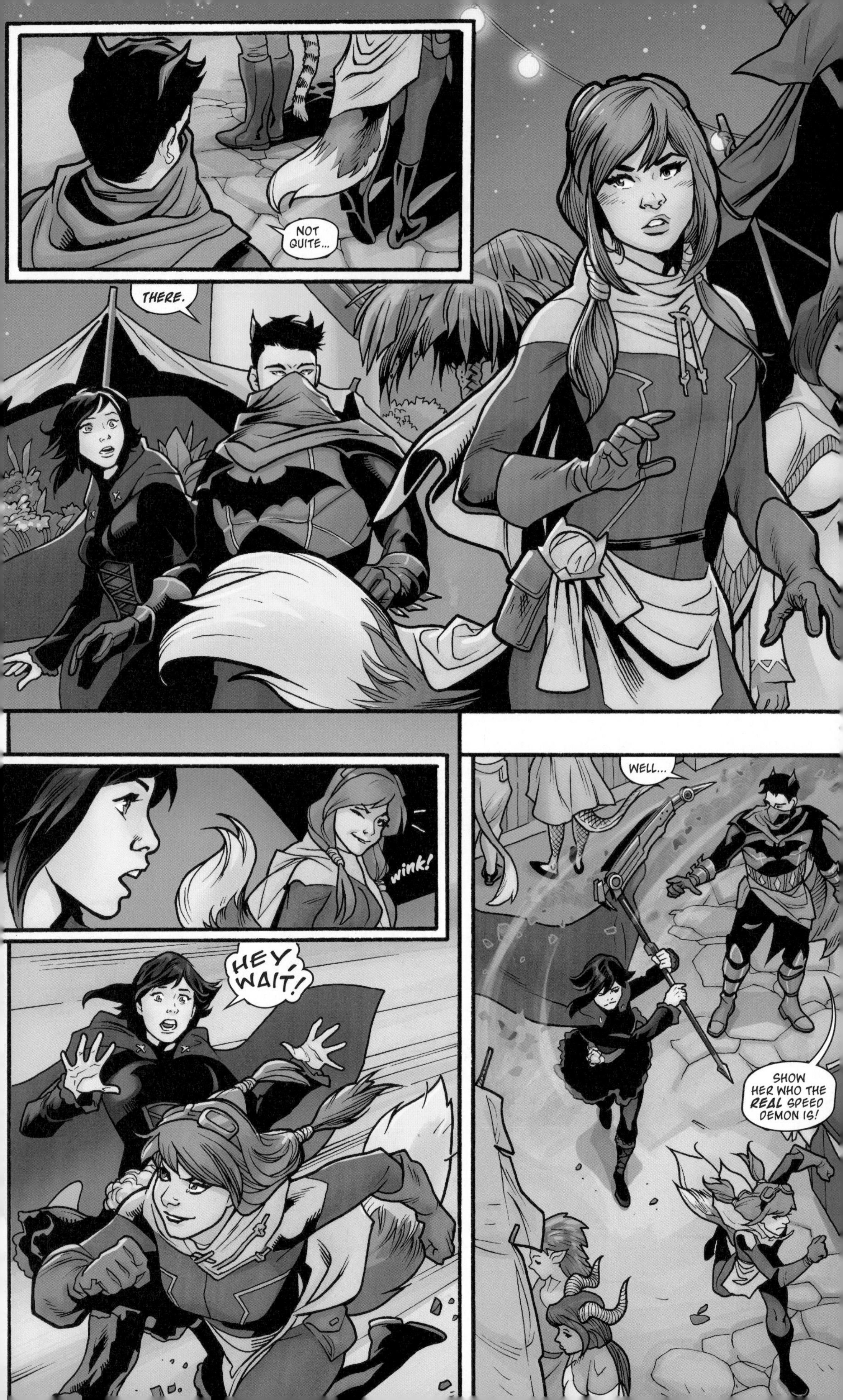
NOT QUITE...
THERE.
wink!
HEY, WAIT!
WELL...
SHOW HER WHO THE REAL SPEED DEMON IS!

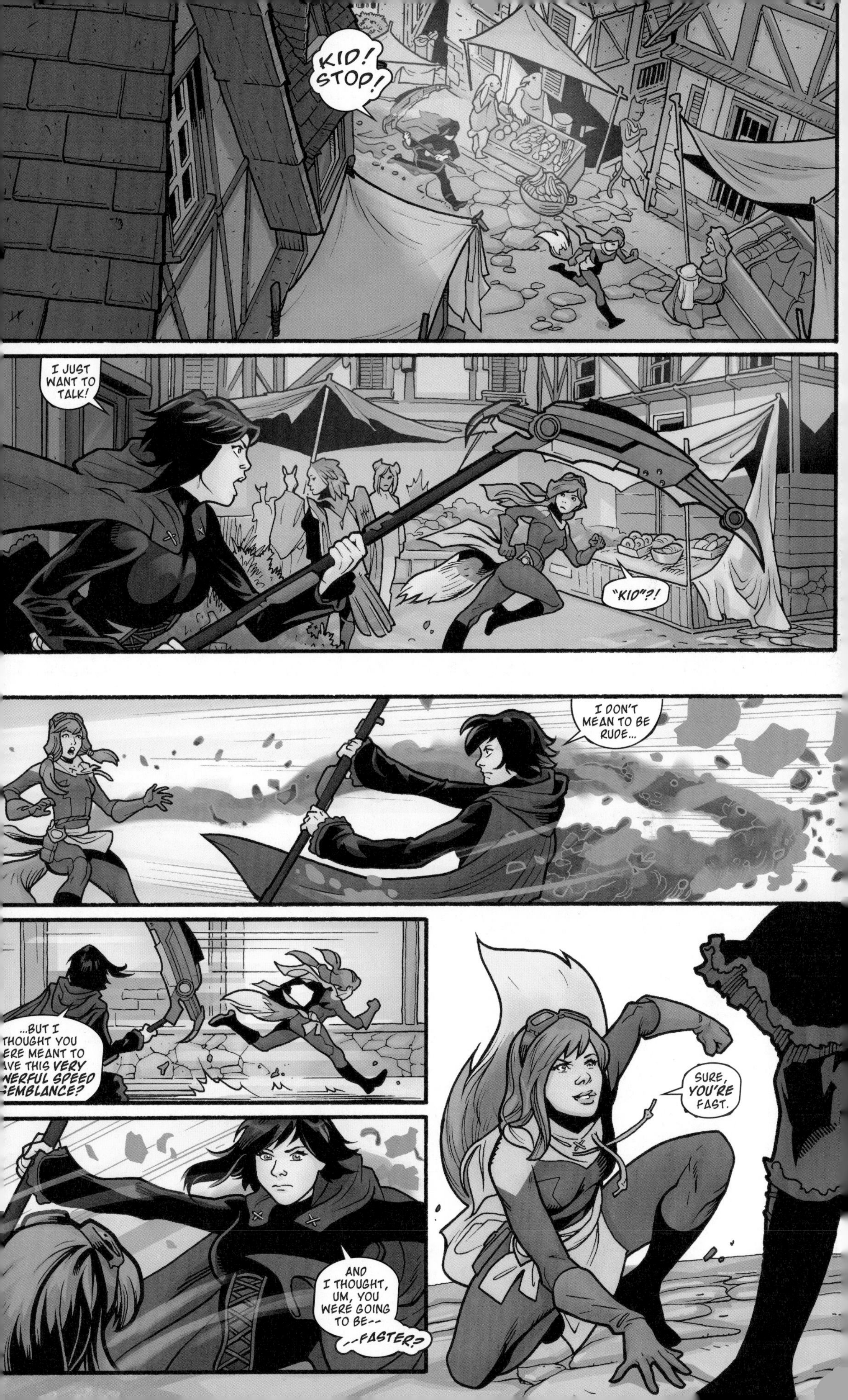
KID! STOP!
I JUST WANT TO TALK!
"KID"?!
I DON'T MEAN TO BE RUDE...
...BUT I THOUGHT YOU ERE MEANT TO AVE THIS VERY WERFUL SPEED SEMBLANCE?
SURE, YOU'RE FAST.
AND I THOUGHT, UM, YOU WERE GOING TO BE--
--FASTER?

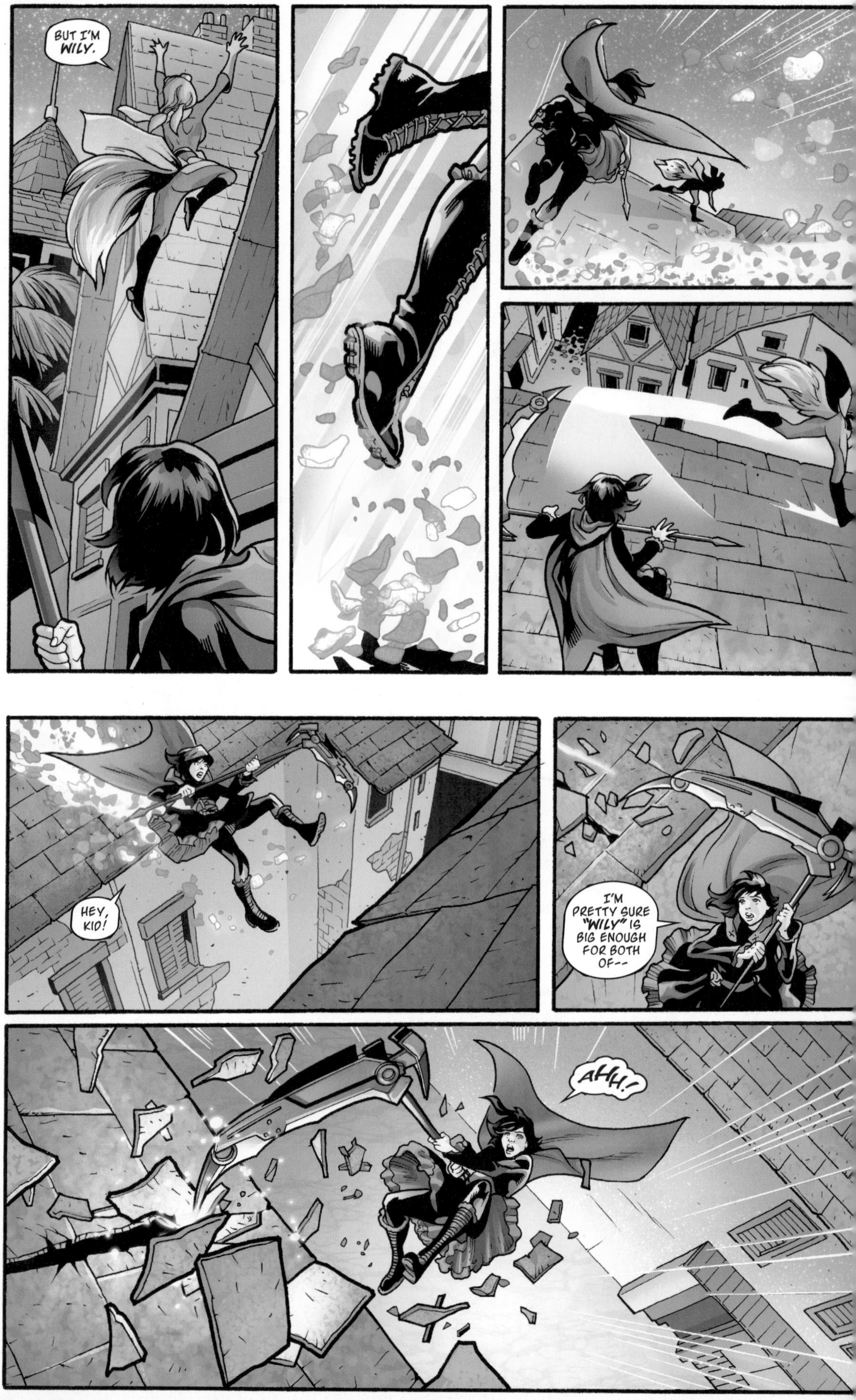
BUT I'M WILY.
HEY, KID!
I'M PRETTY SURE "WILY" IS BIG ENOUGH FOR BOTH OF--
AHH!

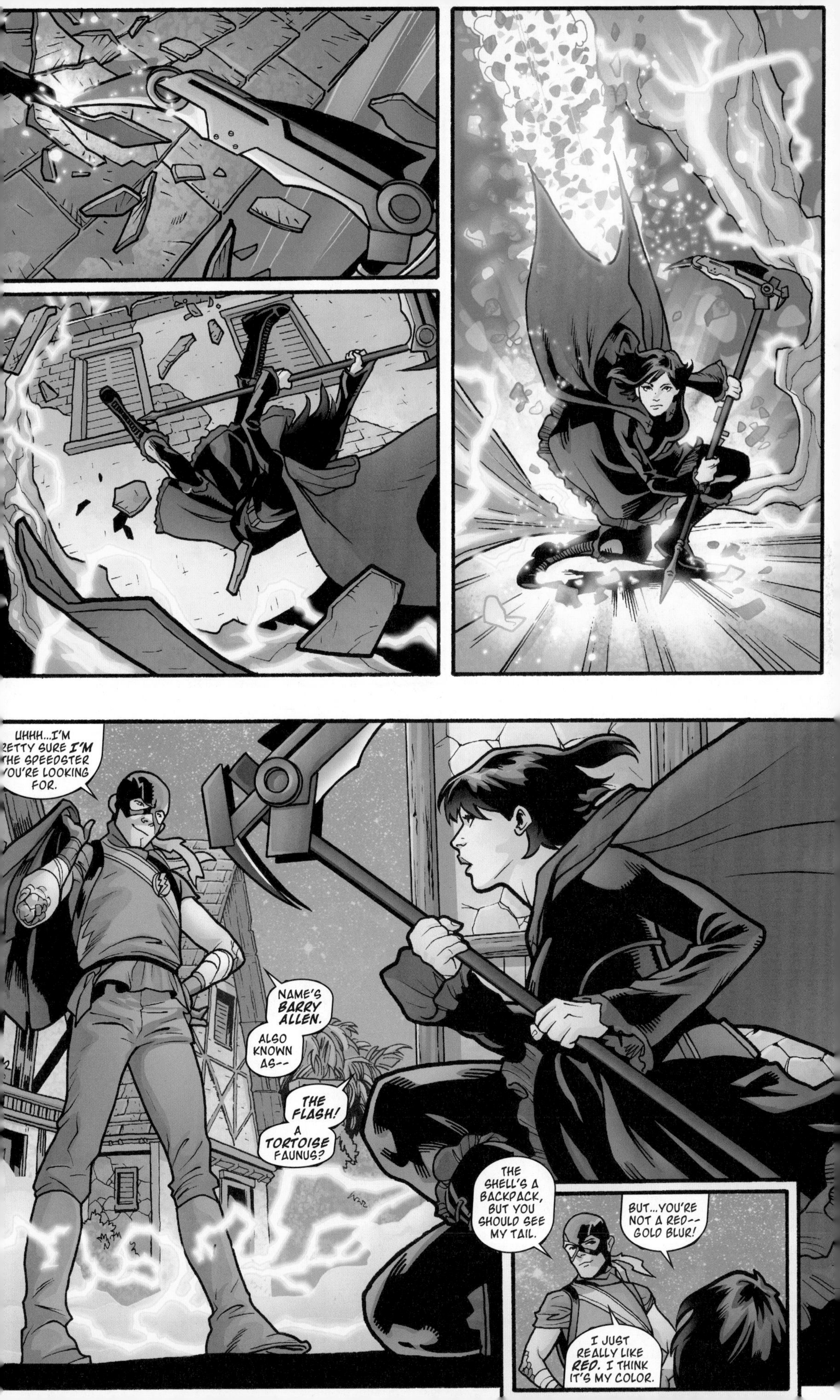

UHHH...I'M PRETTY SURE I'M THE SPEEDSTER YOU'RE LOOKING FOR.
NAME'S BARRY ALLEN.
ALSO KNOWN AS--
THE FLASH!
A TORTOISE FAUNUS?
THE SHELL'S A BACKPACK, BUT YOU SHOULD SEE MY TAIL.
BUT...YOU'RE NOT A RED--GOLD BLUR!
I JUST REALLY LIKE RED. I THINK IT'S MY COLOR.

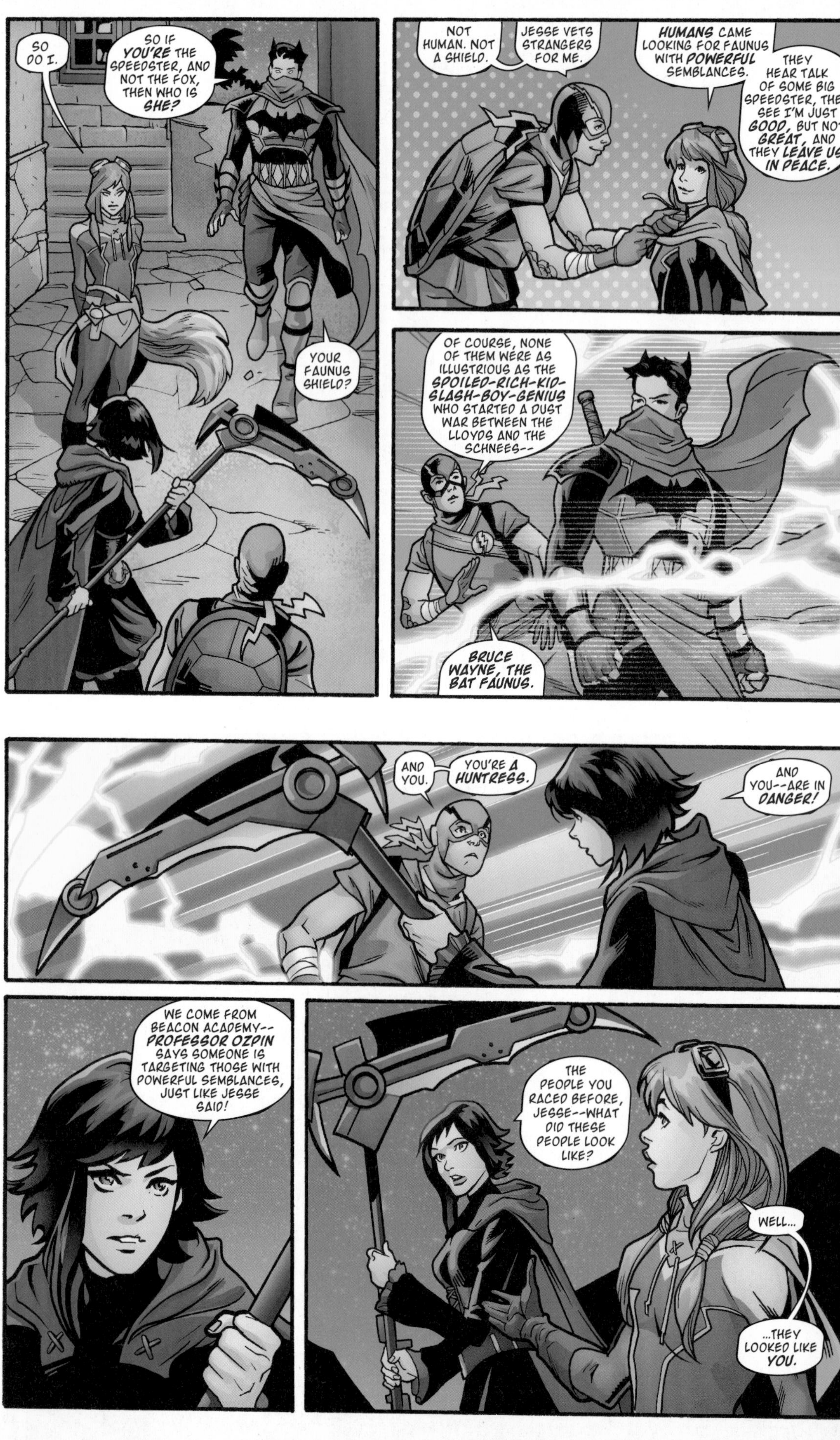
SO DO I.
SO IF YOU'RE THE SPEEDSTER, AND NOT THE FOX, THEN WHO IS SHE?
YOUR FAUNUS SHIELD?
NOT HUMAN. NOT A SHIELD.
JESSE VETS STRANGERS FOR ME.
HUMANS CAME LOOKING FOR FAUNUS WITH POWERFUL SEMBLANCES.
THEY HEAR TALK OF SOME BIG SPEEDSTER, THEN SEE I'M JUST GOOD, BUT NOT GREAT, AND THEY LEAVE US IN PEACE.
OF COURSE, NONE OF THEM WERE AS ILLUSTRIOUS AS THE SPOILED-RICH-KID-SLASH-BOY-GENIUS WHO STARTED A DUST WAR BETWEEN THE LLOYDS AND THE SCHNEES--
BRUCE WAYNE, THE BAT FAUNUS.
AND YOU.
YOU'RE A HUNTRESS.
AND YOU--ARE IN DANGER!
WE COME FROM BEACON ACADEMY--PROFESSOR OZPIN SAYS SOMEONE IS TARGETING THOSE WITH POWERFUL SEMBLANCES, JUST LIKE JESSE SAID!
THE PEOPLE YOU RACED BEFORE, JESSE--WHAT DID THESE PEOPLE LOOK LIKE?
WELL...
...THEY LOOKED LIKE YOU.

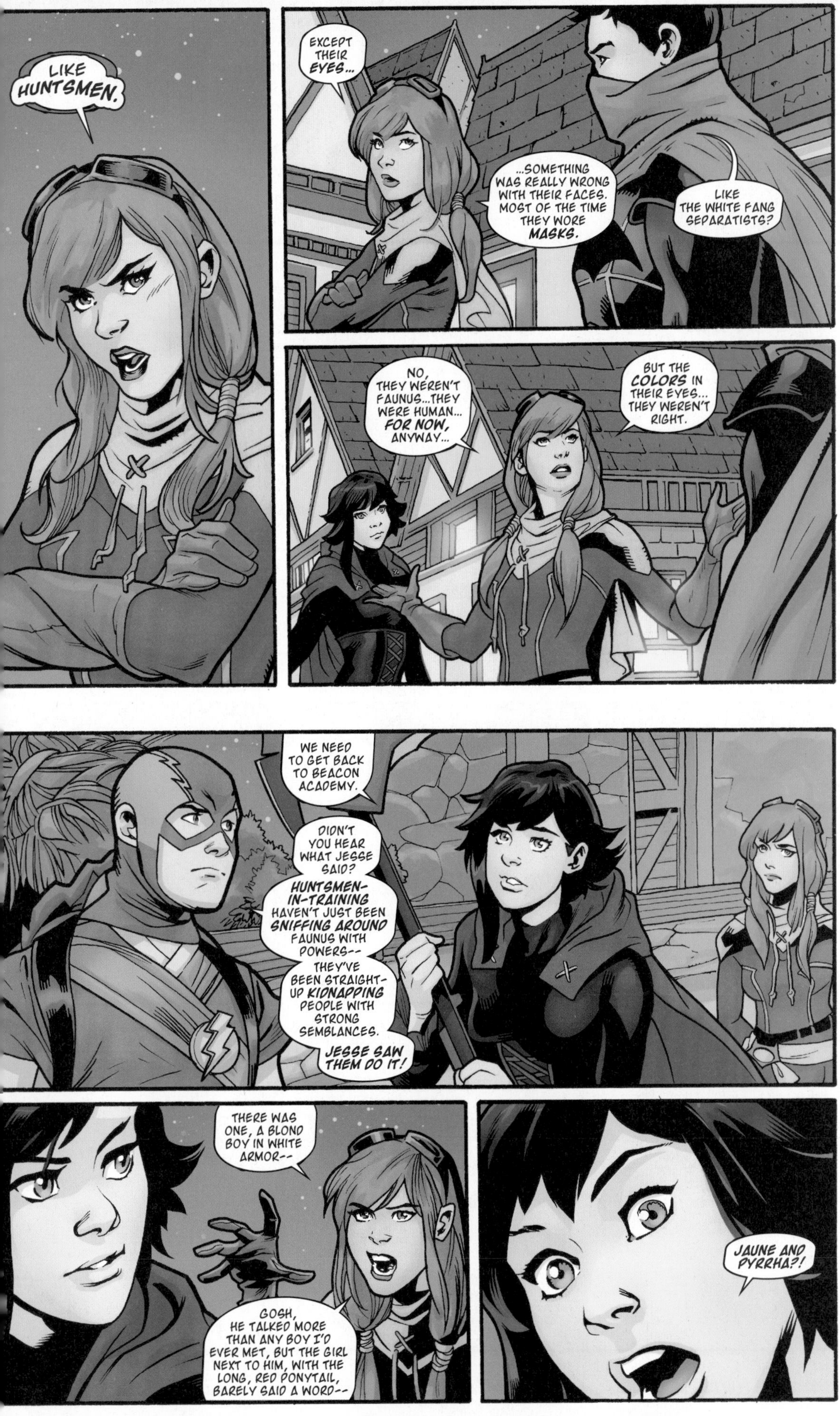
LIKE HUNTSMEN.
EXCEPT THEIR EYES...
...SOMETHING WAS REALLY WRONG WITH THEIR FACES. MOST OF THE TIME THEY WORE MASKS.
LIKE THE WHITE FANG SEPARATISTS?
NO, THEY WEREN'T FAUNUS...THEY WERE HUMAN... FOR NOW, ANYWAY...
BUT THE COLORS IN THEIR EYES... THEY WEREN'T RIGHT.
WE NEED TO GET BACK TO BEACON ACADEMY.
DIDN'T YOU HEAR WHAT JESSE SAID?
HUNTSMEN-IN-TRAINING HAVEN'T JUST BEEN SNIFFING AROUND FAUNUS WITH POWERS--
THEY'VE BEEN STRAIGHT-UP KIDNAPPING PEOPLE WITH STRONG SEMBLANCES.
JESSE SAW THEM DO IT!
THERE WAS ONE, A BLOND BOY IN WHITE ARMOR--
GOSH, HE TALKED MORE THAN ANY BOY I'D EVER MET, BUT THE GIRL NEXT TO HIM, WITH THE LONG, RED PONYTAIL, BARELY SAID A WORD--
JAUNE AND PYRRHA?!

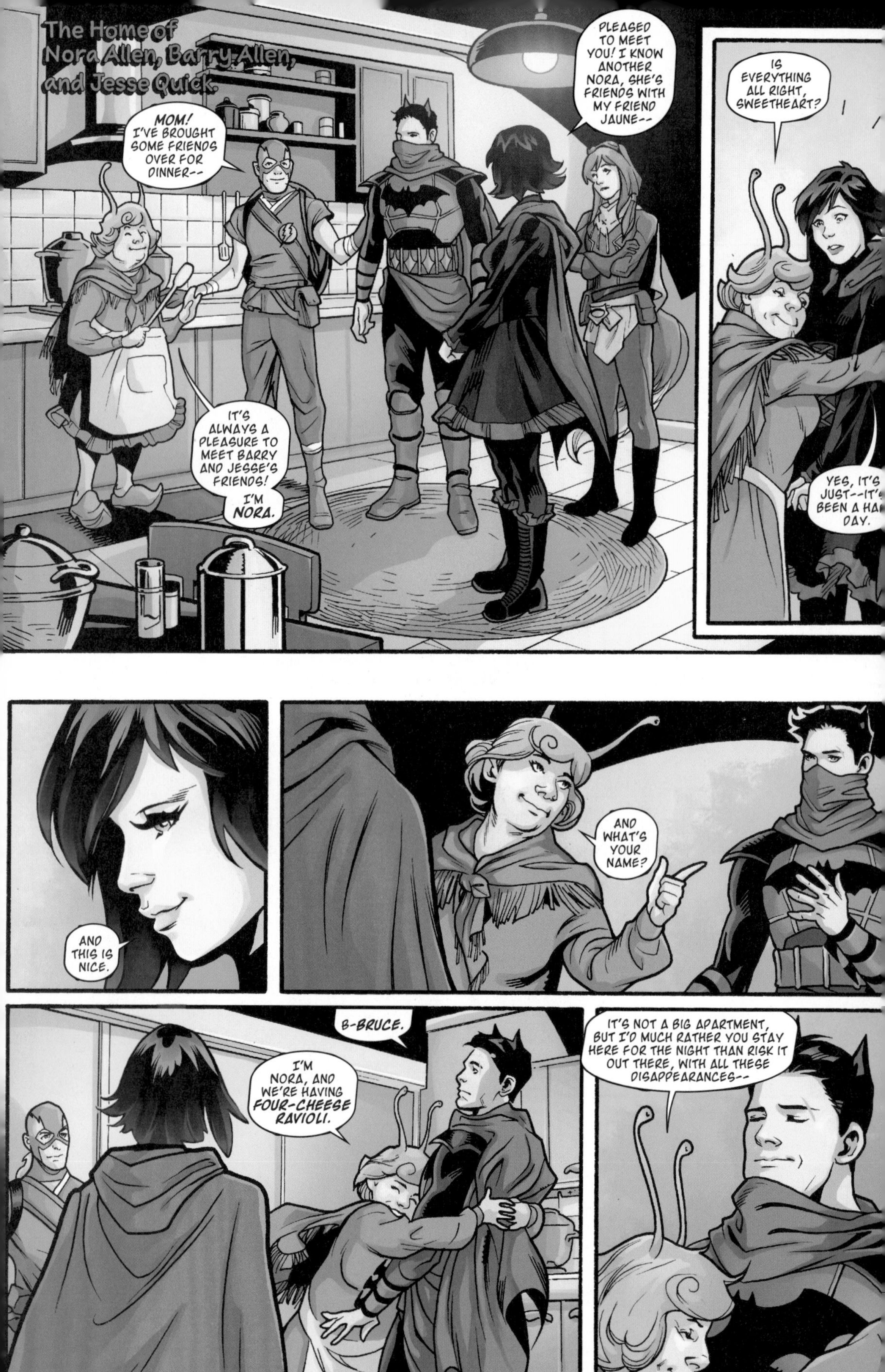
The Home of Nora Allen, Barry Allen, and Jesse Quick.
MOM! I'VE BROUGHT SOME FRIENDS OVER FOR DINNER--
PLEASED TO MEET YOU! I KNOW ANOTHER NORA, SHE'S FRIENDS WITH MY FRIEND JAUNE--
IT'S ALWAYS A PLEASURE TO MEET BARRY AND JESSE'S FRIENDS!
I'M NORA.
IS EVERYTHING ALL RIGHT, SWEETHEART?
YES, IT'S JUST--IT'S BEEN A HA DAY.
AND THIS IS NICE.
AND WHAT'S YOUR NAME?
B-BRUCE.
I'M NORA, AND WE'RE HAVING FOUR-CHEESE RAVIOLI.
IT'S NOT A BIG APARTMENT, BUT I'D MUCH RATHER YOU STAY HERE FOR THE NIGHT THAN RISK IT OUT THERE, WITH ALL THESE DISAPPEARANCES--

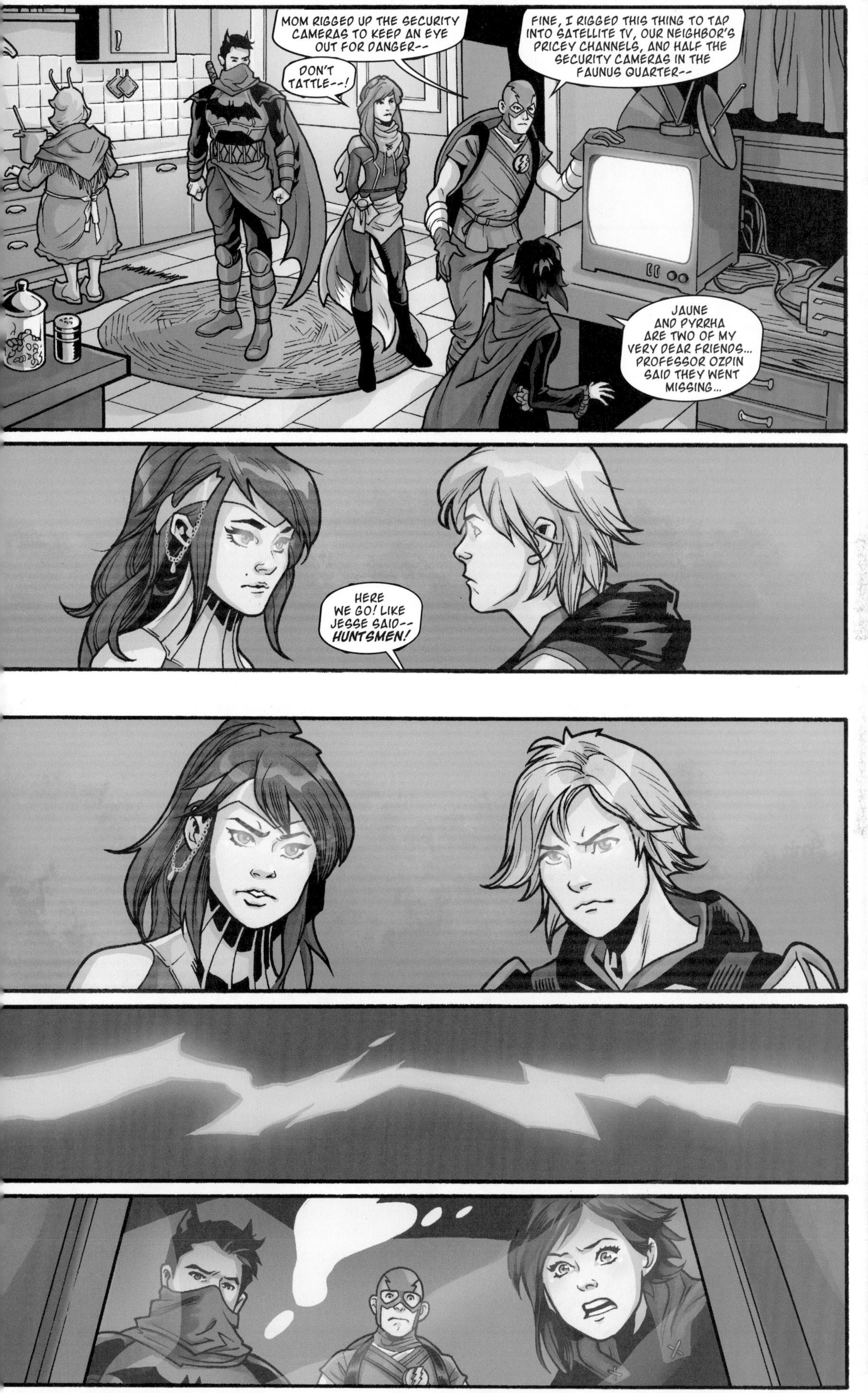
MOM RIGGED UP THE SECURITY CAMERAS TO KEEP AN EYE OUT FOR DANGER--
DON'T TATTLE--!
FINE, I RIGGED THIS THING TO TAP INTO SATELLITE TV, OUR NEIGHBOR'S PRICEY CHANNELS, AND HALF THE SECURITY CAMERAS IN THE FAUNUS QUARTER--
JAUNE AND PYRRHA ARE TWO OF MY VERY DEAR FRIENDS... PROFESSOR OZPIN SAID THEY WENT MISSING...
HERE WE GO! LIKE JESSE SAID-- **HUNTSMEN!**

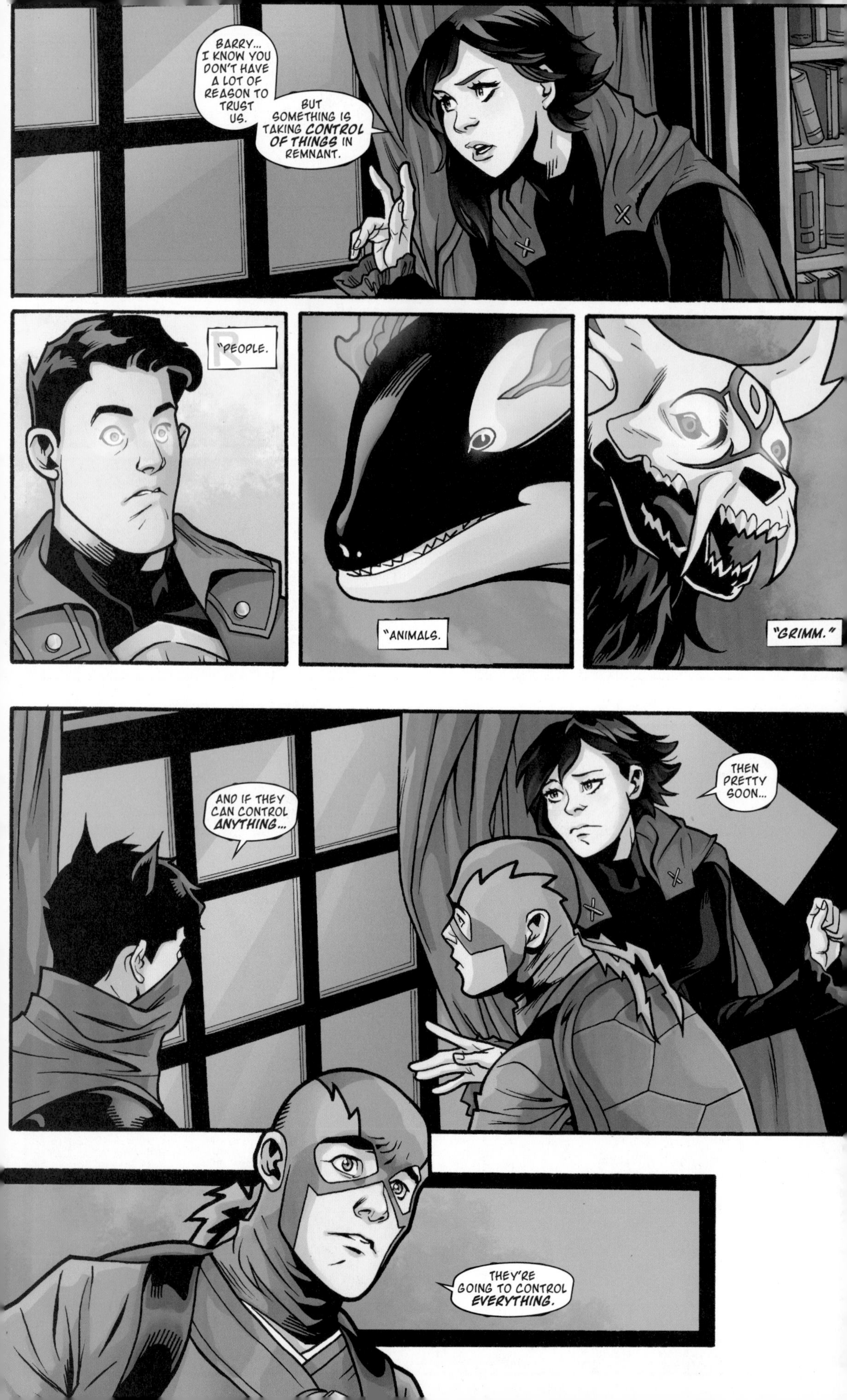
BARRY... I KNOW YOU DON'T HAVE A LOT OF REASON TO TRUST US.
BUT SOMETHING IS TAKING **CONTROL OF THINGS** IN REMNANT.
"PEOPLE.
"ANIMALS.
"GRIMM."
AND IF THEY CAN CONTROL **ANYTHING...**
THEN PRETTY SOON...
THEY'RE GOING TO CONTROL **EVERYTHING.**

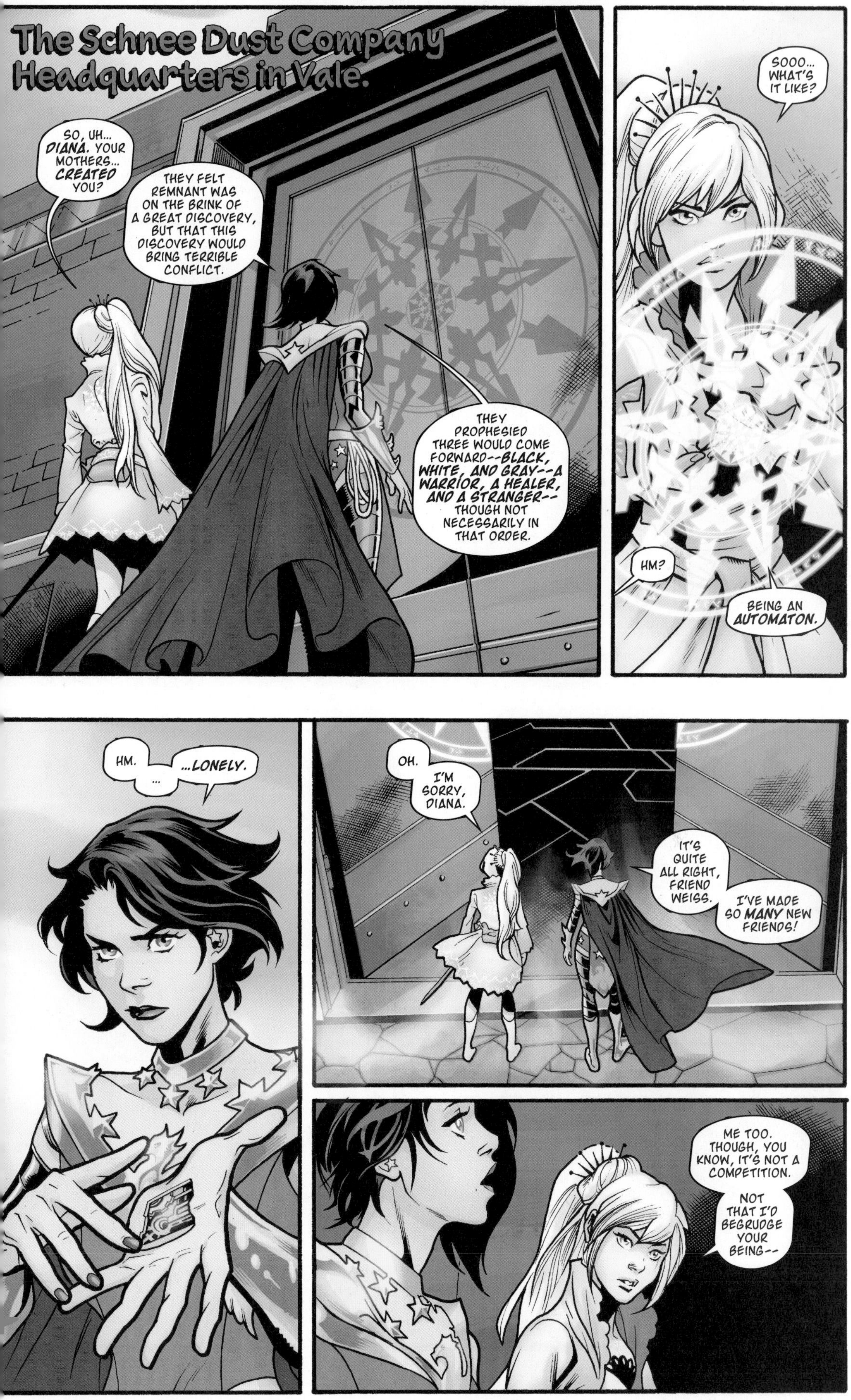
The Schnee Dust Company Headquarters in Vale.
SO, UH... DIANA. YOUR MOTHERS... CREATED YOU?
THEY FELT REMNANT WAS ON THE BRINK OF A GREAT DISCOVERY, BUT THAT THIS DISCOVERY WOULD BRING TERRIBLE CONFLICT.
THEY PROPHESIED THREE WOULD COME FORWARD--BLACK, WHITE, AND GRAY--A WARRIOR, A HEALER, AND A STRANGER--THOUGH NOT NECESSARILY IN THAT ORDER.
SOOO... WHAT'S IT LIKE?
HM?
BEING AN AUTOMATON.
HM.
...
...LONELY.
OH.
I'M SORRY, DIANA.
IT'S QUITE ALL RIGHT, FRIEND WEISS.
I'VE MADE SO MANY NEW FRIENDS!
ME TOO. THOUGH, YOU KNOW, IT'S NOT A COMPETITION.
NOT THAT I'D BEGRUDGE YOUR BEING--

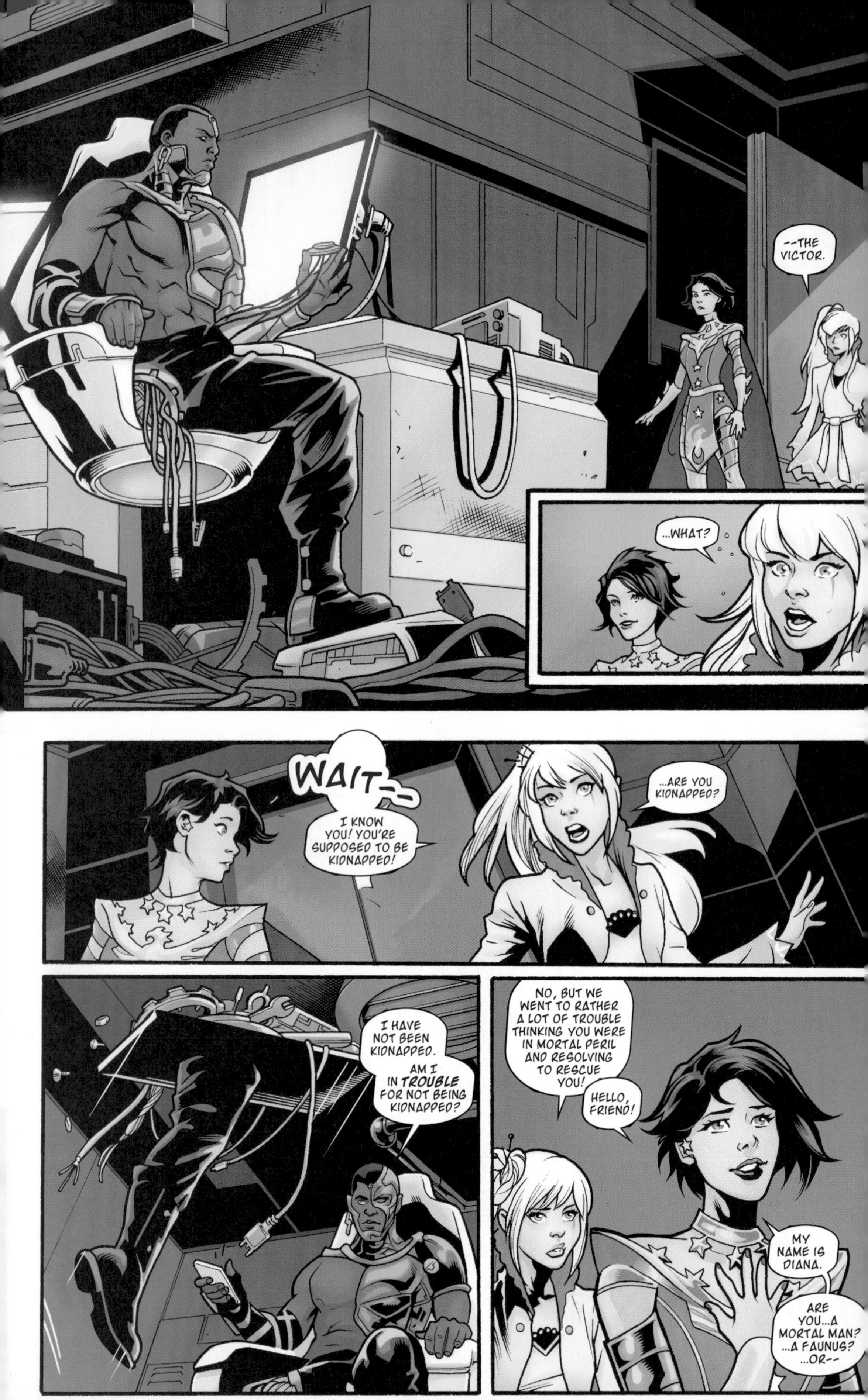
--THE VICTOR.
...WHAT?
WAIT--
I KNOW YOU! YOU'RE SUPPOSED TO BE KIDNAPPED!
...ARE YOU KIDNAPPED?
I HAVE NOT BEEN KIDNAPPED.
AM I IN TROUBLE FOR NOT BEING KIDNAPPED?
NO, BUT WE WENT TO RATHER A LOT OF TROUBLE THINKING YOU WERE IN MORTAL PERIL AND RESOLVING TO RESCUE YOU!
HELLO, FRIEND!
MY NAME IS DIANA.
ARE YOU...A MORTAL MAN? ...A FAUNUS? ...OR--

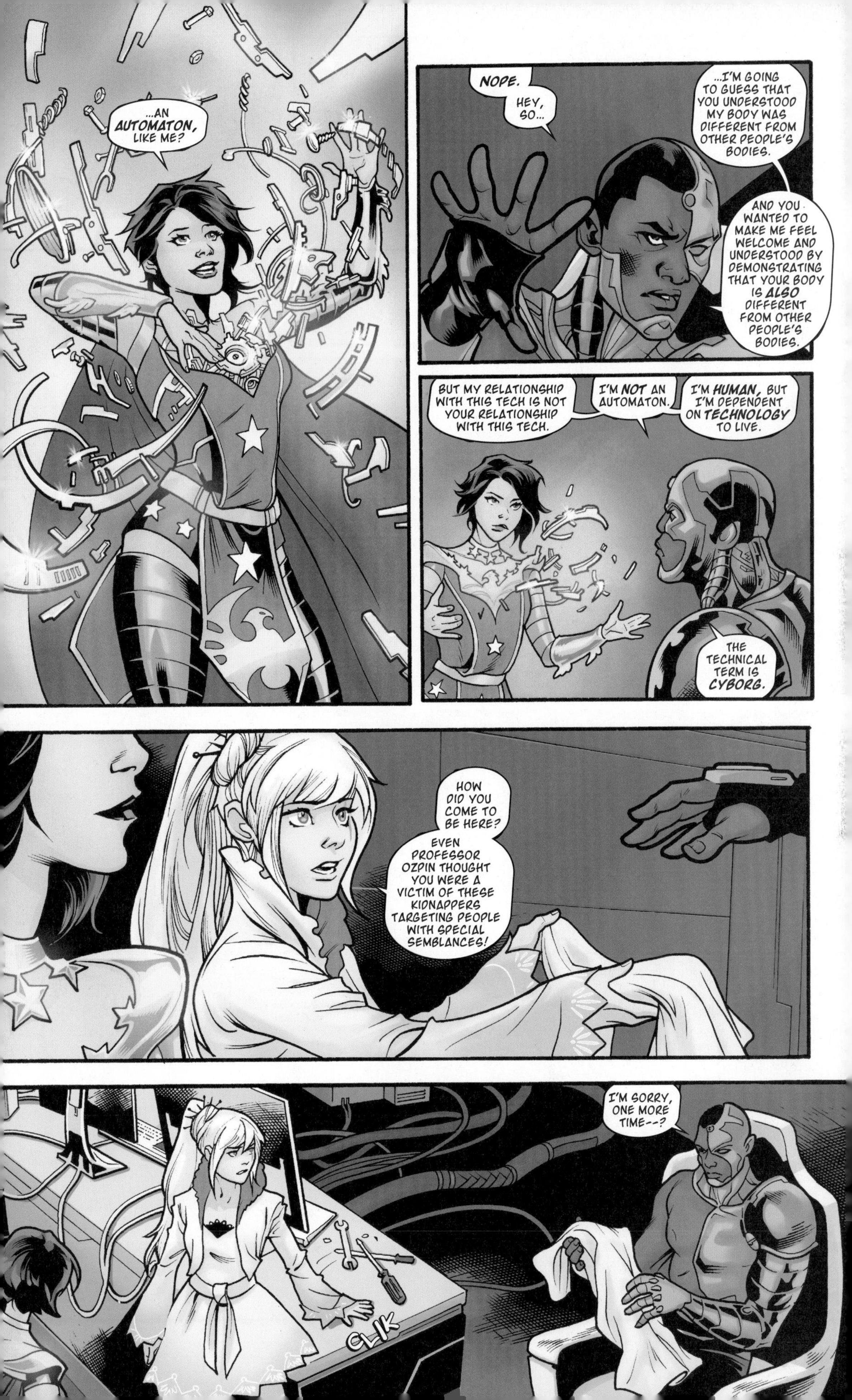
...AN AUTOMATON, LIKE ME?
NOPE.
HEY, SO...
...I'M GOING TO GUESS THAT YOU UNDERSTOOD MY BODY WAS DIFFERENT FROM OTHER PEOPLE'S BODIES.
AND YOU WANTED TO MAKE ME FEEL WELCOME AND UNDERSTOOD BY DEMONSTRATING THAT YOUR BODY IS ALSO DIFFERENT FROM OTHER PEOPLE'S BODIES.
BUT MY RELATIONSHIP WITH THIS TECH IS NOT YOUR RELATIONSHIP WITH THIS TECH.
I'M NOT AN AUTOMATON.
I'M HUMAN, BUT I'M DEPENDENT ON TECHNOLOGY TO LIVE.
THE TECHNICAL TERM IS CYBORG.
HOW DID YOU COME TO BE HERE?
EVEN PROFESSOR OZPIN THOUGHT YOU WERE A VICTIM OF THESE KIDNAPPERS TARGETING PEOPLE WITH SPECIAL SEMBLANCES!
I'M SORRY, ONE MORE TIME--?
CLIK

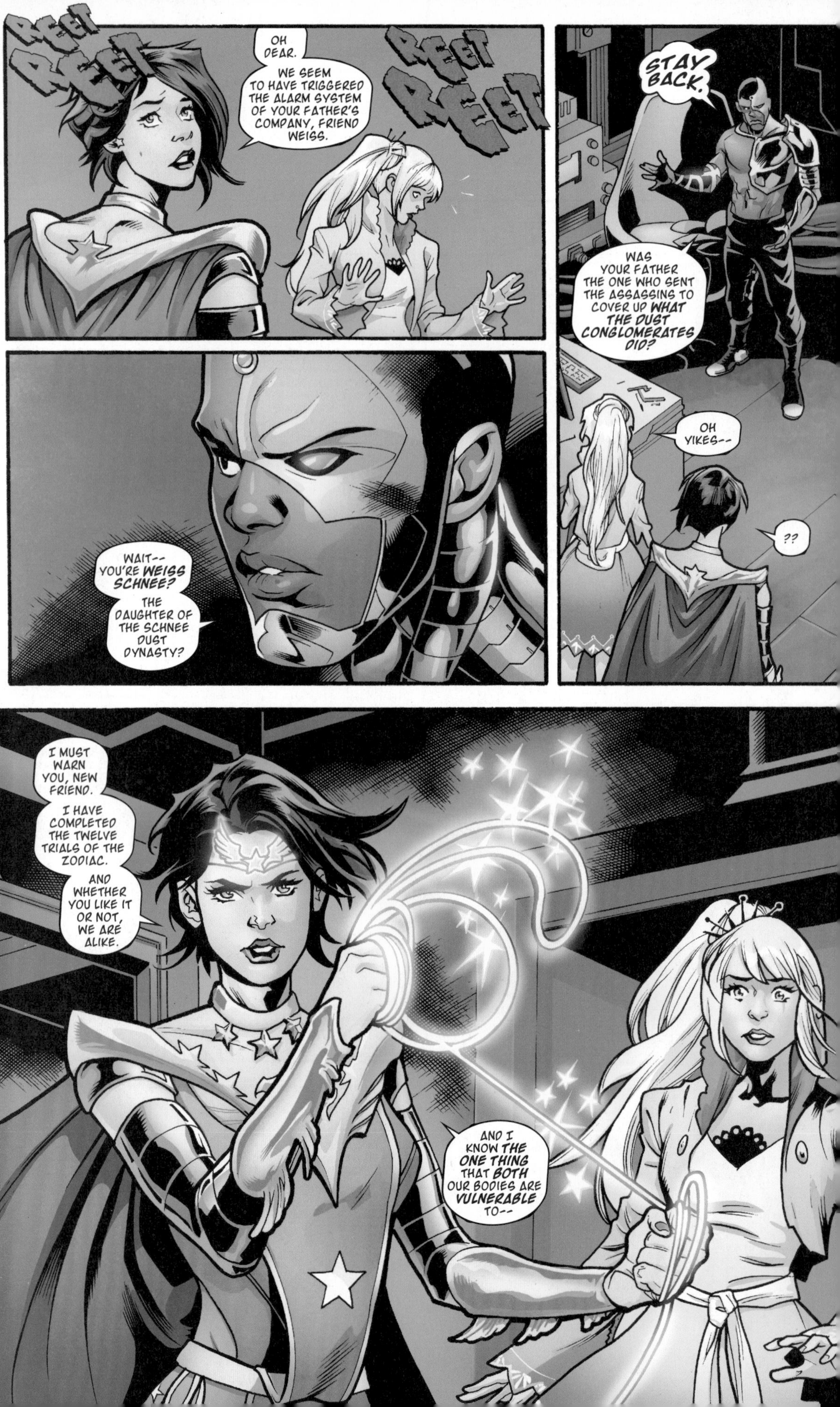
REET REET
OH DEAR.
WE SEEM TO HAVE TRIGGERED THE ALARM SYSTEM OF YOUR FATHER'S COMPANY, FRIEND WEISS.
REET REET
STAY BACK.
WAS YOUR FATHER THE ONE WHO SENT THE ASSASSINS TO COVER UP **WHAT THE DUST CONGLOMERATES DID?**
WAIT-- YOU'RE ***WEISS SCHNEE?***
THE DAUGHTER OF THE SCHNEE DUST DYNASTY?
OH YIKES--
??
I MUST WARN YOU, NEW FRIEND.
I HAVE COMPLETED THE TWELVE TRIALS OF THE ZODIAC.
AND WHETHER YOU LIKE IT OR NOT, WE ARE ALIKE.
AND I KNOW ***THE ONE THING*** THAT ***BOTH*** OUR BODIES ARE ***VULNERABLE*** TO--

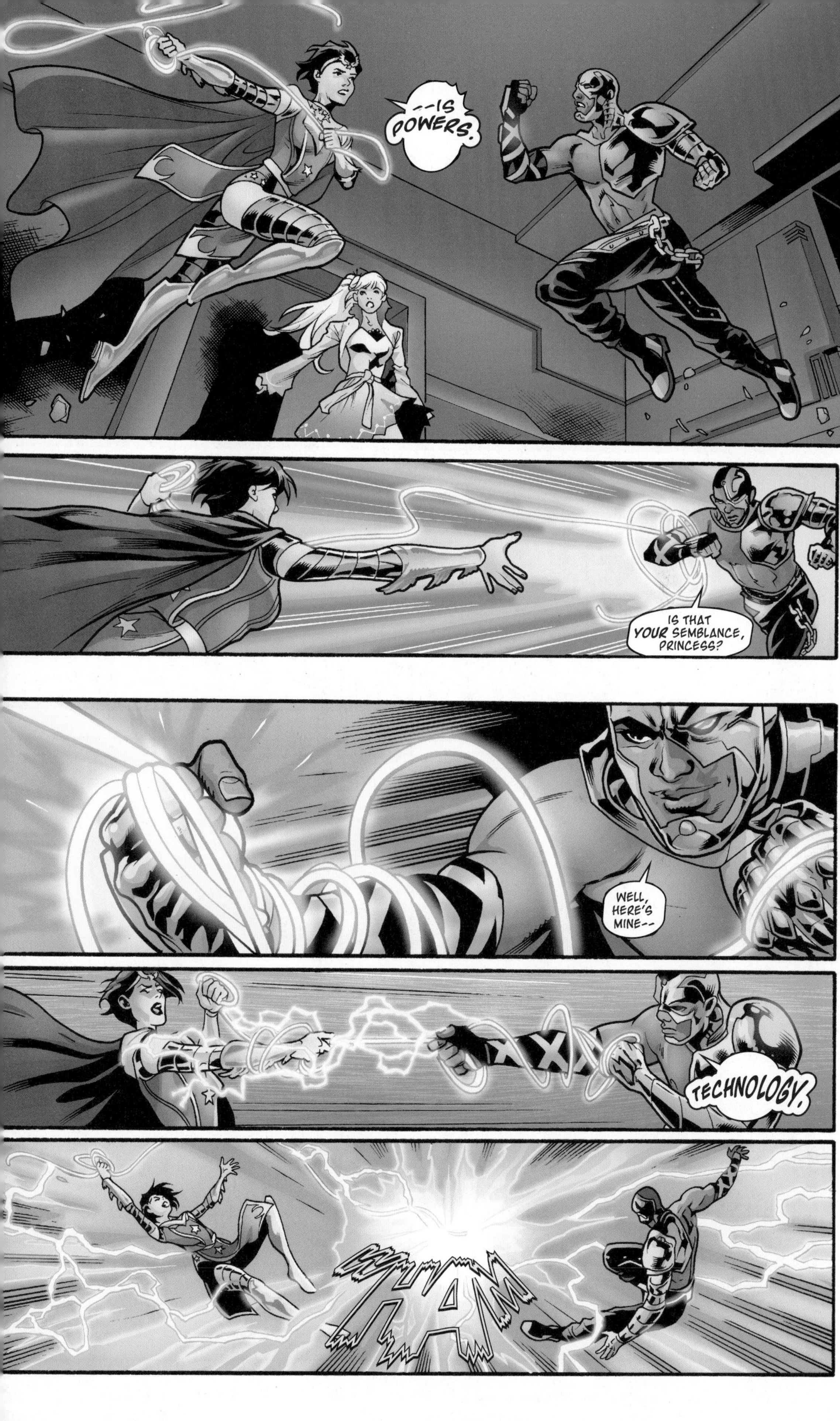
--IS POWERS.
IS THAT YOUR SEMBLANCE, PRINCESS?
WELL, HERE'S MINE--
TECHNOLOGY.
CHYAM

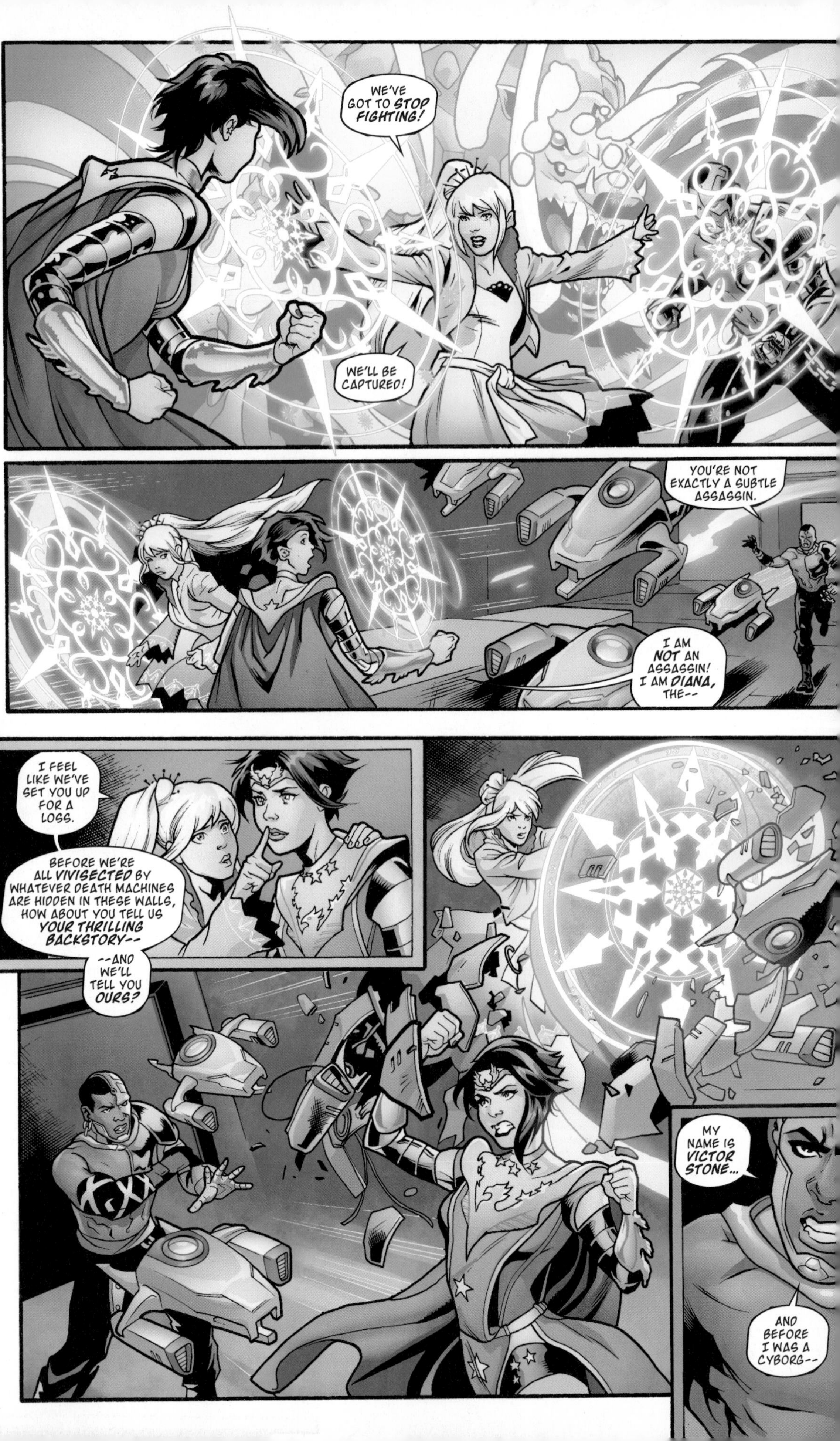
WE'VE GOT TO STOP FIGHTING!
WE'LL BE CAPTURED!
YOU'RE NOT EXACTLY A SUBTLE ASSASSIN.
I AM NOT AN ASSASSIN! I AM DIANA, THE--
I FEEL LIKE WE'VE SET YOU UP FOR A LOSS.
BEFORE WE'RE ALL VIVISECTED BY WHATEVER DEATH MACHINES ARE HIDDEN IN THESE WALLS, HOW ABOUT YOU TELL US YOUR THRILLING BACKSTORY--
--AND WE'LL TELL YOU OURS?
MY NAME IS VICTOR STONE...
AND BEFORE I WAS A CYBORG--

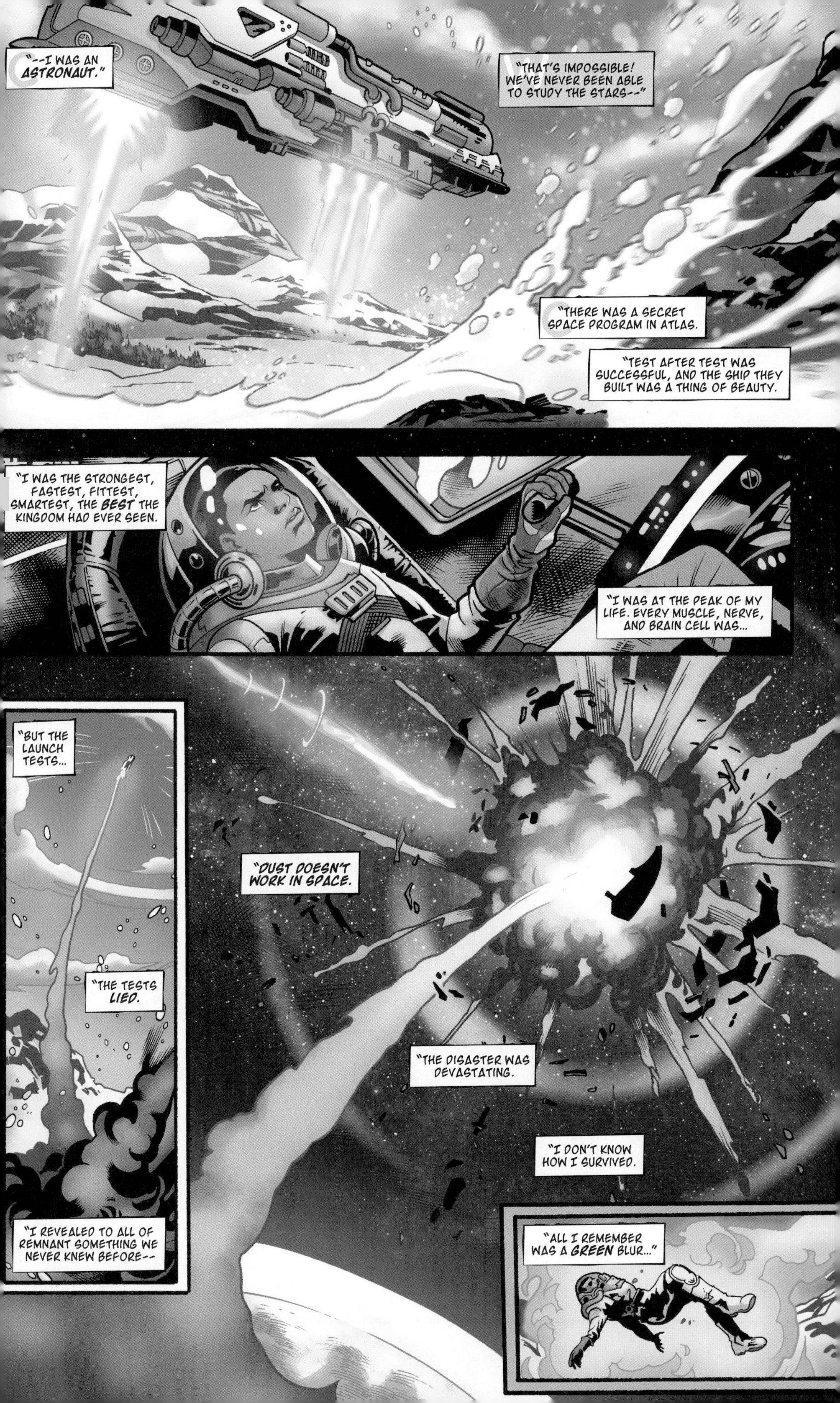
"--I WAS AN ASTRONAUT."
"THAT'S IMPOSSIBLE! WE'VE NEVER BEEN ABLE TO STUDY THE STARS--"
"THERE WAS A SECRET SPACE PROGRAM IN ATLAS.
"TEST AFTER TEST WAS SUCCESSFUL, AND THE SHIP THEY BUILT WAS A THING OF BEAUTY.
"I WAS THE STRONGEST, FASTEST, FITTEST, SMARTEST, THE BEST THE KINGDOM HAD EVER SEEN.
"I WAS AT THE PEAK OF MY LIFE. EVERY MUSCLE, NERVE, AND BRAIN CELL WAS...
"BUT THE LAUNCH TESTS...
"THE TESTS LIED.
"I REVEALED TO ALL OF REMNANT SOMETHING WE NEVER KNEW BEFORE--
"DUST DOESN'T WORK IN SPACE.
"THE DISASTER WAS DEVASTATING.
"I DON'T KNOW HOW I SURVIVED.
"ALL I REMEMBER WAS A GREEN BLUR..."

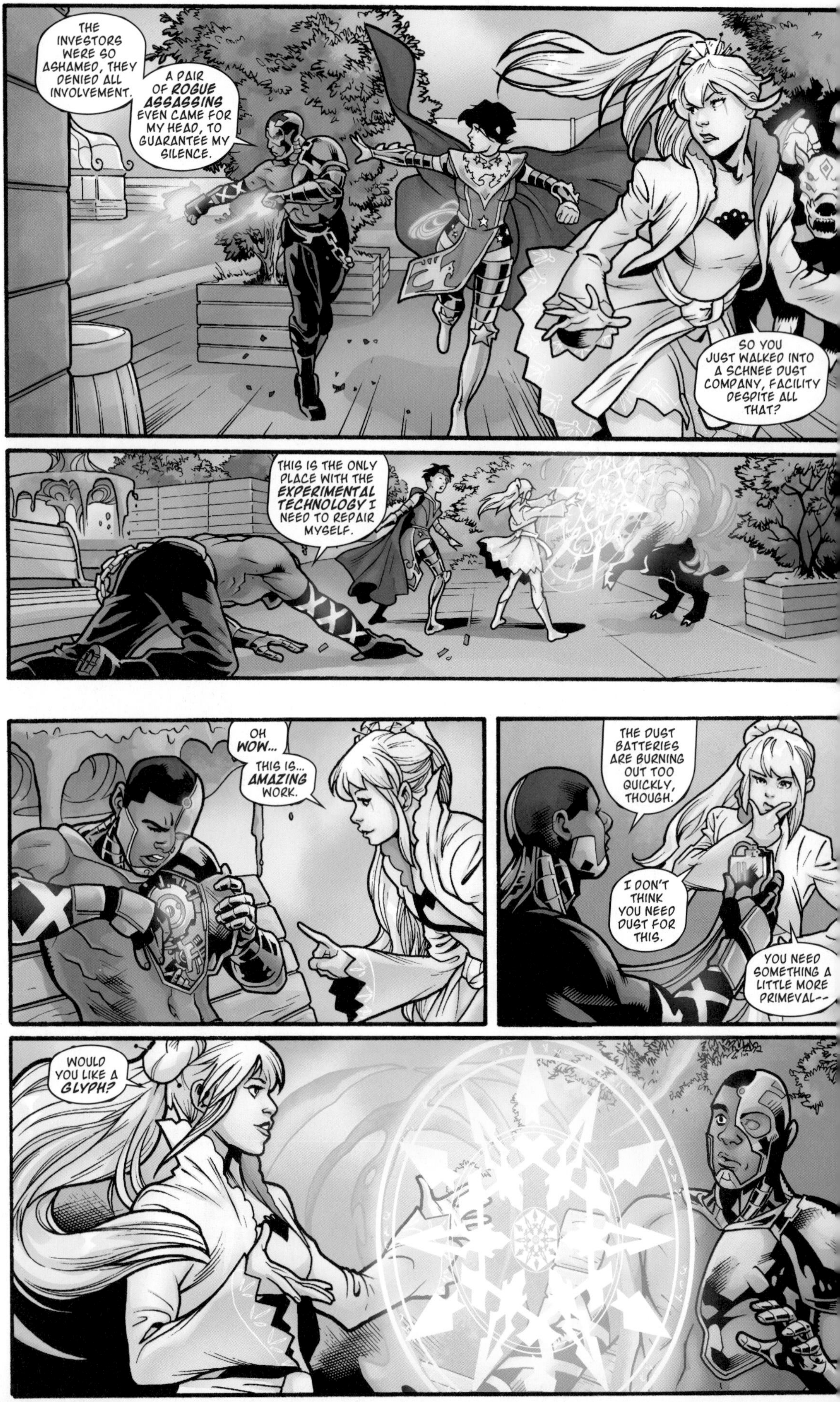

THE INVESTORS WERE SO ASHAMED, THEY DENIED ALL INVOLVEMENT.
A PAIR OF ROGUE ASSASSINS EVEN CAME FOR MY HEAD, TO GUARANTEE MY SILENCE.
SO YOU JUST WALKED INTO A SCHNEE DUST COMPANY, FACILITY DESPITE ALL THAT?
THIS IS THE ONLY PLACE WITH THE EXPERIMENTAL TECHNOLOGY I NEED TO REPAIR MYSELF.
OH WOW...
THIS IS... AMAZING WORK.
THE DUST BATTERIES ARE BURNING OUT TOO QUICKLY, THOUGH.
I DON'T THINK YOU NEED DUST FOR THIS.
YOU NEED SOMETHING A LITTLE MORE PRIMEVAL--
WOULD YOU LIKE A GLYPH?

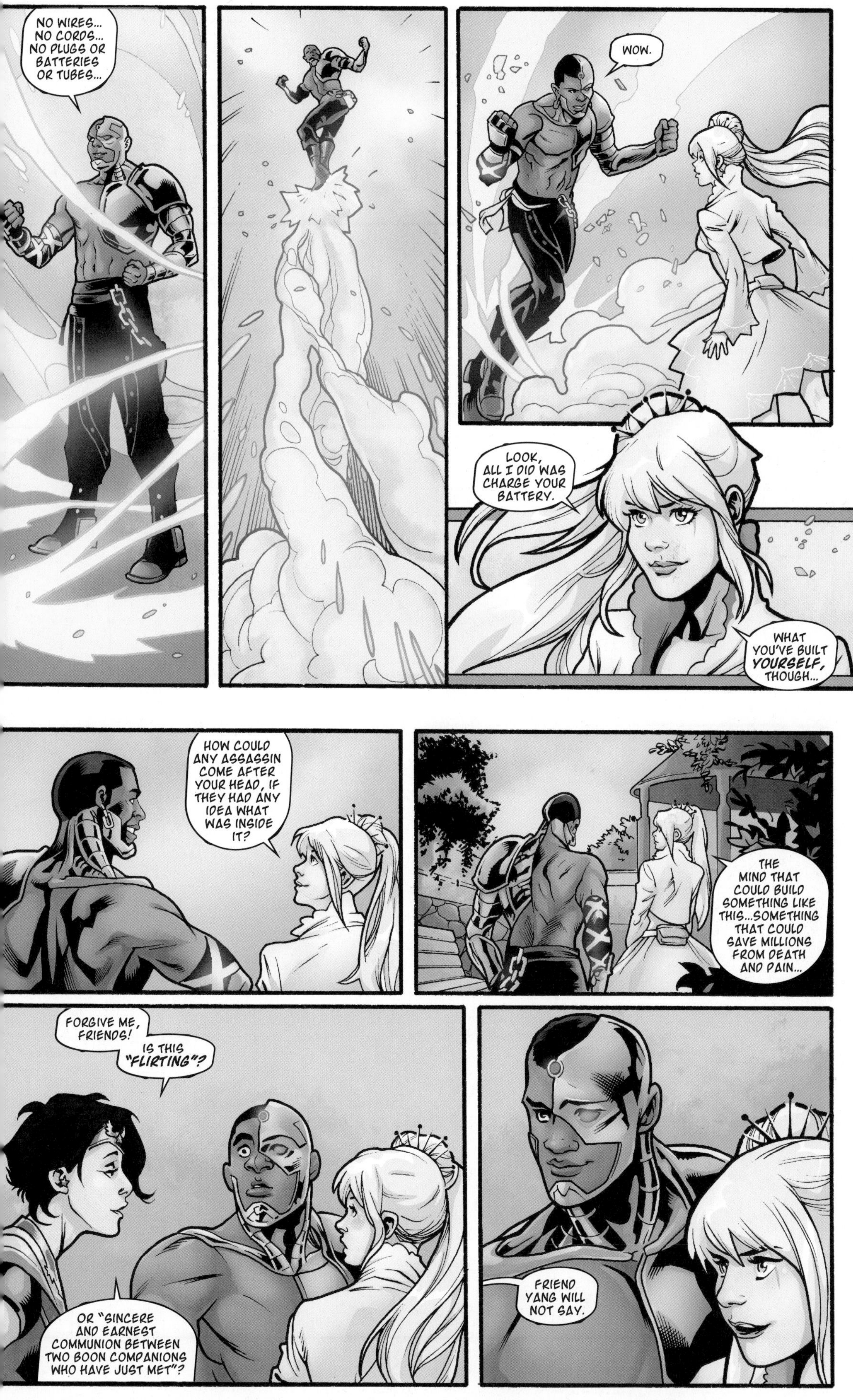
NO WIRES... NO CORDS... NO PLUGS OR BATTERIES OR TUBES...
WOW.
LOOK, ALL I DID WAS CHARGE YOUR BATTERY.
WHAT YOU'VE BUILT **YOURSELF,** THOUGH...
HOW COULD ANY ASSASSIN COME AFTER YOUR HEAD, IF THEY HAD ANY IDEA WHAT WAS INSIDE IT?
THE MIND THAT COULD BUILD SOMETHING LIKE THIS...SOMETHING THAT COULD SAVE MILLIONS FROM DEATH AND PAIN...
FORGIVE ME, FRIENDS!
IS THIS **"FLIRTING"?**
OR "SINCERE AND EARNEST COMMUNION BETWEEN TWO BOON COMPANIONS WHO HAVE JUST MET"?
FRIEND YANG WILL NOT SAY.

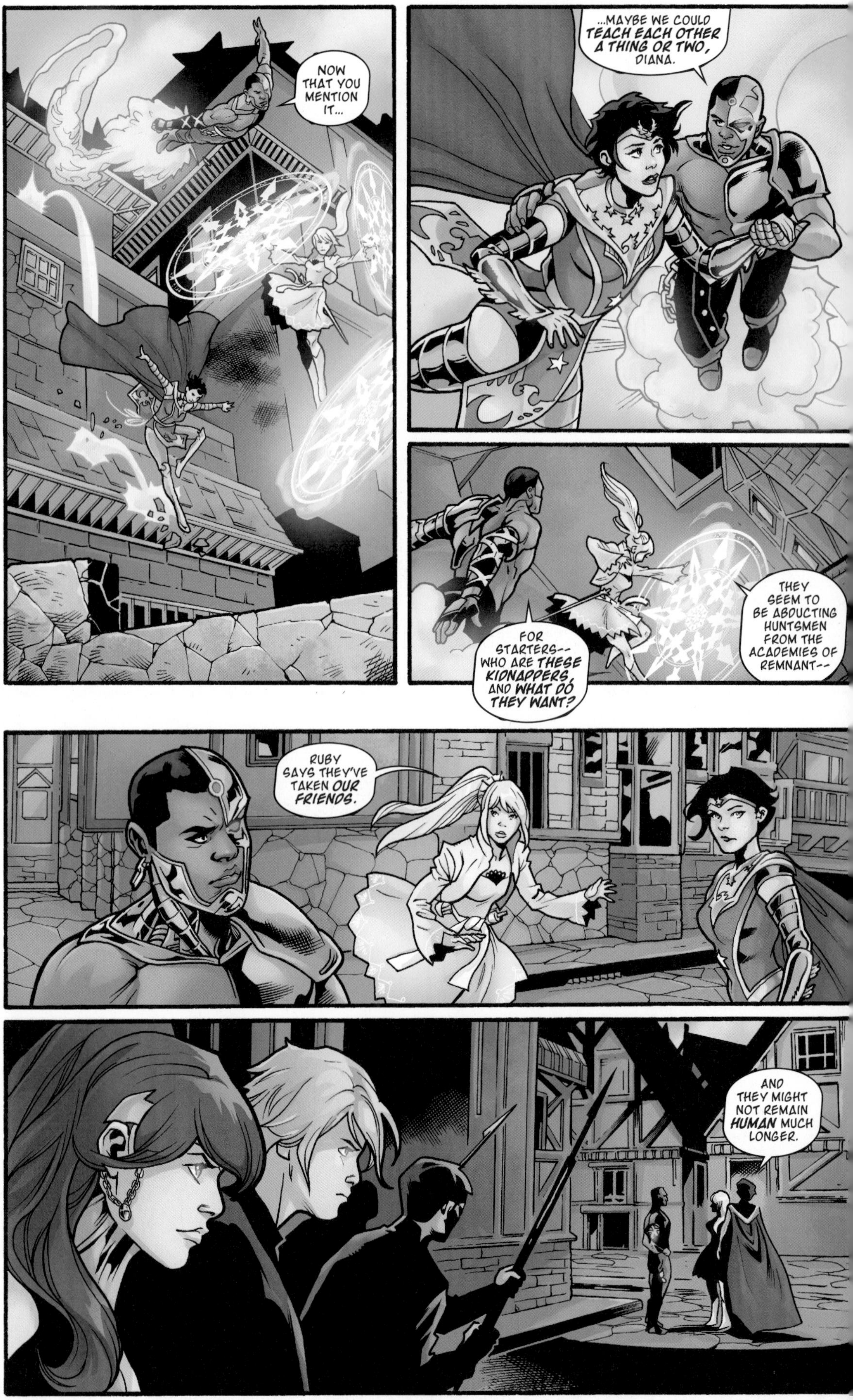
NOW THAT YOU MENTION IT...
...MAYBE WE COULD TEACH EACH OTHER A THING OR TWO, DIANA.
FOR STARTERS-- WHO ARE THESE KIDNAPPERS, AND WHAT DO THEY WANT?
THEY SEEM TO BE ABDUCTING HUNTSMEN FROM THE ACADEMIES OF REMNANT--
RUBY SAYS THEY'VE TAKEN OUR FRIENDS.
AND THEY MIGHT NOT REMAIN HUMAN MUCH LONGER.

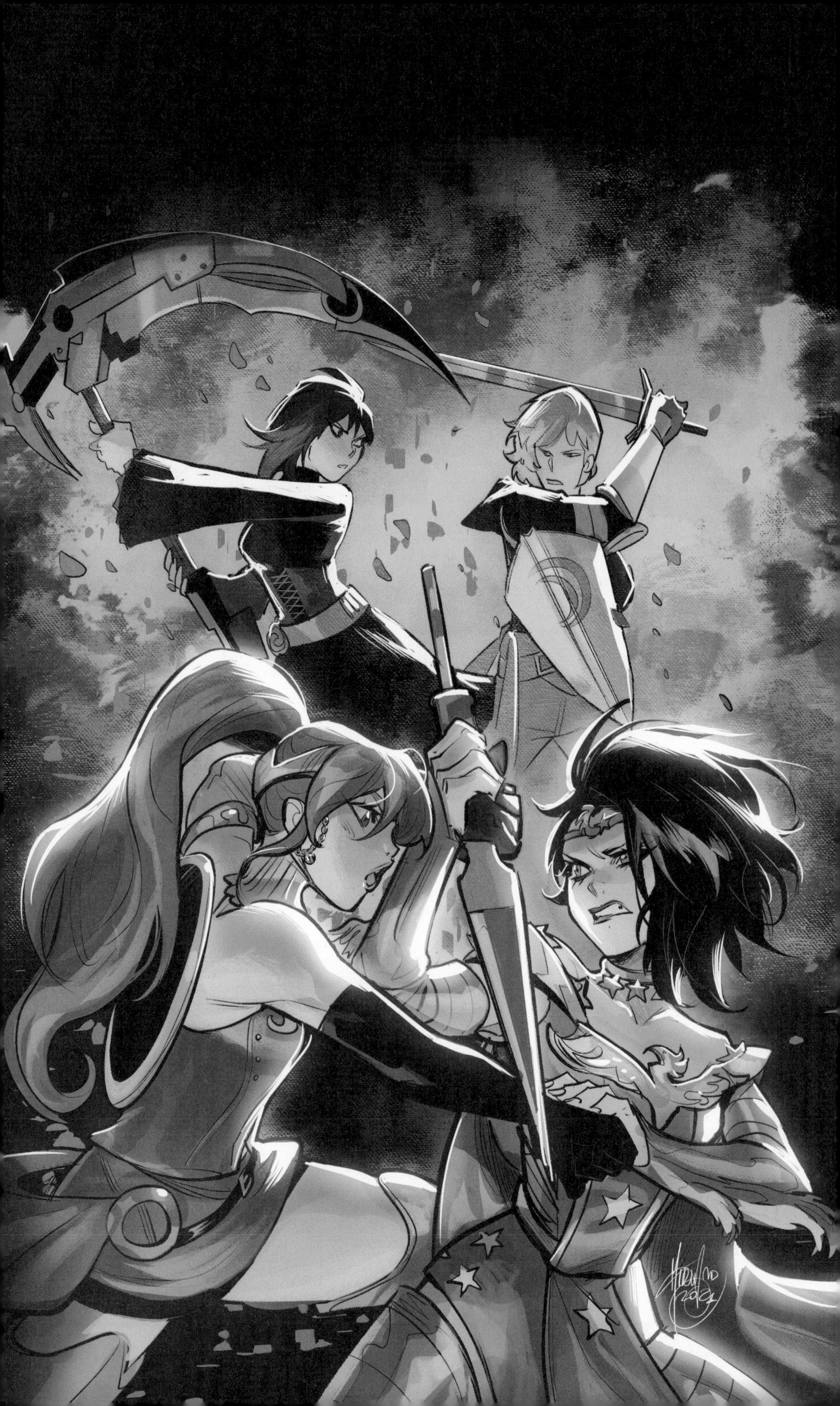

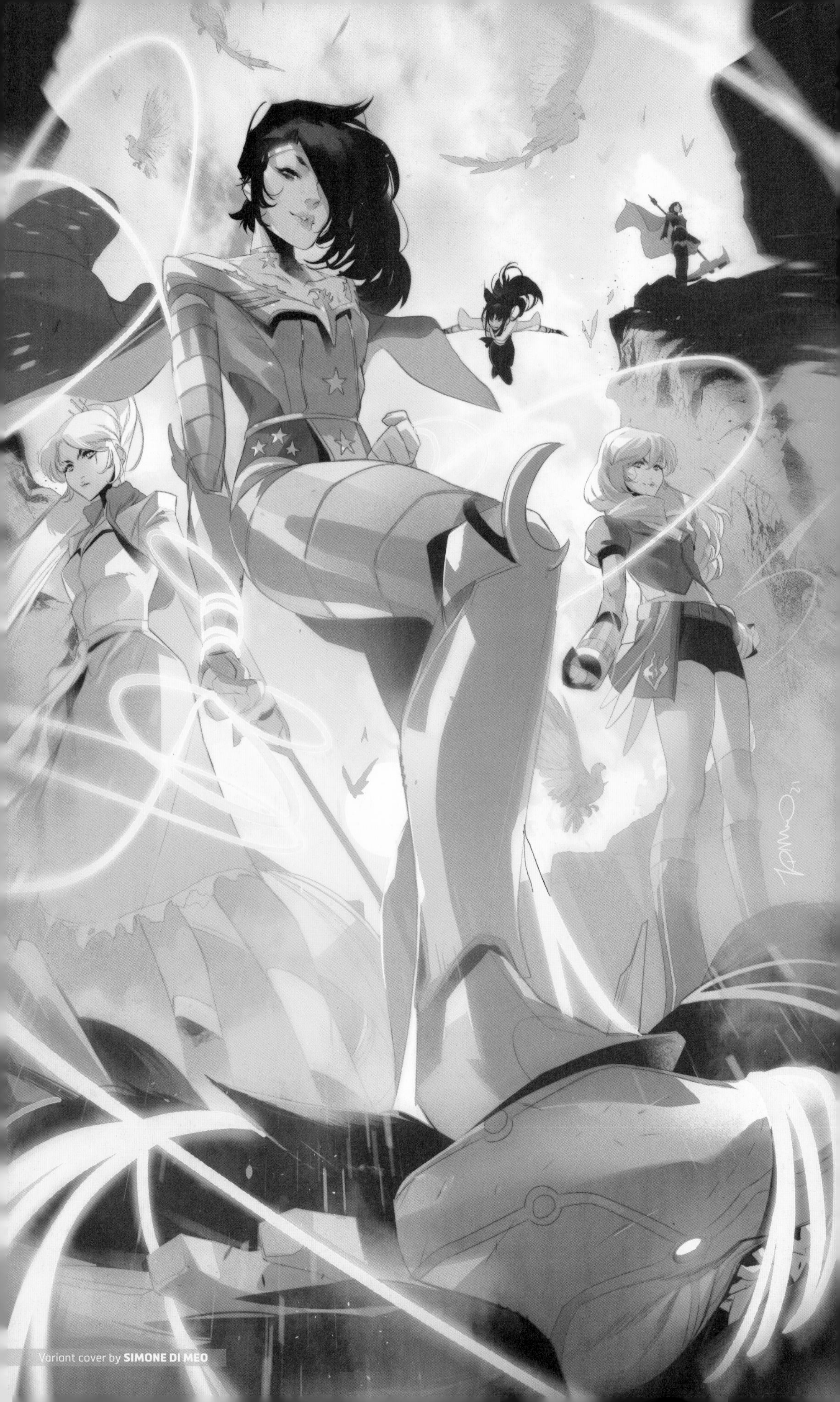

Variant cover by **SIMONE DI MEO**

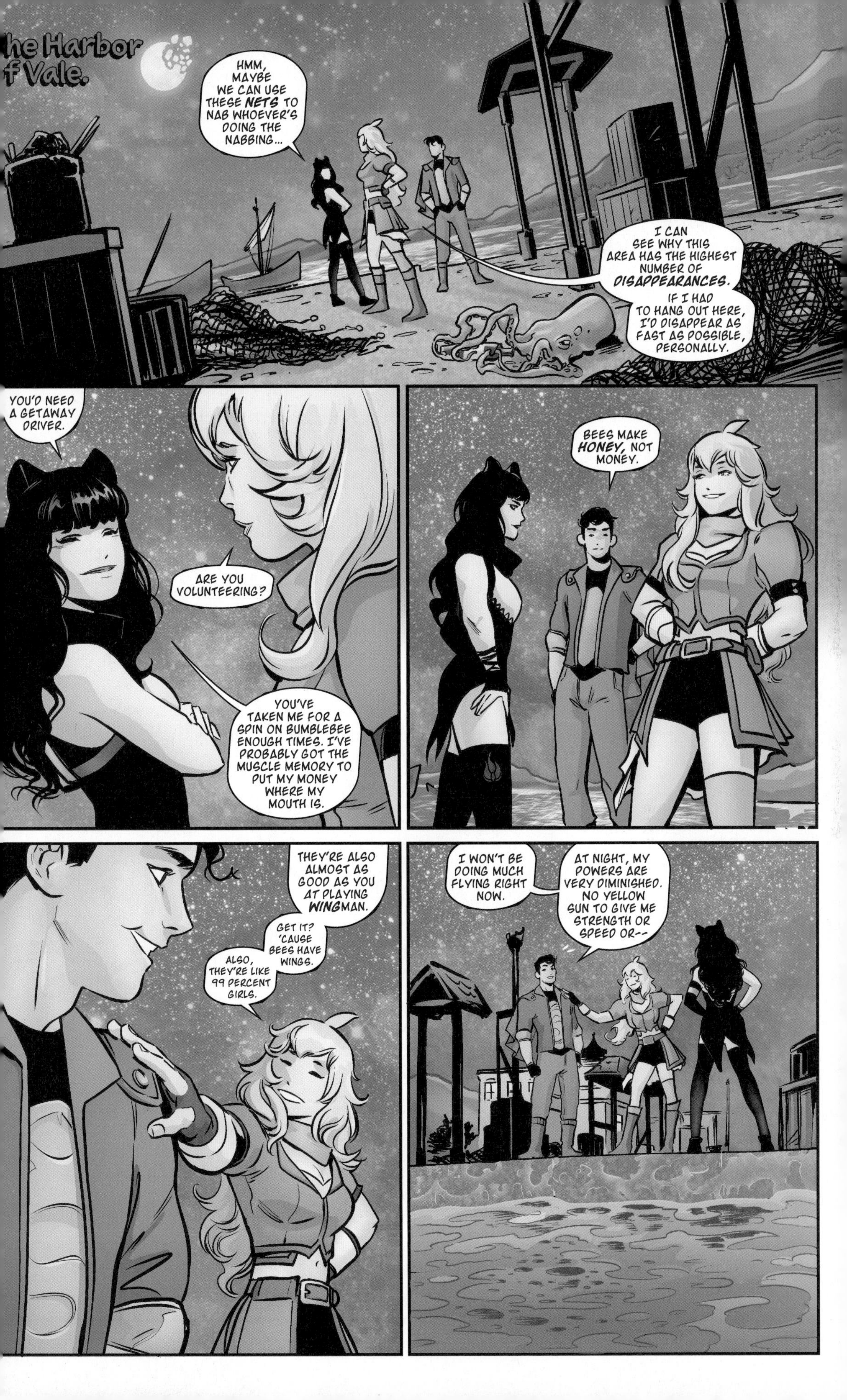
he Harbor
f Vale.
HMM, MAYBE WE CAN USE THESE NETS TO NAB WHOEVER'S DOING THE NABBING...
I CAN SEE WHY THIS AREA HAS THE HIGHEST NUMBER OF DISAPPEARANCES.
IF I HAD TO HANG OUT HERE, I'D DISAPPEAR AS FAST AS POSSIBLE, PERSONALLY.
YOU'D NEED A GETAWAY DRIVER.
ARE YOU VOLUNTEERING?
YOU'VE TAKEN ME FOR A SPIN ON BUMBLEBEE ENOUGH TIMES. I'VE PROBABLY GOT THE MUSCLE MEMORY TO PUT MY MONEY WHERE MY MOUTH IS.
BEES MAKE HONEY, NOT MONEY.
THEY'RE ALSO ALMOST AS GOOD AS YOU AT PLAYING WINGMAN.
GET IT? 'CAUSE BEES HAVE WINGS.
ALSO, THEY'RE LIKE 99 PERCENT GIRLS.
I WON'T BE DOING MUCH FLYING RIGHT NOW.
AT NIGHT, MY POWERS ARE VERY DIMINISHED. NO YELLOW SUN TO GIVE ME STRENGTH OR SPEED OR--

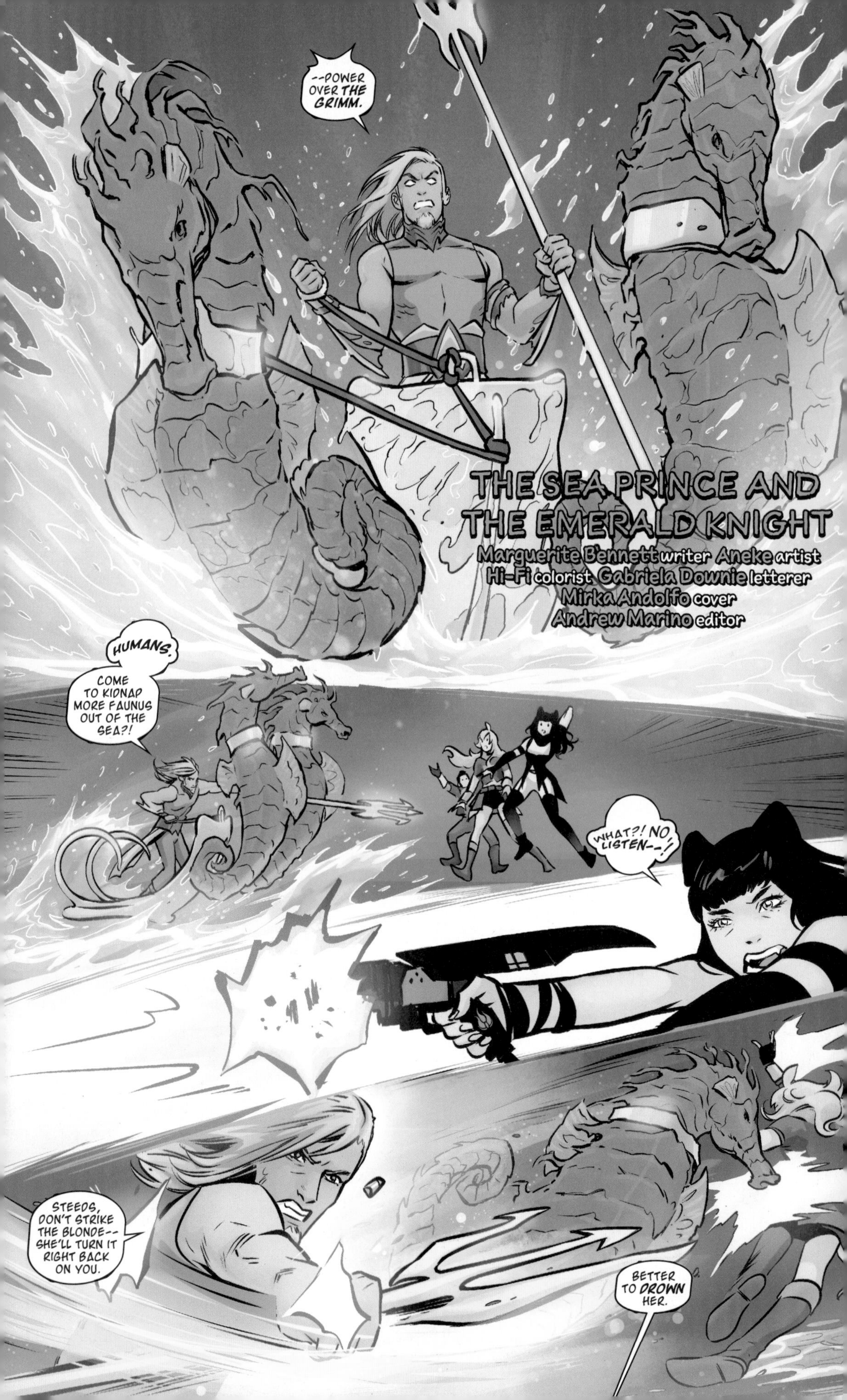

--POWER OVER THE GRIMM.
THE SEA PRINCE AND THE EMERALD KNIGHT
Marguerite Bennett writer Aneke artist
Hi-Fi colorist Gabriela Downie letterer
Mirka Andolfo cover
Andrew Marino editor
HUMANS.
COME TO KIDNAP MORE FAUNUS OUT OF THE SEA?!
WHAT?! NO, LISTEN--!
STEEDS, DON'T STRIKE THE BLONDE--SHE'LL TURN IT RIGHT BACK ON YOU.
BETTER TO DROWN HER.

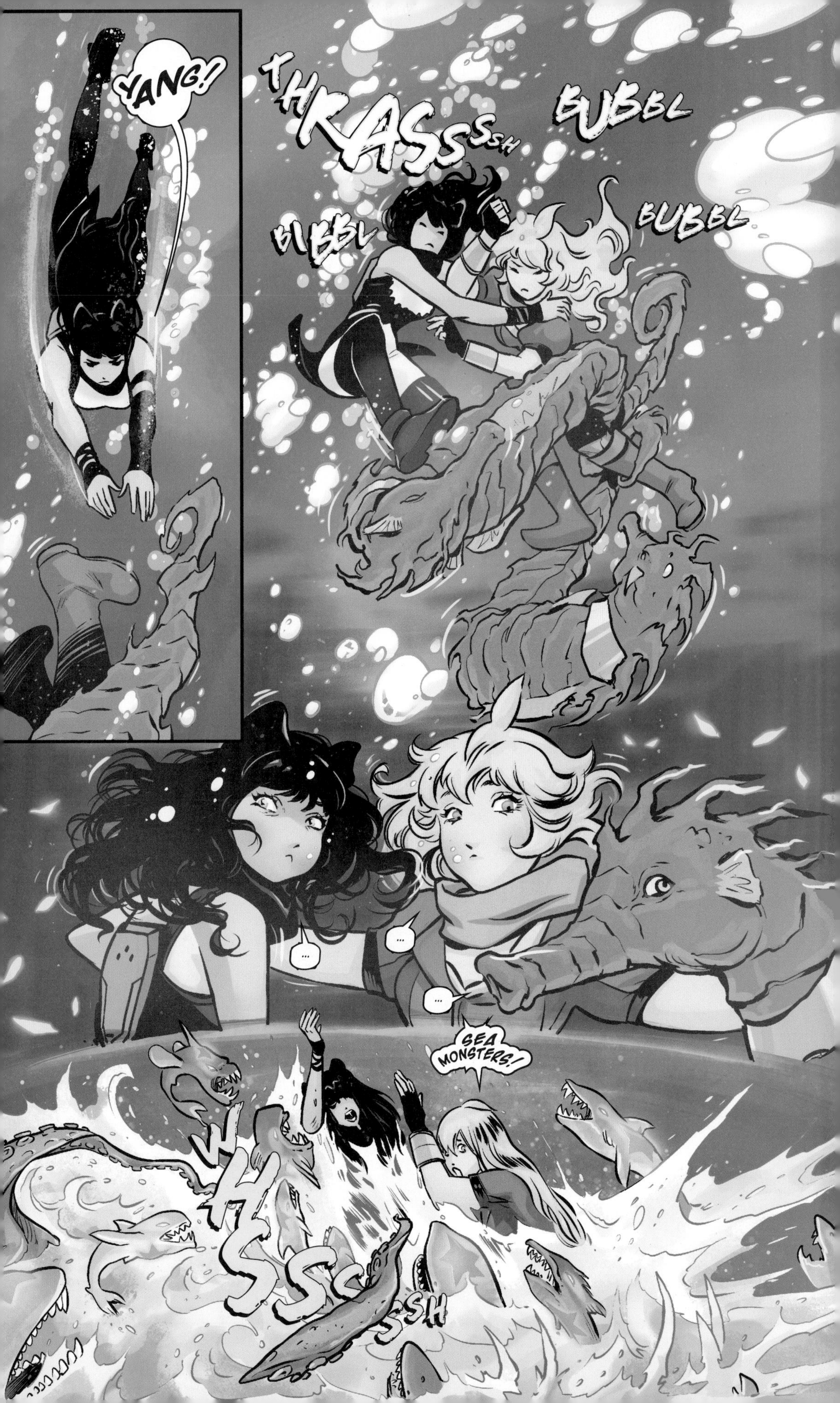
YANG!
THKRASSSSH
BUBBL
BUBBL
BUBBL
...
...
...
SEA MONSTERS!
WHSSSCSSH

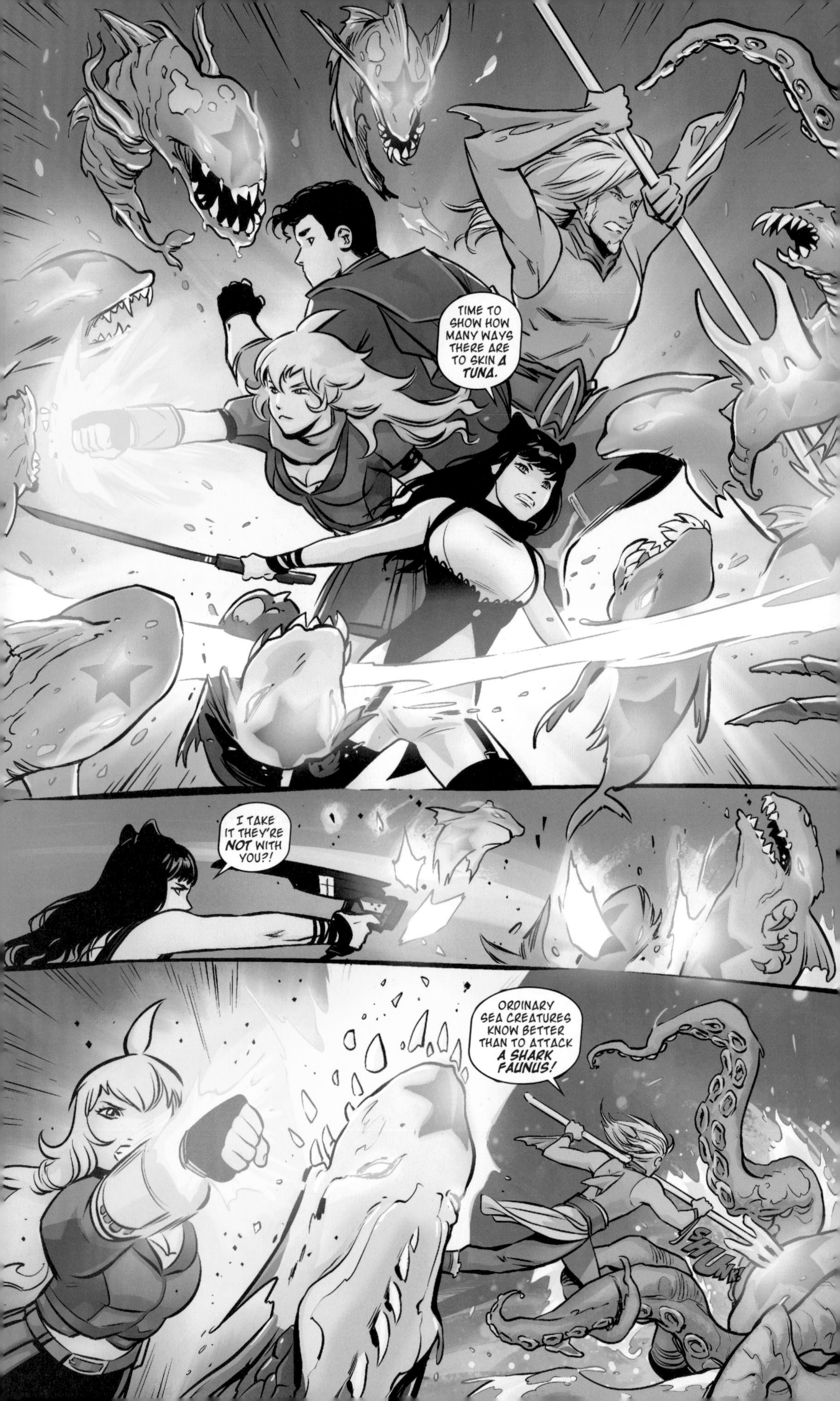
TIME TO SHOW HOW MANY WAYS THERE ARE TO SKIN A TUNA.
I TAKE IT THEY'RE NOT WITH YOU?!
ORDINARY SEA CREATURES KNOW BETTER THAN TO ATTACK A SHARK FAUNUS!
SHUNK!

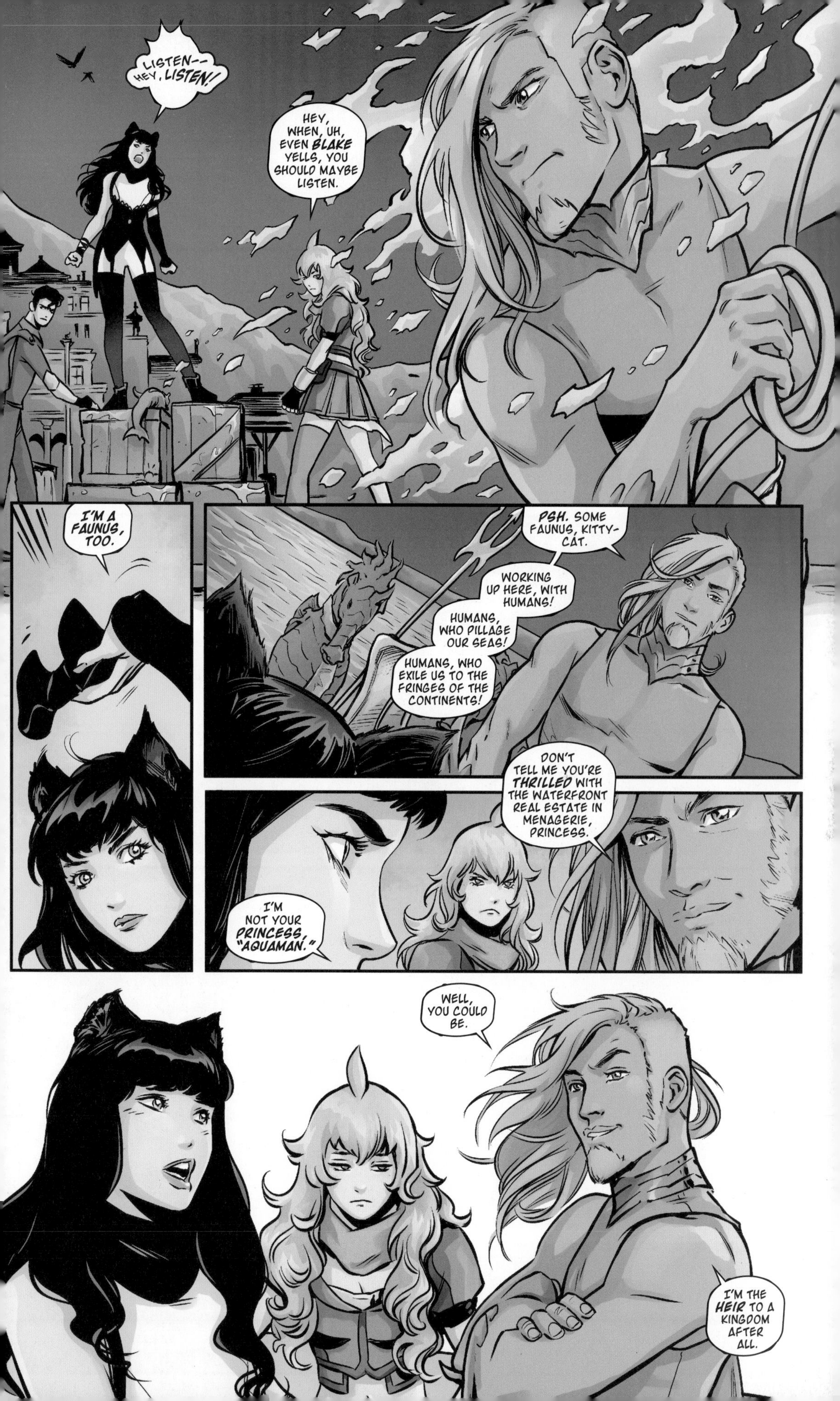

LISTEN--
HEY, LISTEN!
HEY, WHEN, UH, EVEN BLAKE YELLS, YOU SHOULD MAYBE LISTEN.
I'M A FAUNUS, TOO.
PSH. SOME FAUNUS, KITTY-CAT.
WORKING UP HERE, WITH HUMANS!
HUMANS, WHO PILLAGE OUR SEAS!
HUMANS, WHO EXILE US TO THE FRINGES OF THE CONTINENTS!
DON'T TELL ME YOU'RE THRILLED WITH THE WATERFRONT REAL ESTATE IN MENAGERIE, PRINCESS.
I'M NOT YOUR PRINCESS, "AQUAMAN."
WELL, YOU COULD BE.
I'M THE HEIR TO A KINGDOM AFTER ALL.

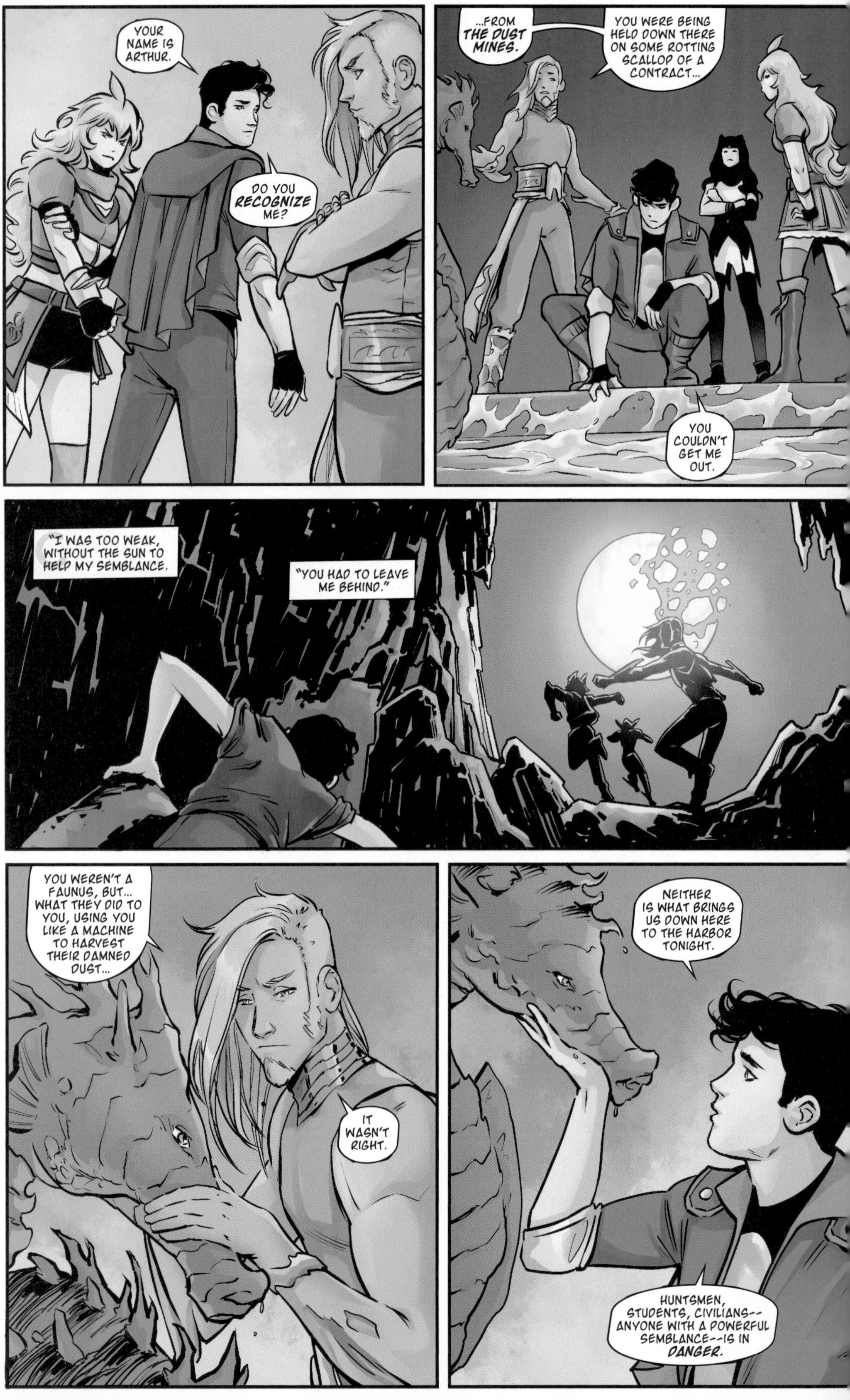

YOUR NAME IS ARTHUR.
DO YOU RECOGNIZE ME?
...FROM THE DUST MINES.
YOU WERE BEING HELD DOWN THERE ON SOME ROTTING SCALLOP OF A CONTRACT...
YOU COULDN'T GET ME OUT.
"I WAS TOO WEAK, WITHOUT THE SUN TO HELP MY SEMBLANCE.
"YOU HAD TO LEAVE ME BEHIND."
YOU WEREN'T A FAUNUS, BUT... WHAT THEY DID TO YOU, USING YOU LIKE A MACHINE TO HARVEST THEIR DAMNED DUST...
IT WASN'T RIGHT.
NEITHER IS WHAT BRINGS US DOWN HERE TO THE HARBOR TONIGHT.
HUNTSMEN, STUDENTS, CIVILIANS--ANYONE WITH A POWERFUL SEMBLANCE--IS IN DANGER.

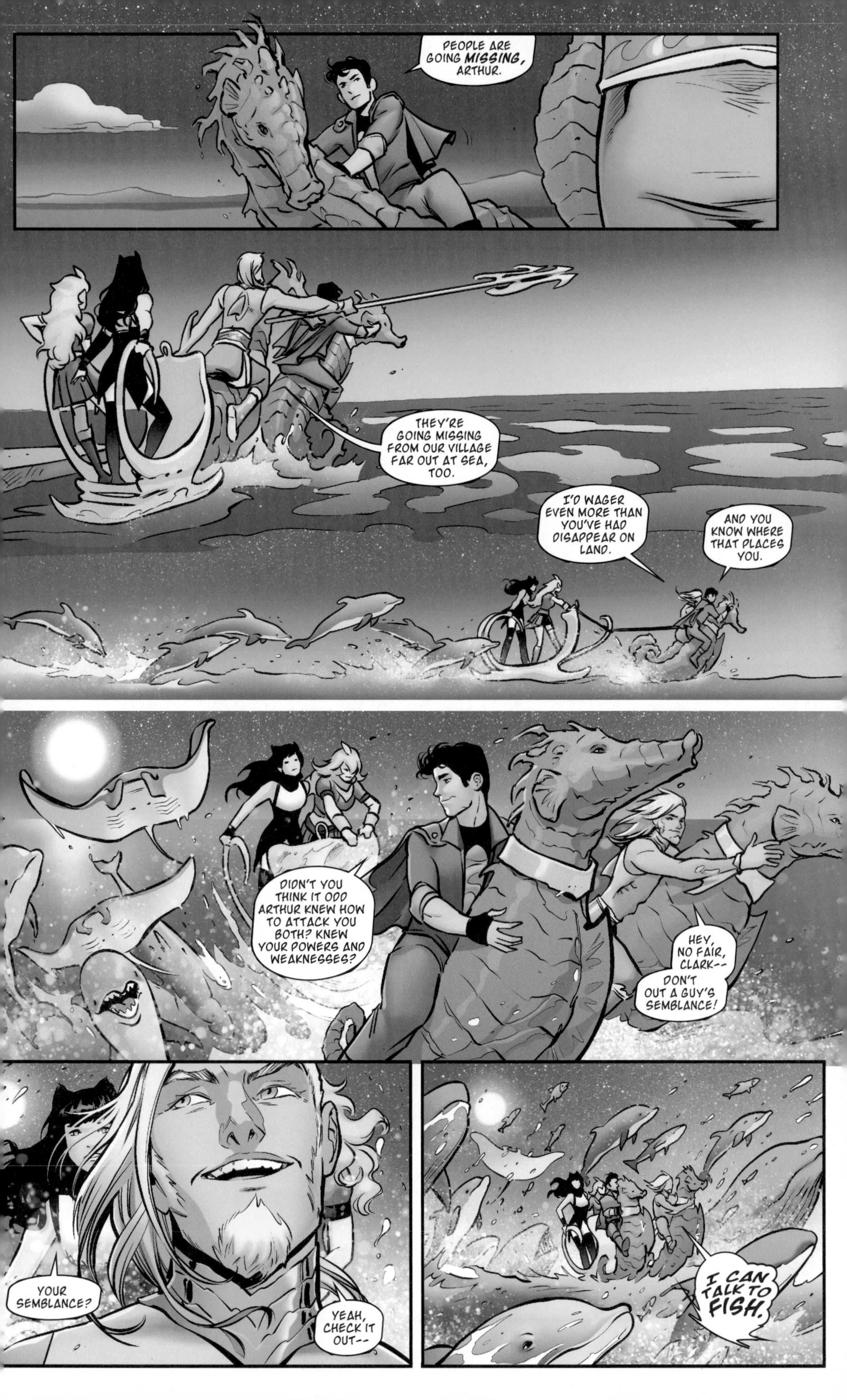
PEOPLE ARE GOING MISSING, ARTHUR.
THEY'RE GOING MISSING FROM OUR VILLAGE FAR OUT AT SEA, TOO.
I'D WAGER EVEN MORE THAN YOU'VE HAD DISAPPEAR ON LAND.
AND YOU KNOW WHERE THAT PLACES YOU.
DIDN'T YOU THINK IT ODD ARTHUR KNEW HOW TO ATTACK YOU BOTH? KNEW YOUR POWERS AND WEAKNESSES?
HEY, NO FAIR, CLARK--
DON'T OUT A GUY'S SEMBLANCE!
YOUR SEMBLANCE?
YEAH, CHECK IT OUT--
I CAN TALK TO FISH.

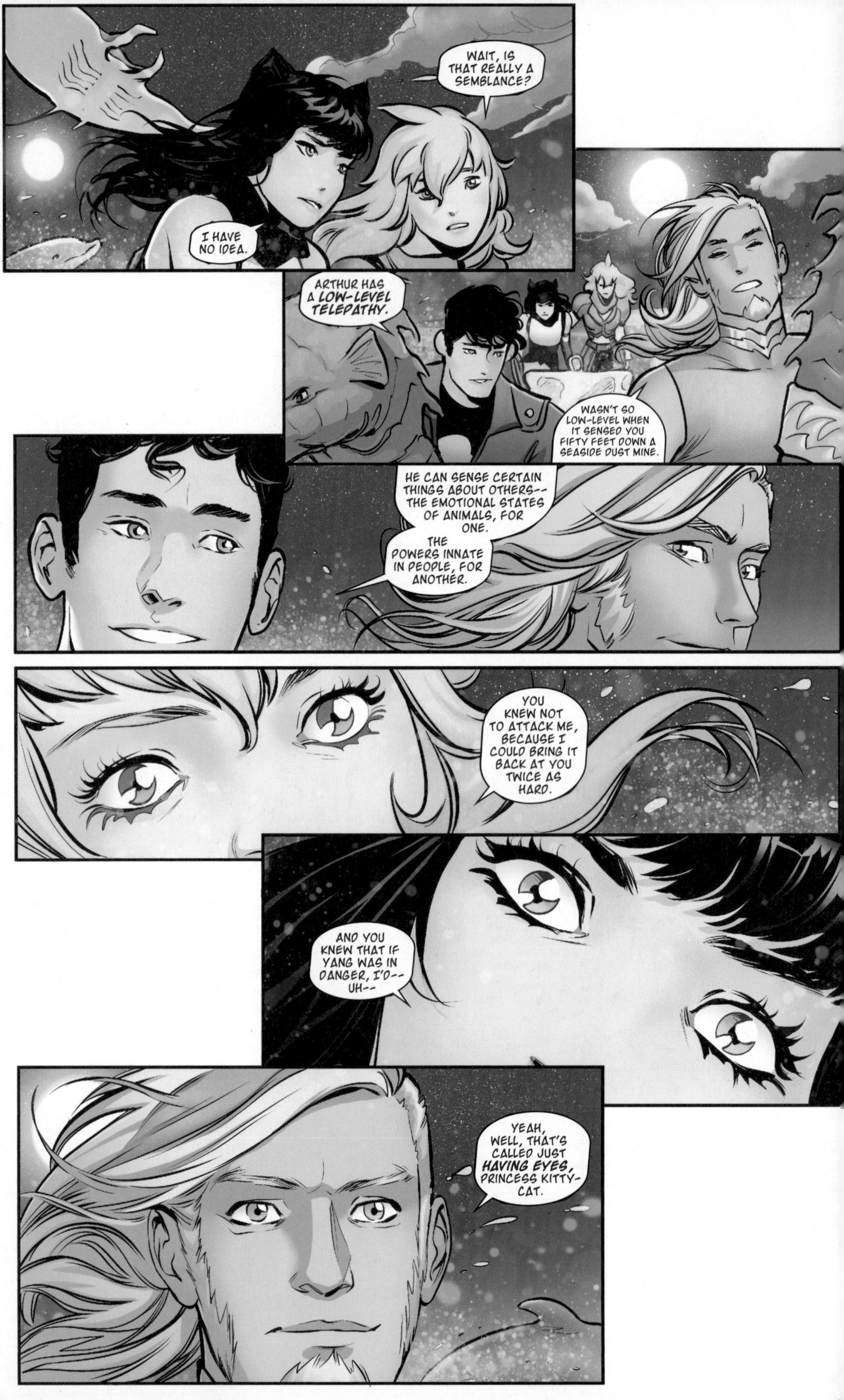
WAIT, IS THAT REALLY A SEMBLANCE?
I HAVE NO IDEA.
ARTHUR HAS A **LOW-LEVEL TELEPATHY.**
WASN'T SO LOW-LEVEL WHEN IT SENSED YOU FIFTY FEET DOWN A SEASIDE DUST MINE.
HE CAN SENSE CERTAIN THINGS ABOUT OTHERS-- THE EMOTIONAL STATES OF ANIMALS, FOR ONE.
THE POWERS INNATE IN PEOPLE, FOR ANOTHER.
YOU KNEW NOT TO ATTACK ME, BECAUSE I COULD BRING IT BACK AT YOU TWICE AS HARD.
AND YOU KNEW THAT IF YANG WAS IN DANGER, I'D-- UH--
YEAH, WELL, THAT'S CALLED JUST **HAVING EYES,** PRINCESS KITTY-CAT.

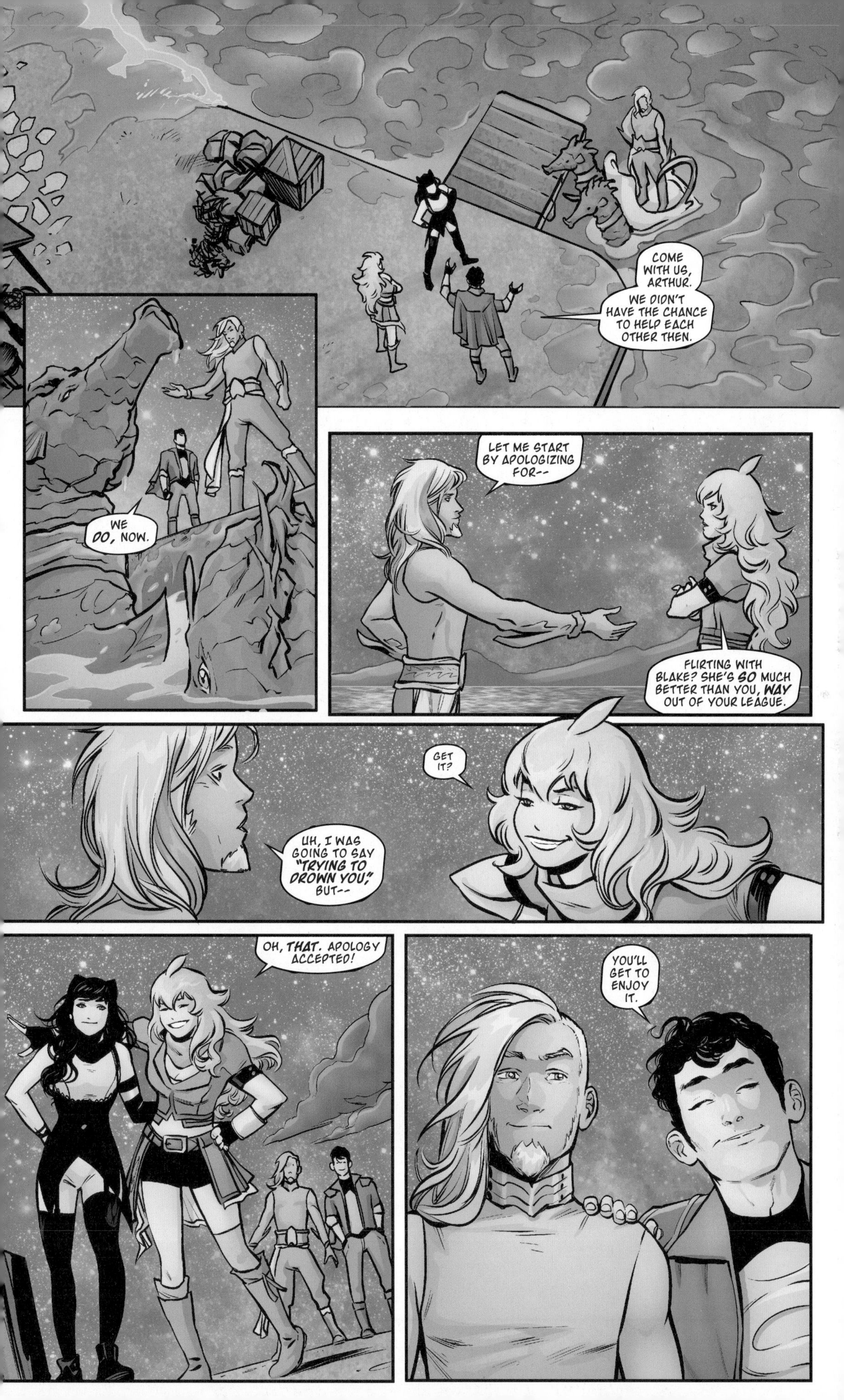
COME WITH US, ARTHUR.
WE DIDN'T HAVE THE CHANCE TO HELP EACH OTHER THEN.
WE DO, NOW.
LET ME START BY APOLOGIZING FOR--
FLIRTING WITH BLAKE? SHE'S SO MUCH BETTER THAN YOU, WAY OUT OF YOUR LEAGUE.
GET IT?
UH, I WAS GOING TO SAY "TRYING TO DROWN YOU," BUT--
OH, THAT. APOLOGY ACCEPTED!
YOU'LL GET TO ENJOY IT.

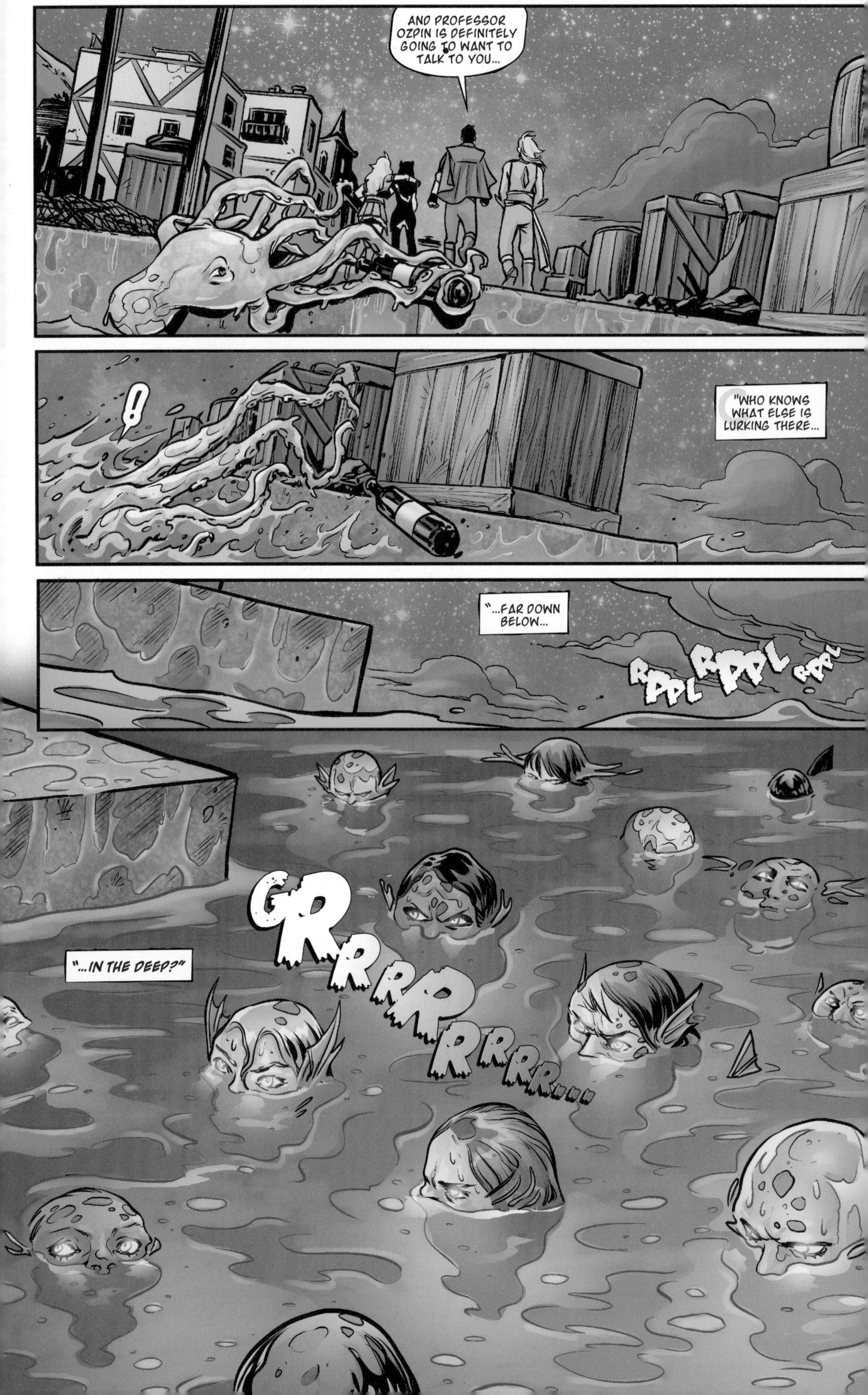
AND PROFESSOR OZPIN IS DEFINITELY GOING TO WANT TO TALK TO YOU...
!
"WHO KNOWS WHAT ELSE IS LURKING THERE...
"...FAR DOWN BELOW...
RPPL RPPL RPPL
"...IN THE DEEP?"
GRRRRRRRR...

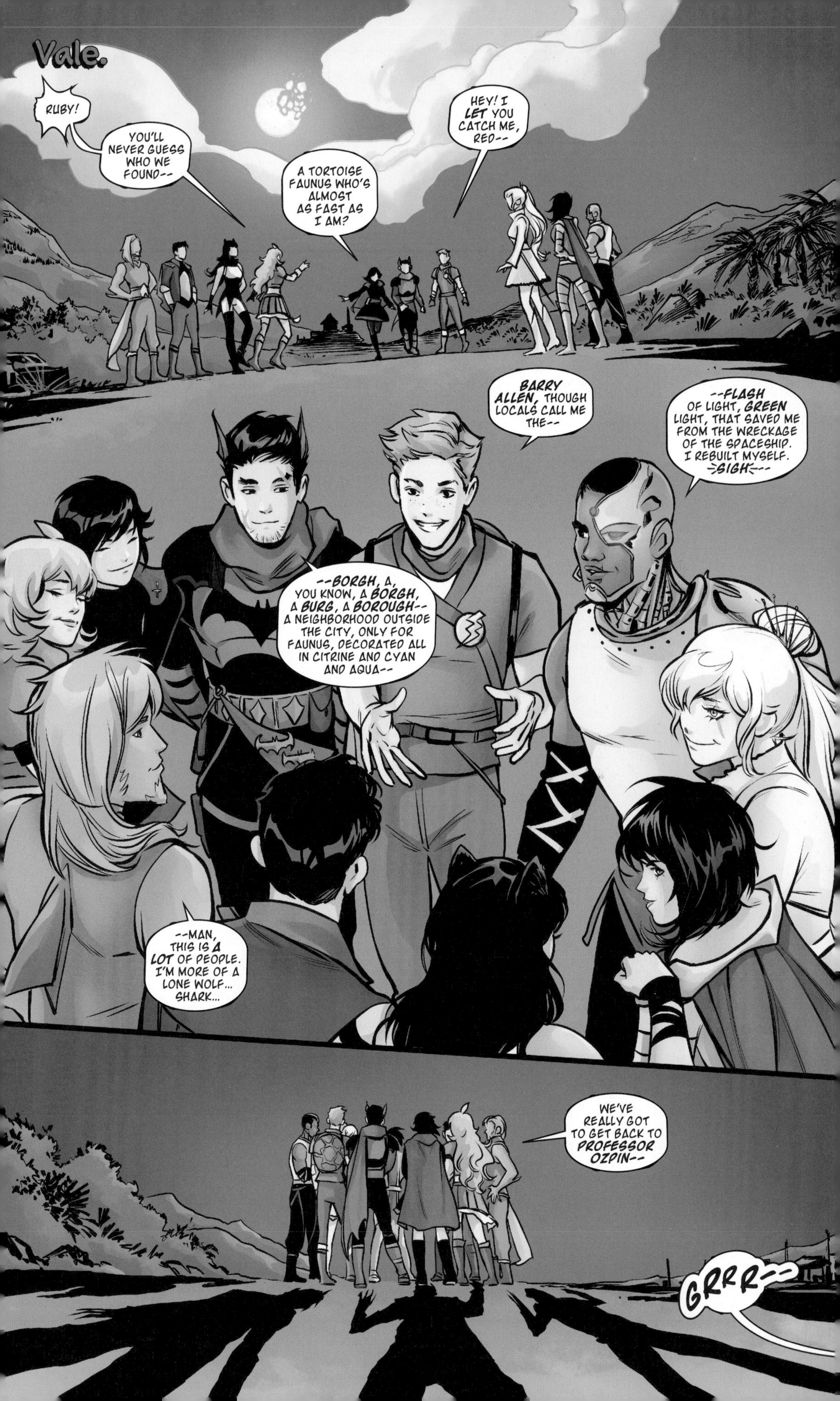
Vale.
RUBY!
YOU'LL NEVER GUESS WHO WE FOUND--
A TORTOISE FAUNUS WHO'S ALMOST AS FAST AS I AM?
HEY! I LET YOU CATCH ME, RED--
BARRY ALLEN, THOUGH LOCALS CALL ME THE--
--FLASH OF LIGHT, GREEN LIGHT, THAT SAVED ME FROM THE WRECKAGE OF THE SPACESHIP. I REBUILT MYSELF. SIGH--
--BORGH, A, YOU KNOW, A BORGH, A BURG, A BOROUGH-- A NEIGHBORHOOD OUTSIDE THE CITY, ONLY FOR FAUNUS, DECORATED ALL IN CITRINE AND CYAN AND AQUA--
--MAN, THIS IS A LOT OF PEOPLE. I'M MORE OF A LONE WOLF... SHARK...
WE'VE REALLY GOT TO GET BACK TO PROFESSOR OZPIN--
GRRR--

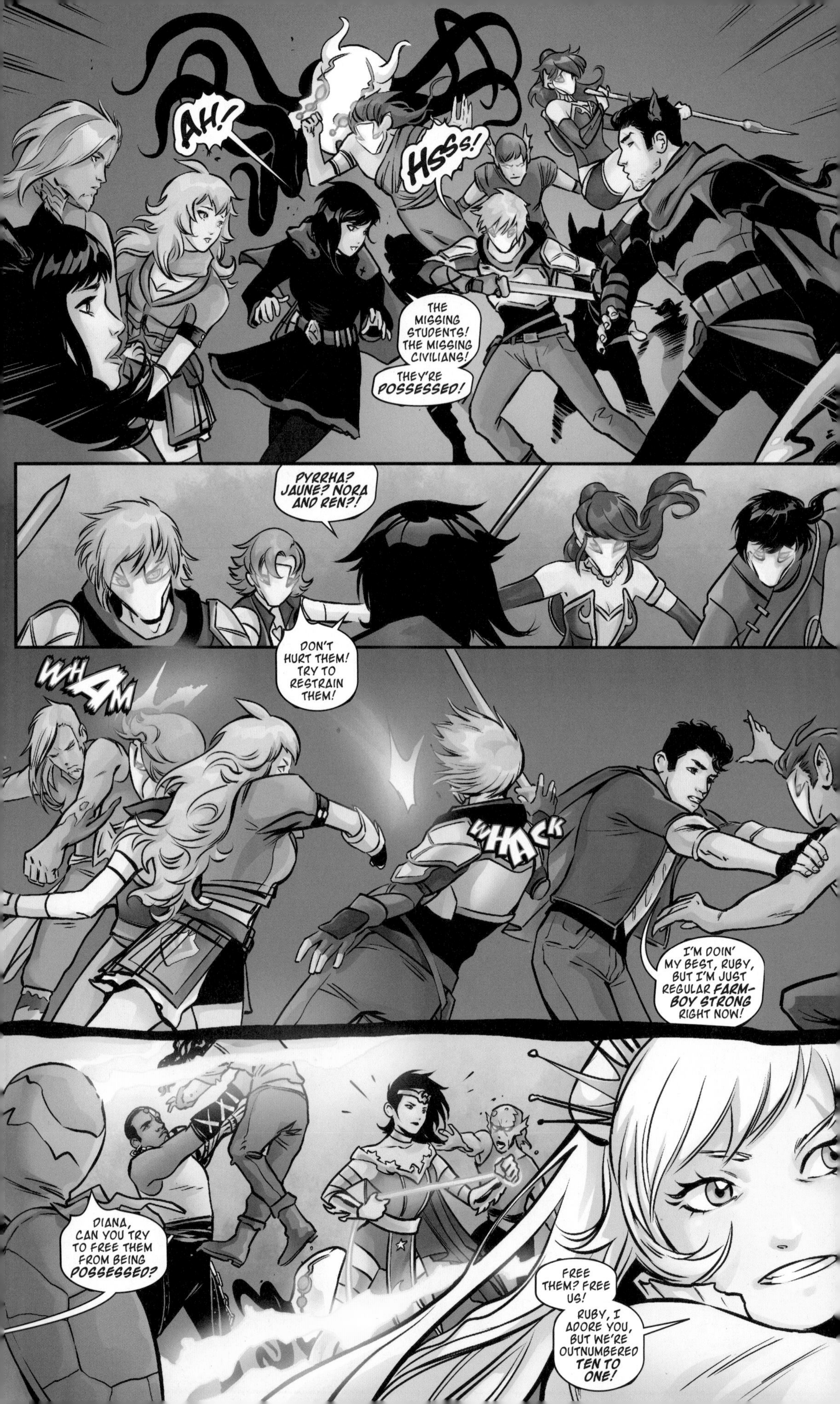
AH!
HSSS!
THE MISSING STUDENTS! THE MISSING CIVILIANS!
THEY'RE POSSESSED!
PYRRHA? JAUNE? NORA AND REN?!
DON'T HURT THEM! TRY TO RESTRAIN THEM!
WHAM
WHACK
I'M DOIN' MY BEST, RUBY, BUT I'M JUST REGULAR FARM-BOY STRONG RIGHT NOW!
DIANA, CAN YOU TRY TO FREE THEM FROM BEING POSSESSED?
FREE THEM? FREE US!
RUBY, I ADORE YOU, BUT WE'RE OUTNUMBERED TEN TO ONE!

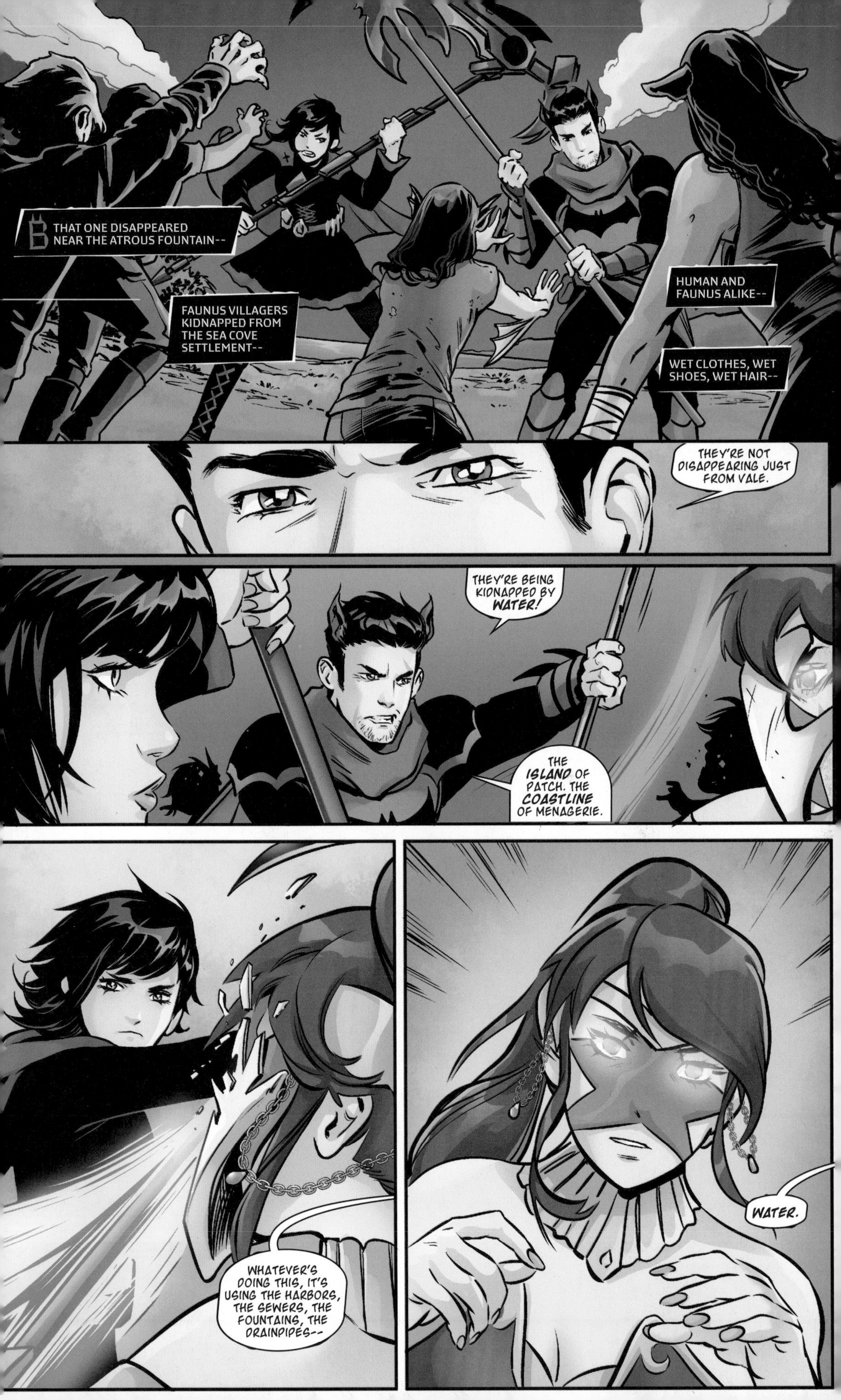
THAT ONE DISAPPEARED NEAR THE ATROUS FOUNTAIN--
FAUNUS VILLAGERS KIDNAPPED FROM THE SEA COVE SETTLEMENT--
HUMAN AND FAUNUS ALIKE--
WET CLOTHES, WET SHOES, WET HAIR--
THEY'RE NOT DISAPPEARING JUST FROM VALE.
THEY'RE BEING KIDNAPPED BY WATER!
THE ISLAND OF PATCH. THE COASTLINE OF MENAGERIE.
WHATEVER'S DOING THIS, IT'S USING THE HARBORS, THE SEWERS, THE FOUNTAINS, THE DRAINPIPES--
WATER.

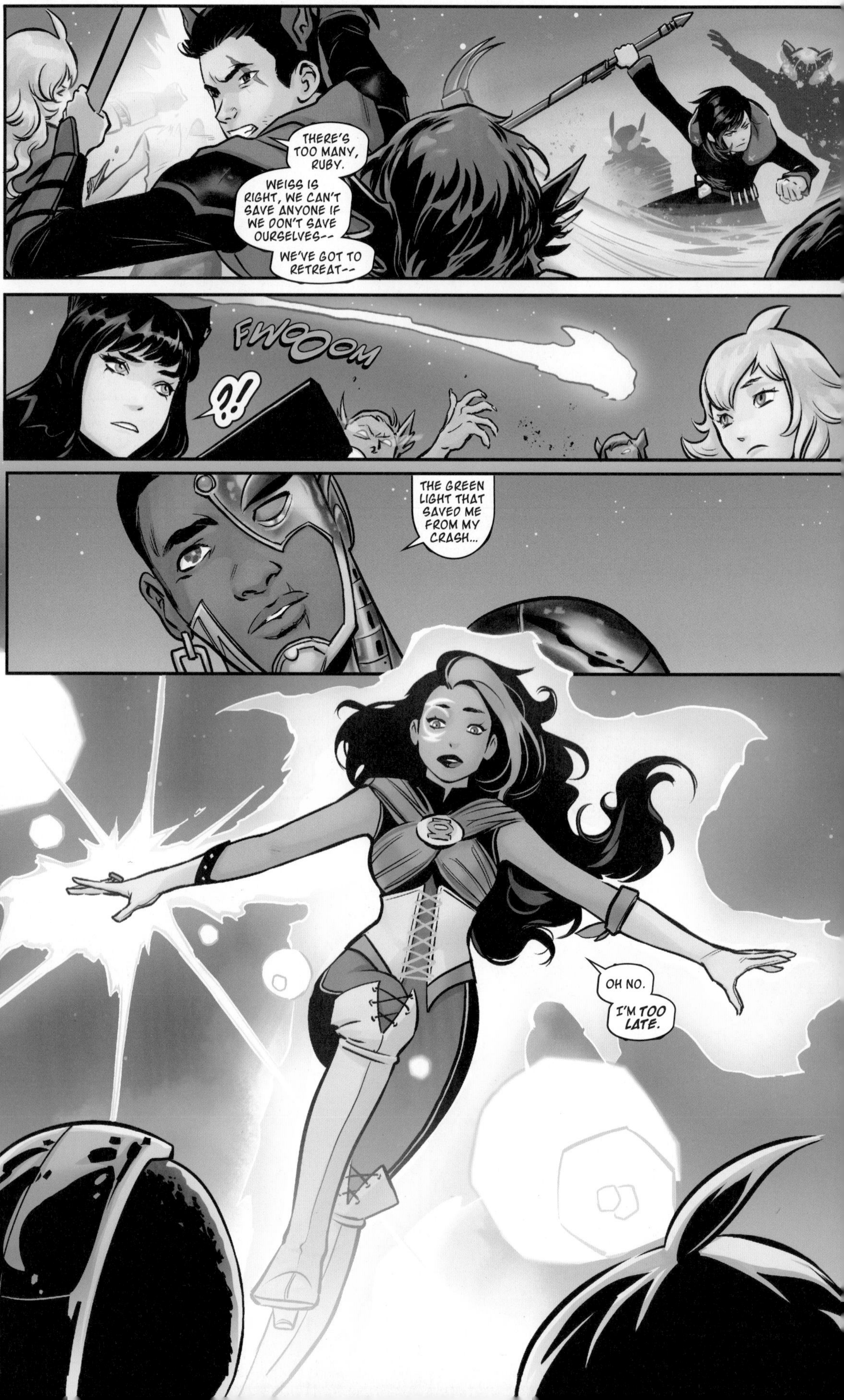
THERE'S TOO MANY, RUBY.
WEISS IS RIGHT, WE CAN'T SAVE ANYONE IF WE DON'T SAVE OURSELVES--
WE'VE GOT TO RETREAT--
FWOOOM
?!
THE GREEN LIGHT THAT SAVED ME FROM MY CRASH...
OH NO.
I'M TOO LATE.

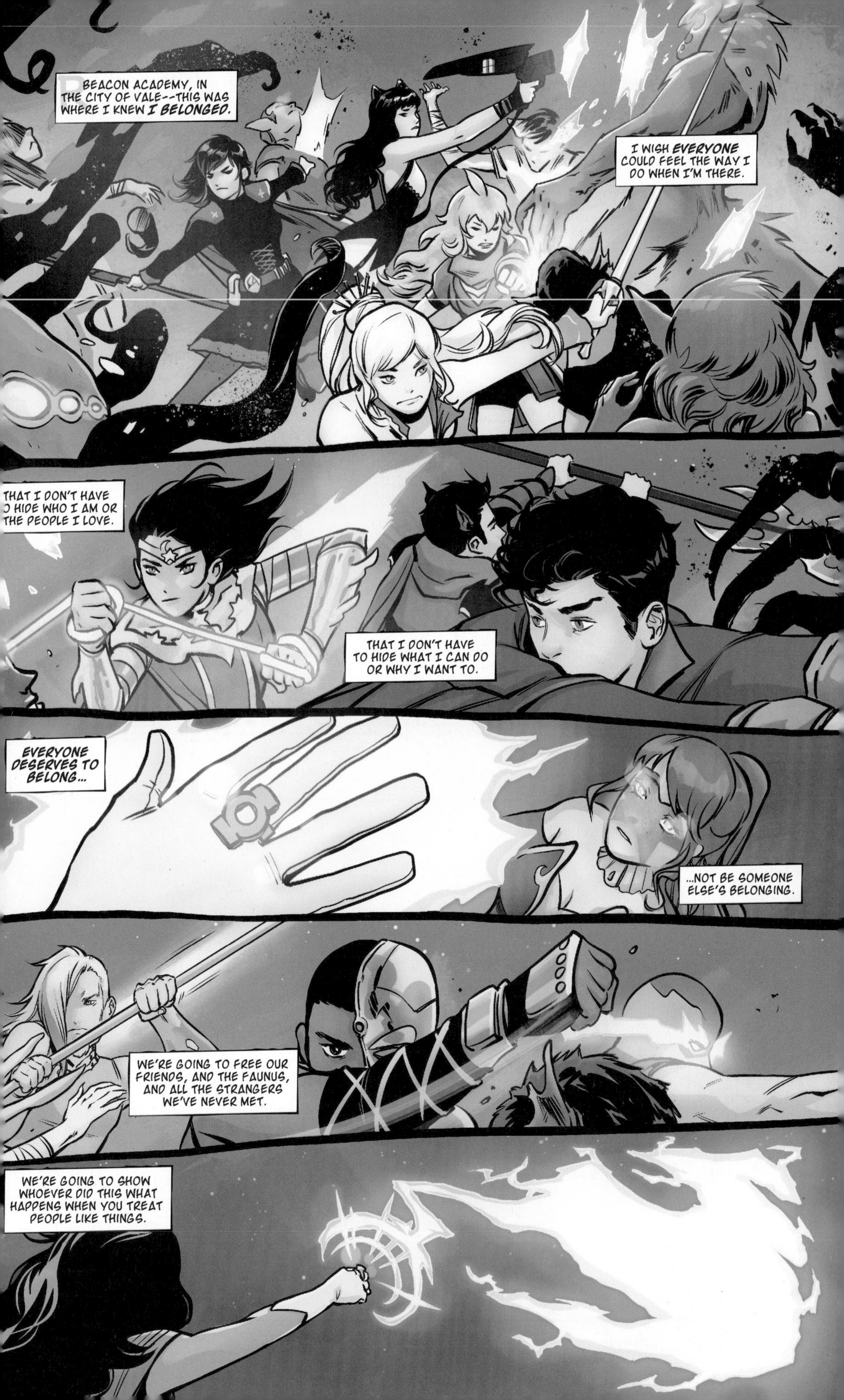
BEACON ACADEMY, IN THE CITY OF VALE--THIS WAS WHERE I KNEW I BELONGED.
I WISH EVERYONE COULD FEEL THE WAY I DO WHEN I'M THERE.
THAT I DON'T HAVE TO HIDE WHO I AM OR THE PEOPLE I LOVE.
THAT I DON'T HAVE TO HIDE WHAT I CAN DO OR WHY I WANT TO.
EVERYONE DESERVES TO BELONG...
...NOT BE SOMEONE ELSE'S BELONGING.
WE'RE GOING TO FREE OUR FRIENDS, AND THE FAUNUS, AND ALL THE STRANGERS WE'VE NEVER MET.
WE'RE GOING TO SHOW WHOEVER DID THIS WHAT HAPPENS WHEN YOU TREAT PEOPLE LIKE THINGS.

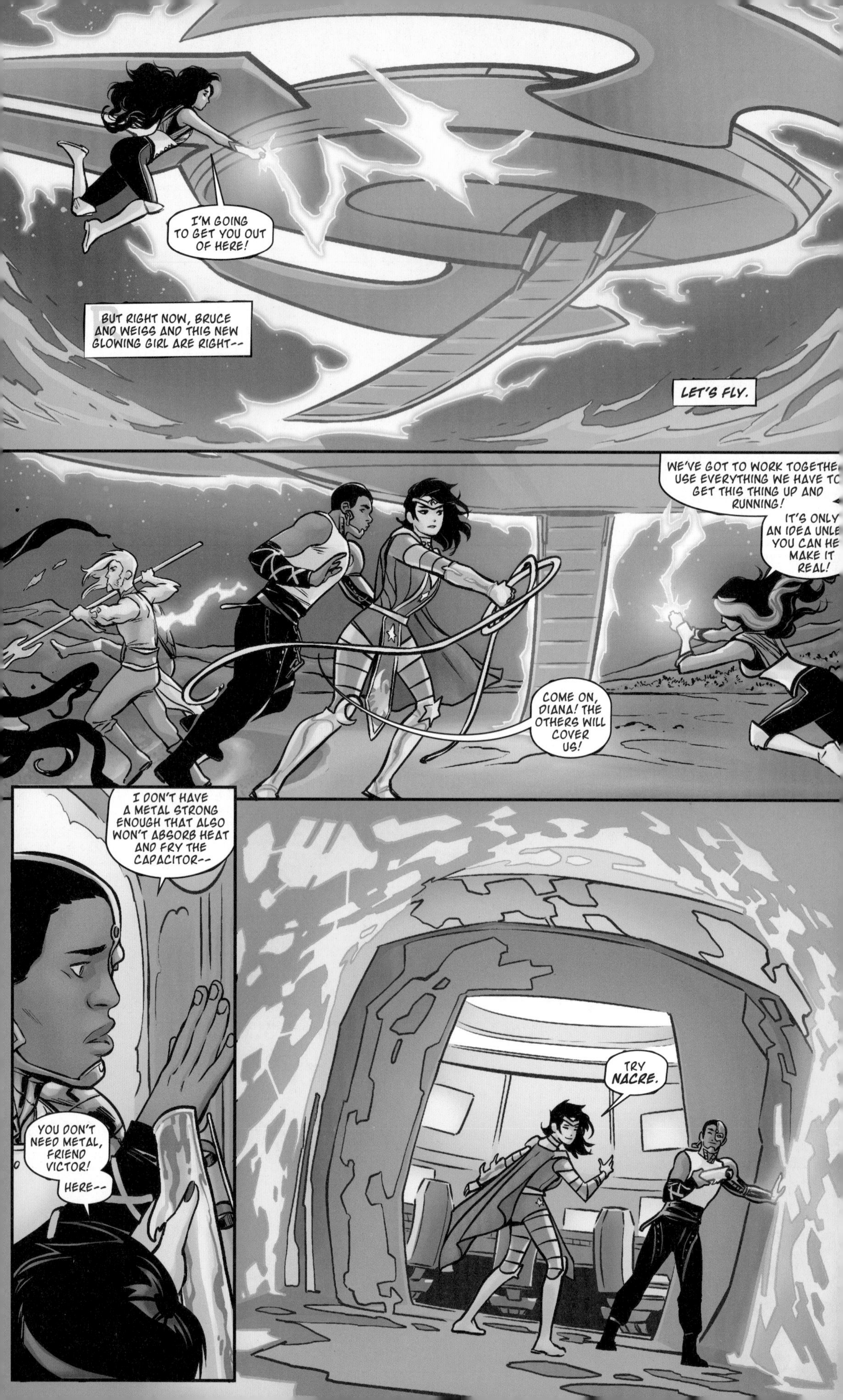
I'M GOING TO GET YOU OUT OF HERE!
BUT RIGHT NOW, BRUCE AND WEISS AND THIS NEW GLOWING GIRL ARE RIGHT--
LET'S FLY.
WE'VE GOT TO WORK TOGETHE USE EVERYTHING WE HAVE TO GET THIS THING UP AND RUNNING!
IT'S ONLY AN IDEA UNLE YOU CAN HE MAKE IT REAL!
COME ON, DIANA! THE OTHERS WILL COVER US!
I DON'T HAVE A METAL STRONG ENOUGH THAT ALSO WON'T ABSORB HEAT AND FRY THE CAPACITOR--
YOU DON'T NEED METAL, FRIEND VICTOR!
HERE--
TRY NACRE.

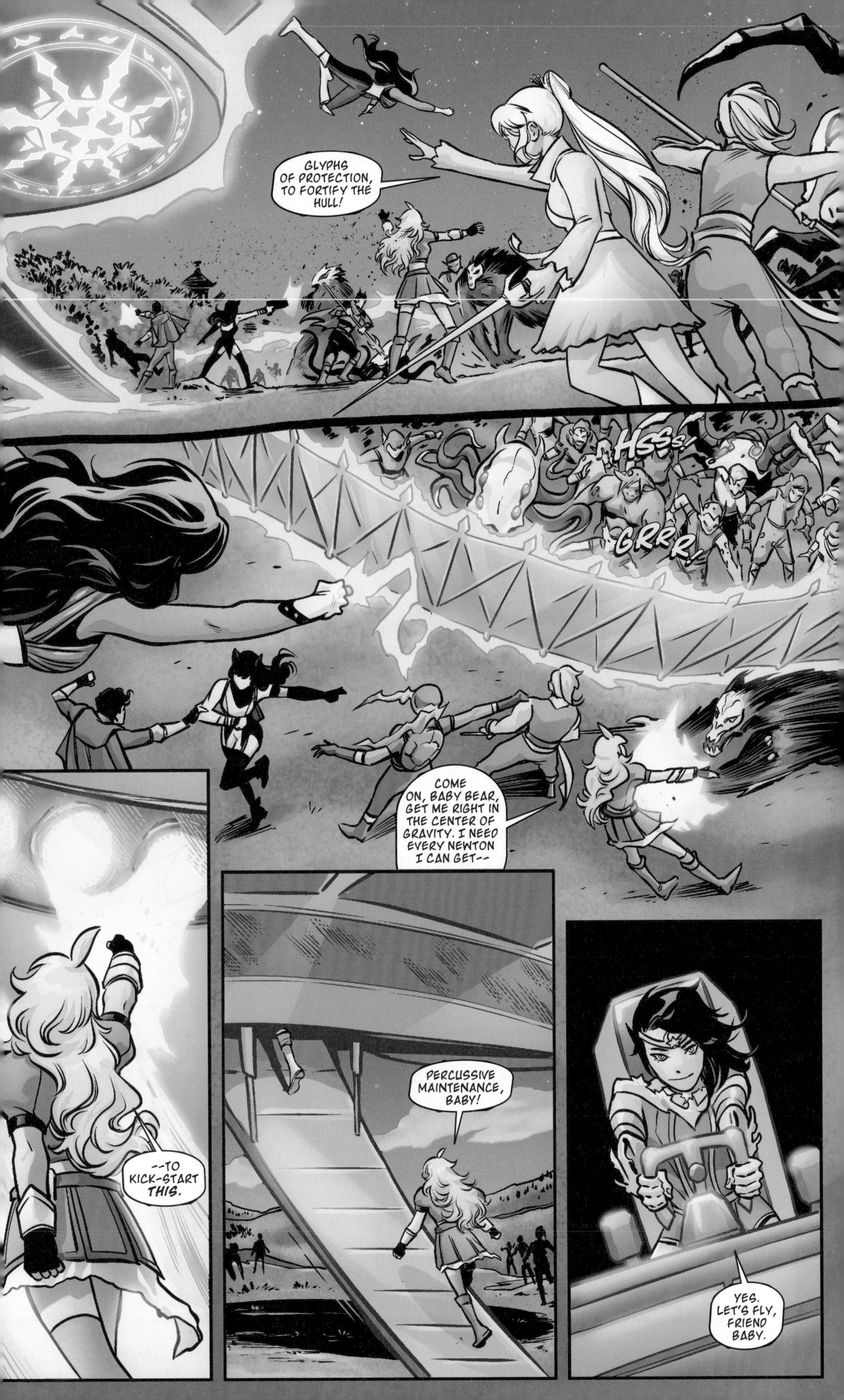
GLYPHS OF PROTECTION, TO FORTIFY THE HULL!
HSSS!
GRRR!
COME ON, BABY BEAR, GET ME RIGHT IN THE CENTER OF GRAVITY. I NEED EVERY NEWTON I CAN GET--
--TO KICK-START THIS.
PERCUSSIVE MAINTENANCE, BABY!
YES. LET'S FLY, FRIEND BABY.

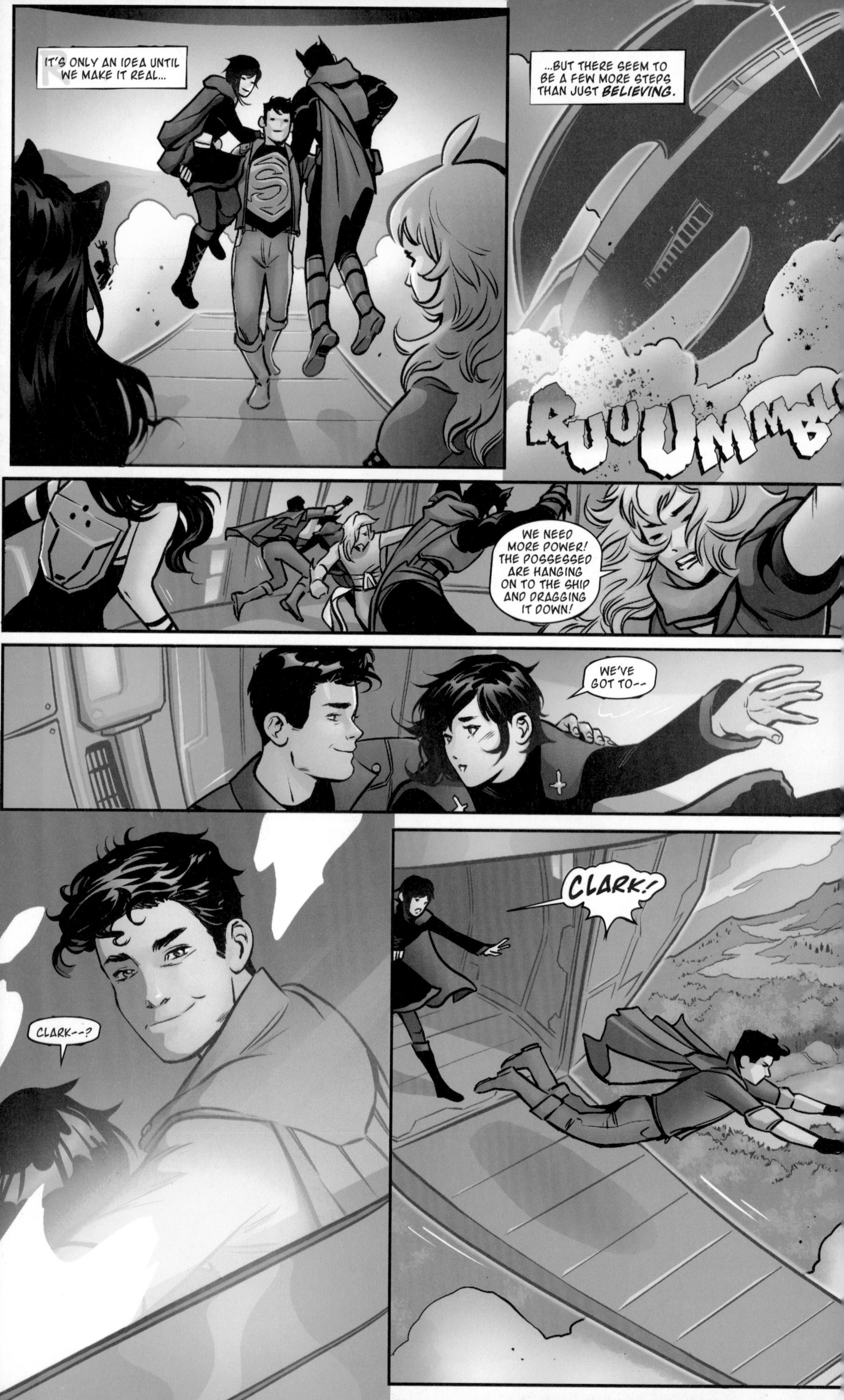
IT'S ONLY AN IDEA UNTIL WE MAKE IT REAL...
...BUT THERE SEEM TO BE A FEW MORE STEPS THAN JUST BELIEVING.
RUUUMMBL
WE NEED MORE POWER! THE POSSESSED ARE HANGING ON TO THE SHIP AND DRAGGING IT DOWN!
WE'VE GOT TO--
CLARK--?
CLARK!

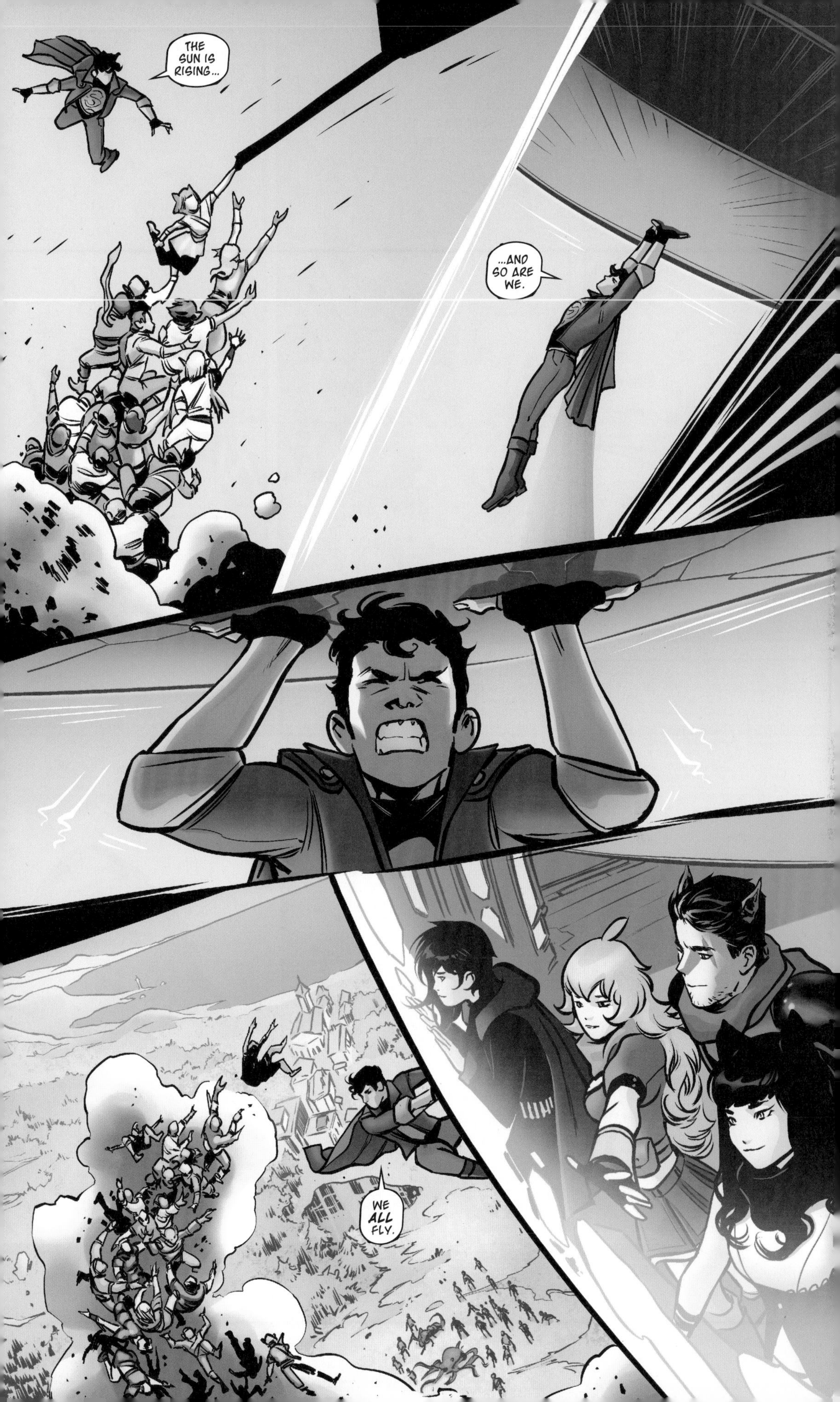
THE SUN IS RISING...
...AND SO ARE WE.
WE ALL FLY.

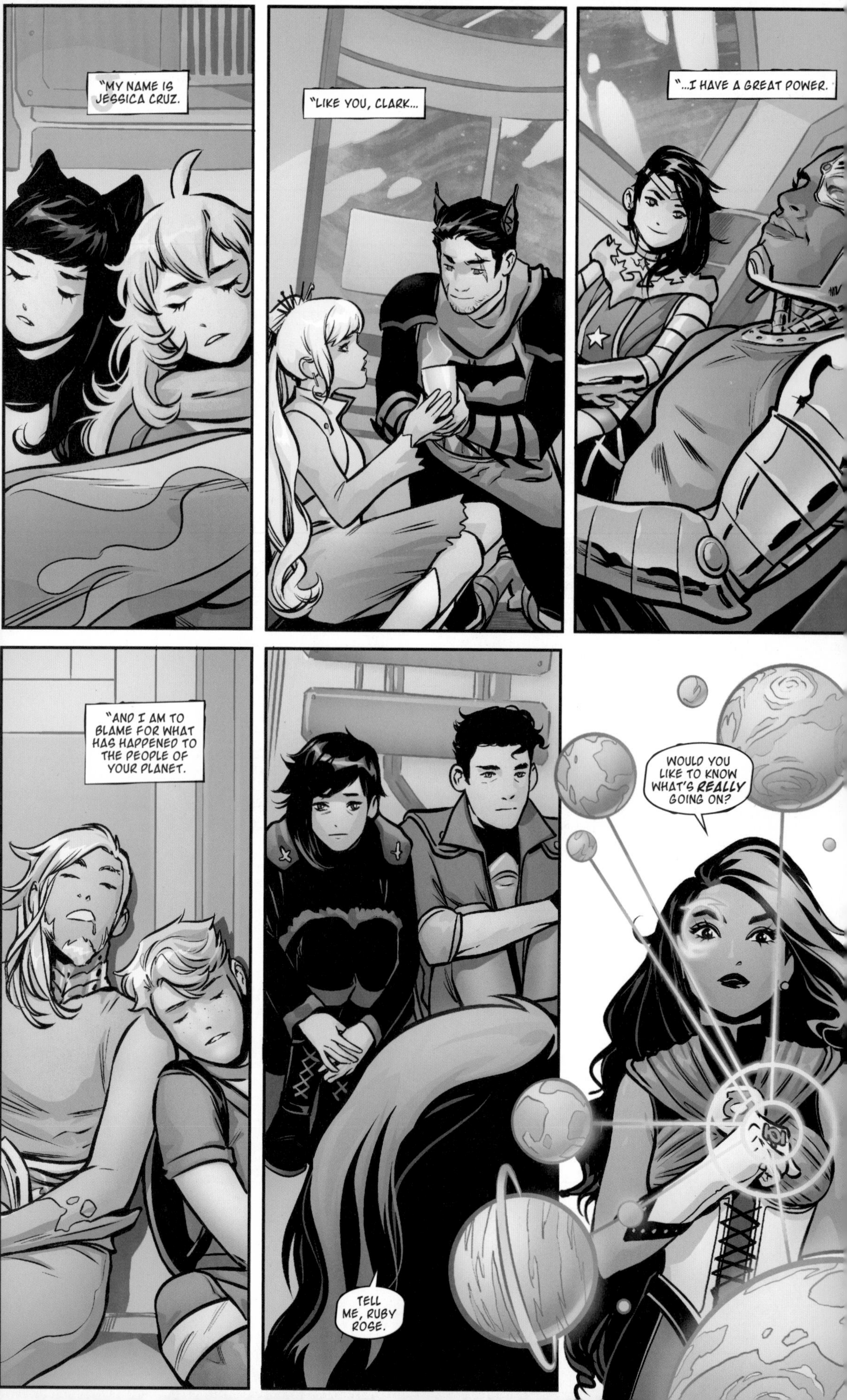

"MY NAME IS JESSICA CRUZ.
"LIKE YOU, CLARK...
"...I HAVE A GREAT POWER.
"AND I AM TO BLAME FOR WHAT HAS HAPPENED TO THE PEOPLE OF YOUR PLANET.
TELL ME, RUBY ROSE.
WOULD YOU LIKE TO KNOW WHAT'S REALLY GOING ON?

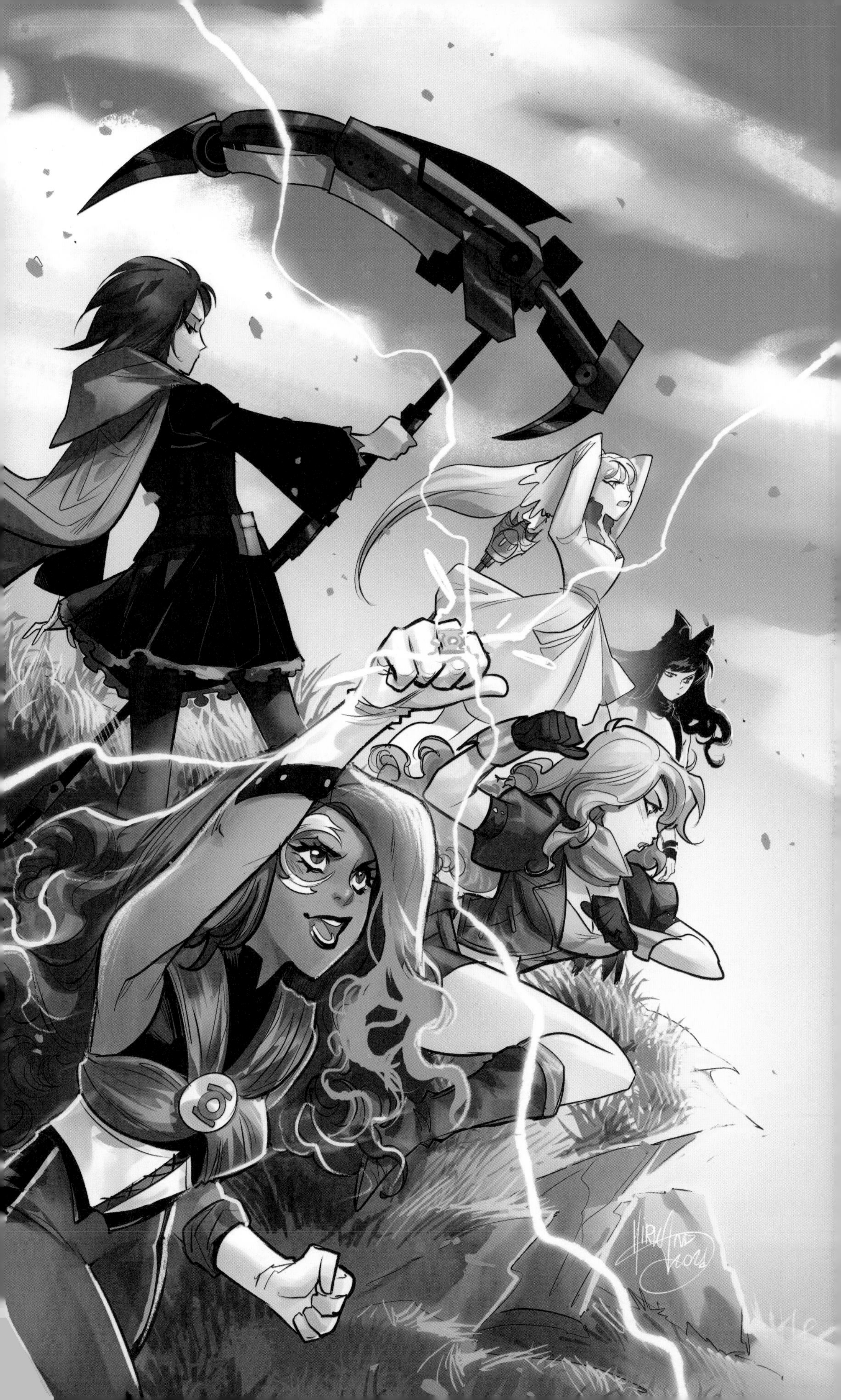

Variant cover by **VASCO GEORGIEV**

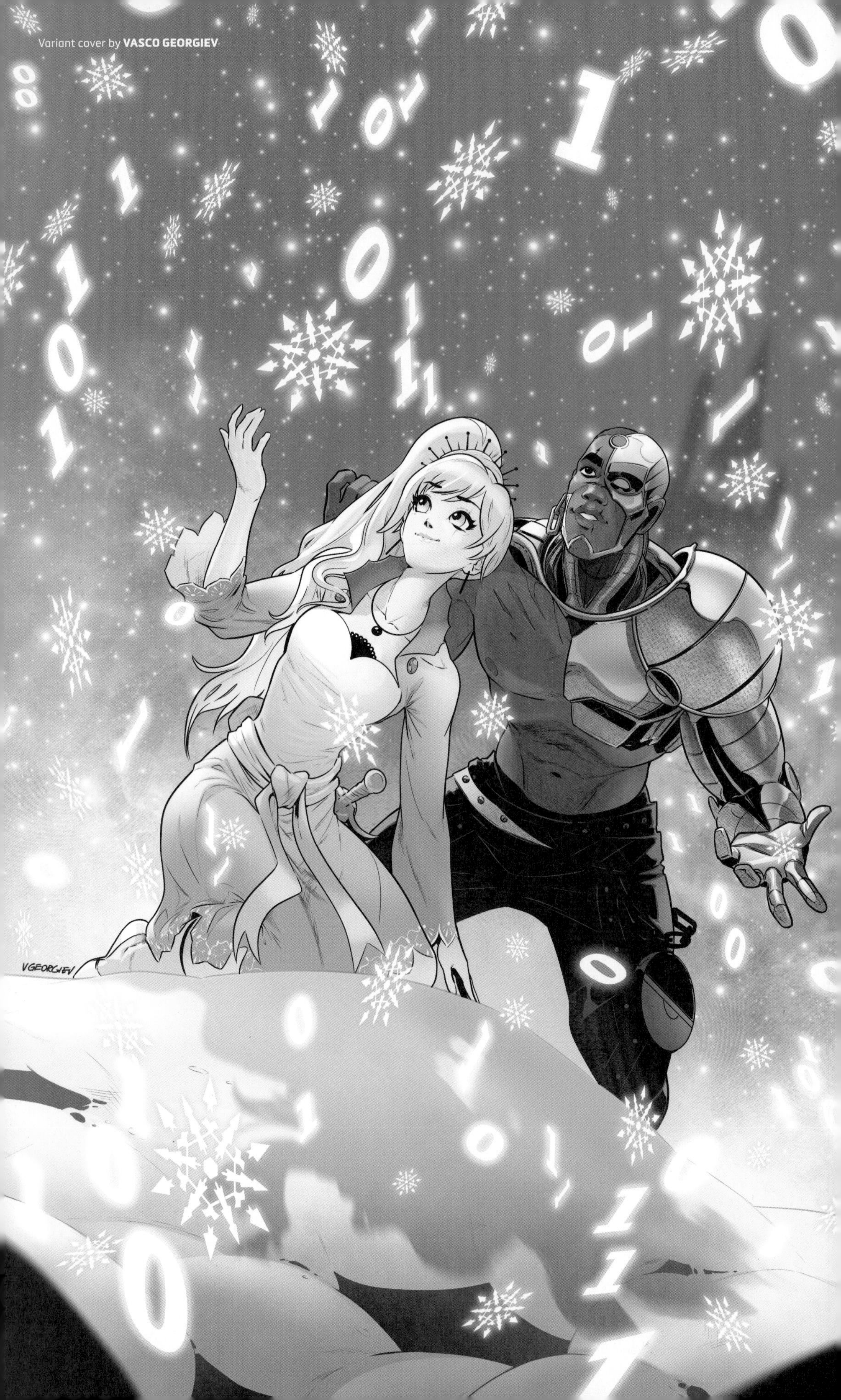
VGEORGIEV

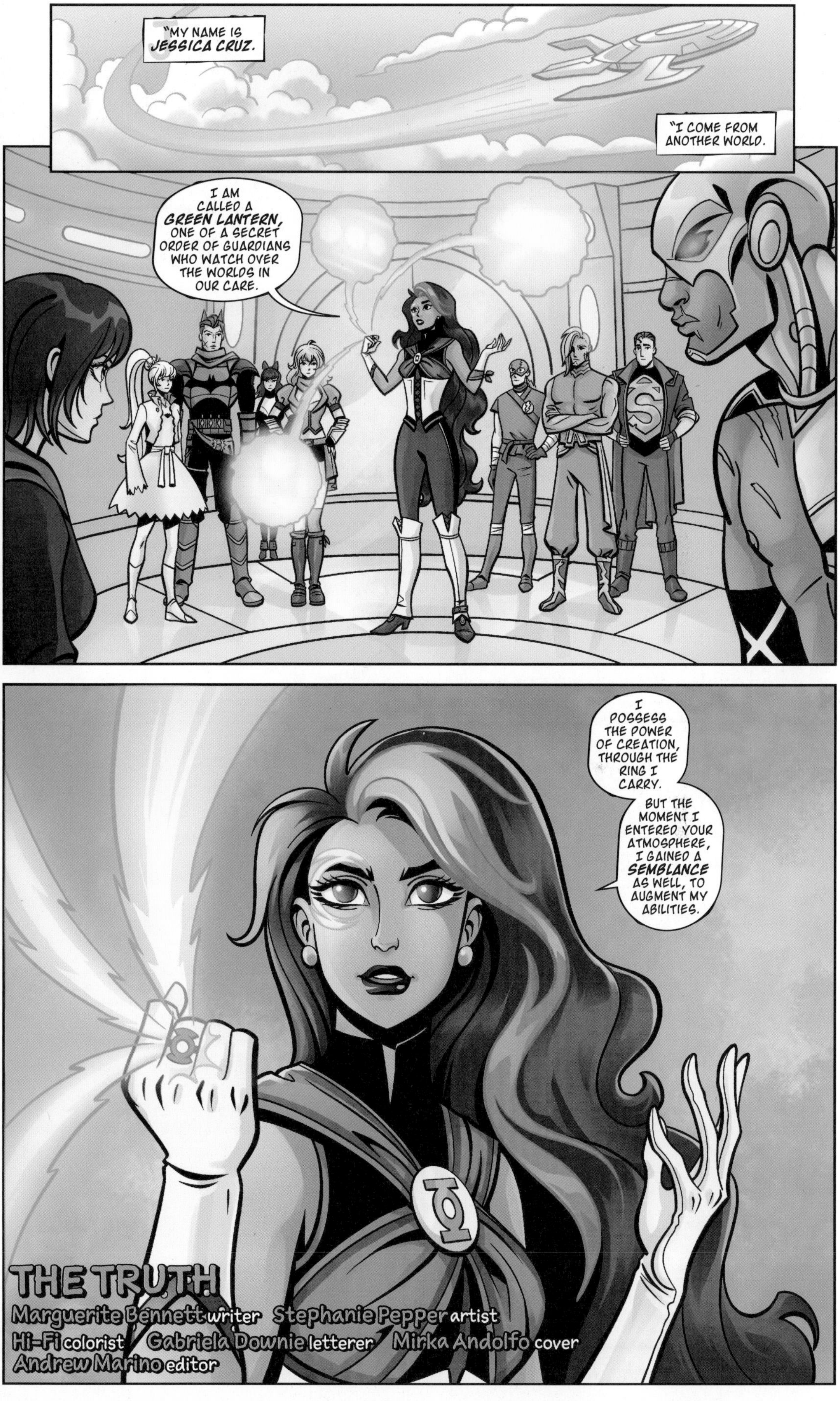

"MY NAME IS JESSICA CRUZ.
"I COME FROM ANOTHER WORLD.
I AM CALLED A GREEN LANTERN, ONE OF A SECRET ORDER OF GUARDIANS WHO WATCH OVER THE WORLDS IN OUR CARE.
I POSSESS THE POWER OF CREATION, THROUGH THE RING I CARRY.
BUT THE MOMENT I ENTERED YOUR ATMOSPHERE, I GAINED A SEMBLANCE AS WELL, TO AUGMENT MY ABILITIES.
THE TRUTH
Marguerite Bennett writer Stephanie Pepper artist
Hi-Fi colorist Gabriela Downie letterer Mirka Andolfo cover
Andrew Marino editor

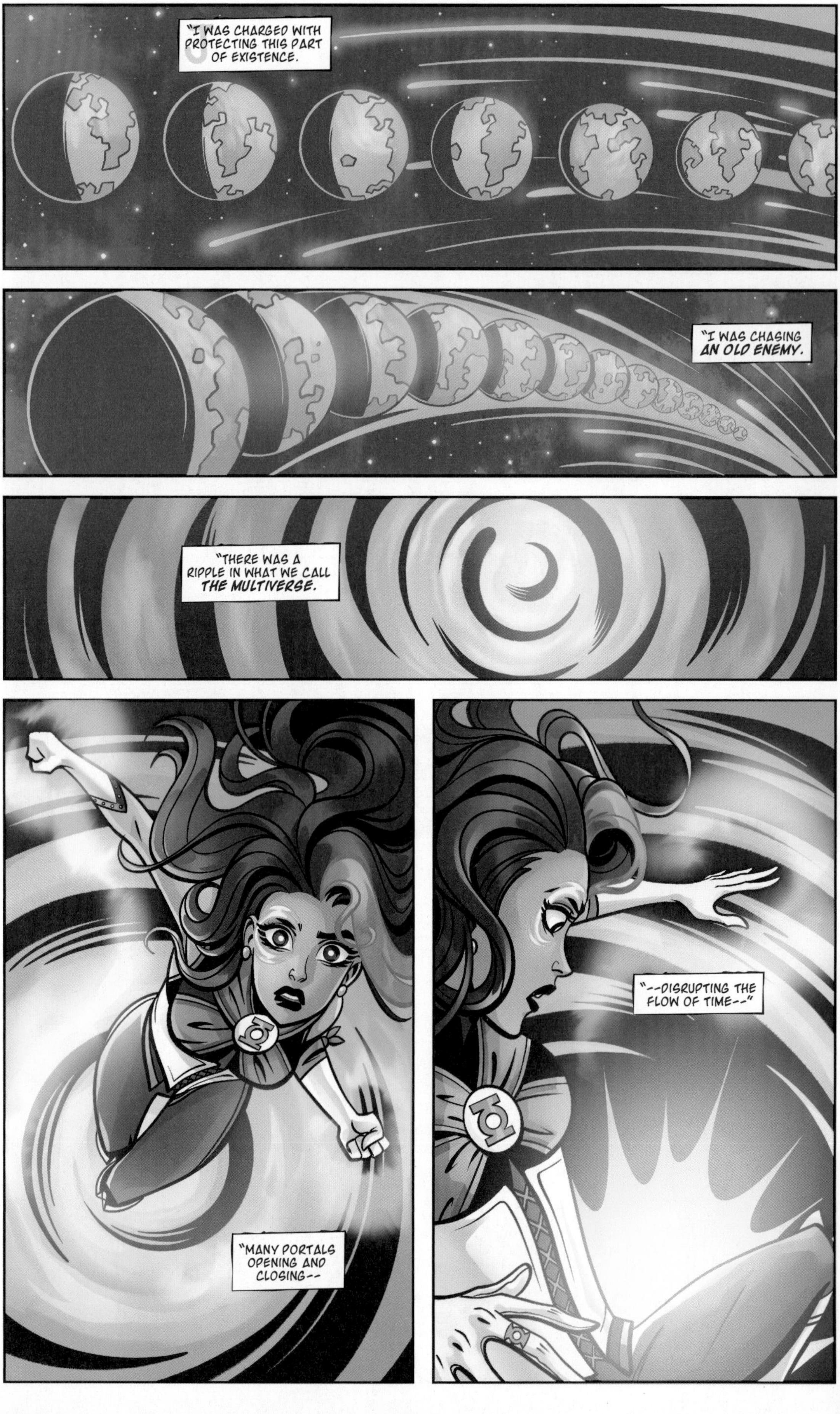
"I WAS CHARGED WITH PROTECTING THIS PART OF EXISTENCE.
"I WAS CHASING *AN OLD ENEMY*.
"THERE WAS A RIPPLE IN WHAT WE CALL *THE MULTIVERSE*.
"MANY PORTALS OPENING AND CLOSING--
"--DISRUPTING THE FLOW OF TIME--"

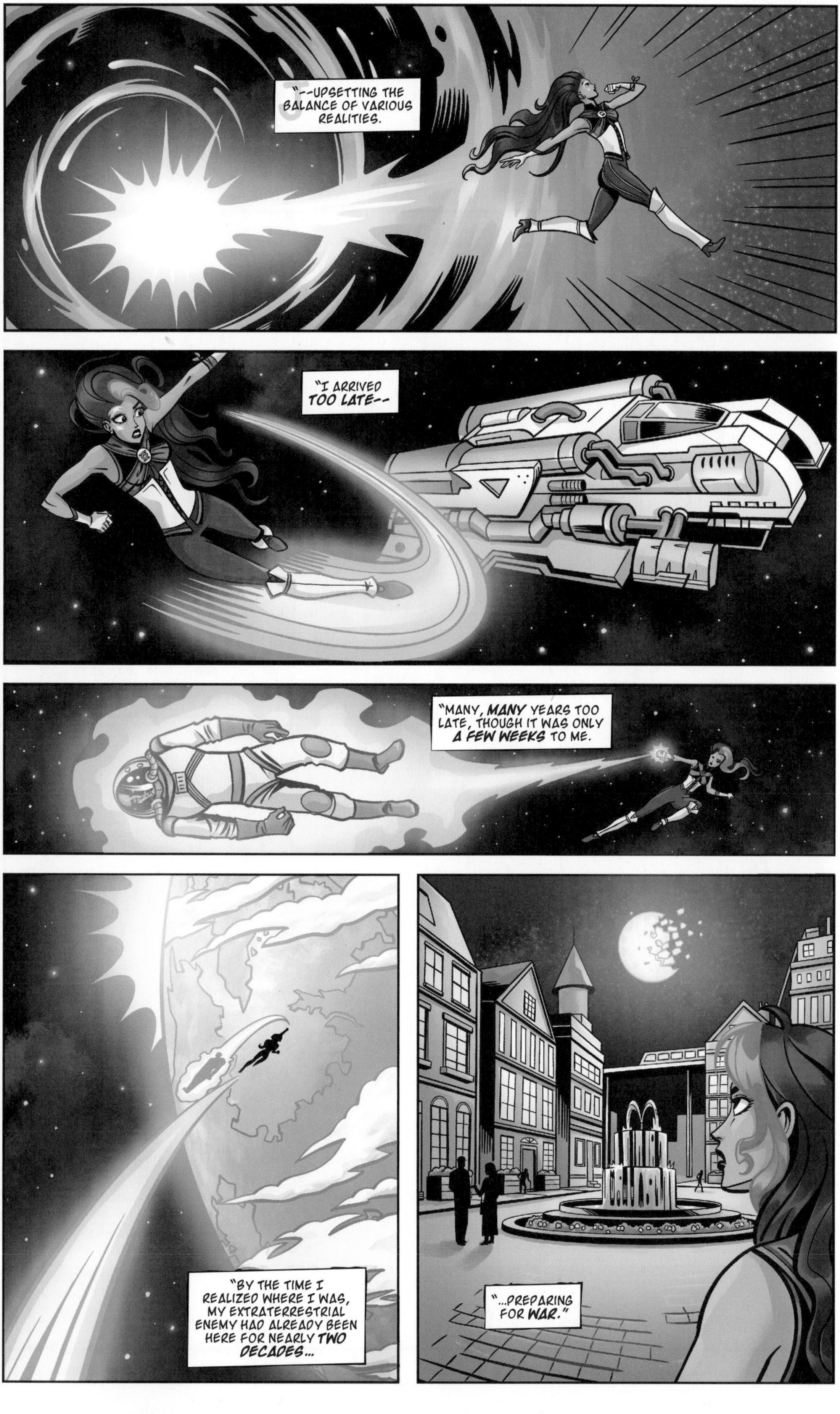
"--UPSETTING THE BALANCE OF VARIOUS REALITIES.
"I ARRIVED TOO LATE--
"MANY, MANY YEARS TOO LATE, THOUGH IT WAS ONLY A FEW WEEKS TO ME.
"BY THE TIME I REALIZED WHERE I WAS, MY EXTRATERRESTRIAL ENEMY HAD ALREADY BEEN HERE FOR NEARLY TWO DECADES...
"...PREPARING FOR WAR."

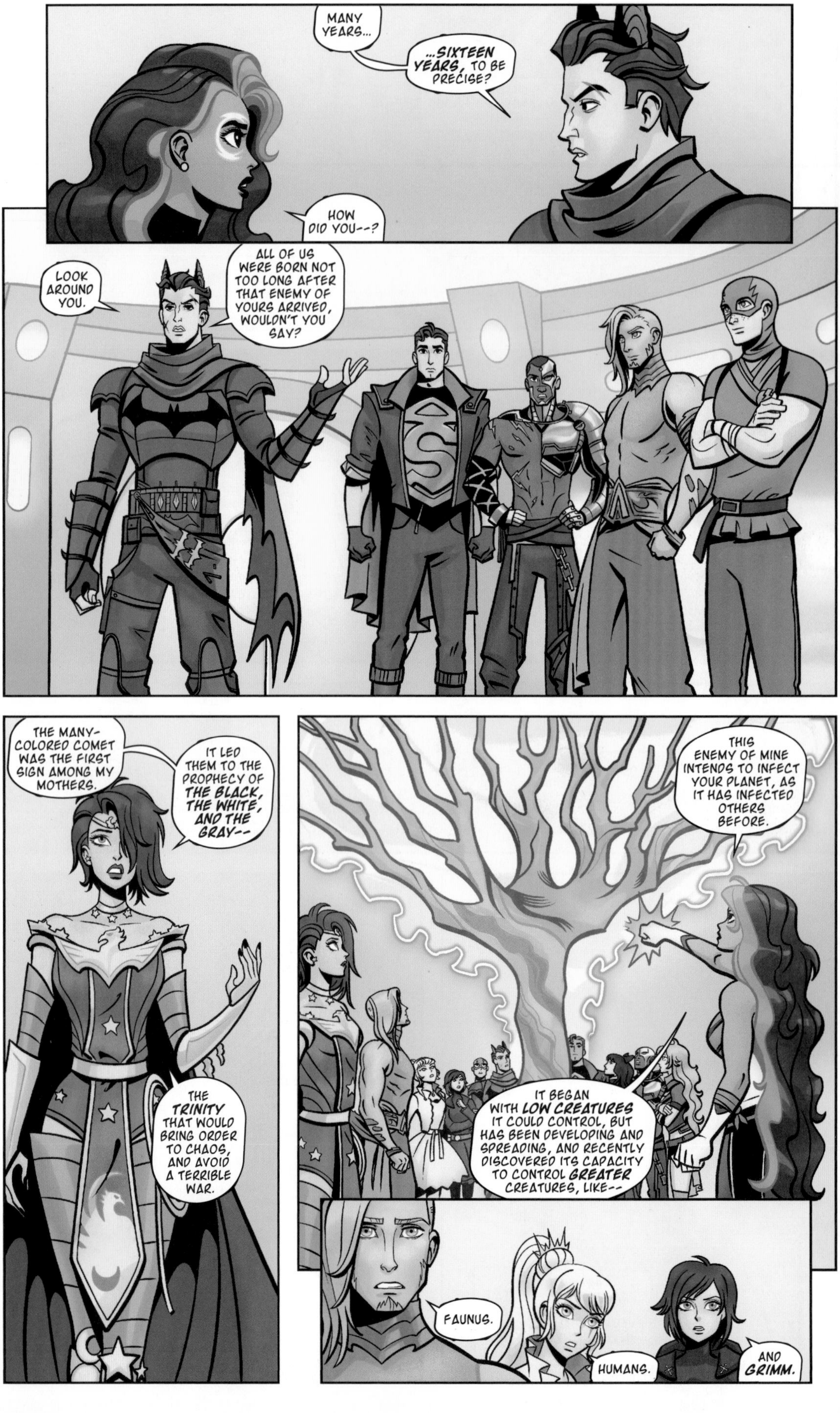
MANY YEARS...
...SIXTEEN YEARS, TO BE PRECISE?
HOW DID YOU--?
LOOK AROUND YOU.
ALL OF US WERE BORN NOT TOO LONG AFTER THAT ENEMY OF YOURS ARRIVED, WOULDN'T YOU SAY?
THE MANY-COLORED COMET WAS THE FIRST SIGN AMONG MY MOTHERS.
IT LED THEM TO THE PROPHECY OF THE BLACK, THE WHITE, AND THE GRAY--
THE TRINITY THAT WOULD BRING ORDER TO CHAOS, AND AVOID A TERRIBLE WAR.
THIS ENEMY OF MINE INTENDS TO INFECT YOUR PLANET, AS IT HAS INFECTED OTHERS BEFORE.
IT BEGAN WITH LOW CREATURES IT COULD CONTROL, BUT HAS BEEN DEVELOPING AND SPREADING, AND RECENTLY DISCOVERED ITS CAPACITY TO CONTROL GREATER CREATURES, LIKE--
FAUNUS.
HUMANS.
AND GRIMM.

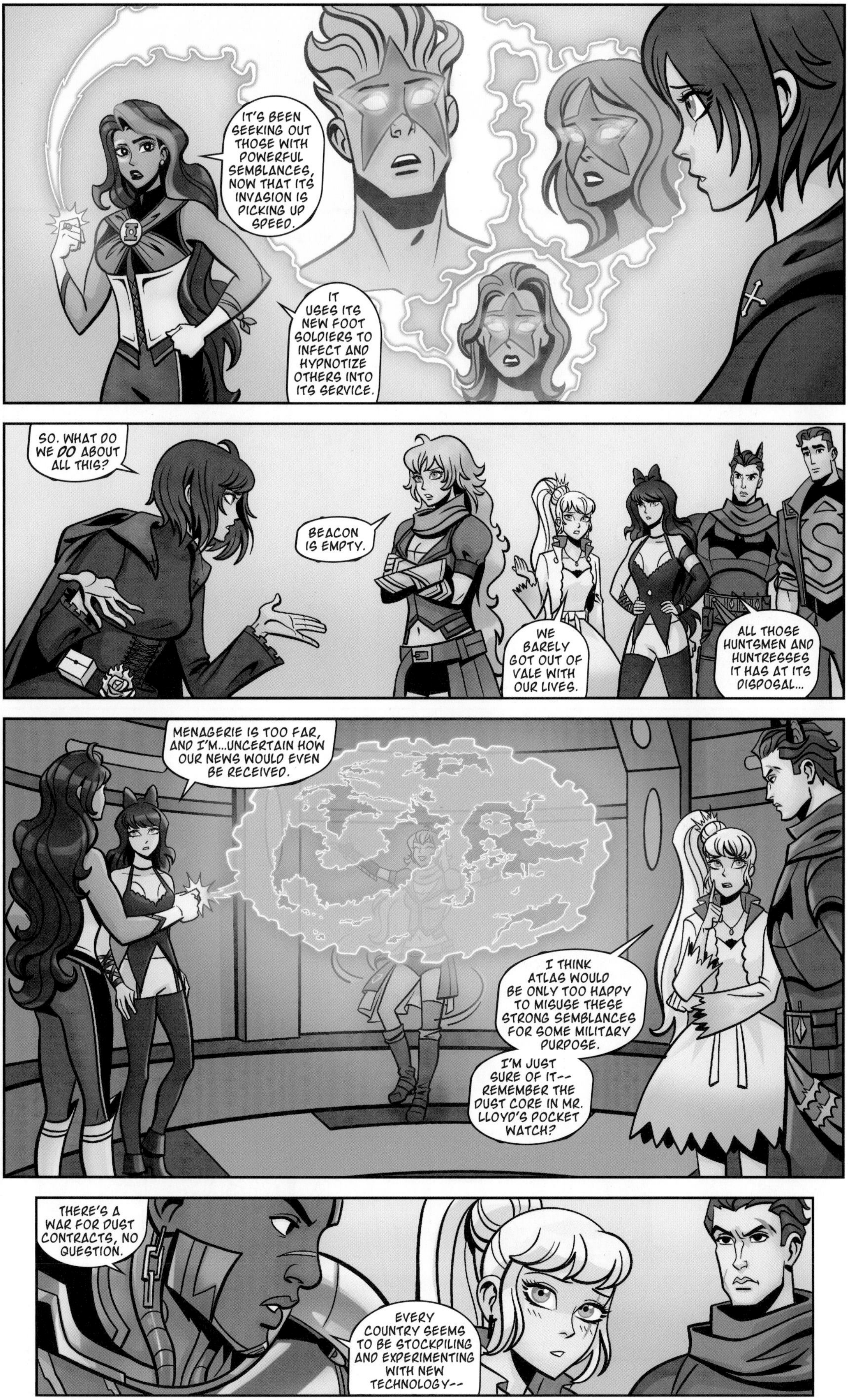
IT'S BEEN SEEKING OUT THOSE WITH POWERFUL SEMBLANCES, NOW THAT ITS INVASION IS PICKING UP SPEED.
IT USES ITS NEW FOOT SOLDIERS TO INFECT AND HYPNOTIZE OTHERS INTO ITS SERVICE.
SO. WHAT DO WE DO ABOUT ALL THIS?
BEACON IS EMPTY.
WE BARELY GOT OUT OF VALE WITH OUR LIVES.
ALL THOSE HUNTSMEN AND HUNTRESSES IT HAS AT ITS DISPOSAL...
MENAGERIE IS TOO FAR, AND I'M...UNCERTAIN HOW OUR NEWS WOULD EVEN BE RECEIVED.
I THINK ATLAS WOULD BE ONLY TOO HAPPY TO MISUSE THESE STRONG SEMBLANCES FOR SOME MILITARY PURPOSE.
I'M JUST SURE OF IT-- REMEMBER THE DUST CORE IN MR. LLOYD'S POCKET WATCH?
THERE'S A WAR FOR DUST CONTRACTS, NO QUESTION.
EVERY COUNTRY SEEMS TO BE STOCKPILING AND EXPERIMENTING WITH NEW TECHNOLOGY--

UNDER THE COMMAND AND CONTROL OF THIS ENEMY OF MINE.

MR. LLOYD IS WORKING WITH AN ALIEN INVADER?!

NO. ONE OF THE POSSESSED, HIGHER UP, TOLD HIM THAT HE WOULD BE PAID HANDSOMELY FOR EVERY DUST WEAPON HE TURNED OVER.

WELL, I DON'T THINK THERE'S MUCH I CAN DO AGAINST SUCH A MASSIVE MILITARY FORCE.

I'M TECHNICALLY A WANTED FUGITIVE WHO ABSCONDED FROM AN INDENTURED WORK CONTRACT IN A DUST MINE.

I HAVE THE POWER OF THE WAYNE NAME AND FORTUNE, BUT NOW THAT WORD IS OUT I'M A FAUNUS...

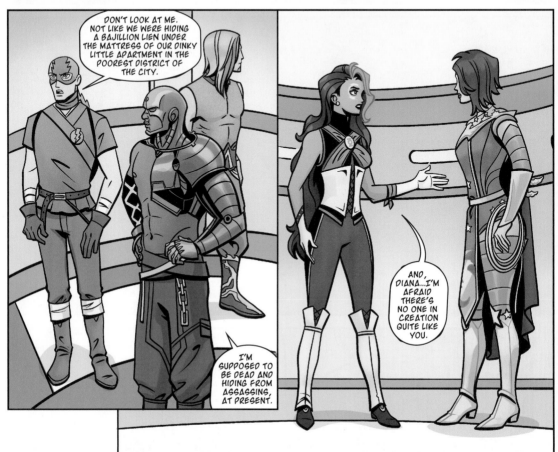

DON'T LOOK AT ME. NOT LIKE WE WERE HIDING A BAJILLION LIEN UNDER THE MATTRESS OF OUR DINKY LITTLE APARTMENT IN THE POOREST DISTRICT OF THE CITY.

I'M SUPPOSED TO BE DEAD AND HIDING FROM ASSASSINS, AT PRESENT.

AND, DIANA...I'M AFRAID THERE'S NO ONE IN CREATION QUITE LIKE YOU.

MY MOTHERS THOUGHT I WAS READY TO GO INTO THE WORLD.

THEY KNEW I WOULD NOT BELONG.

THEY KNEW I WOULD BE SINGULAR AND ALONE.

I NEVER EXPECTED TO FIND FRIENDS.

AND THOUGH WE HAVE ONLY JUST MET, YOU ARE EACH MORE DEAR TO ME THAN YOU SHALL EVER KNOW.

AND WHEN I SAY I WILL RISK YOU, RISK MY HEART'S DESIRE TO DO THE RIGHT THING, I KNOW WHAT IT IS I ASK.

"I HAVE LEARNED THAT THERE IS MORE TO LIFE THAN *BELONGING*.

"I HAVE LEARNED THERE IS BELIEVING--

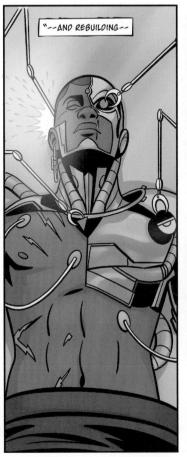

"--AND REBUILDING--

"--AND *BECOMING*."

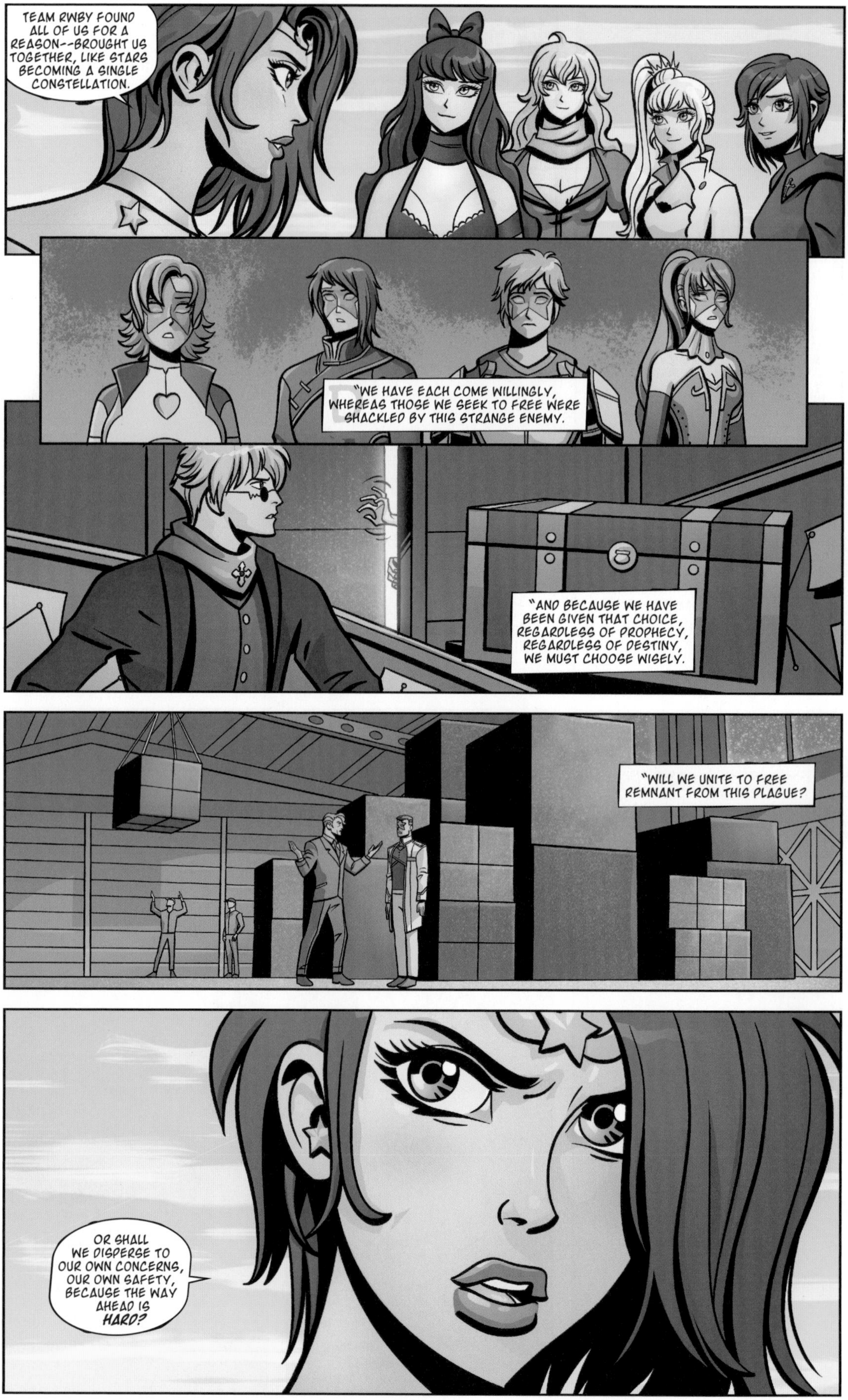
TEAM RWBY FOUND ALL OF US FOR A REASON--BROUGHT US TOGETHER, LIKE STARS BECOMING A SINGLE CONSTELLATION.
"WE HAVE EACH COME WILLINGLY, WHEREAS THOSE WE SEEK TO FREE WERE SHACKLED BY THIS STRANGE ENEMY.
"AND BECAUSE WE HAVE BEEN GIVEN THAT CHOICE, REGARDLESS OF PROPHECY, REGARDLESS OF DESTINY, WE MUST CHOOSE WISELY.
"WILL WE UNITE TO FREE REMNANT FROM THIS PLAGUE?
OR SHALL WE DISPERSE TO OUR OWN CONCERNS, OUR OWN SAFETY, BECAUSE THE WAY AHEAD IS *HARD?*

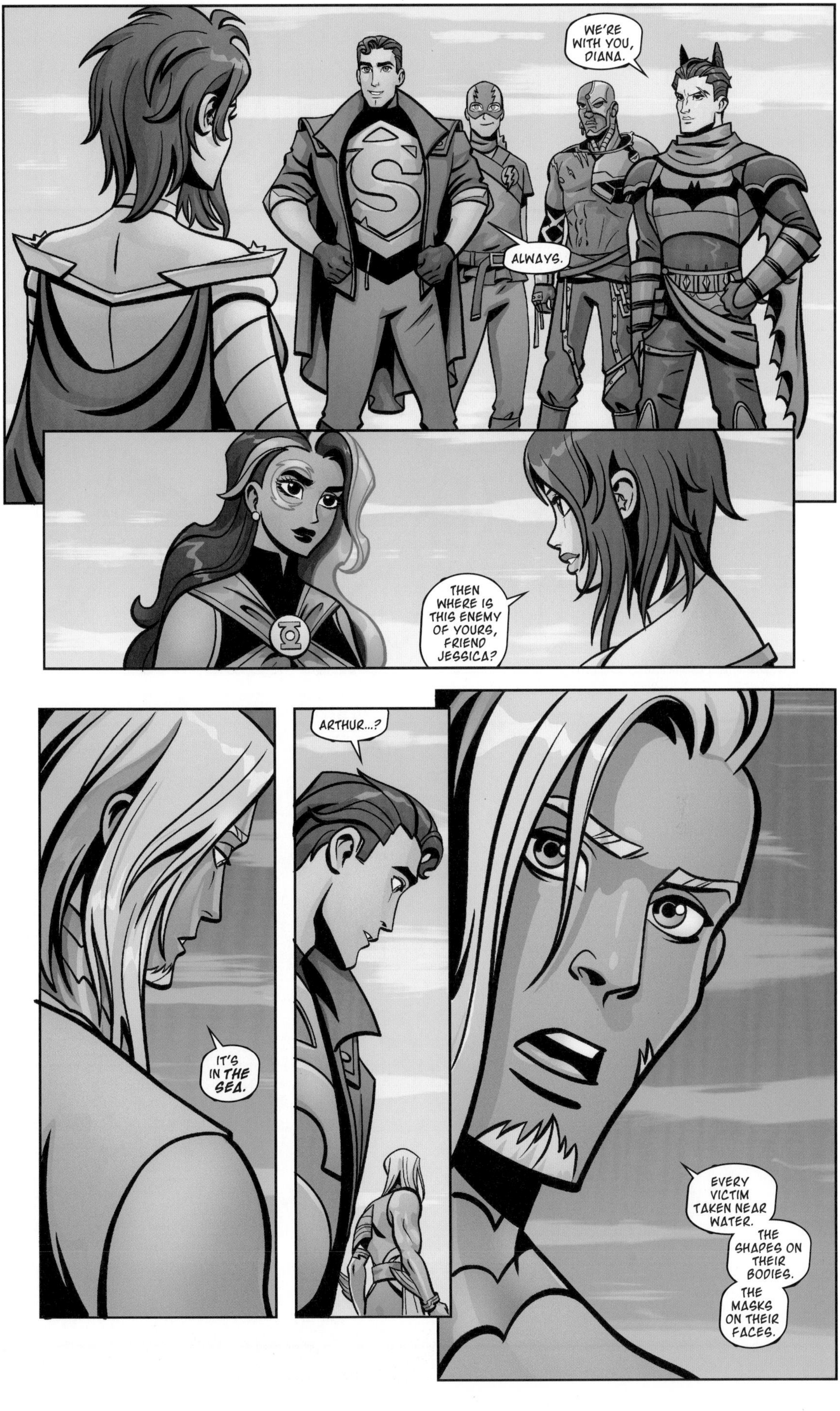
WE'RE WITH YOU, DIANA.
ALWAYS.
THEN WHERE IS THIS ENEMY OF YOURS, FRIEND JESSICA?
IT'S IN THE SEA.
ARTHUR...?
EVERY VICTIM TAKEN NEAR WATER.
THE SHAPES ON THEIR BODIES.
THE MASKS ON THEIR FACES.

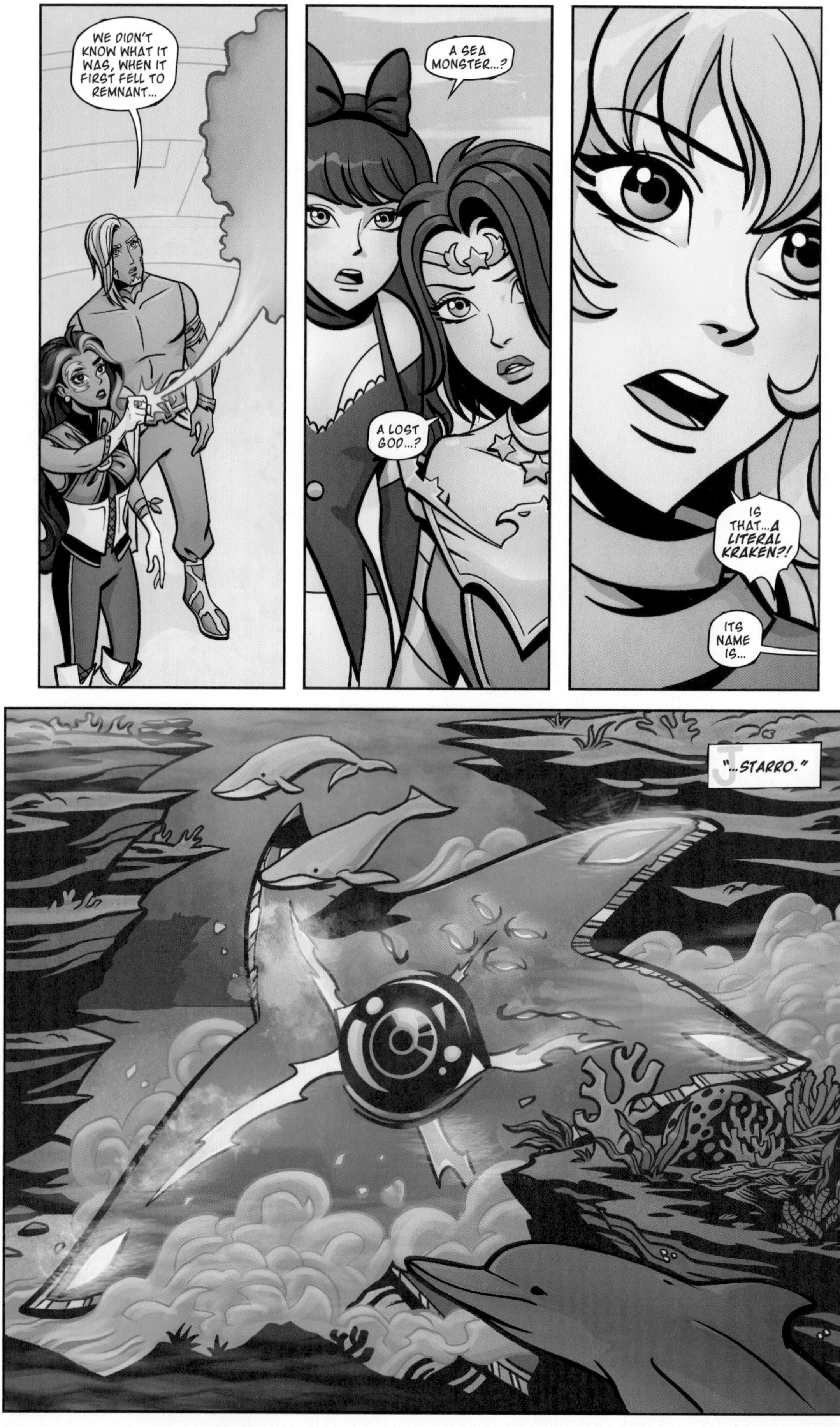
WE DIDN'T KNOW WHAT IT WAS, WHEN IT FIRST FELL TO REMNANT...
A SEA MONSTER...?
A LOST GOD...?
IS THAT...A LITERAL KRAKEN?!
ITS NAME IS...
"...STARRO."

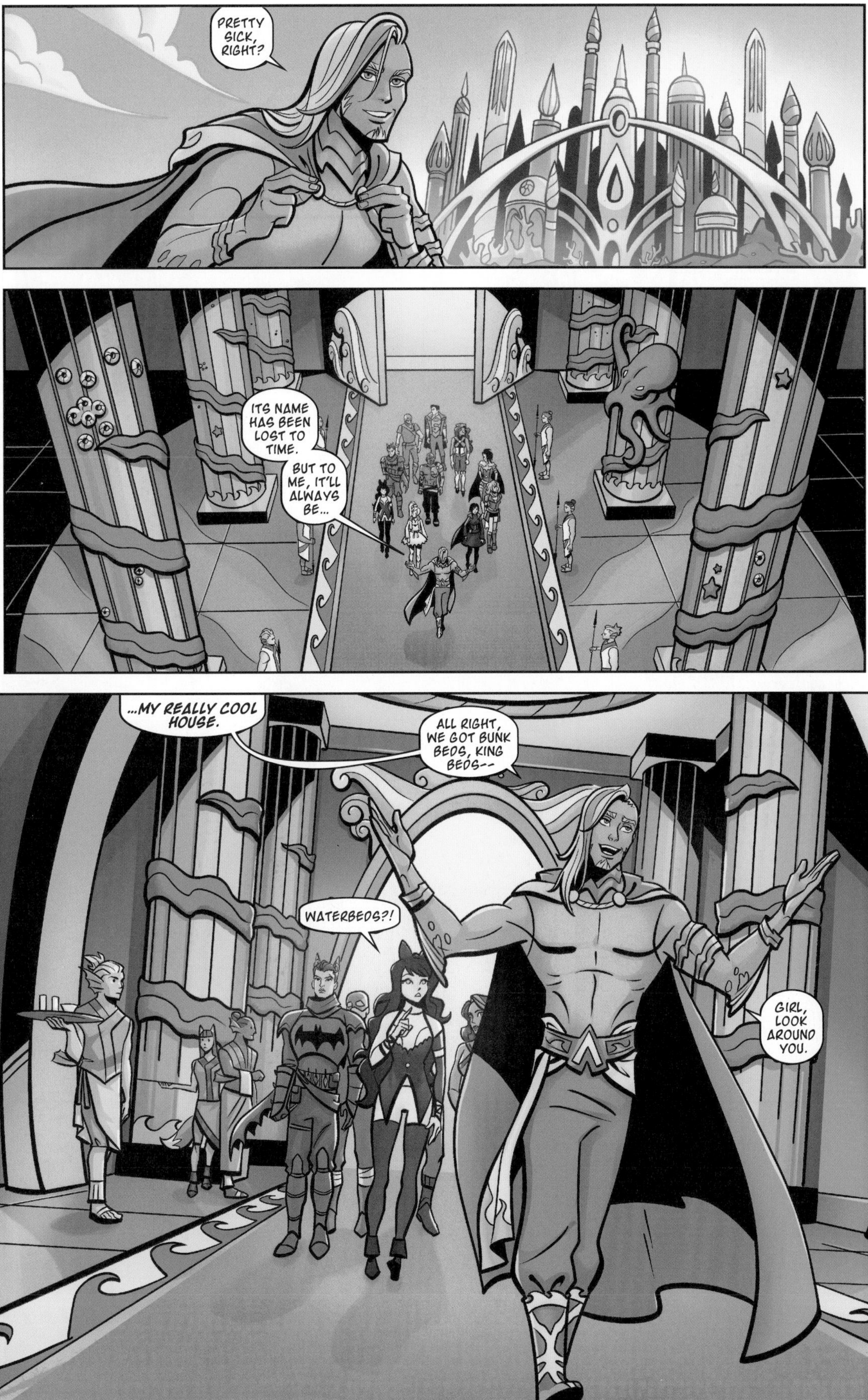
PRETTY SICK, RIGHT?
ITS NAME HAS BEEN LOST TO TIME.
BUT TO ME, IT'LL ALWAYS BE...
...MY REALLY COOL HOUSE.
ALL RIGHT, WE GOT BUNK BEDS, KING BEDS--
WATERBEDS?!
GIRL, LOOK AROUND YOU.

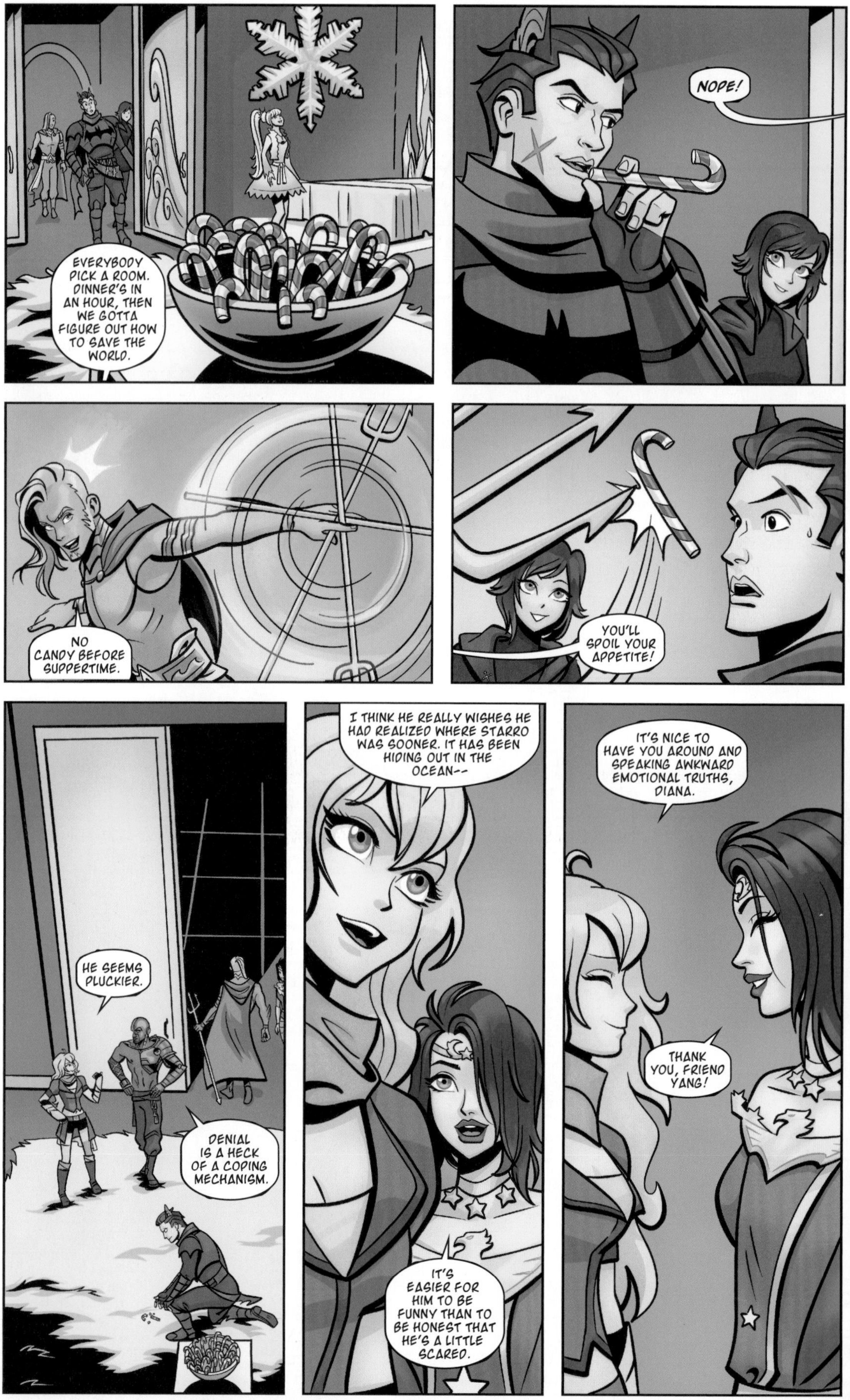
EVERYBODY PICK A ROOM. DINNER'S IN AN HOUR, THEN WE GOTTA FIGURE OUT HOW TO SAVE THE WORLD.
NOPE!
NO CANDY BEFORE SUPPERTIME.
YOU'LL SPOIL YOUR APPETITE!
HE SEEMS PLUCKIER.
DENIAL IS A HECK OF A COPING MECHANISM.
I THINK HE REALLY WISHES HE HAD REALIZED WHERE STARRO WAS SOONER. IT HAS BEEN HIDING OUT IN THE OCEAN--
IT'S EASIER FOR HIM TO BE FUNNY THAN TO BE HONEST THAT HE'S A LITTLE SCARED.
IT'S NICE TO HAVE YOU AROUND AND SPEAKING AWKWARD EMOTIONAL TRUTHS, DIANA.
THANK YOU, FRIEND YANG!

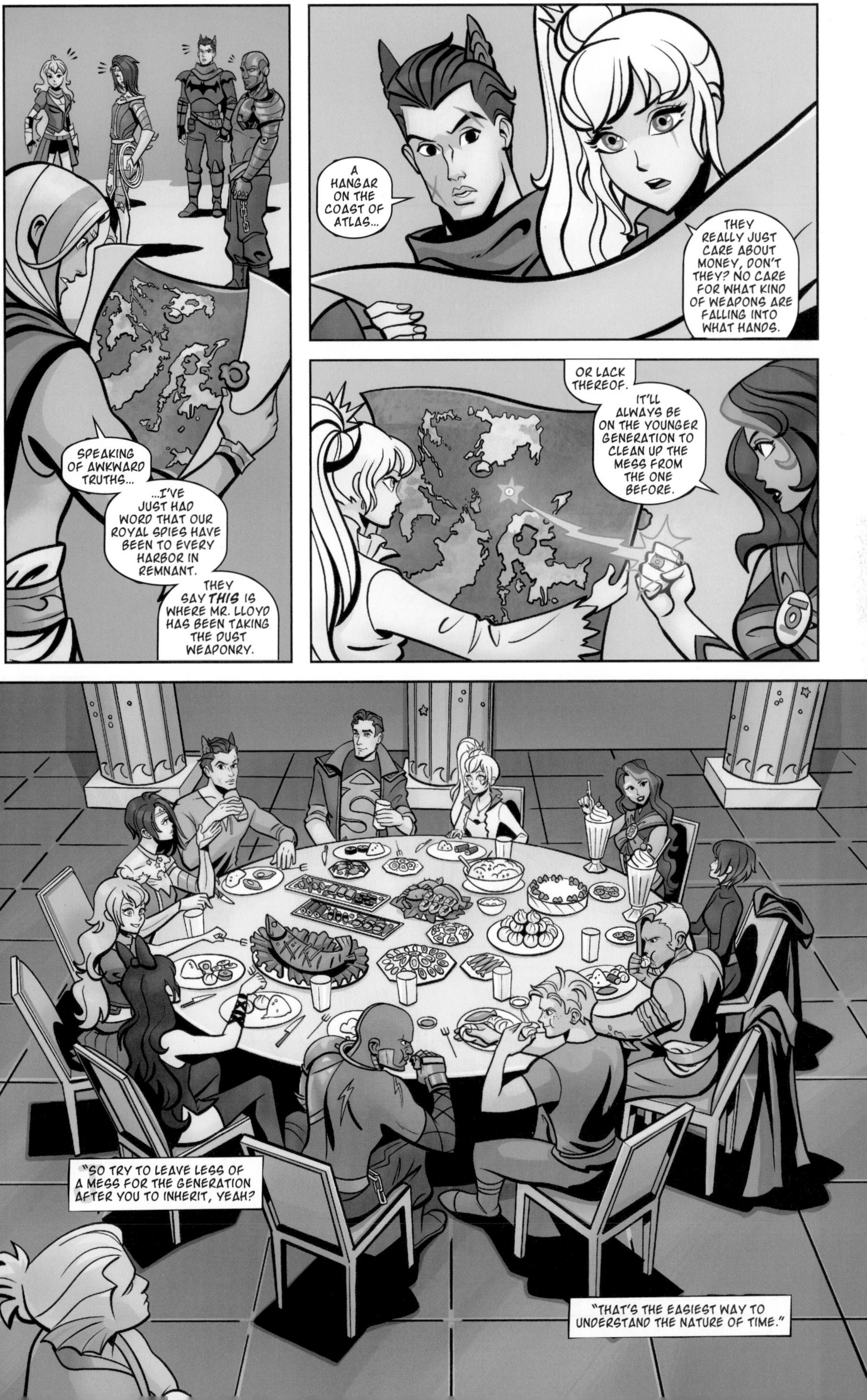

A HANGAR ON THE COAST OF ATLAS...
THEY REALLY JUST CARE ABOUT MONEY, DON'T THEY? NO CARE FOR WHAT KIND OF WEAPONS ARE FALLING INTO WHAT HANDS.
SPEAKING OF AWKWARD TRUTHS...
...I'VE JUST HAD WORD THAT OUR ROYAL SPIES HAVE BEEN TO EVERY HARBOR IN REMNANT.
THEY SAY THIS IS WHERE MR. LLOYD HAS BEEN TAKING THE DUST WEAPONRY.
OR LACK THEREOF.
IT'LL ALWAYS BE ON THE YOUNGER GENERATION TO CLEAN UP THE MESS FROM THE ONE BEFORE.
"SO TRY TO LEAVE LESS OF A MESS FOR THE GENERATION AFTER YOU TO INHERIT, YEAH?
"THAT'S THE EASIEST WAY TO UNDERSTAND THE NATURE OF TIME."

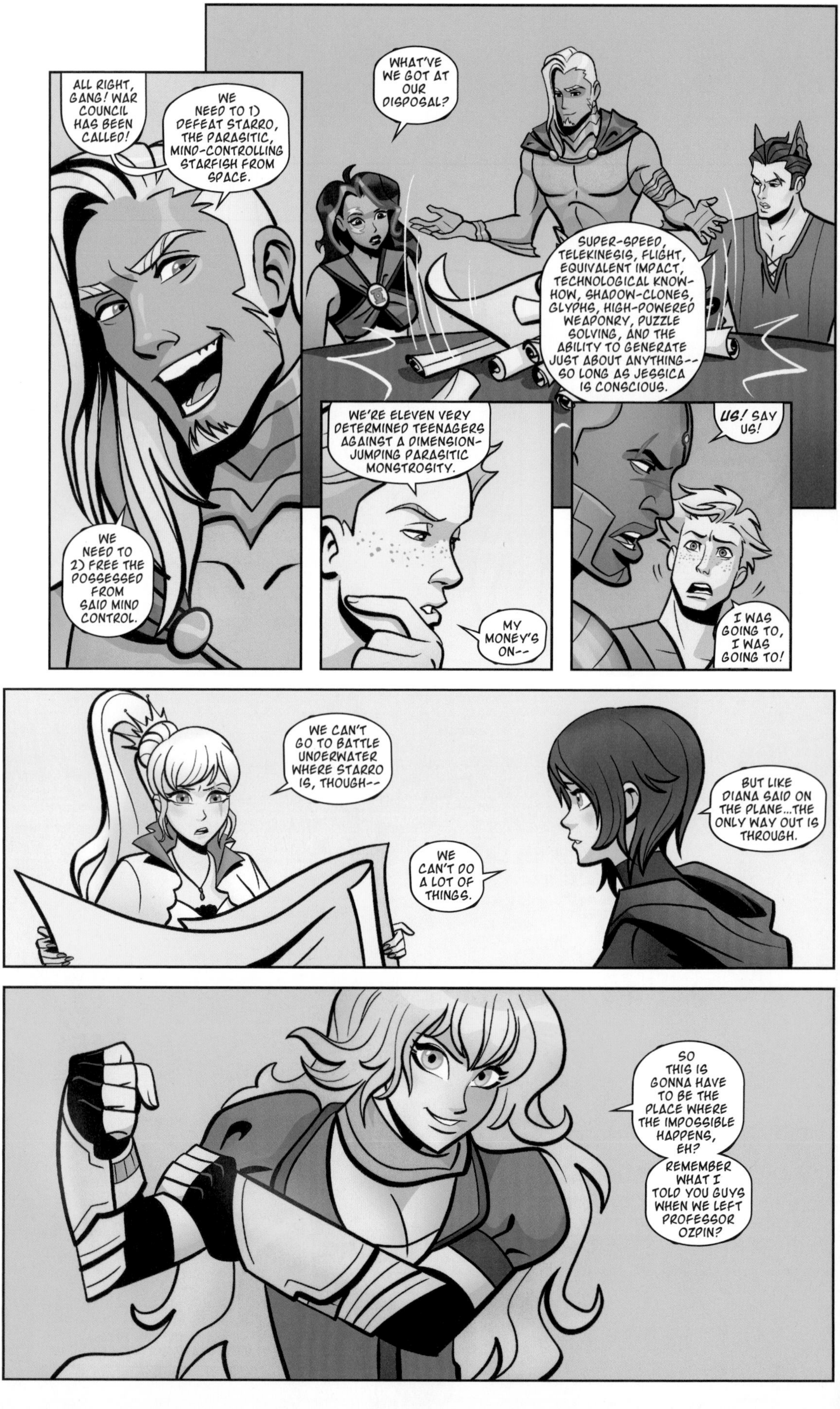
ALL RIGHT, GANG! WAR COUNCIL HAS BEEN CALLED!
WE NEED TO 1) DEFEAT STARRO, THE PARASITIC, MIND-CONTROLLING STARFISH FROM SPACE.
WE NEED TO 2) FREE THE POSSESSED FROM SAID MIND CONTROL.
WHAT'VE WE GOT AT OUR DISPOSAL?
SUPER-SPEED, TELEKINESIS, FLIGHT, EQUIVALENT IMPACT, TECHNOLOGICAL KNOW-HOW, SHADOW-CLONES, GLYPHS, HIGH-POWERED WEAPONRY, PUZZLE SOLVING, AND THE ABILITY TO GENERATE JUST ABOUT ANYTHING--SO LONG AS JESSICA IS CONSCIOUS.
WE'RE ELEVEN VERY DETERMINED TEENAGERS AGAINST A DIMENSION-JUMPING PARASITIC MONSTROSITY.
MY MONEY'S ON--
US! SAY US!
I WAS GOING TO, I WAS GOING TO!
WE CAN'T GO TO BATTLE UNDERWATER WHERE STARRO IS, THOUGH--
WE CAN'T DO A LOT OF THINGS.
BUT LIKE DIANA SAID ON THE PLANE...THE ONLY WAY OUT IS THROUGH.
SO THIS IS GONNA HAVE TO BE THE PLACE WHERE THE IMPOSSIBLE HAPPENS, EH?
REMEMBER WHAT I TOLD YOU GUYS WHEN WE LEFT PROFESSOR OZPIN?

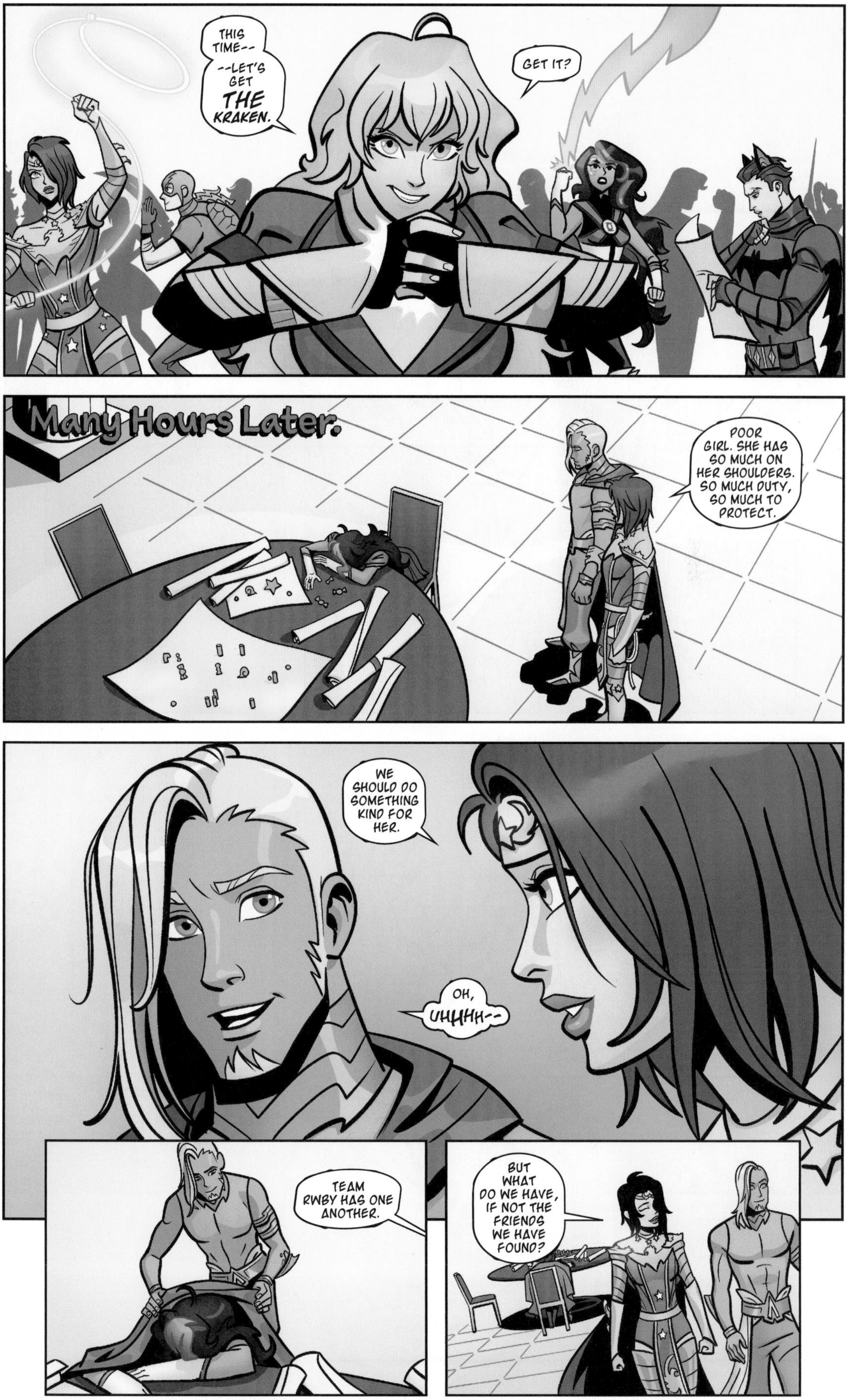

THIS TIME-- --LET'S GET THE KRAKEN.
GET IT?
Many Hours Later.
POOR GIRL. SHE HAS SO MUCH ON HER SHOULDERS. SO MUCH DUTY, SO MUCH TO PROTECT.
WE SHOULD DO SOMETHING KIND FOR HER.
OH, UHHHH--
TEAM RWBY HAS ONE ANOTHER.
BUT WHAT DO WE HAVE, IF NOT THE FRIENDS WE HAVE FOUND?

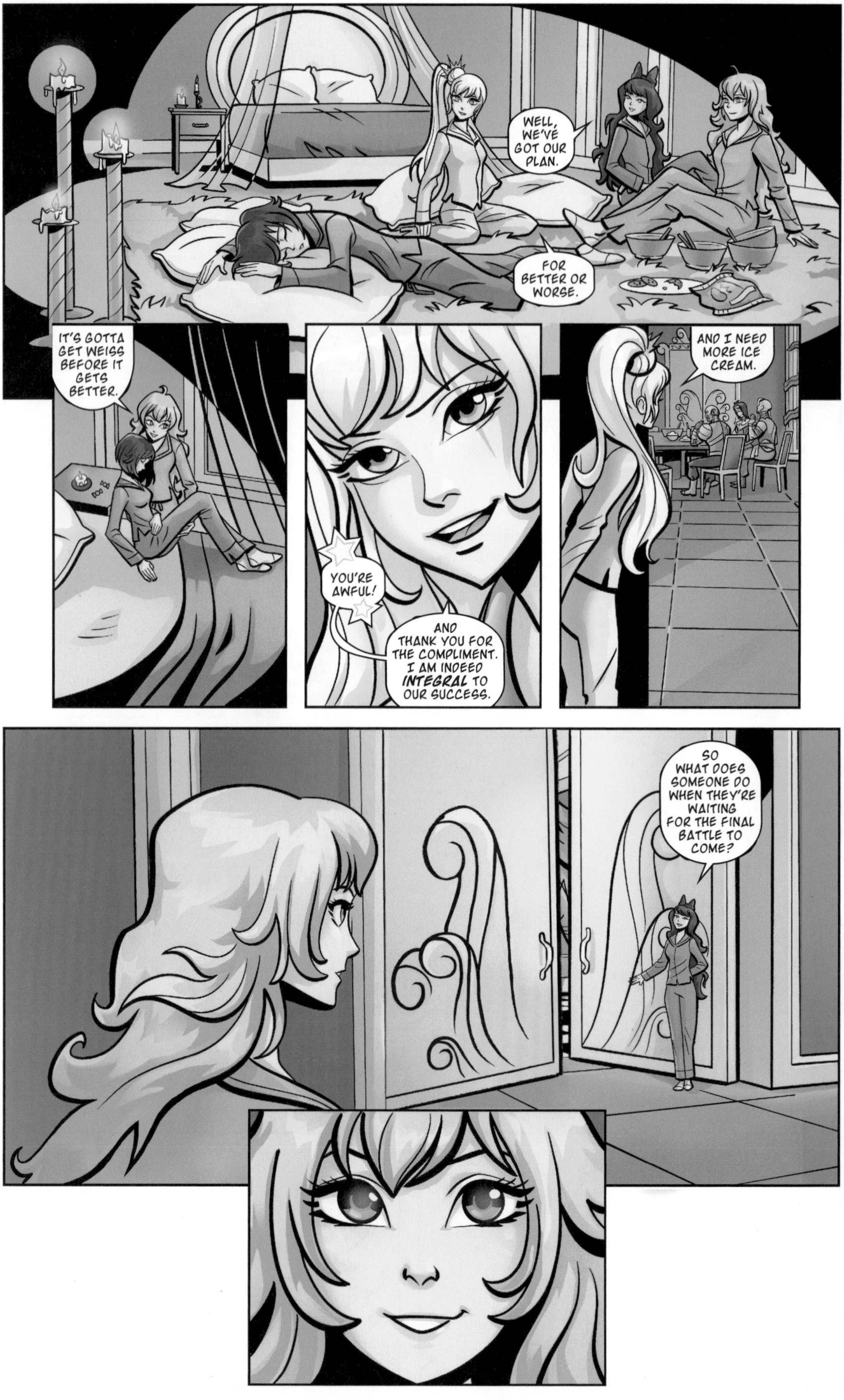
WELL, WE'VE GOT OUR PLAN.
FOR BETTER OR WORSE.
IT'S GOTTA GET WEISS BEFORE IT GETS BETTER.
YOU'RE AWFUL!
AND THANK YOU FOR THE COMPLIMENT. I AM INDEED INTEGRAL TO OUR SUCCESS.
AND I NEED MORE ICE CREAM.
SO WHAT DOES SOMEONE DO WHEN THEY'RE WAITING FOR THE FINAL BATTLE TO COME?

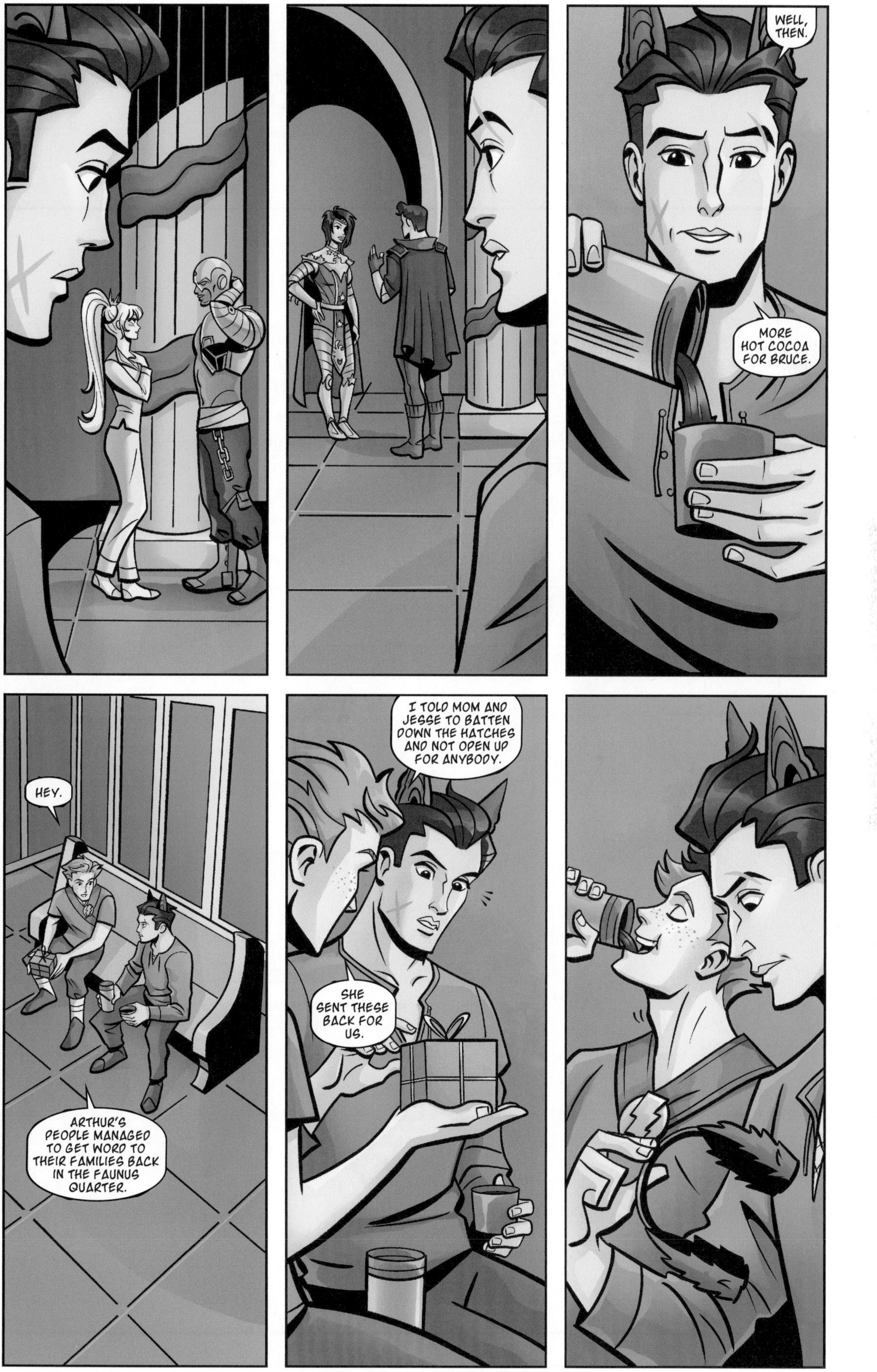
WELL, THEN.
MORE HOT COCOA FOR BRUCE.
HEY.
ARTHUR'S PEOPLE MANAGED TO GET WORD TO THEIR FAMILIES BACK IN THE FAUNUS QUARTER.
I TOLD MOM AND JESSE TO BATTEN DOWN THE HATCHES AND NOT OPEN UP FOR ANYBODY.
SHE SENT THESE BACK FOR US.

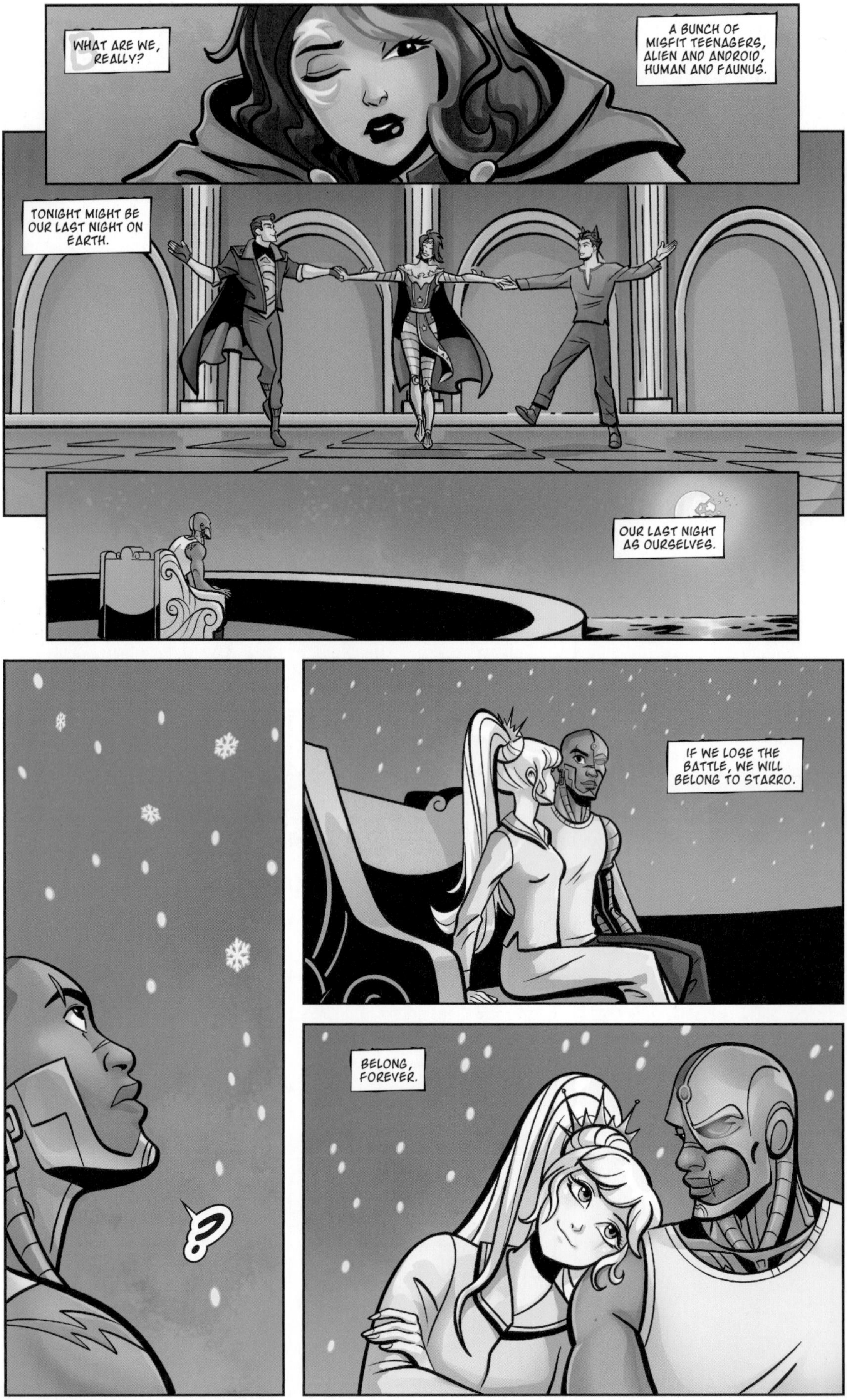
WHAT ARE WE, REALLY?
A BUNCH OF MISFIT TEENAGERS, ALIEN AND ANDROID, HUMAN AND FAUNUS.
TONIGHT MIGHT BE OUR LAST NIGHT ON EARTH.
OUR LAST NIGHT AS OURSELVES.
?
IF WE LOSE THE BATTLE, WE WILL BELONG TO STARRO.
BELONG, FOREVER.

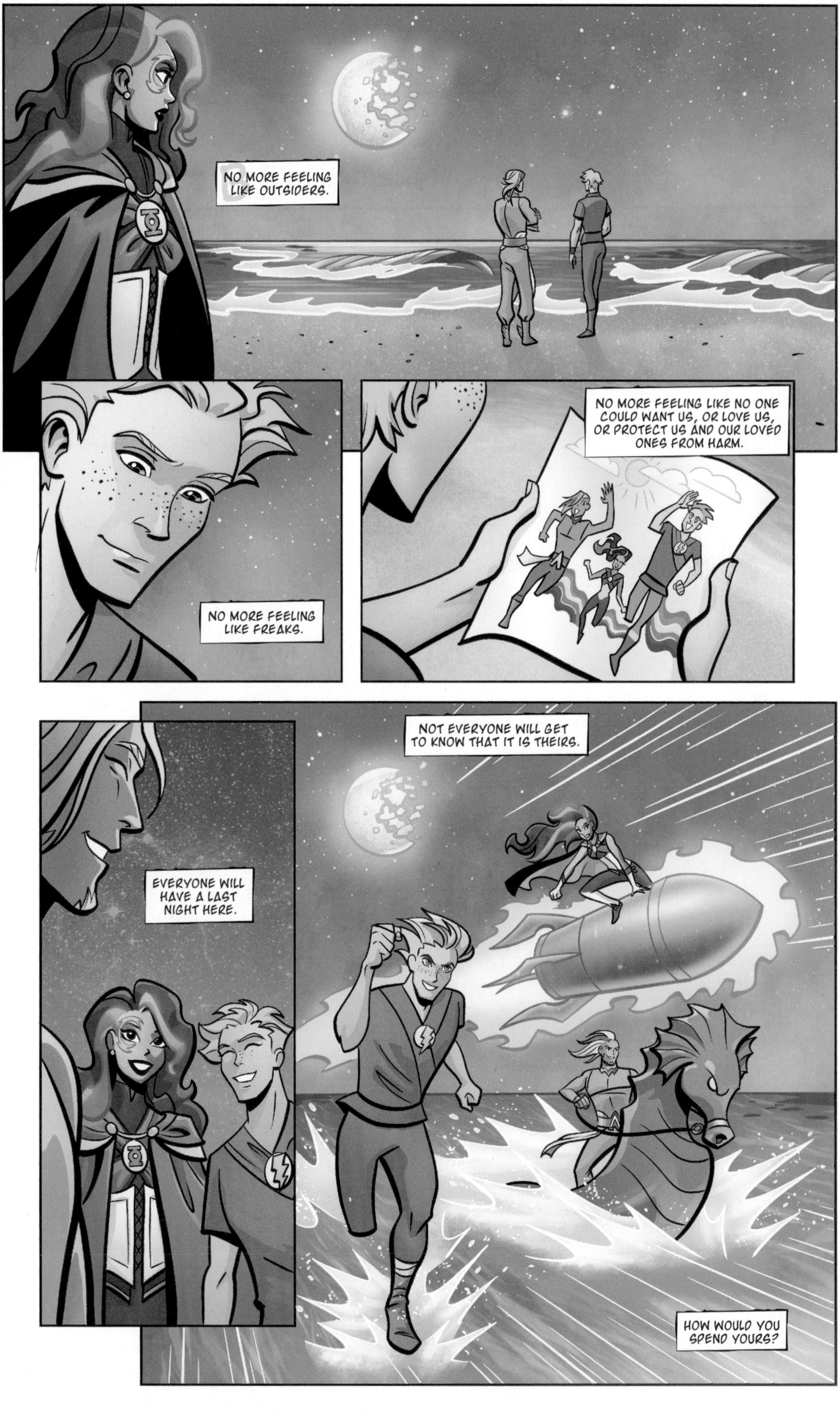
NO MORE FEELING LIKE OUTSIDERS.
NO MORE FEELING LIKE FREAKS.
NO MORE FEELING LIKE NO ONE COULD WANT US, OR LOVE US, OR PROTECT US AND OUR LOVED ONES FROM HARM.
EVERYONE WILL HAVE A LAST NIGHT HERE.
NOT EVERYONE WILL GET TO KNOW THAT IT IS THEIRS.
HOW WOULD YOU SPEND YOURS?

"LAST NIGHT...

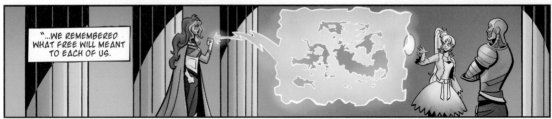

"...WE REMEMBERED WHAT FREE WILL MEANT TO EACH OF US.

"BUT *TODAY*...

...WE **SUCKER-PUNCH** AN ALIEN GOD.

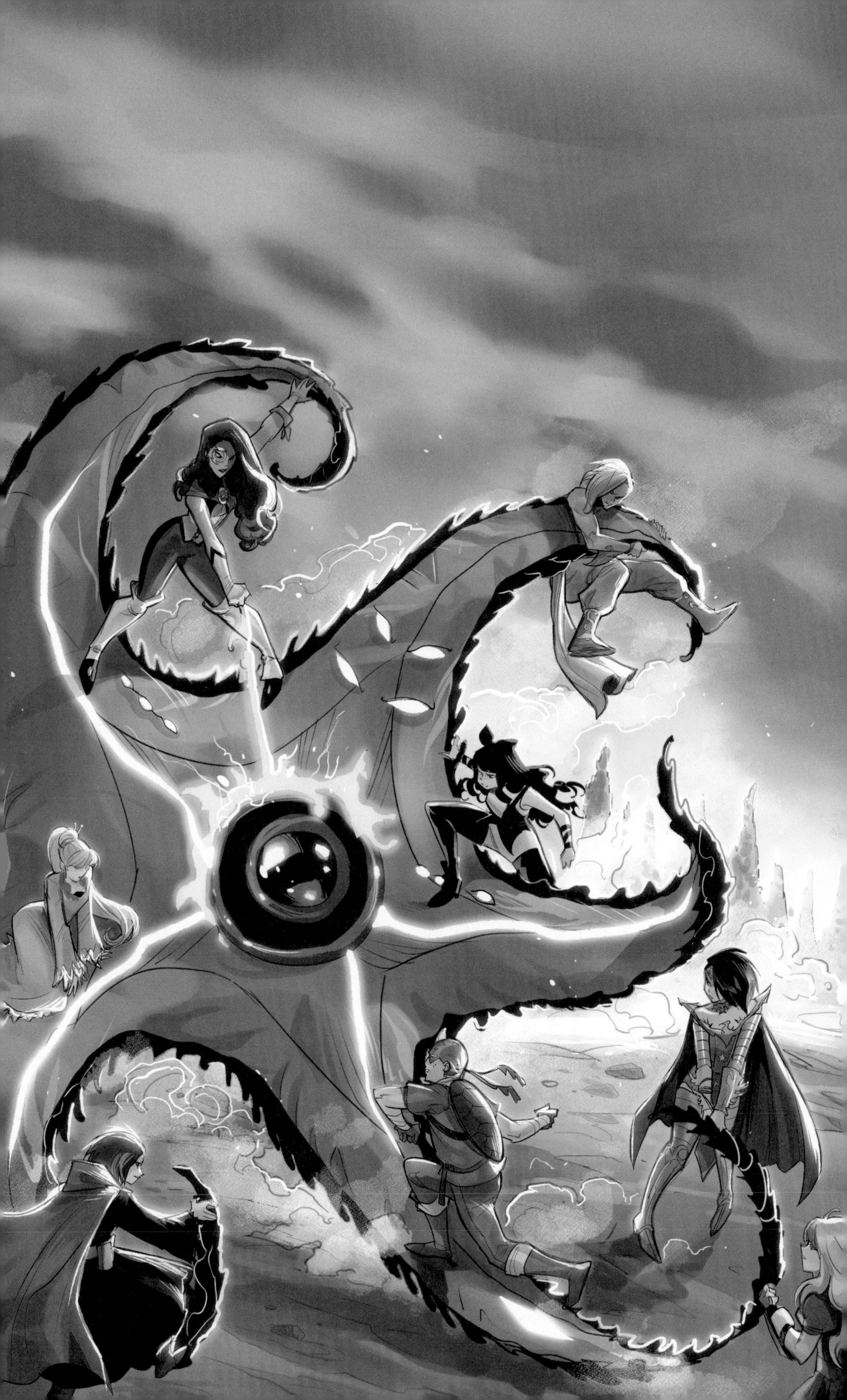

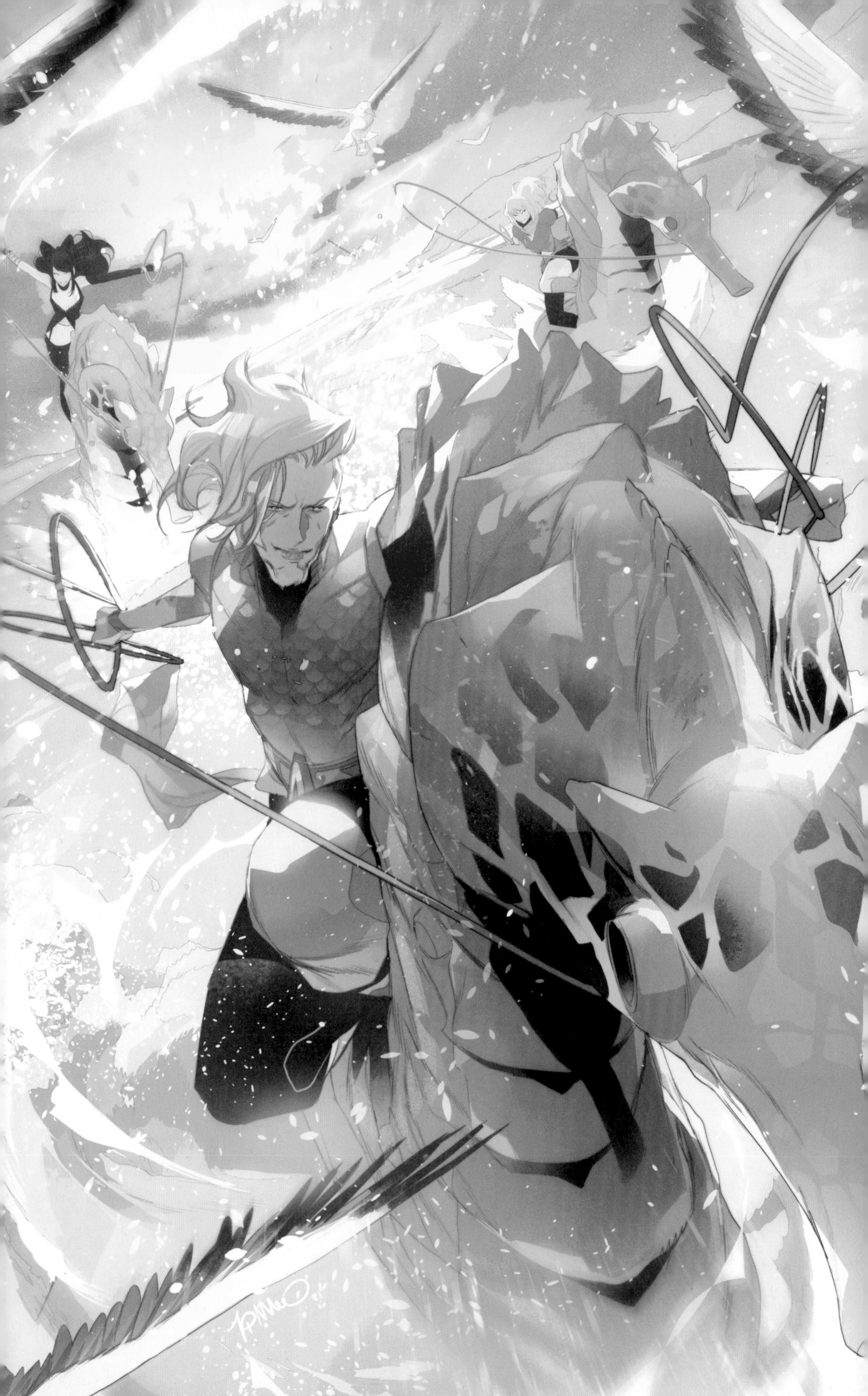

Variant cover by **SIMONE DI MEO**

THE TIME TO FREE REMNANT FROM STARRO'S GRASP HAS COME.

NONE OF US CAN FIGHT SO DEEP, IN THE CRUSHING, PRESSURIZED DARKNESS OF THE OCEAN FLOOR...

...EXCEPT FOR OUR AUTOMATON.

EXCEPT FOR DIANA.

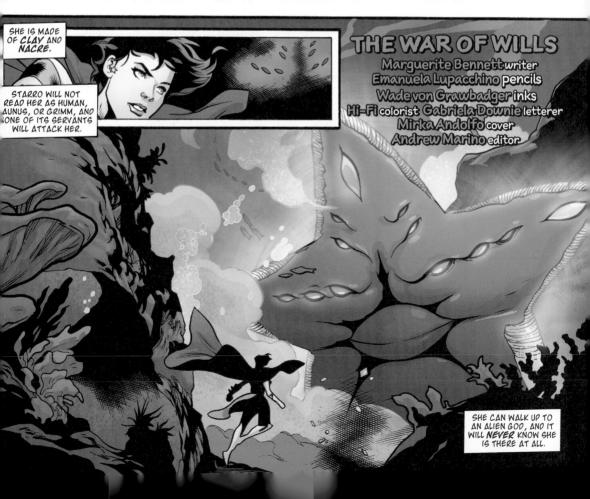

SHE IS MADE OF CLAY AND NACRE.

STARRO WILL NOT READ HER AS HUMAN, AUNUS, OR GRIMM, AND NONE OF ITS SERVANTS WILL ATTACK HER.

THE WAR OF WILLS

Marguerite Bennett writer
Emanuela Lupacchino pencils
Wade von Grawbadger inks
Hi-Fi colorist Gabriela Downie letterer
Mirka Andolfo cover
Andrew Marino editor

SHE CAN WALK UP TO AN ALIEN GOD, AND IT WILL NEVER KNOW SHE IS THERE AT ALL.

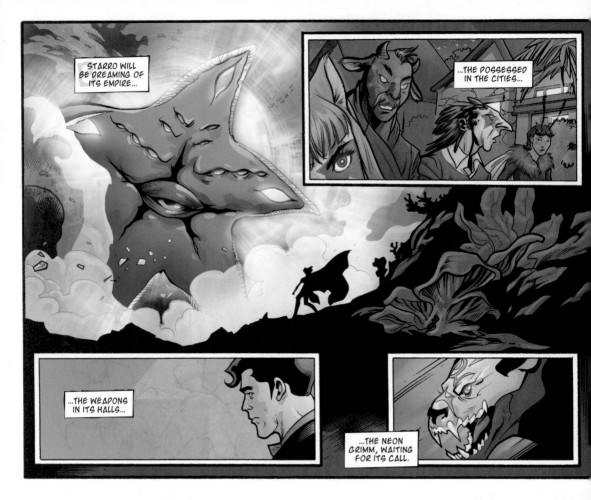

STARRO WILL BE DREAMING OF ITS EMPIRE...

...THE POSSESSED IN THE CITIES...

...THE WEAPONS IN ITS HALLS...

...THE NEON GRIMM, WAITING FOR ITS CALL.

WE'RE GOING TO END THOSE DARK DREAMS--

--ONCE AND FOR ALL.

DIANA IS *THE STICK*, DRIVING STARRO SKYWARD--

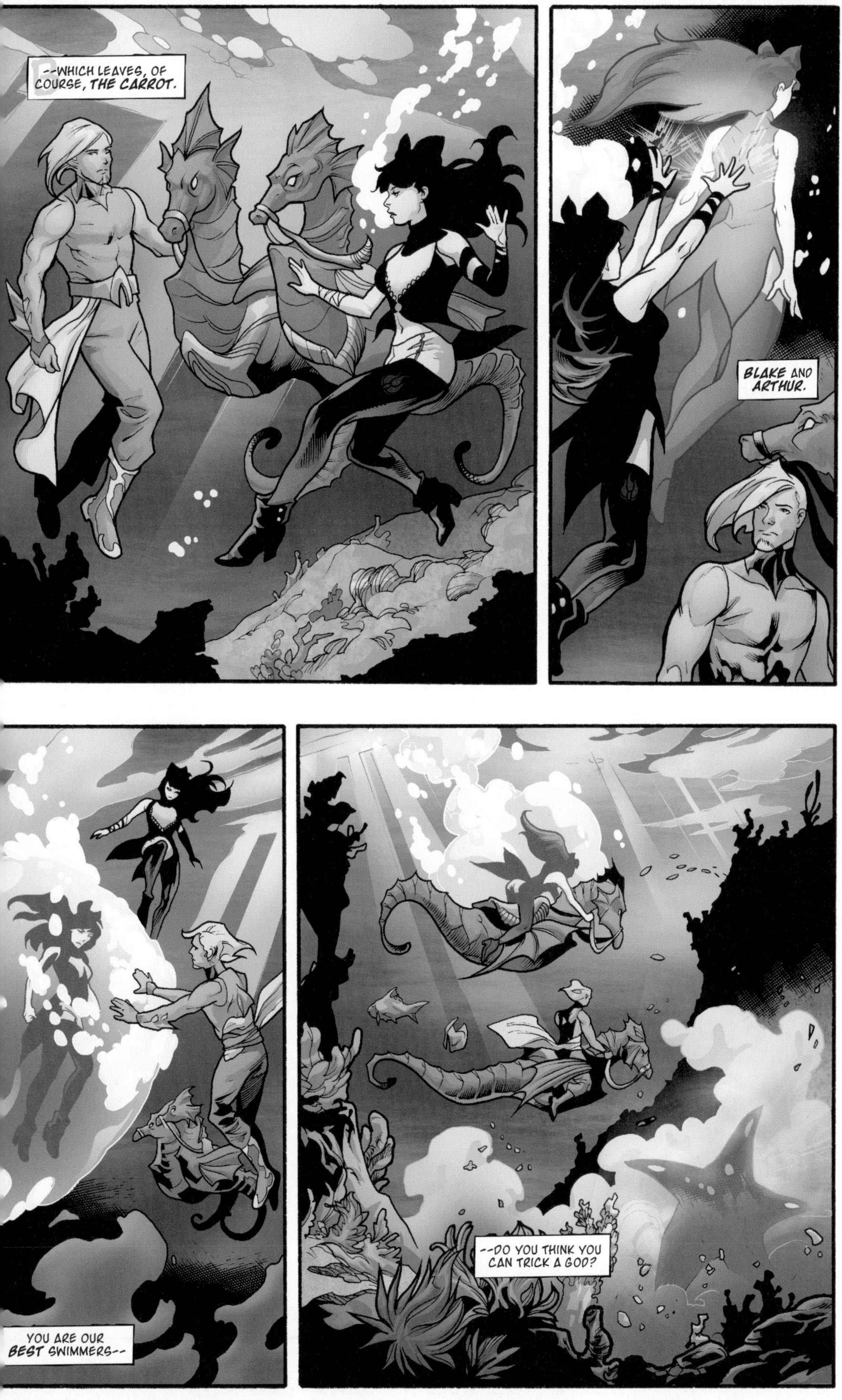
--WHICH LEAVES, OF COURSE, THE CARROT.
BLAKE AND ARTHUR.
YOU ARE OUR BEST SWIMMERS--
--DO YOU THINK YOU CAN TRICK A GOD?

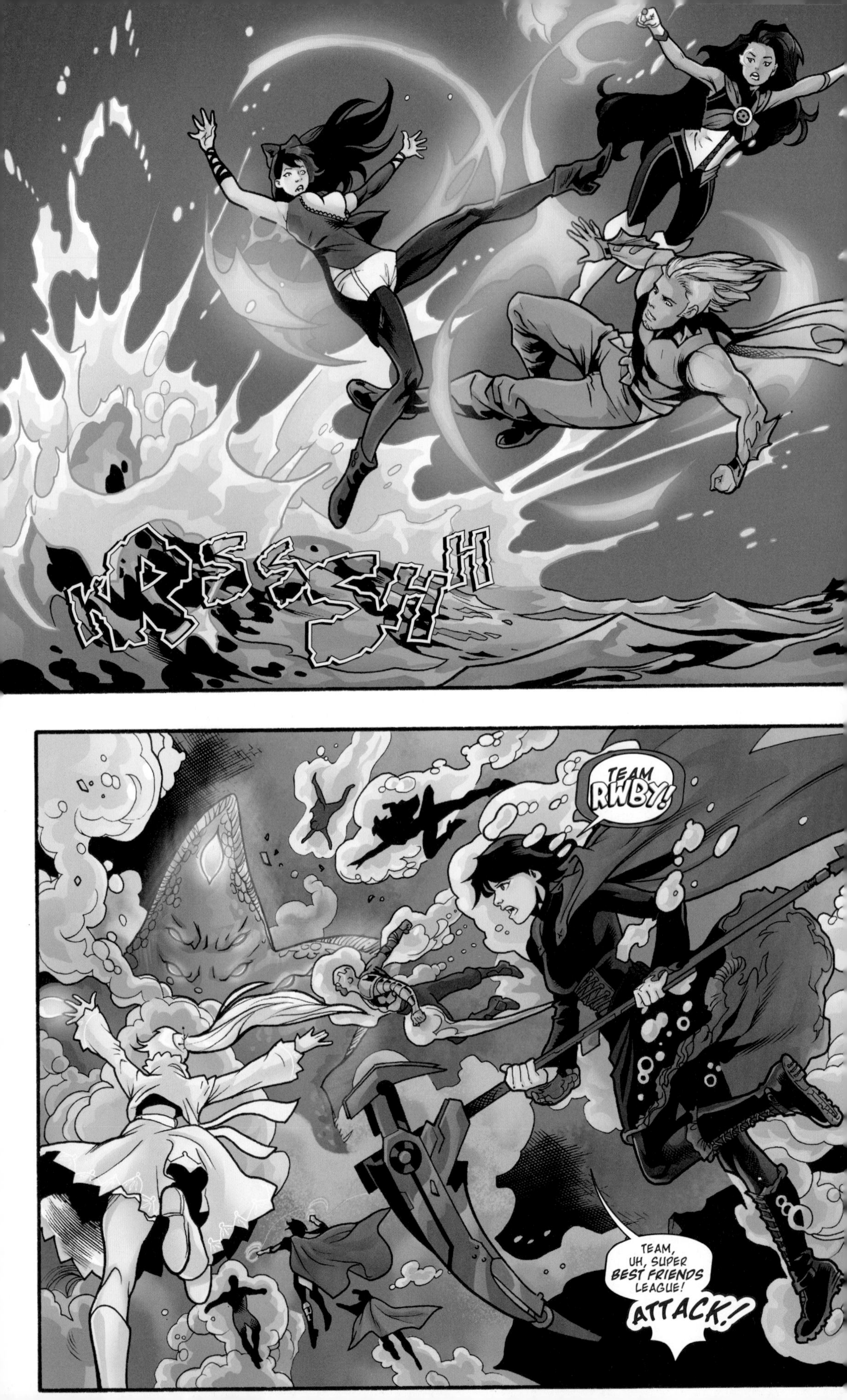
KRSSSHH
TEAM RWBY!
TEAM, UH, SUPER BEST FRIENDS LEAGUE! ATTACK!

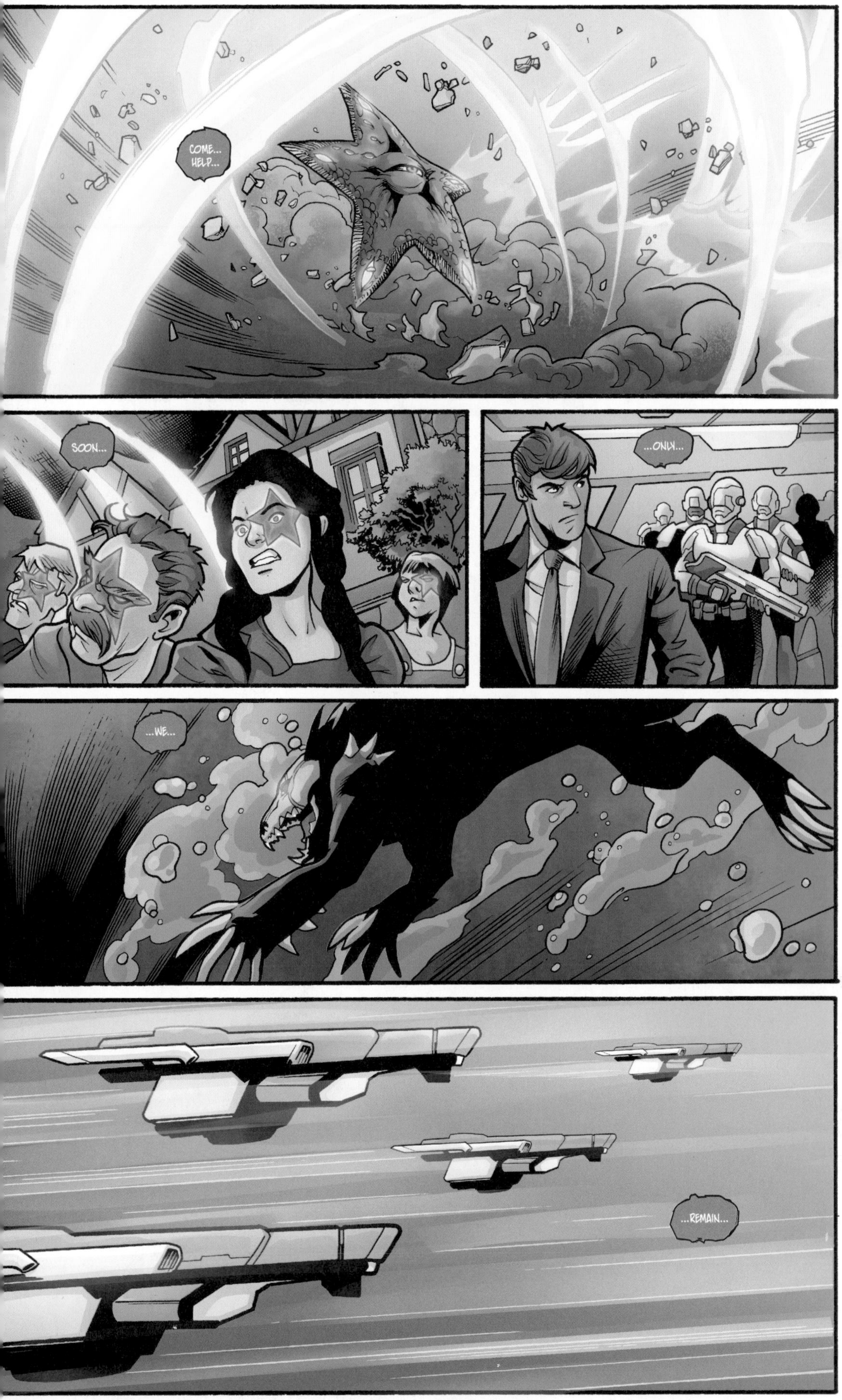
COME... HELP...
SOON...
...ONLY...
...WE...
...REMAIN...

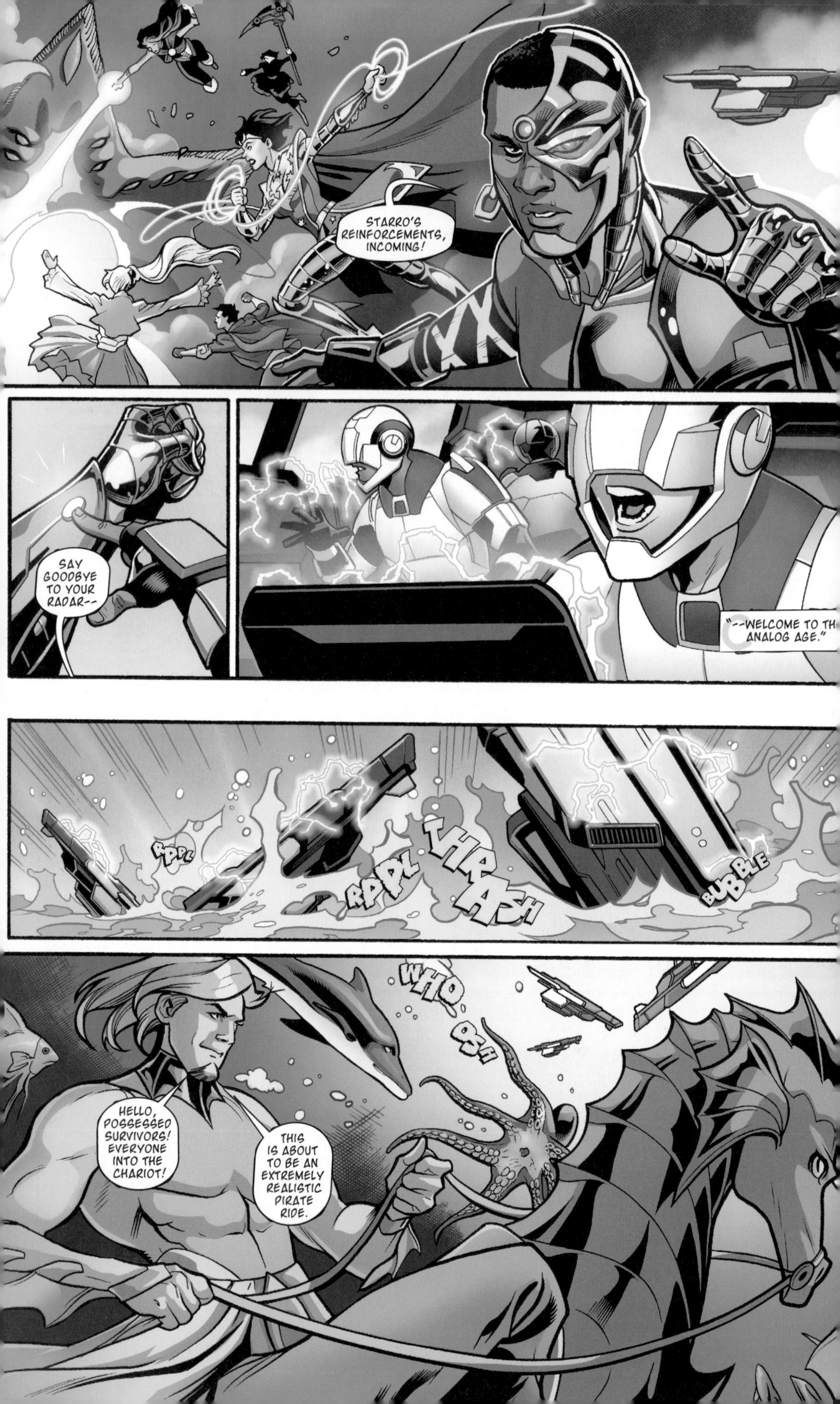
STARRO'S REINFORCEMENTS, INCOMING!
SAY GOODBYE TO YOUR RADAR--
"--WELCOME TO TH ANALOG AGE."
RPPL
RPPL
THRASH
BUBBLE
WHOOSH!!
HELLO, POSSESSED SURVIVORS! EVERYONE INTO THE CHARIOT!
THIS IS ABOUT TO BE AN EXTREMELY REALISTIC PIRATE RIDE.

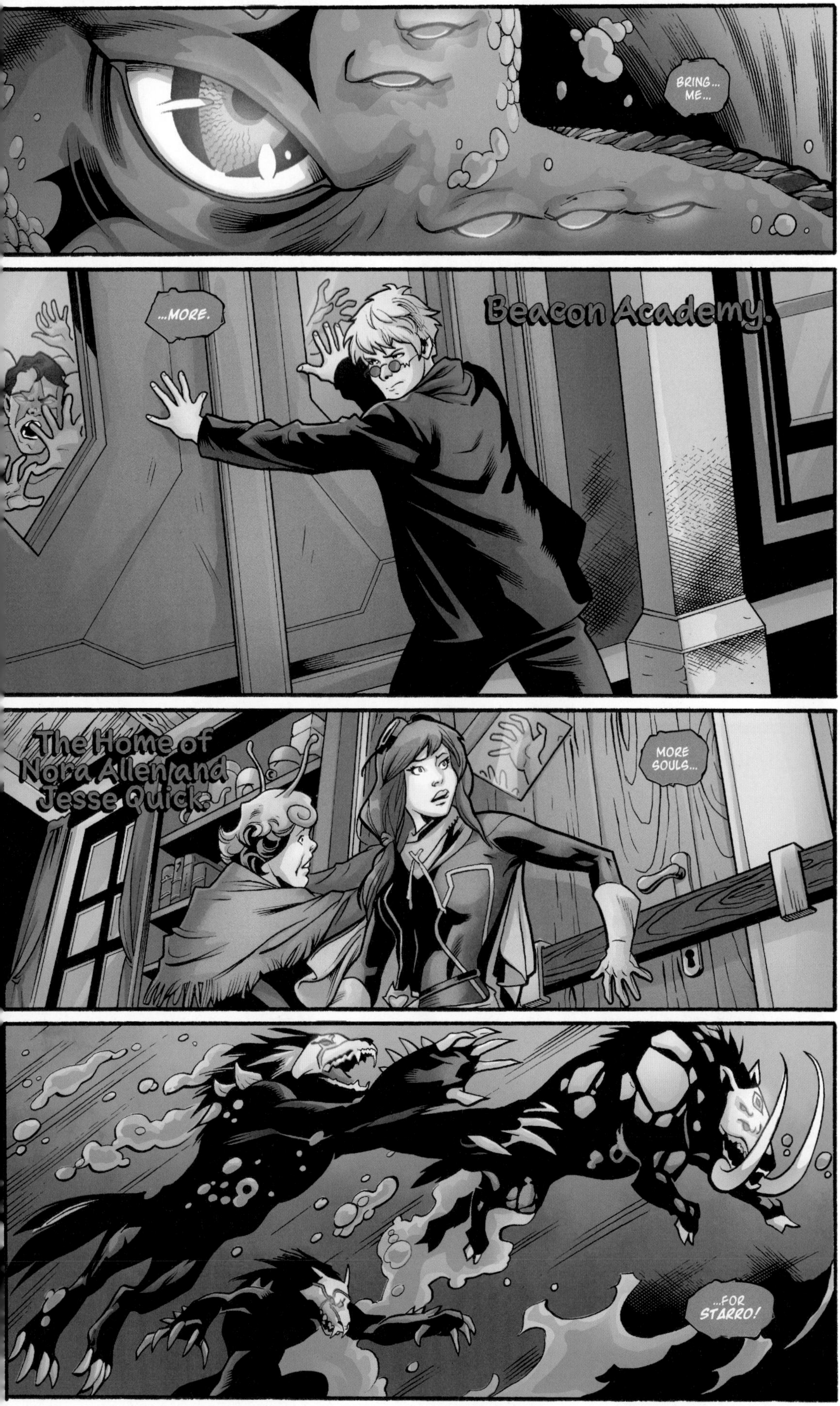
BRING... ME...
...MORE.
Beacon Academy.
The Home of Nora Allen and Jesse Quick.
MORE SOULS...
...FOR STARRO!

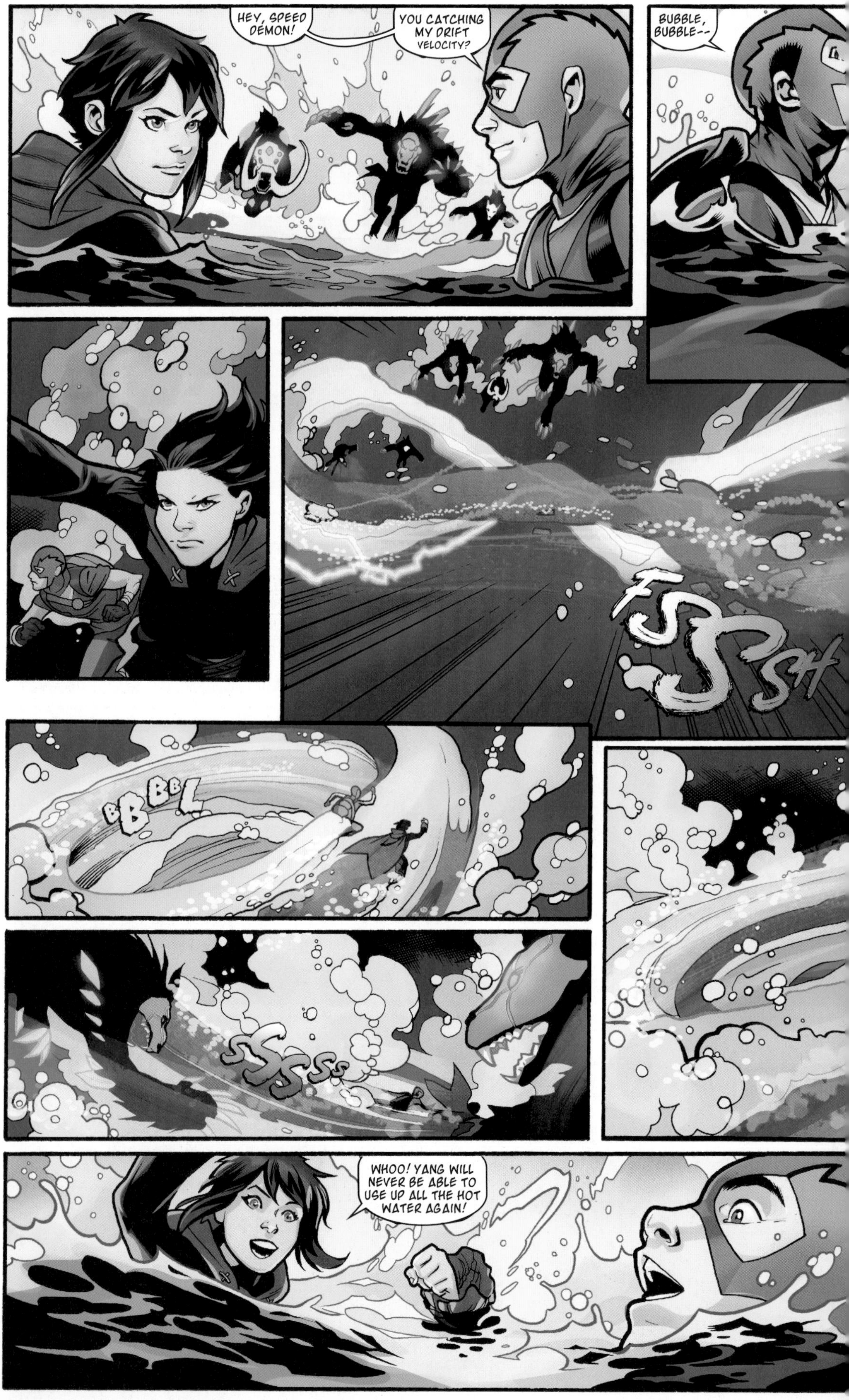
HEY, SPEED DEMON!
YOU CATCHING MY DRIFT VELOCITY?
BUBBLE, BUBBLE--
FSSSH
BBBL
SSSSs
WHOO! YANG WILL NEVER BE ABLE TO USE UP ALL THE HOT WATER AGAIN!

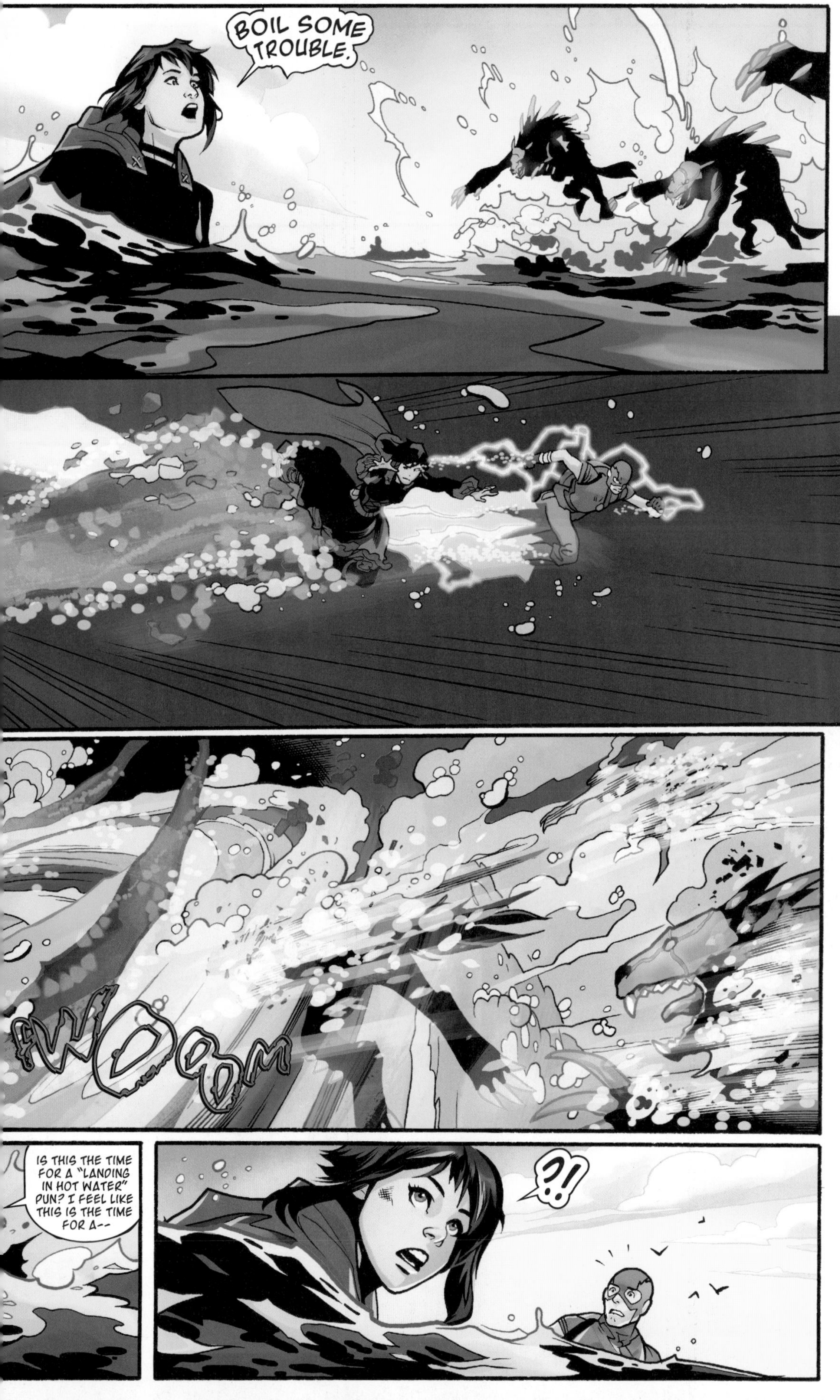

BOIL SOME TROUBLE.
FWOOOM
IS THIS THE TIME FOR A "LANDING IN HOT WATER" PUN? I FEEL LIKE THIS IS THE TIME FOR A--
?!

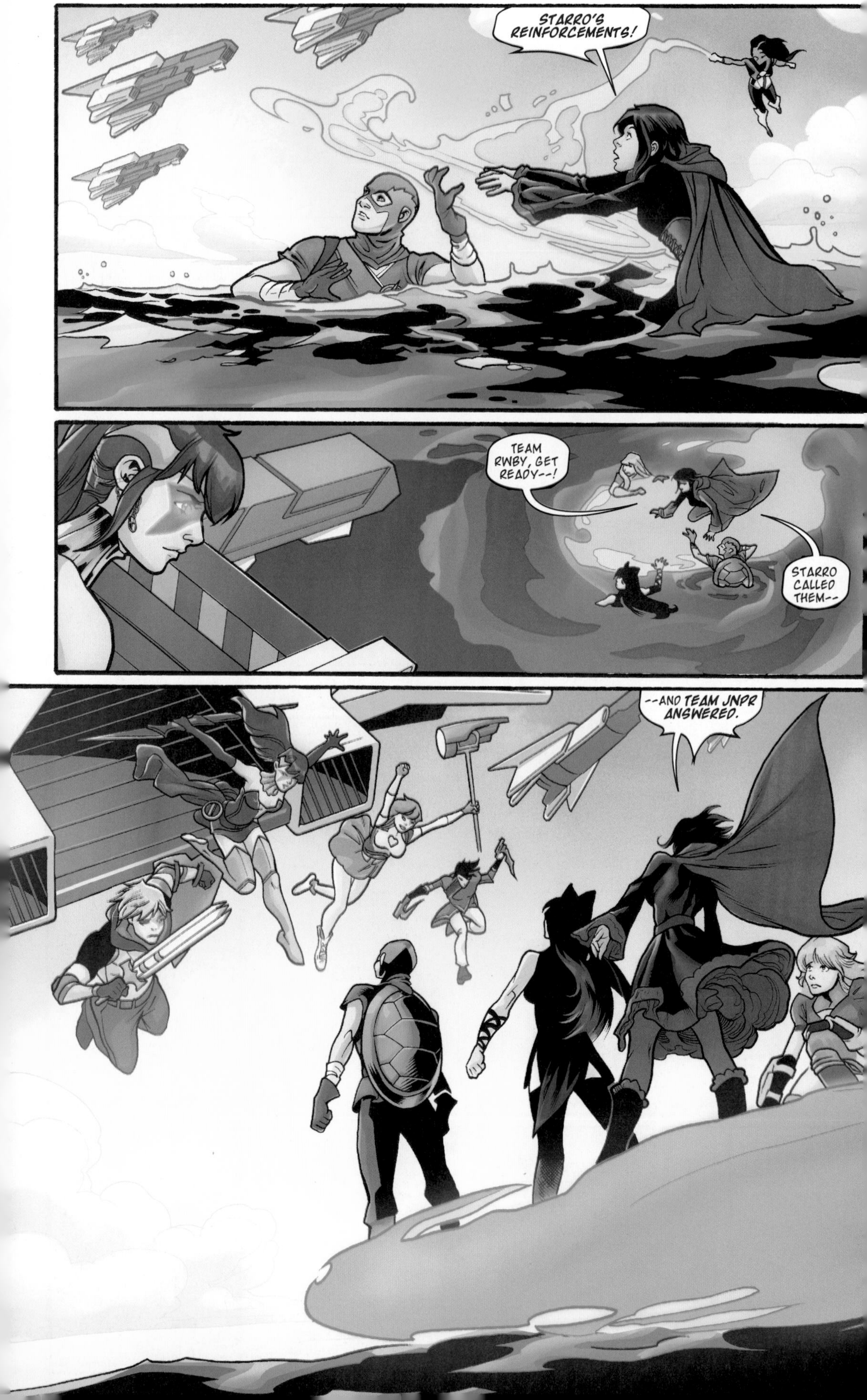

STARRO'S REINFORCEMENTS!
TEAM RWBY, GET READY--!
STARRO CALLED THEM--
--AND TEAM JNPR ANSWERED.

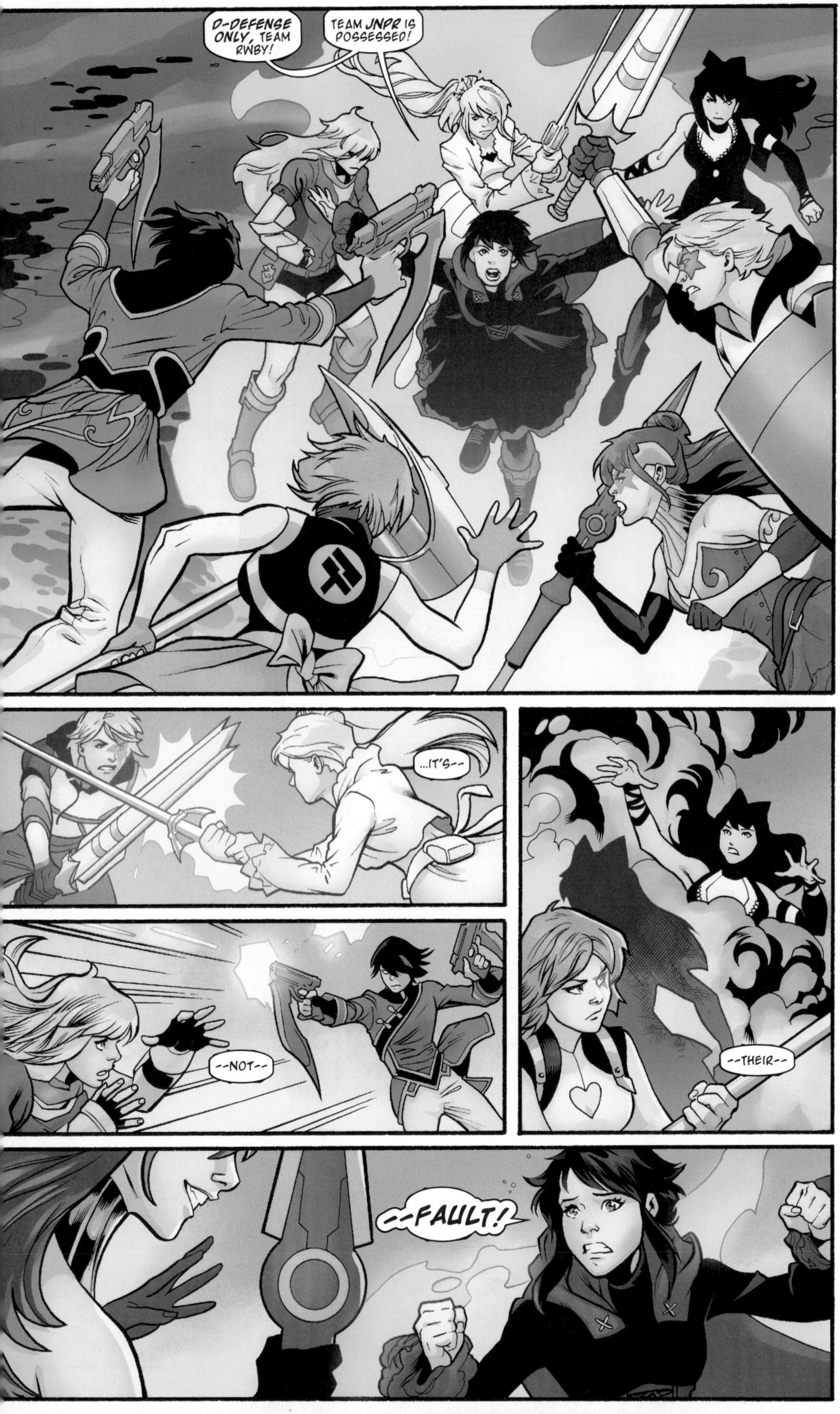
D-DEFENSE ONLY, TEAM RWBY!
TEAM JNPR IS POSSESSED!
...IT'S--
--NOT--
--THEIR--
--FAULT!

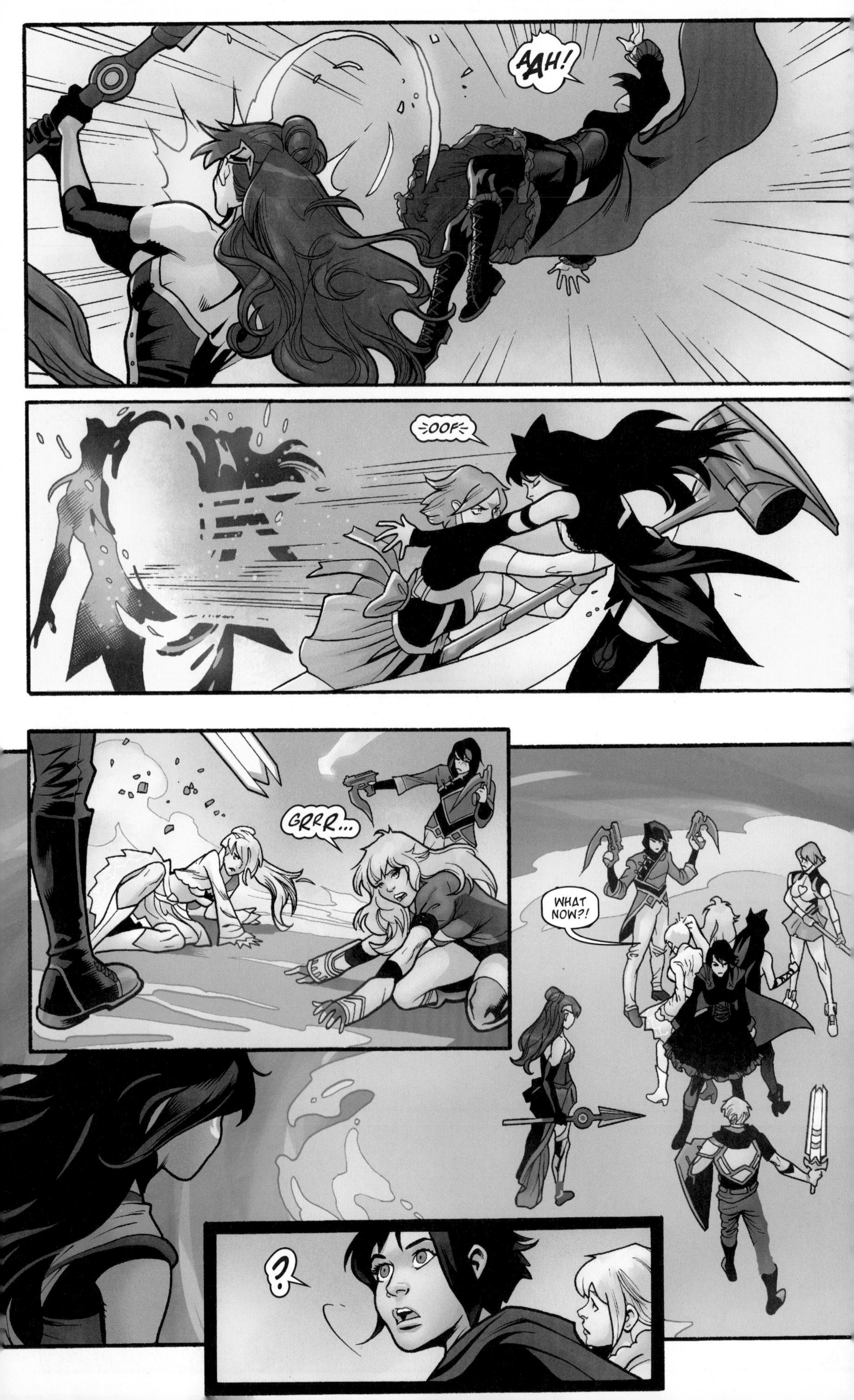
AAH!
OOF
GRRR...
WHAT NOW?!
?

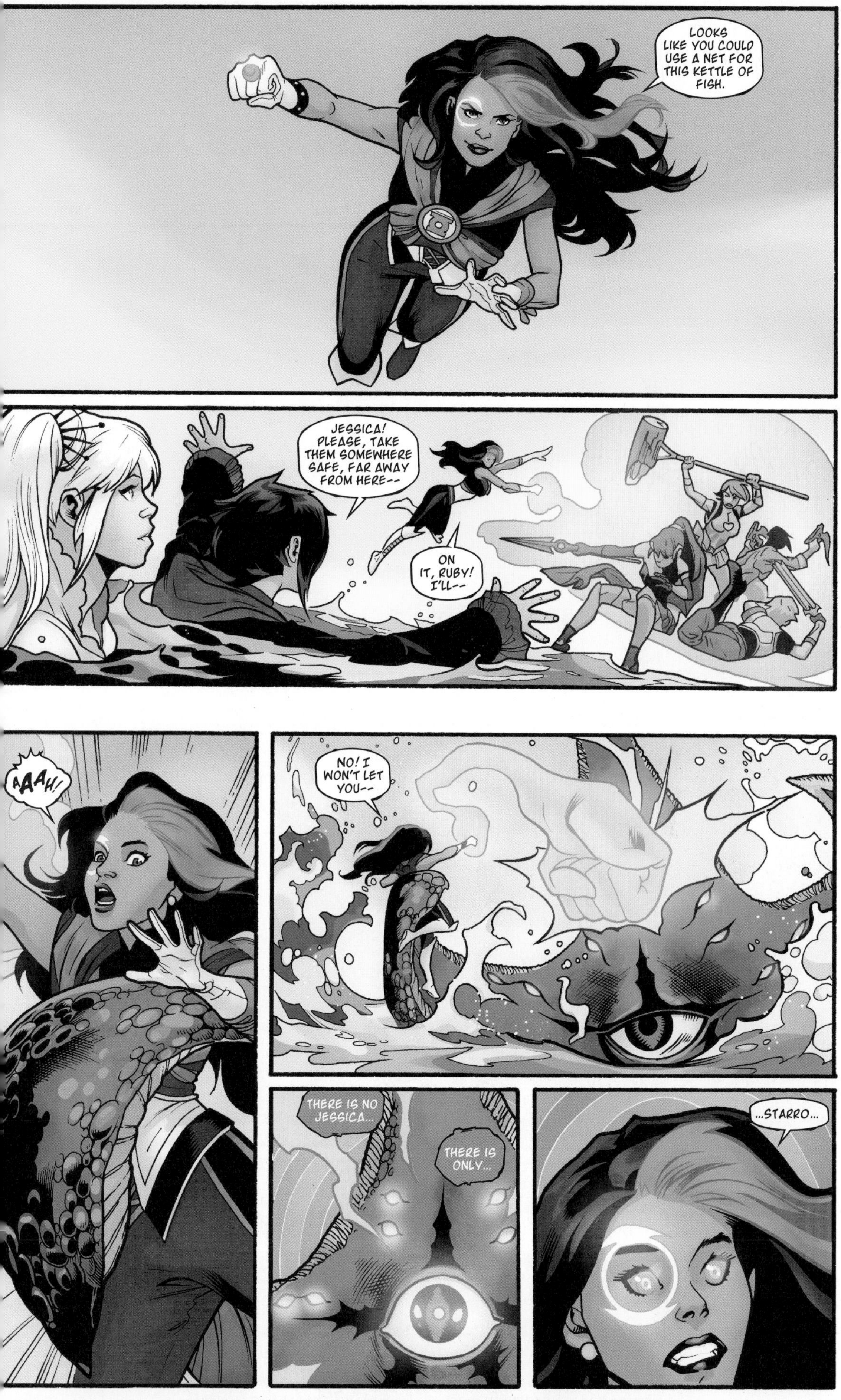
LOOKS LIKE YOU COULD USE A NET FOR THIS KETTLE OF FISH.
JESSICA! PLEASE, TAKE THEM SOMEWHERE SAFE, FAR AWAY FROM HERE--
ON IT, RUBY! I'LL--
AAAH!
NO! I WON'T LET YOU--
THERE IS NO JESSICA...
THERE IS ONLY...
...STARRO...

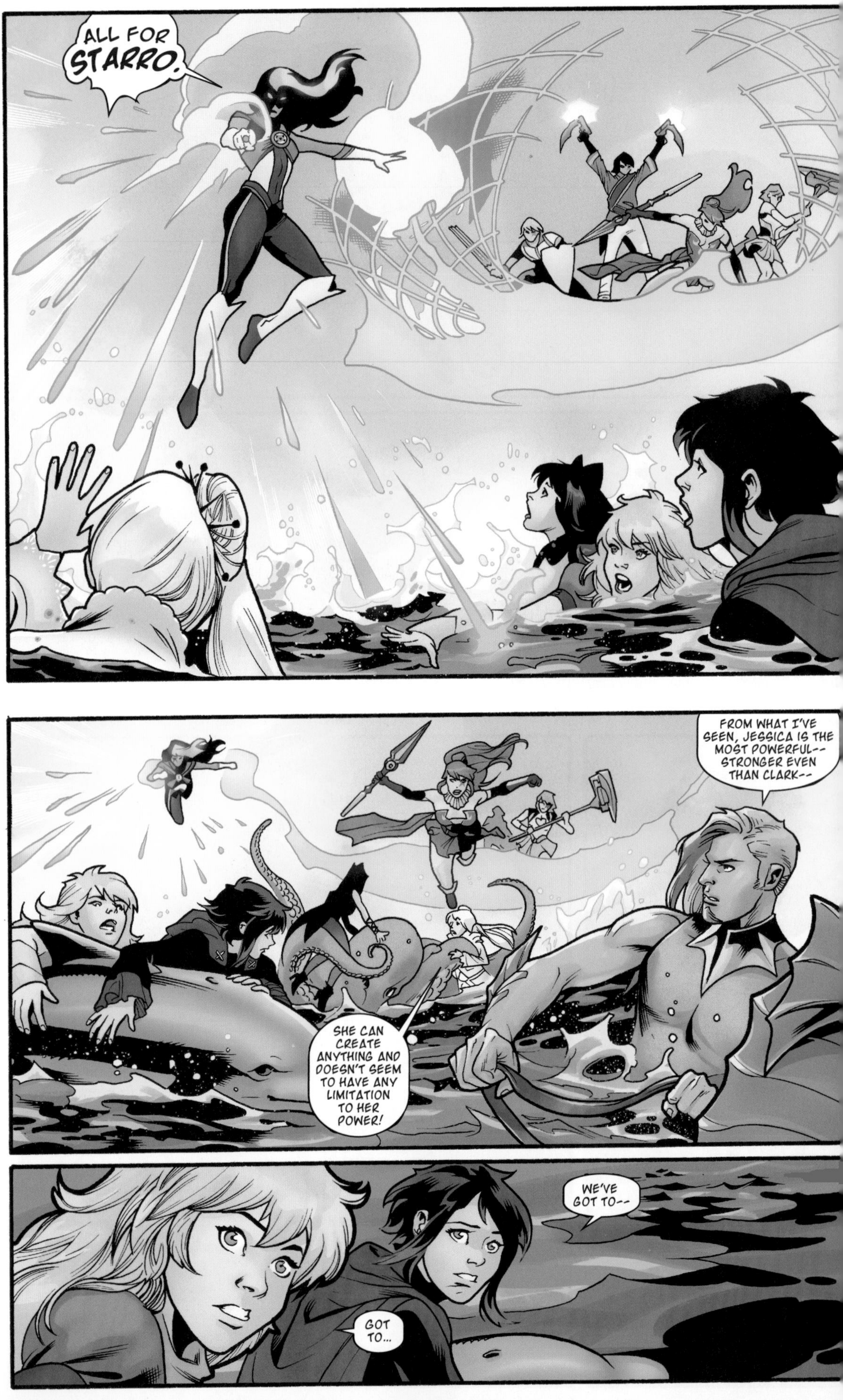
ALL FOR STARRO.
FROM WHAT I'VE SEEN, JESSICA IS THE MOST POWERFUL-- STRONGER EVEN THAN CLARK--
SHE CAN CREATE ANYTHING AND DOESN'T SEEM TO HAVE ANY LIMITATION TO HER POWER!
WE'VE GOT TO--
GOT TO...

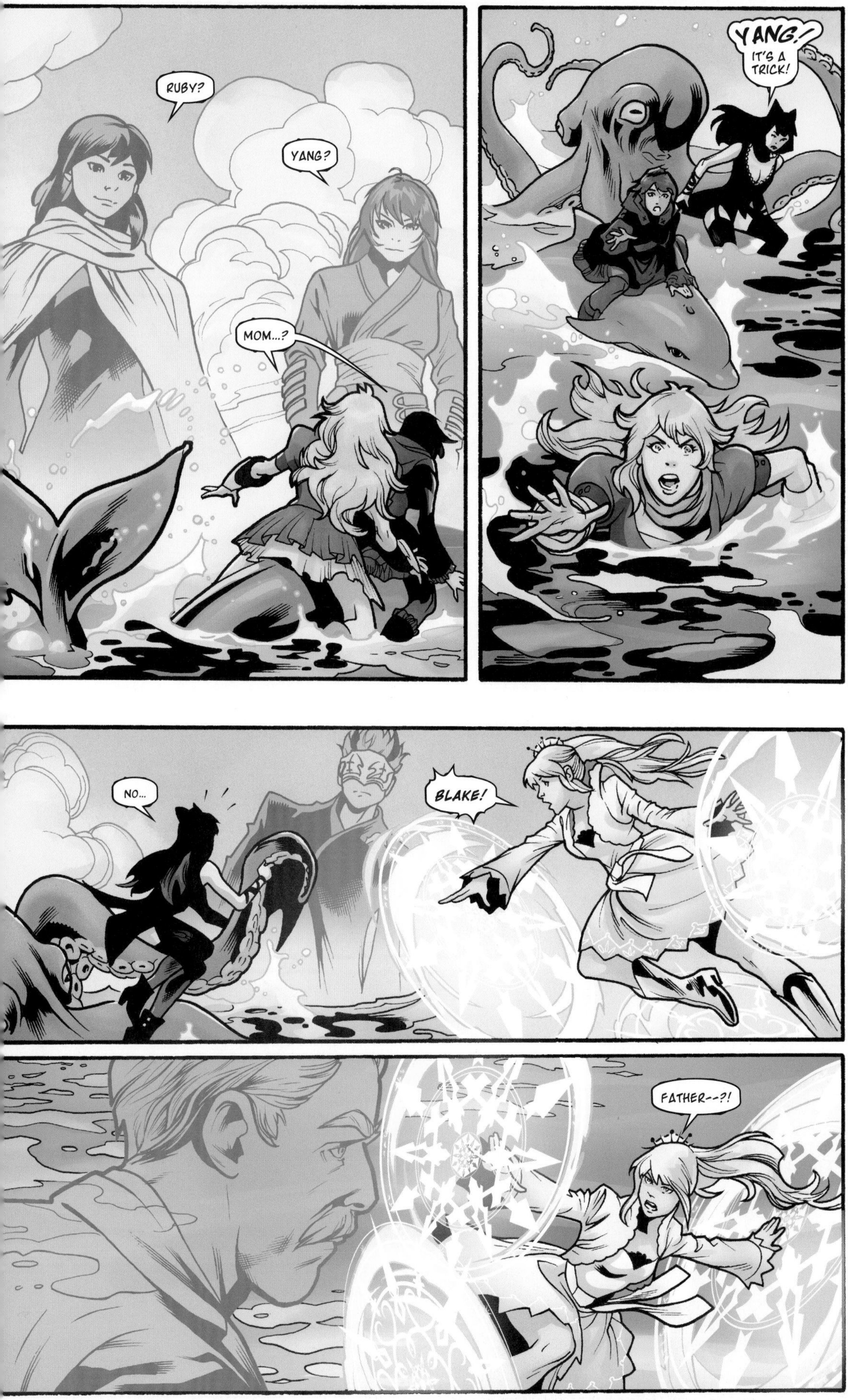
RUBY?
YANG?
MOM...?
YANG! IT'S A TRICK!
NO...
BLAKE!
FATHER--?!

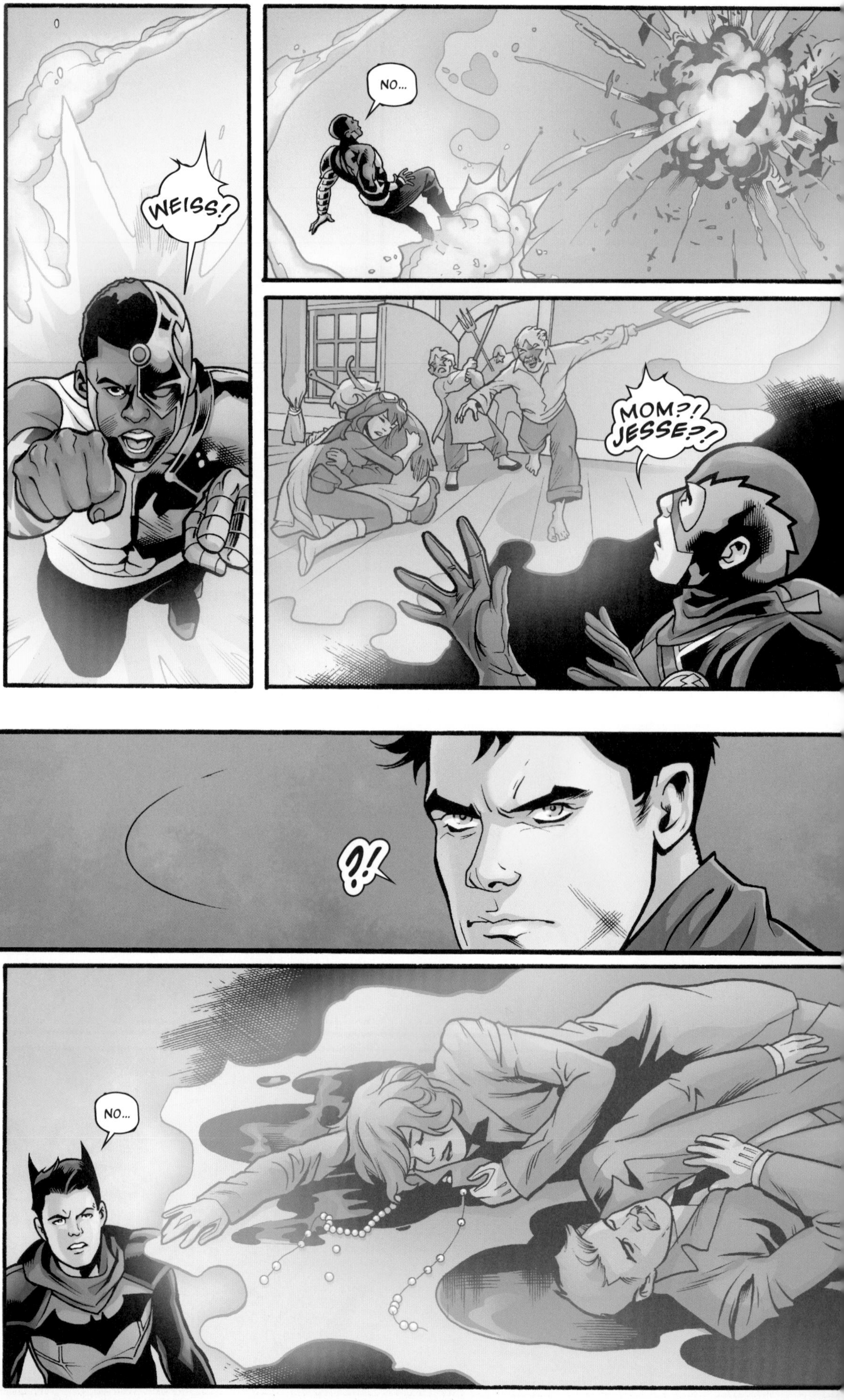
WEISS!
NO...
MOM?! JESSE?!
?!
NO...

FRIEND BRUCE!

SLICE

THEY'RE NOT REAL!

...

BUT THAT IS.

JOIN US, OUTSIDER...

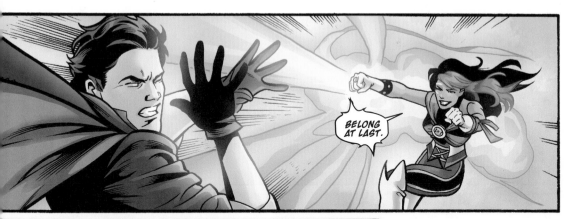

BELONG AT LAST.

WHAM

CLARK!

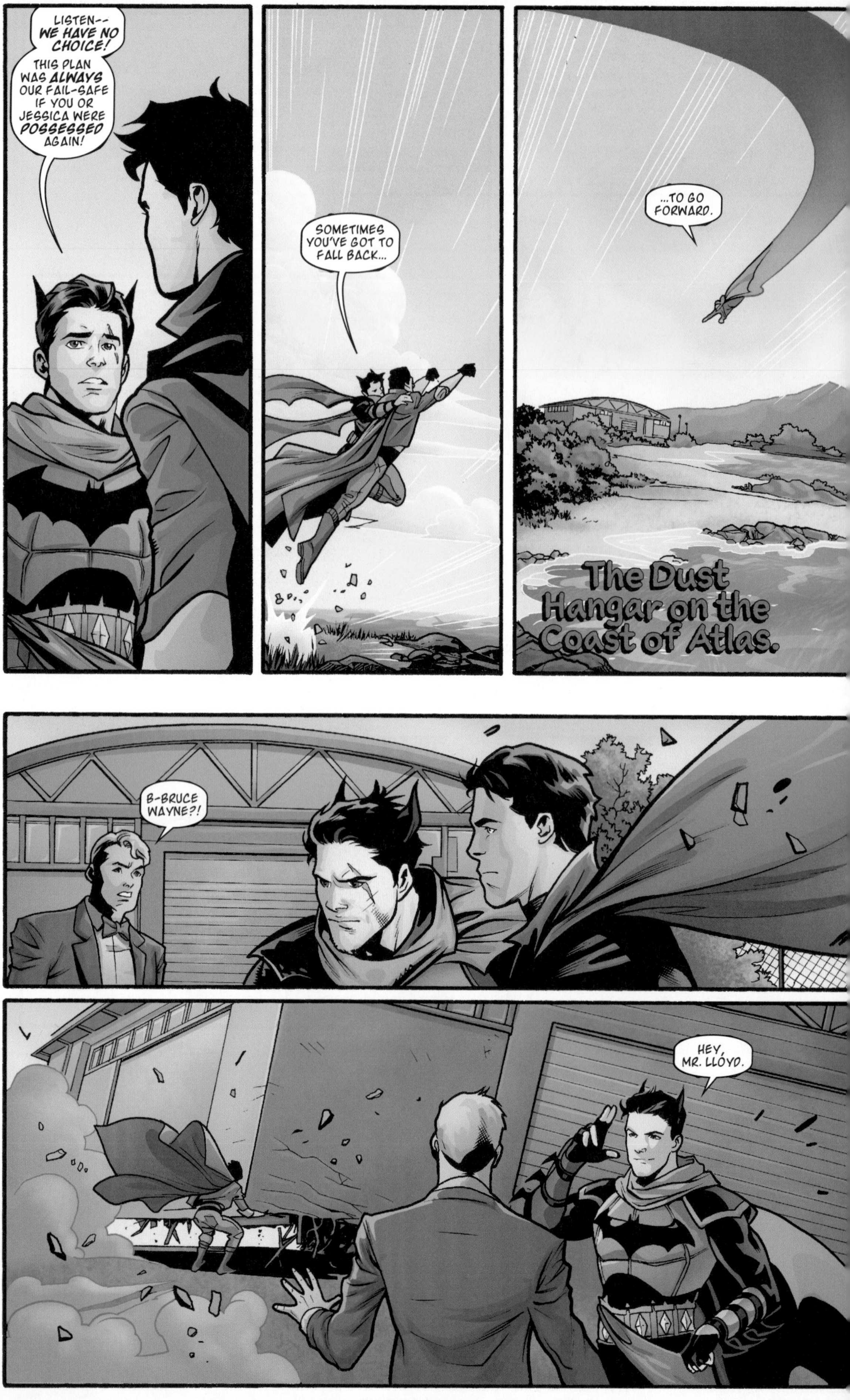
LISTEN-- WE HAVE NO CHOICE!
THIS PLAN WAS ALWAYS OUR FAIL-SAFE IF YOU OR JESSICA WERE POSSESSED AGAIN!
SOMETIMES YOU'VE GOT TO FALL BACK...
...TO GO FORWARD.
The Dust Hangar on the Coast of Atlas.
B-BRUCE WAYNE?!
HEY, MR. LLOYD.

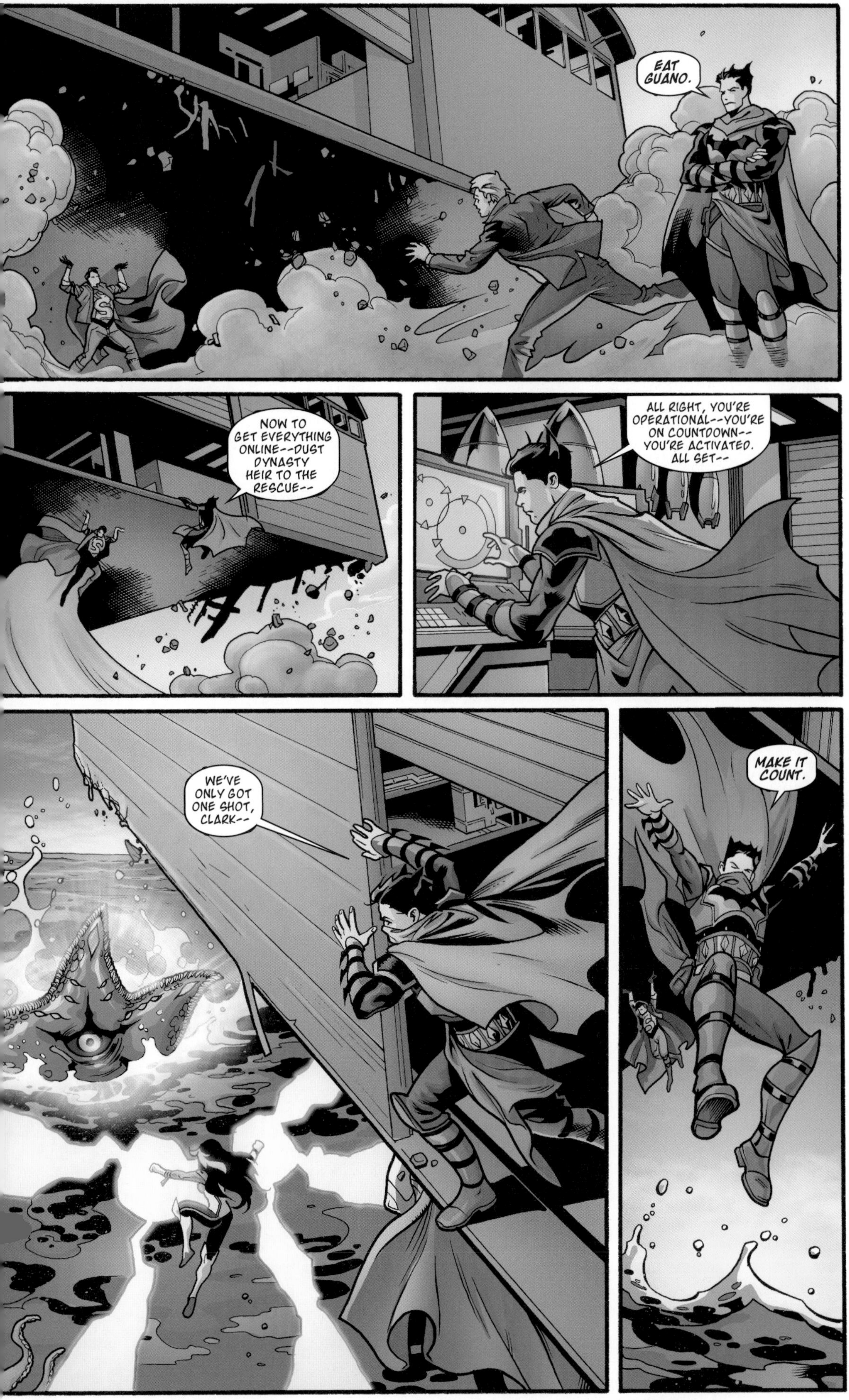
EAT GUANO.
NOW TO GET EVERYTHING ONLINE--DUST DYNASTY HEIR TO THE RESCUE--
ALL RIGHT, YOU'RE OPERATIONAL--YOU'RE ON COUNTDOWN--YOU'RE ACTIVATED. ALL SET--
WE'VE ONLY GOT ONE SHOT, CLARK--
MAKE IT COUNT.

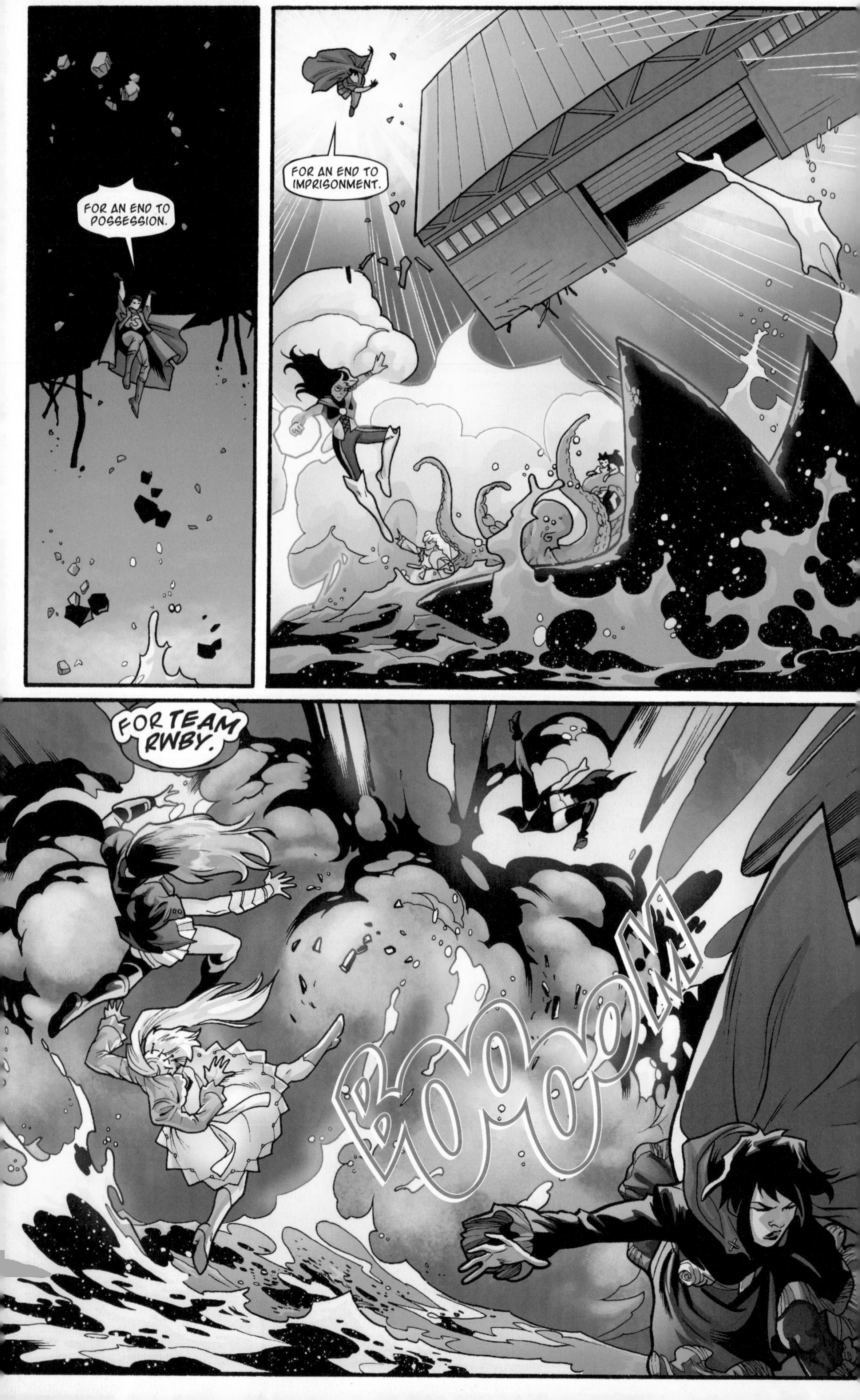
FOR AN END TO POSSESSION.
FOR AN END TO IMPRISONMENT.
FOR TEAM RWBY.
BOOOOOM

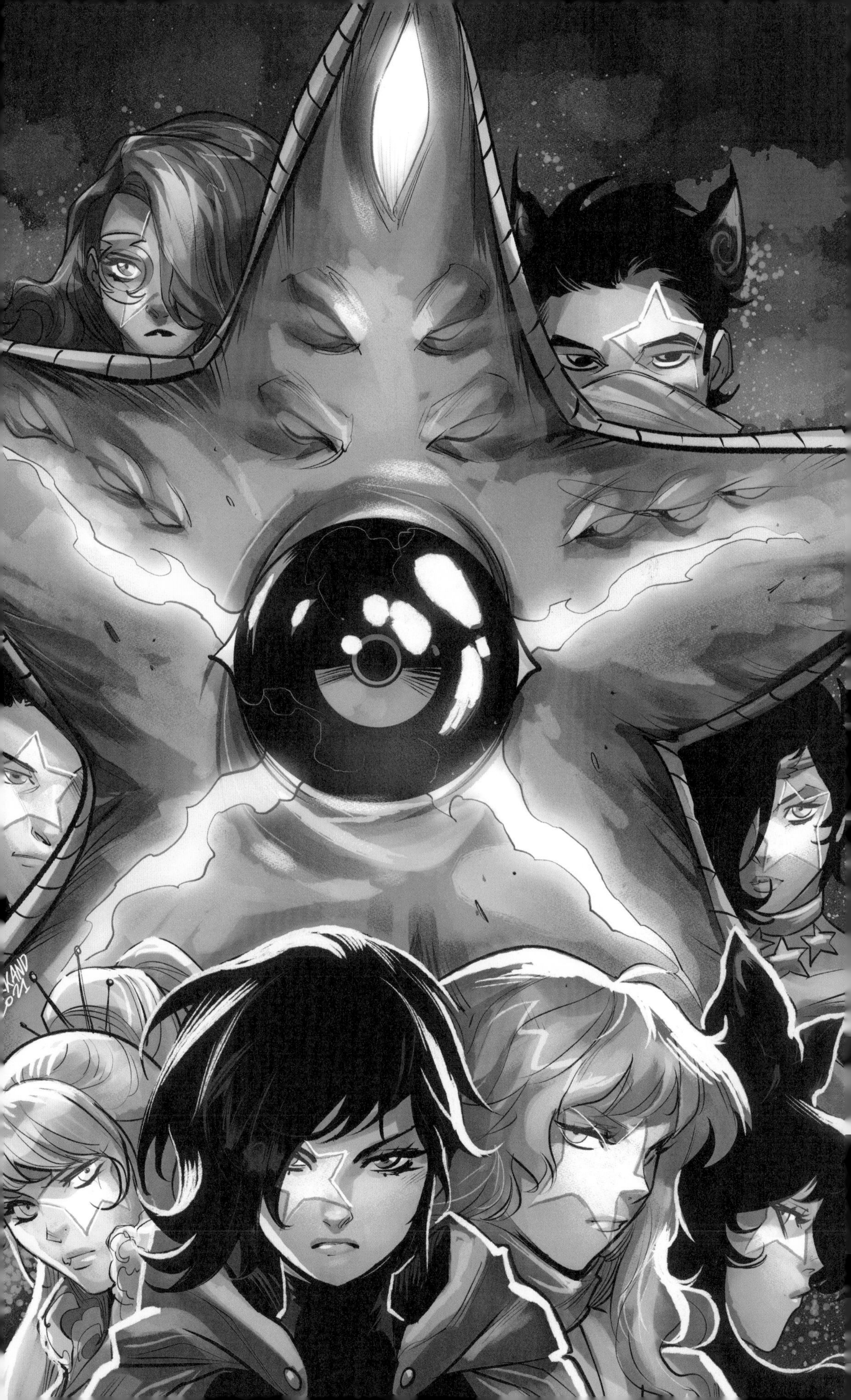

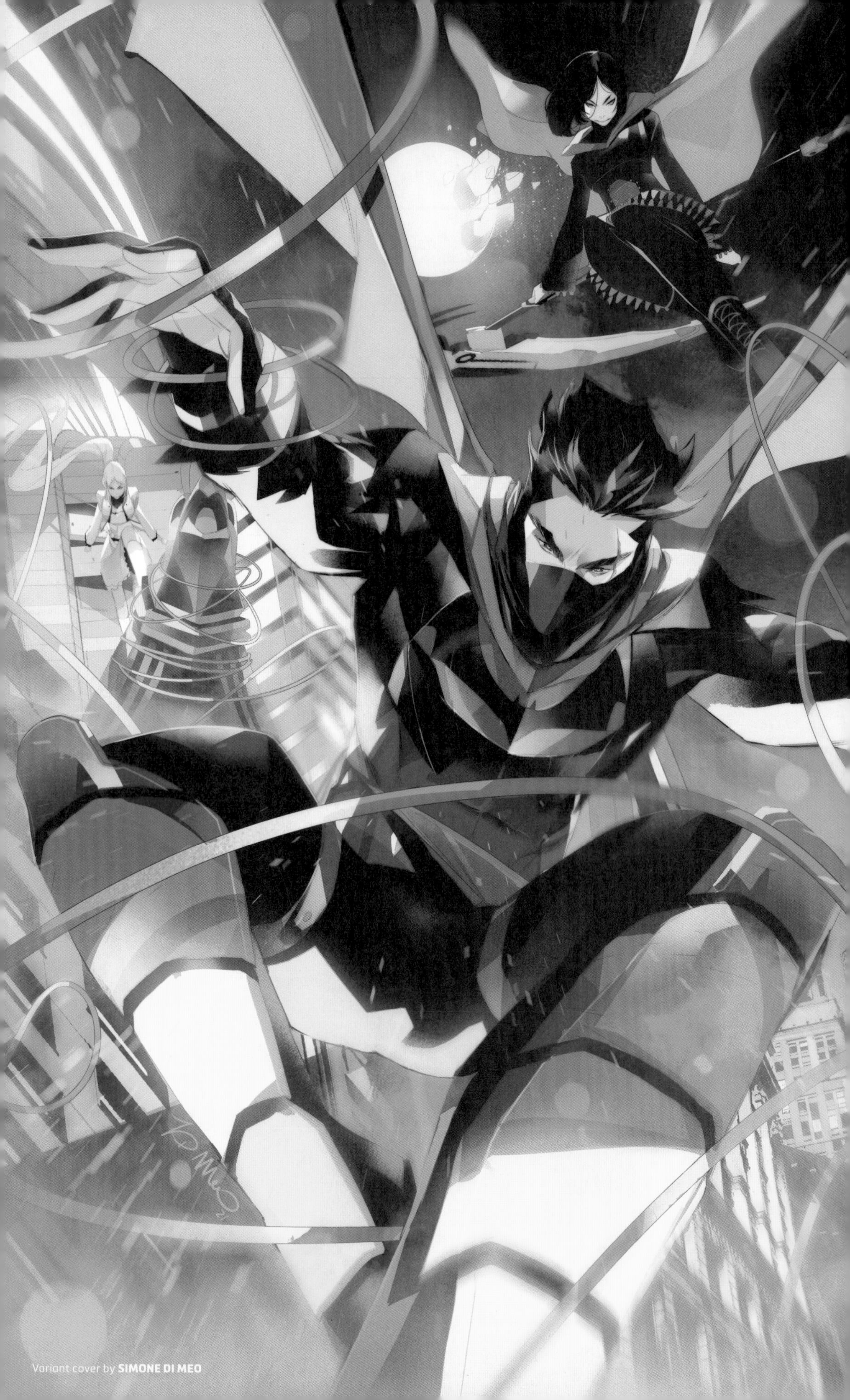

Variant cover by **SIMONE DI MEO**

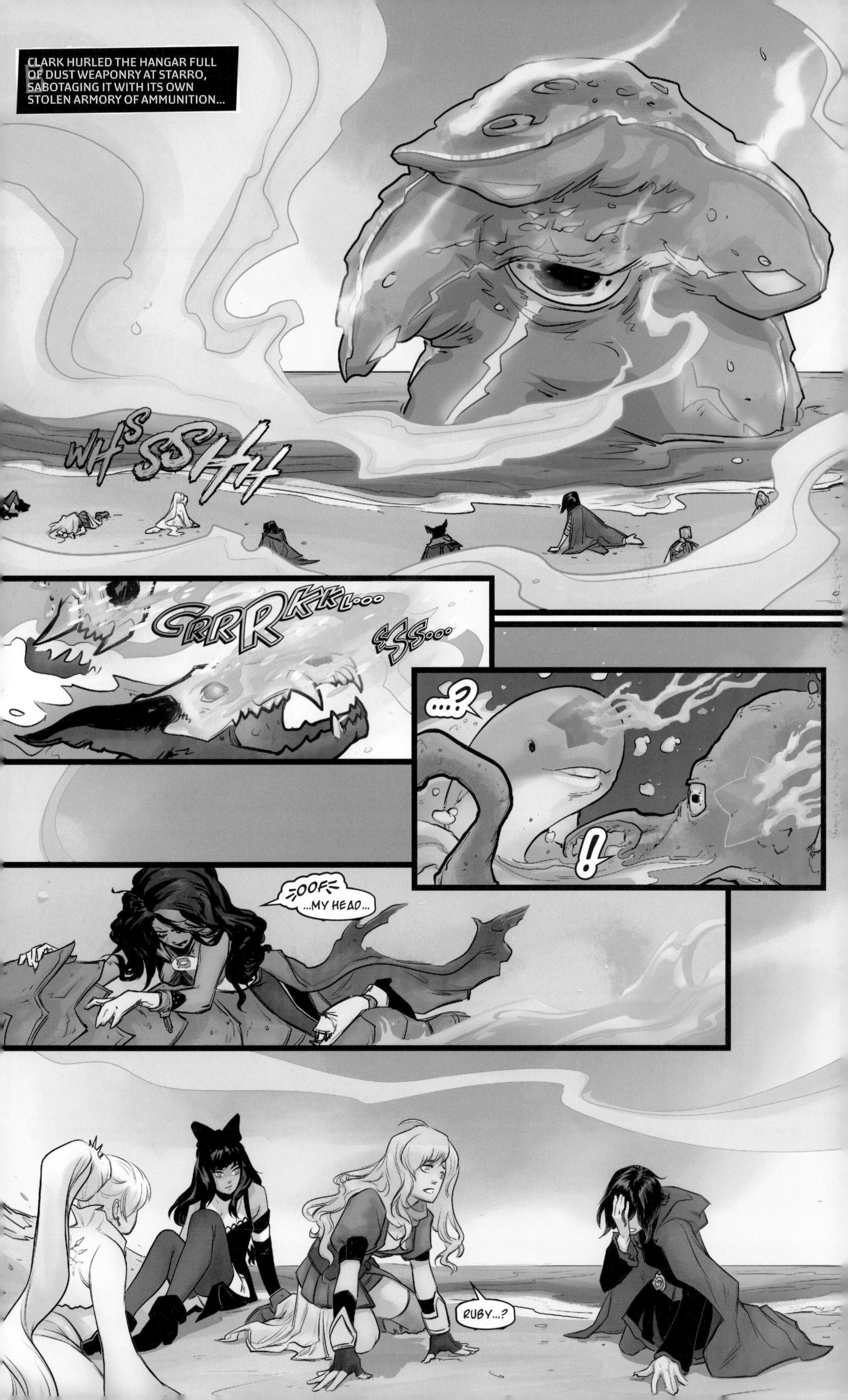
CLARK HURLED THE HANGAR FULL OF DUST WEAPONRY AT STARRO, SABOTAGING IT WITH ITS OWN STOLEN ARMORY OF AMMUNITION...
WHSSSHH
CRRRKKKL...
SSS...
...?
!
OOF
...MY HEAD...
RUBY...?

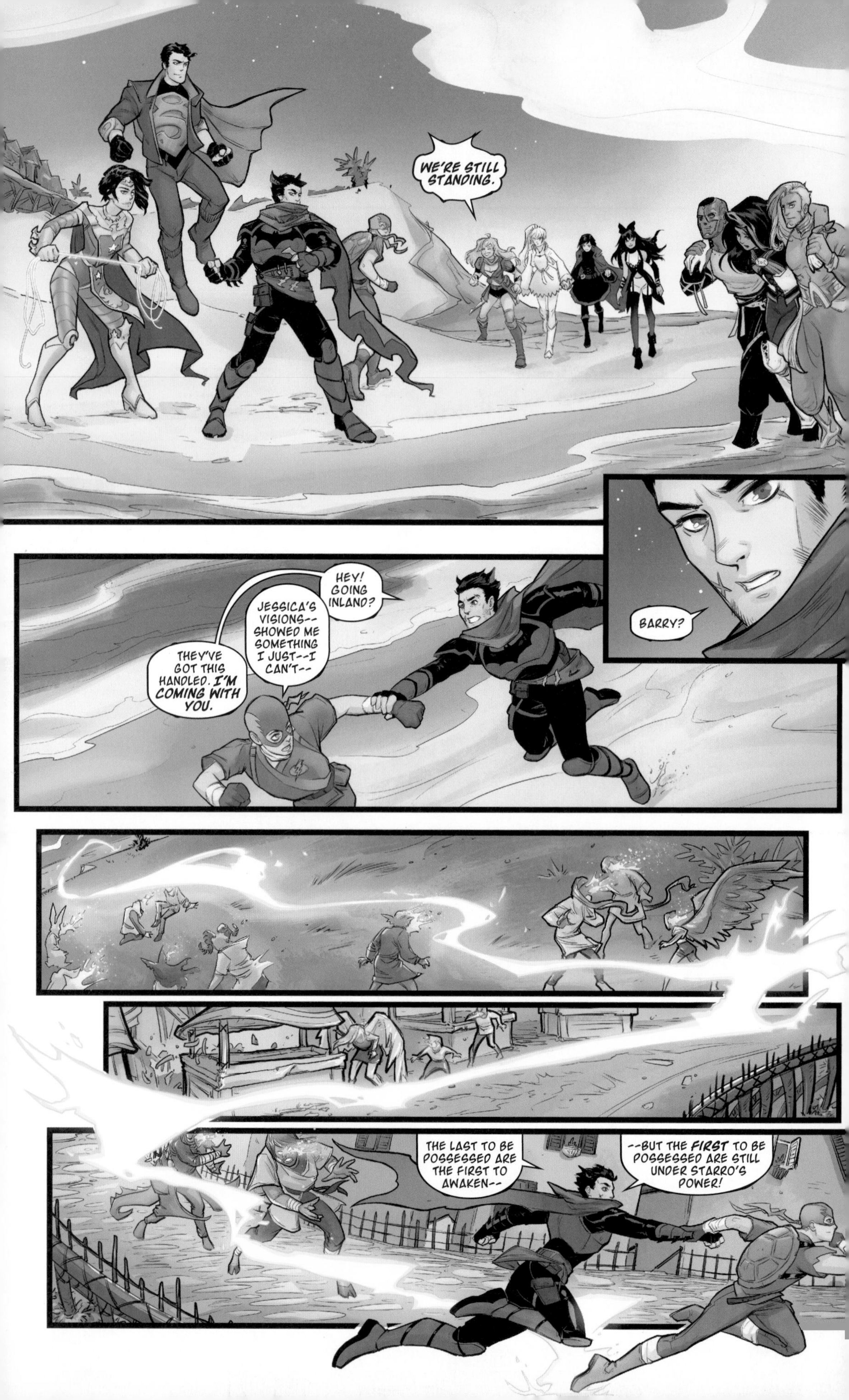
WE'RE STILL STANDING.
BARRY?
HEY! GOING INLAND?
JESSICA'S VISIONS--SHOWED ME SOMETHING I JUST--I CAN'T--
THEY'VE GOT THIS HANDLED. I'M COMING WITH YOU.
THE LAST TO BE POSSESSED ARE THE FIRST TO AWAKEN--
--BUT THE FIRST TO BE POSSESSED ARE STILL UNDER STARRO'S POWER!

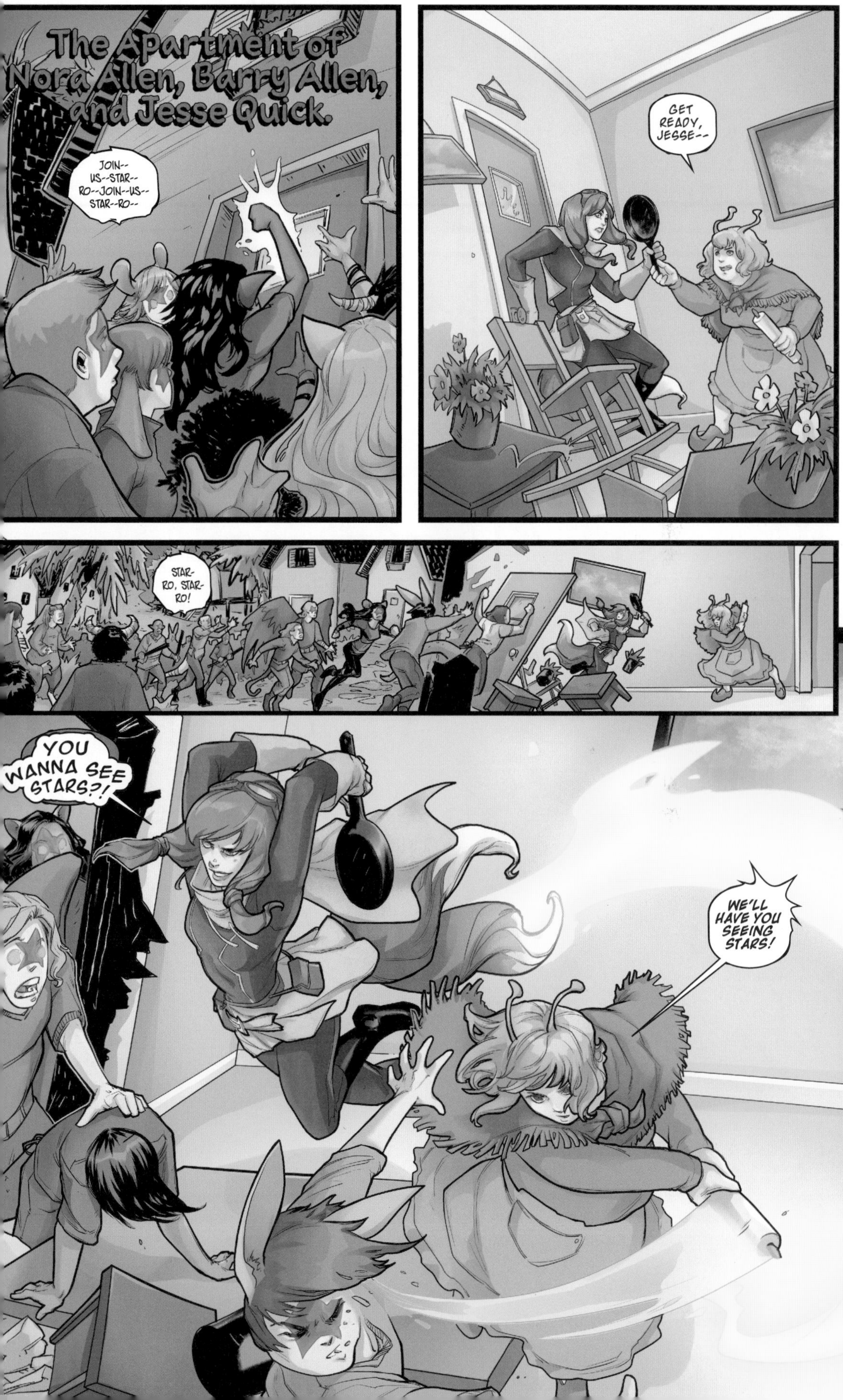
The Apartment of Nora Allen, Barry Allen, and Jesse Quick.
JOIN-- US--STAR-- RO--JOIN--US-- STAR--RO--
GET READY, JESSE--
STAR-RO, STAR-RO!
YOU WANNA SEE STARS?!
WE'LL HAVE YOU SEEING STARS!

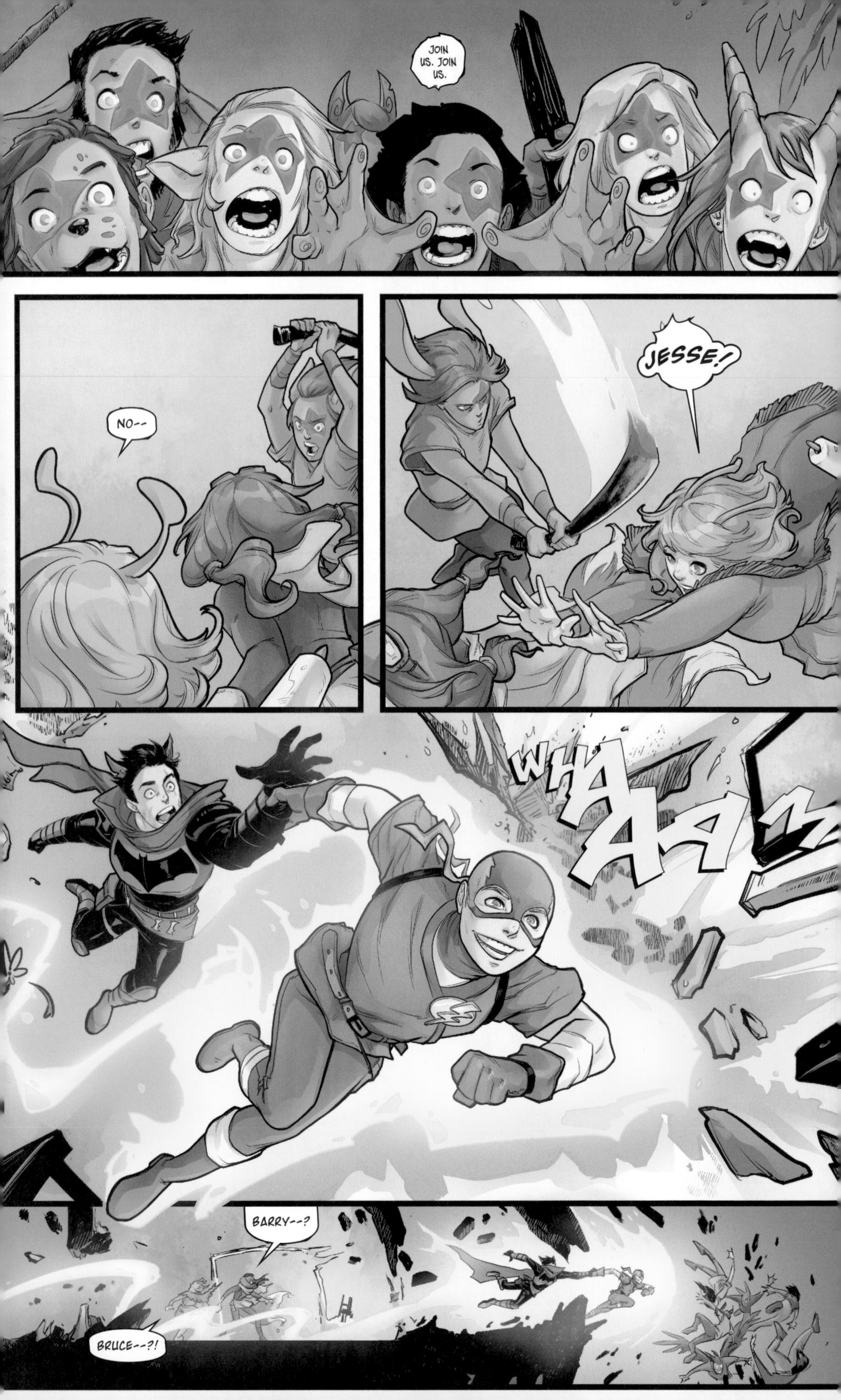
JOIN US. JOIN US.
NO--
JESSE!
WHAAAZ
BARRY--?
BRUCE--?!

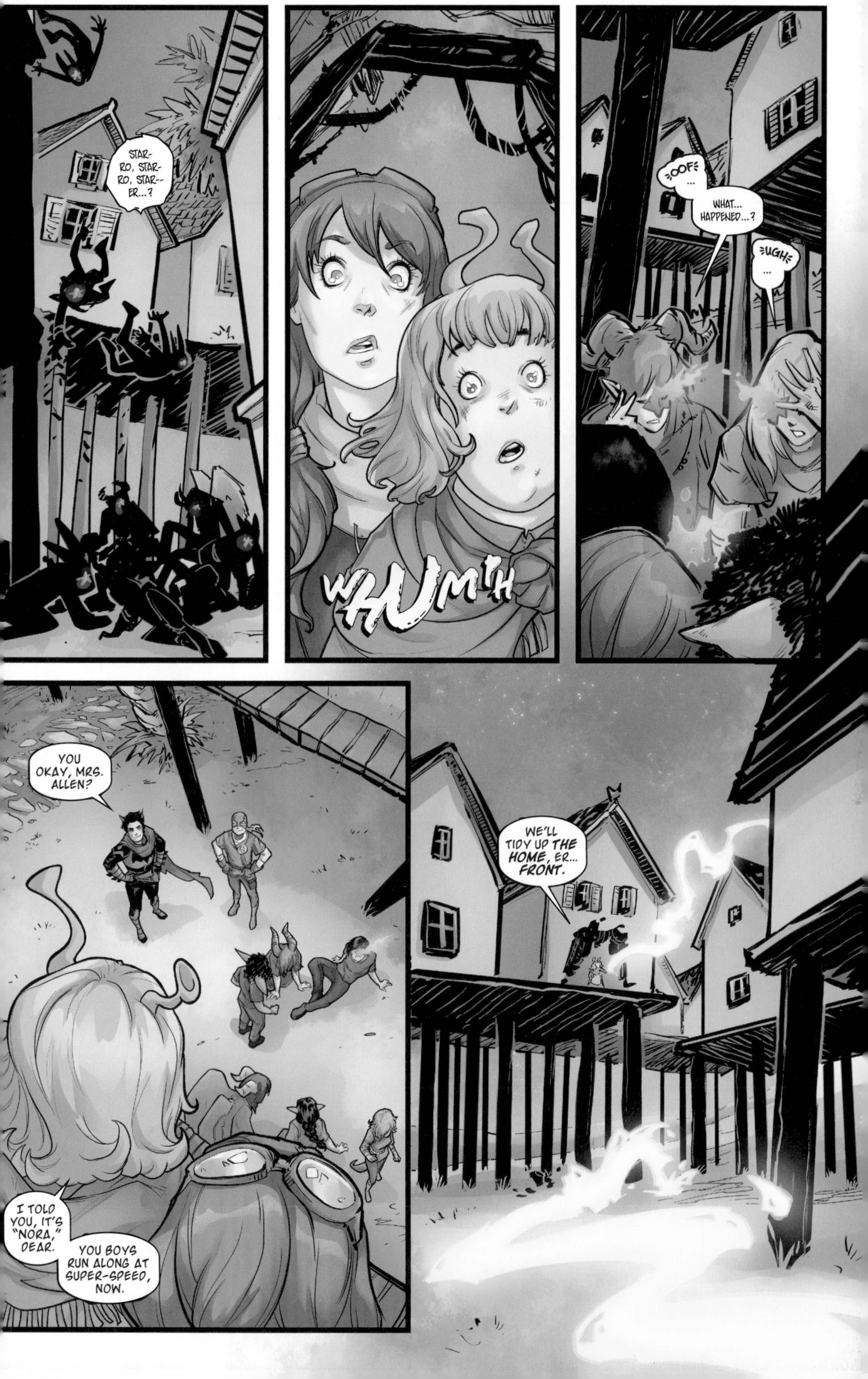

STAR-RO, STAR-RO, STAR-- ER...?
WHUMPH
OOF ...
WHAT... HAPPENED...?
UGH ...
YOU OKAY, MRS. ALLEN?
I TOLD YOU, IT'S "NORA," DEAR.
YOU BOYS RUN ALONG AT SUPER-SPEED, NOW.
WE'LL TIDY UP THE HOME, ER... FRONT.

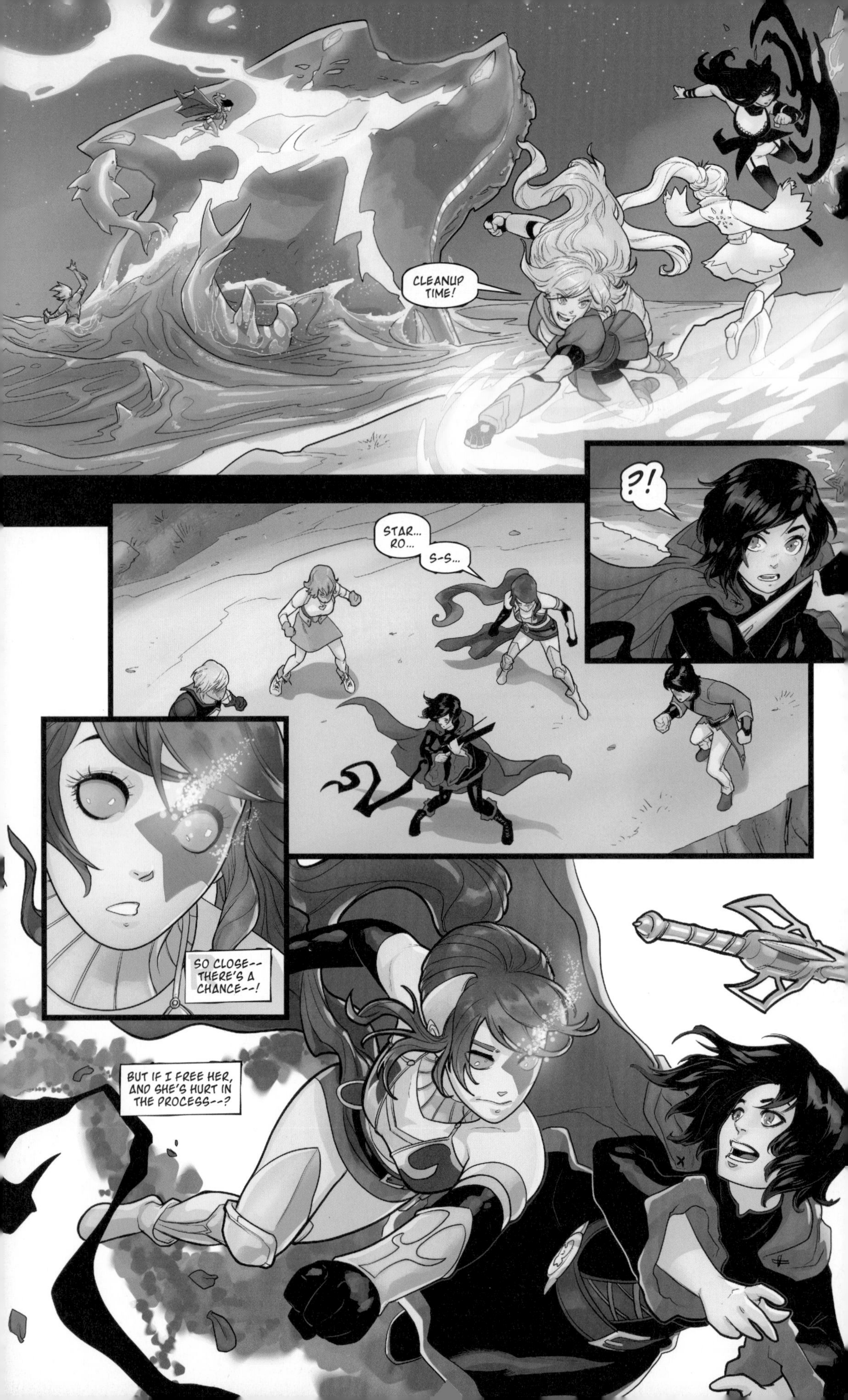
CLEANUP TIME!
?!
STAR... RO...
S-S...
SO CLOSE-- THERE'S A CHANCE--!
BUT IF I FREE HER, AND SHE'S HURT IN THE PROCESS--?

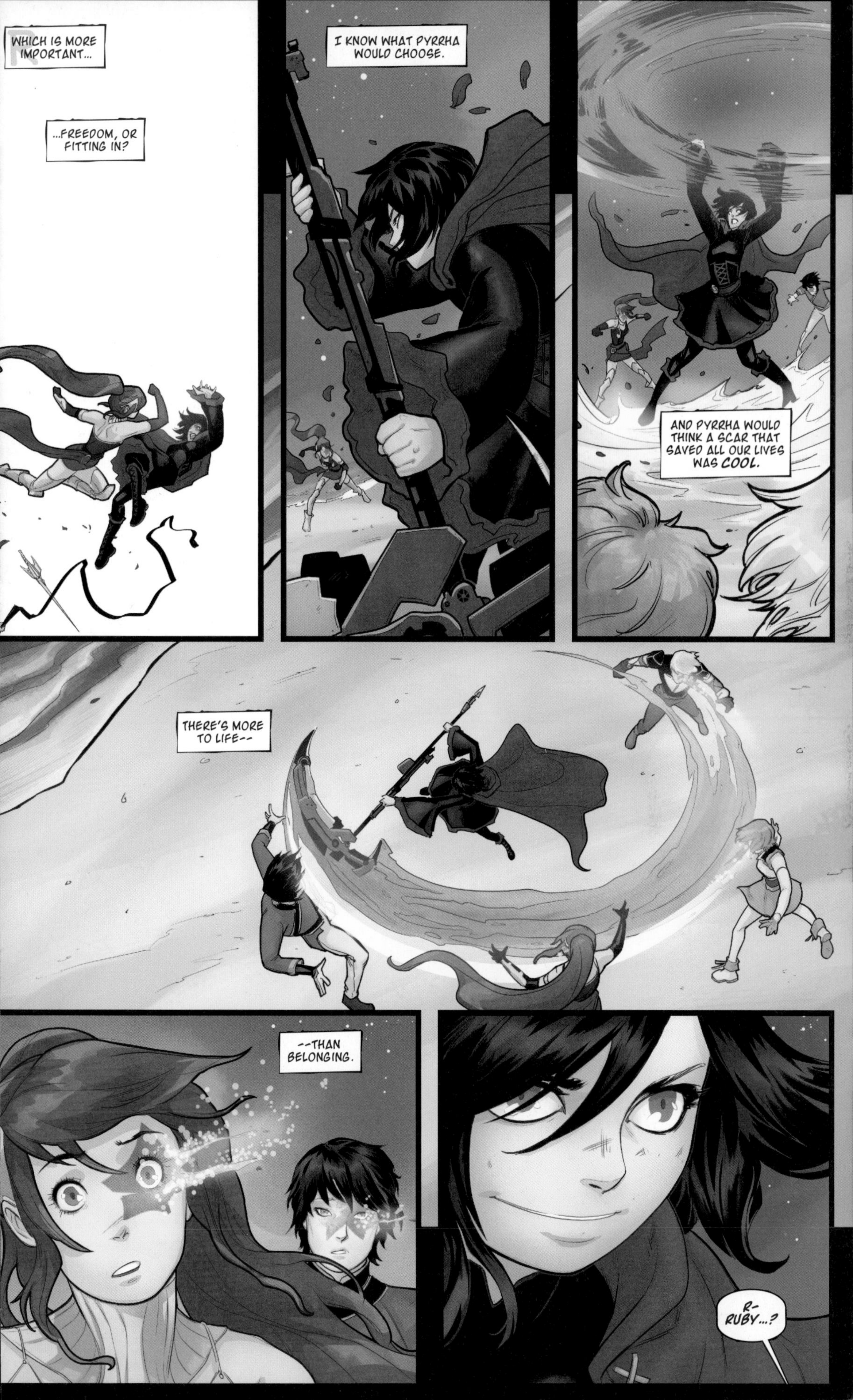
WHICH IS MORE IMPORTANT...
...FREEDOM, OR FITTING IN?
I KNOW WHAT PYRRHA WOULD CHOOSE.
AND PYRRHA WOULD THINK A SCAR THAT SAVED ALL OUR LIVES WAS COOL.
THERE'S MORE TO LIFE--
--THAN BELONGING.
R-RUBY...?

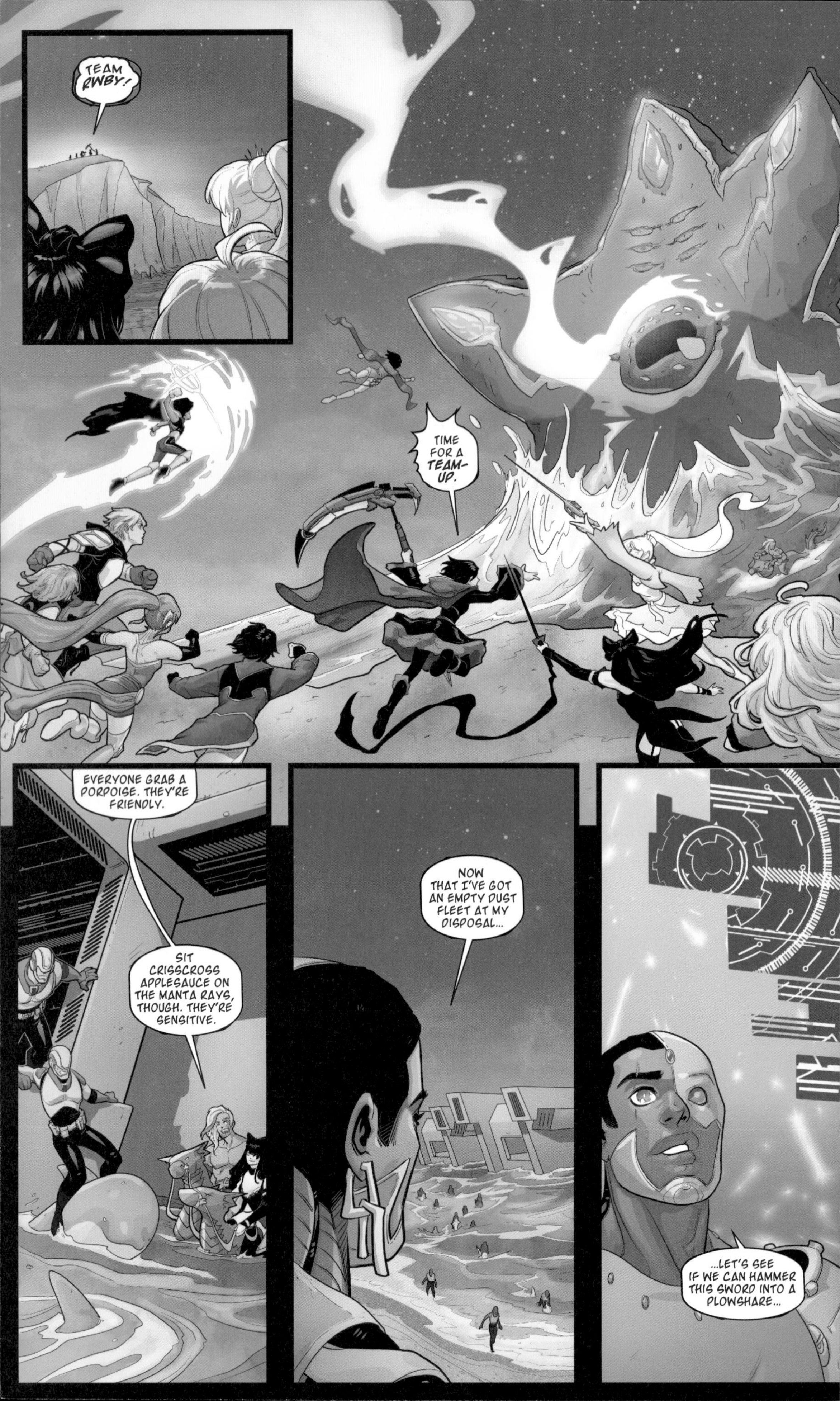
TEAM RWBY!
TIME FOR A TEAM-UP.
EVERYONE GRAB A PORPOISE. THEY'RE FRIENDLY.
SIT CRISSCROSS APPLESAUCE ON THE MANTA RAYS, THOUGH. THEY'RE SENSITIVE.
NOW THAT I'VE GOT AN EMPTY DUST FLEET AT MY DISPOSAL...
...LET'S SEE IF WE CAN HAMMER THIS SWORD INTO A PLOWSHARE...

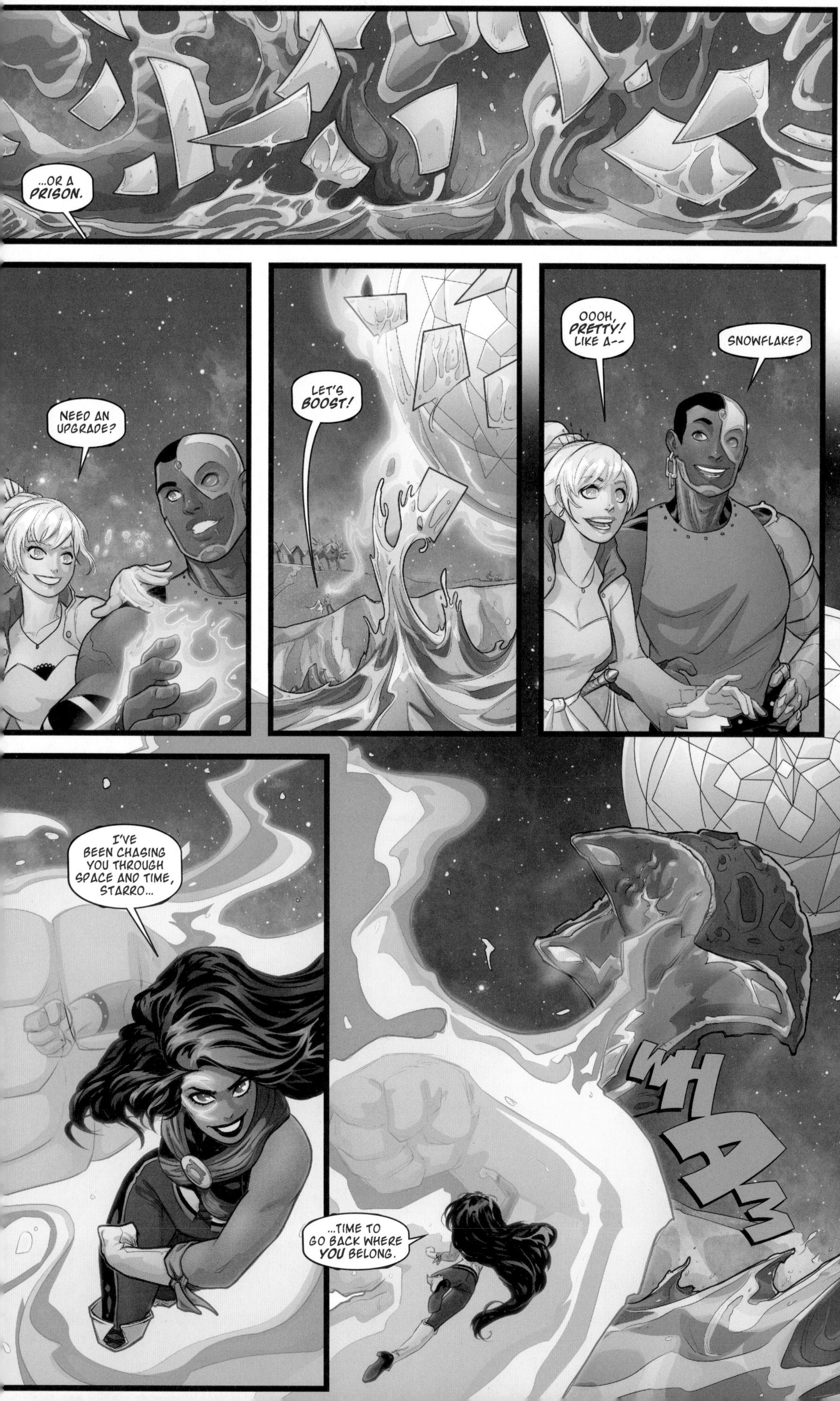
...OR A PRISON.
NEED AN UPGRADE?
LET'S BOOST!
OOOH, PRETTY! LIKE A--
SNOWFLAKE?
I'VE BEEN CHASING YOU THROUGH SPACE AND TIME, STARRO...
WHAM
...TIME TO GO BACK WHERE YOU BELONG.

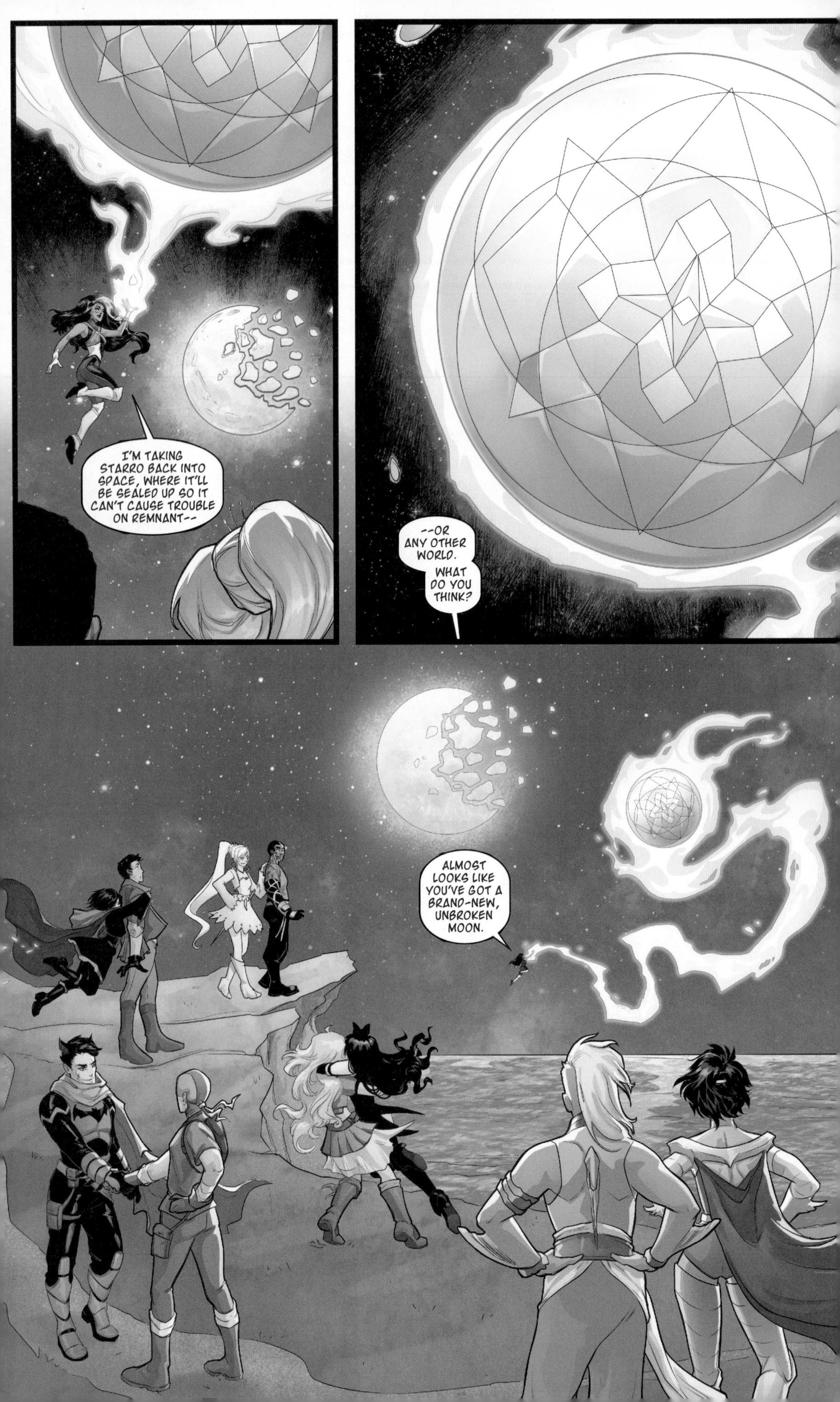
I'M TAKING STARRO BACK INTO SPACE, WHERE IT'LL BE SEALED UP SO IT CAN'T CAUSE TROUBLE ON REMNANT--
--OR ANY OTHER WORLD.
WHAT DO YOU THINK?
ALMOST LOOKS LIKE YOU'VE GOT A BRAND-NEW, UNBROKEN MOON.

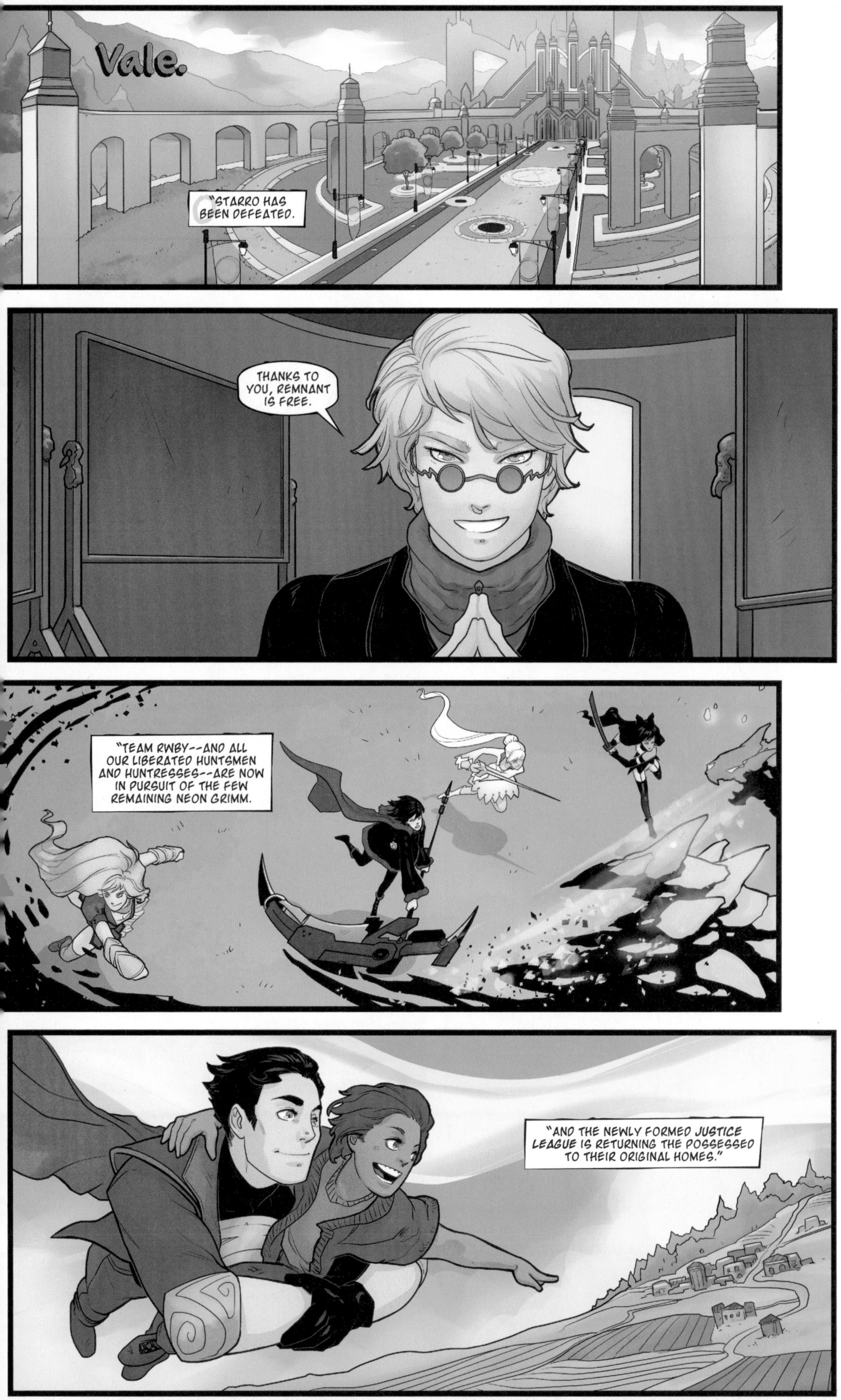
Vale.
"STARRO HAS BEEN DEFEATED.
THANKS TO YOU, REMNANT IS FREE.
"TEAM RWBY--AND ALL OUR LIBERATED HUNTSMEN AND HUNTRESSES--ARE NOW IN PURSUIT OF THE FEW REMAINING NEON GRIMM.
"AND THE NEWLY FORMED JUSTICE LEAGUE IS RETURNING THE POSSESSED TO THEIR ORIGINAL HOMES."

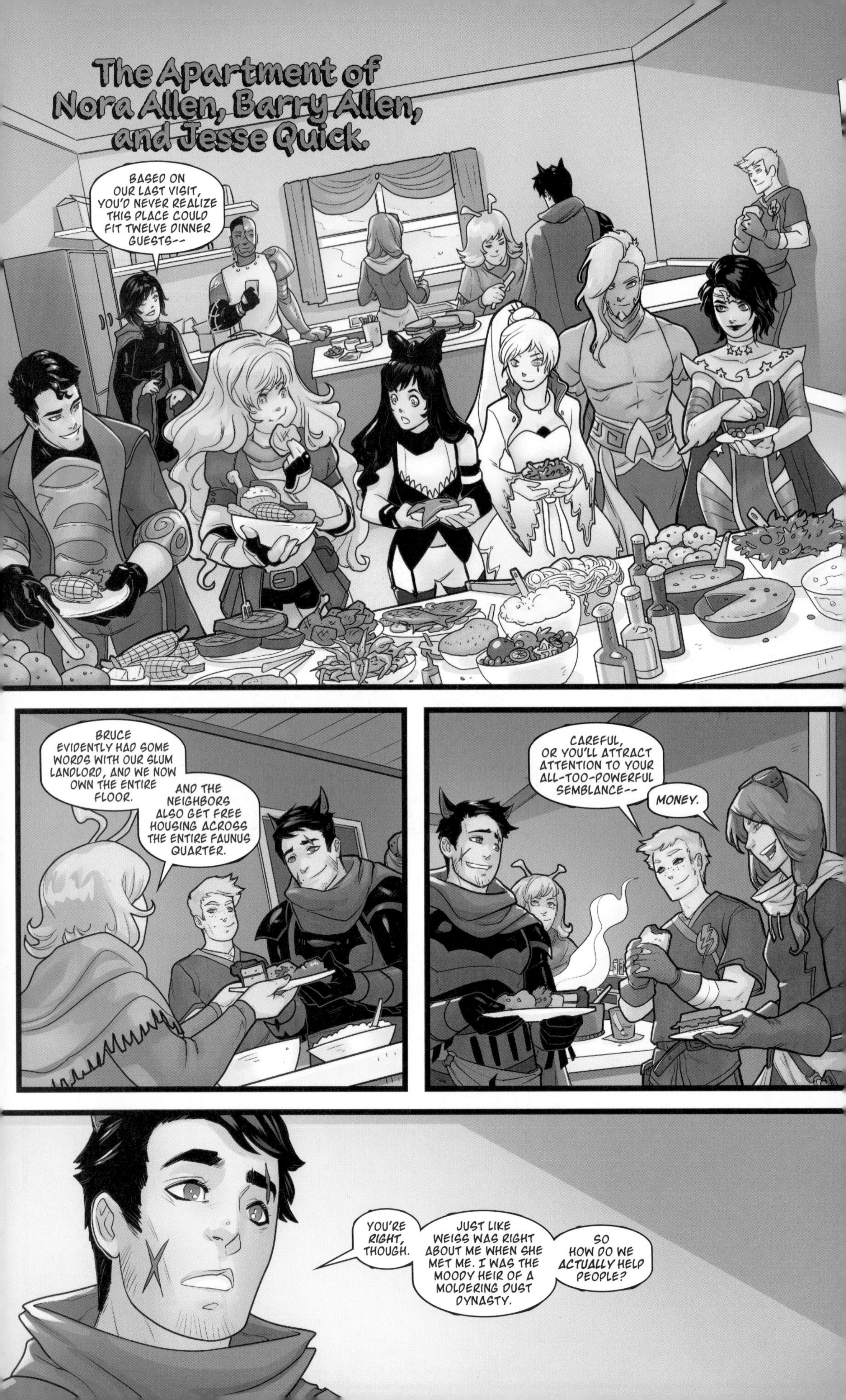
The Apartment of Nora Allen, Barry Allen, and Jesse Quick.
BASED ON OUR LAST VISIT, YOU'D NEVER REALIZE THIS PLACE COULD FIT TWELVE DINNER GUESTS--
BRUCE EVIDENTLY HAD SOME WORDS WITH OUR SLUM LANDLORD, AND WE NOW OWN THE ENTIRE FLOOR.
AND THE NEIGHBORS ALSO GET FREE HOUSING ACROSS THE ENTIRE FAUNUS QUARTER.
CAREFUL, OR YOU'LL ATTRACT ATTENTION TO YOUR ALL-TOO-POWERFUL SEMBLANCE--
MONEY.
YOU'RE RIGHT, THOUGH.
JUST LIKE WEISS WAS RIGHT ABOUT ME WHEN SHE MET ME. I WAS THE MOODY HEIR OF A MOLDERING DUST DYNASTY.
SO HOW DO WE ACTUALLY HELP PEOPLE?

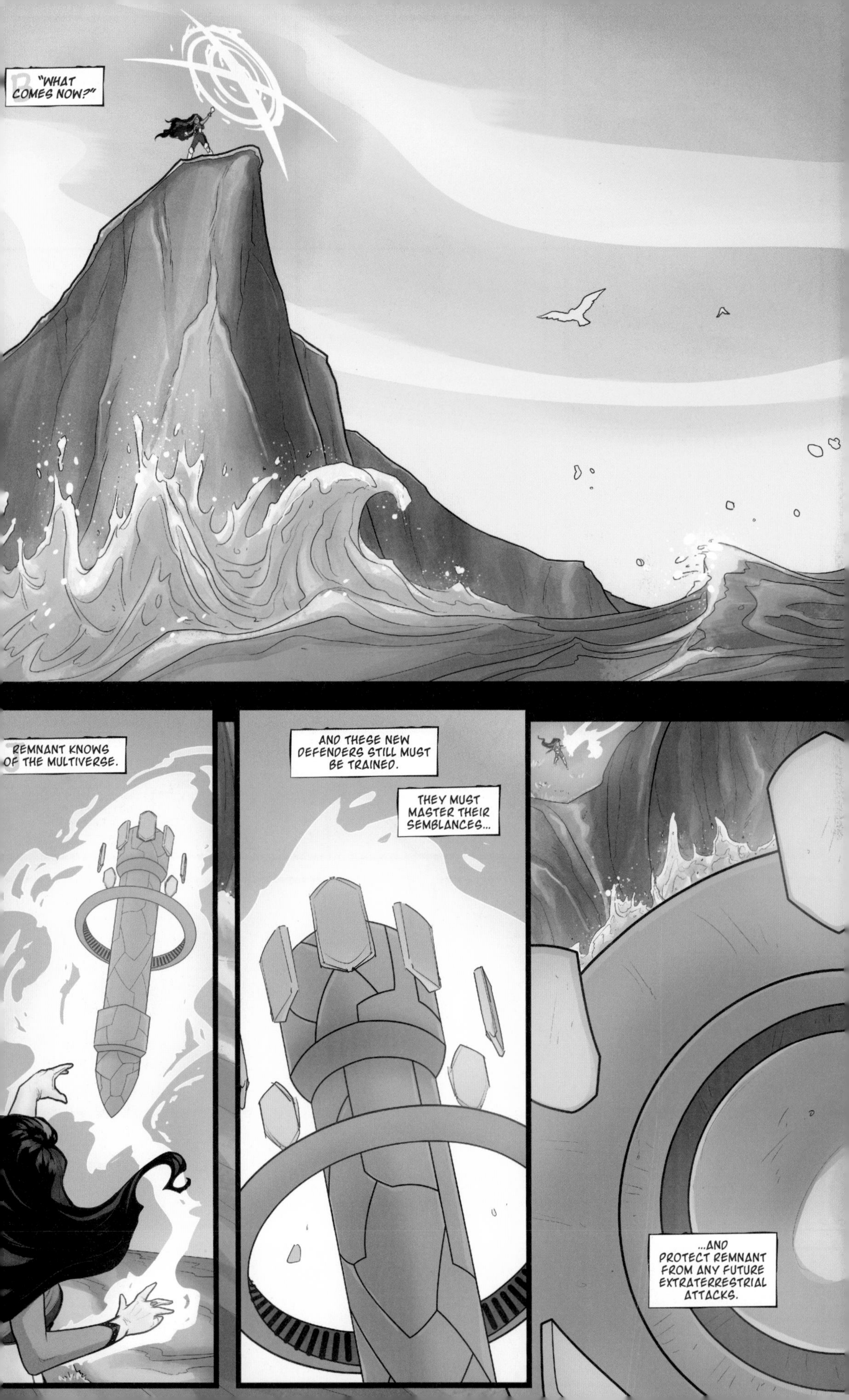
"WHAT COMES NOW?"
REMNANT KNOWS OF THE MULTIVERSE.
AND THESE NEW DEFENDERS STILL MUST BE TRAINED.
THEY MUST MASTER THEIR SEMBLANCES...
...AND PROTECT REMNANT FROM ANY FUTURE EXTRATERRESTRIAL ATTACKS.

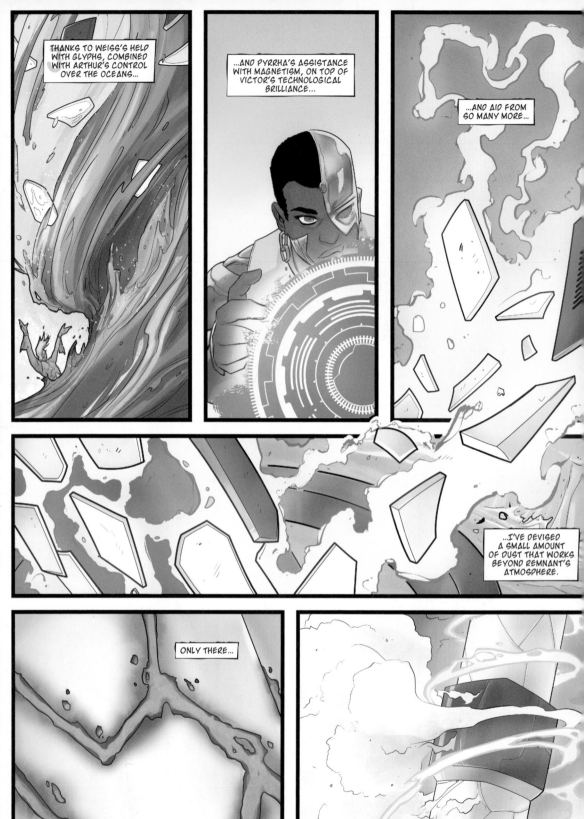

THANKS TO WEISS'S HELP WITH GLYPHS, COMBINED WITH ARTHUR'S CONTROL OVER THE OCEANS...

...AND PYRRHA'S ASSISTANCE WITH MAGNETISM, ON TOP OF VICTOR'S TECHNOLOGICAL BRILLIANCE...

...AND AID FROM SO MANY MORE...

...I'VE DEVISED A SMALL AMOUNT OF DUST THAT WORKS BEYOND REMNANT'S ATMOSPHERE.

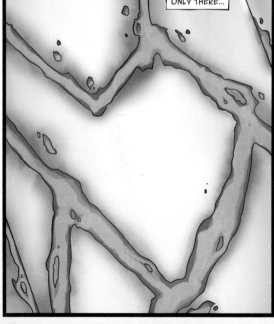

ONLY THERE...

...AND NO FARTHER.

OUR HOME.

AND IN MY ABSENCE, THE COUNCIL SHOULD CONTINUE STEWARDSHIP--

WAR WAS AVERTED, MOTHERS, BUT OTHER DANGERS MAY YET COME.

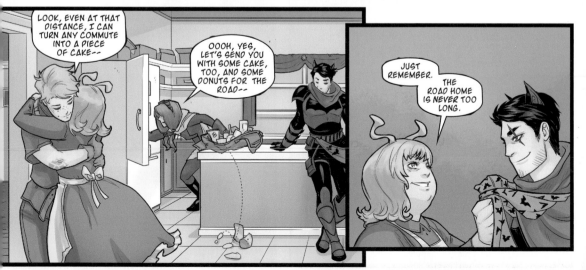

LOOK, EVEN AT THAT DISTANCE, I CAN TURN ANY COMMUTE INTO A PIECE OF CAKE--

OOOH, YES, LET'S SEND YOU WITH SOME CAKE, TOO, AND SOME DONUTS FOR THE ROAD--

JUST REMEMBER. THE ROAD HOME IS NEVER TOO LONG.

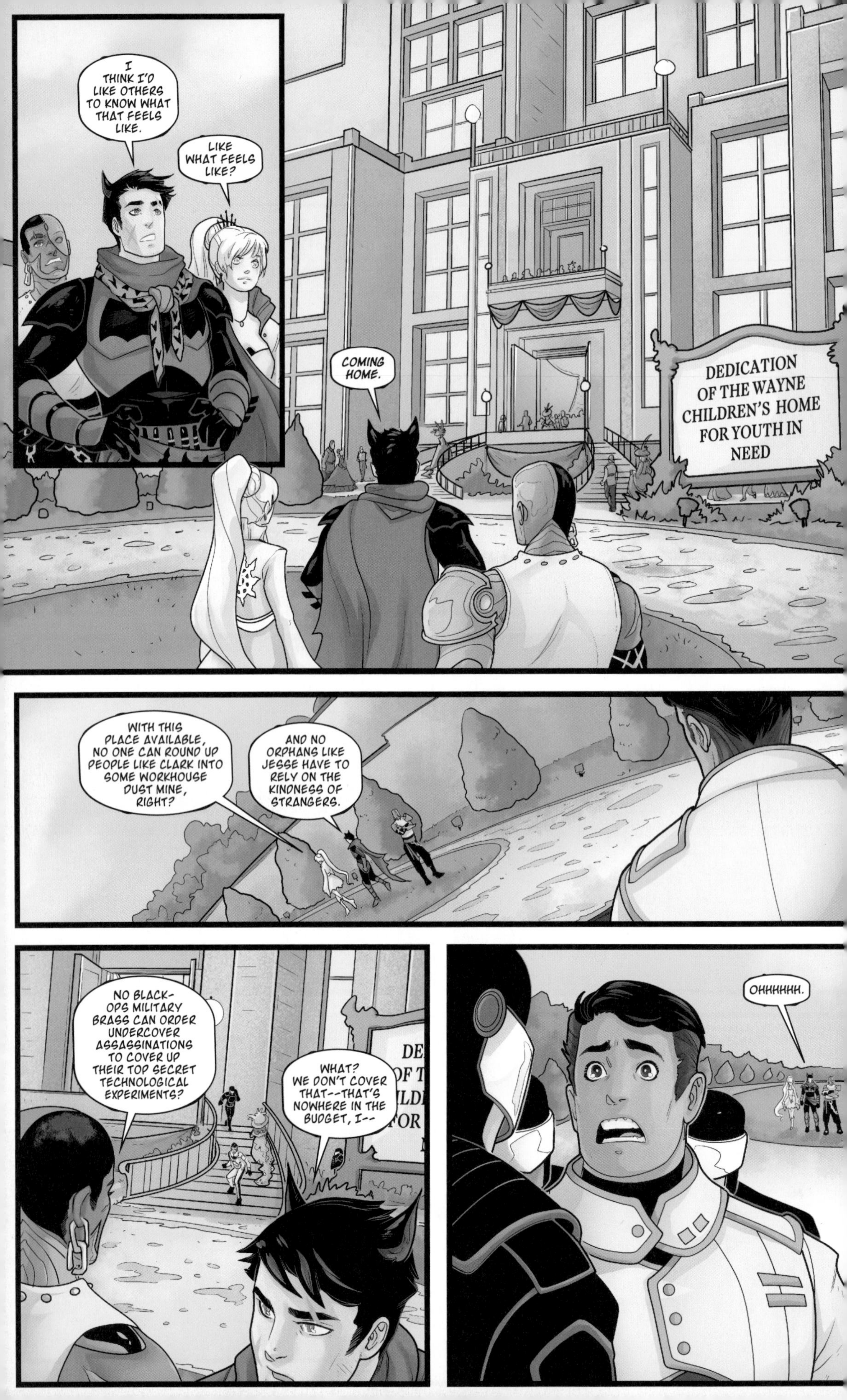
I THINK I'D LIKE OTHERS TO KNOW WHAT THAT FEELS LIKE.
LIKE WHAT FEELS LIKE?
COMING HOME.
DEDICATION OF THE WAYNE CHILDREN'S HOME FOR YOUTH IN NEED
WITH THIS PLACE AVAILABLE, NO ONE CAN ROUND UP PEOPLE LIKE CLARK INTO SOME WORKHOUSE DUST MINE, RIGHT?
AND NO ORPHANS LIKE JESSE HAVE TO RELY ON THE KINDNESS OF STRANGERS.
NO BLACK-OPS MILITARY BRASS CAN ORDER UNDERCOVER ASSASSINATIONS TO COVER UP THEIR TOP SECRET TECHNOLOGICAL EXPERIMENTS?
WHAT? WE DON'T COVER THAT--THAT'S NOWHERE IN THE BUDGET, I--
OHHHHHH.

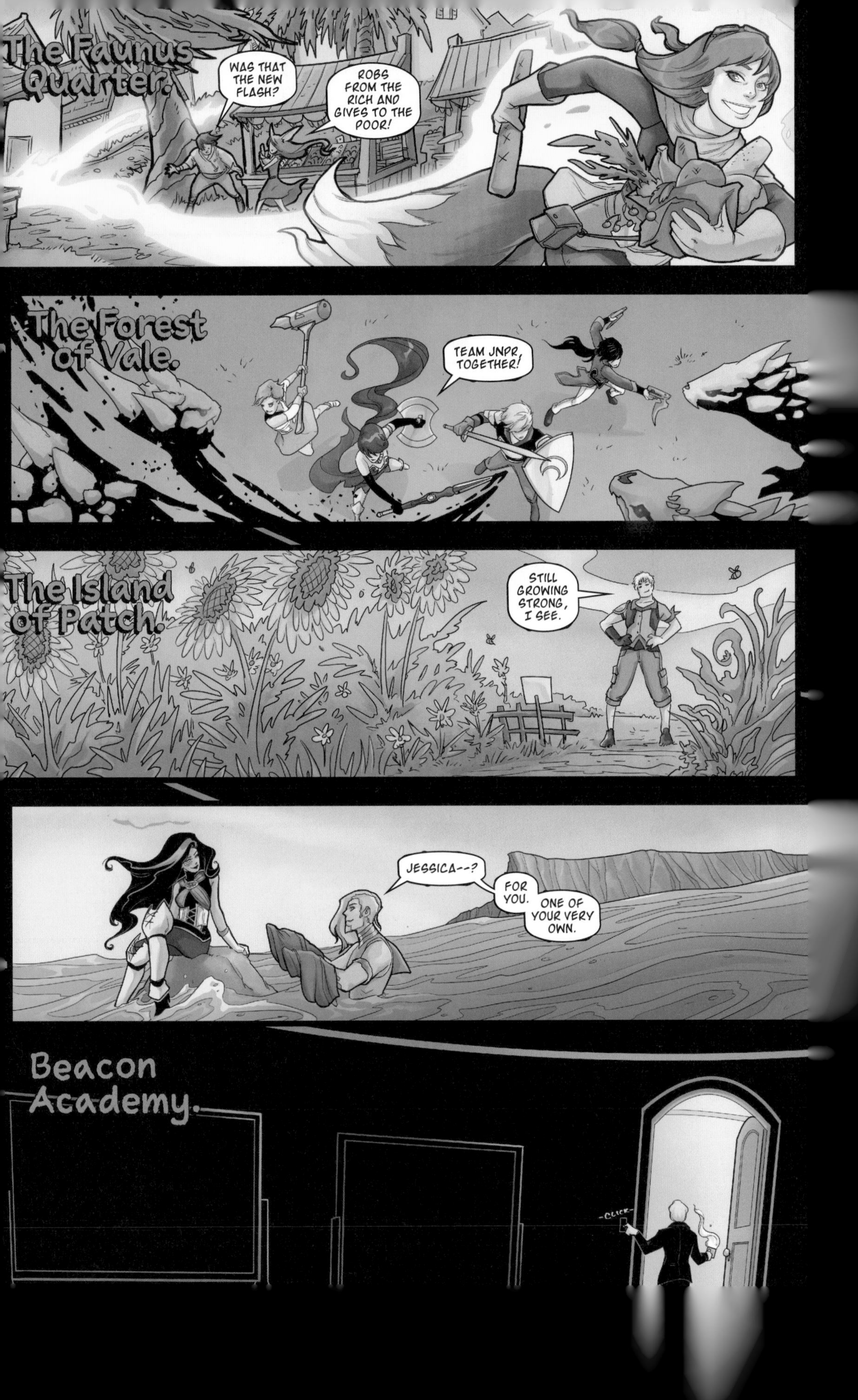
The Faunus Quarter.
WAS THAT THE NEW FLASH?
ROBS FROM THE RICH AND GIVES TO THE POOR!
The Forest of Vale.
TEAM JNPR, TOGETHER!
The Island of Patch.
STILL GROWING STRONG, I SEE.
JESSICA--?
FOR YOU.
ONE OF YOUR VERY OWN.
Beacon Academy.
-CLICK-

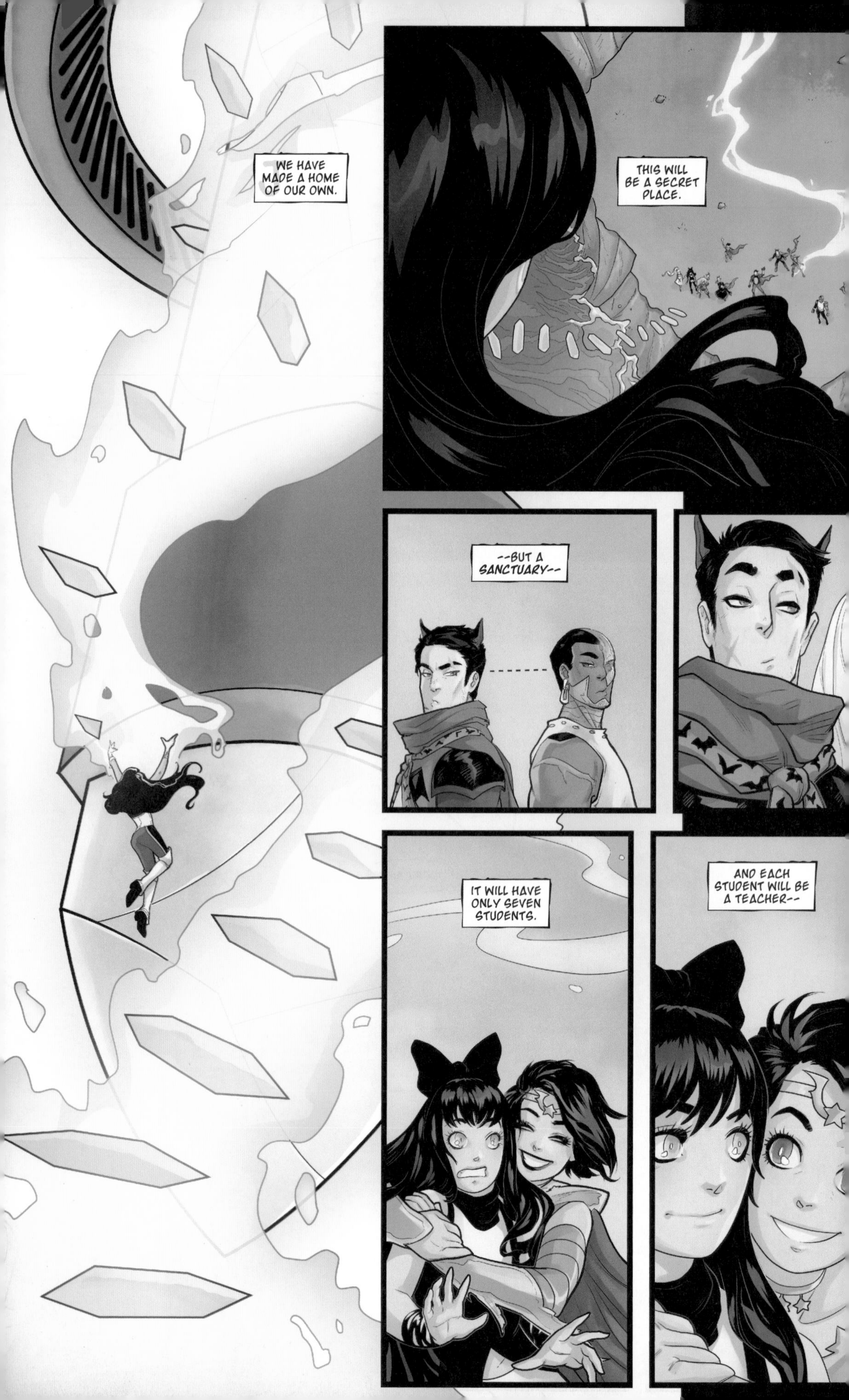
WE HAVE MADE A HOME OF OUR OWN.
THIS WILL BE A SECRET PLACE.
--BUT A SANCTUARY--
IT WILL HAVE ONLY SEVEN STUDENTS.
AND EACH STUDENT WILL BE A TEACHER--

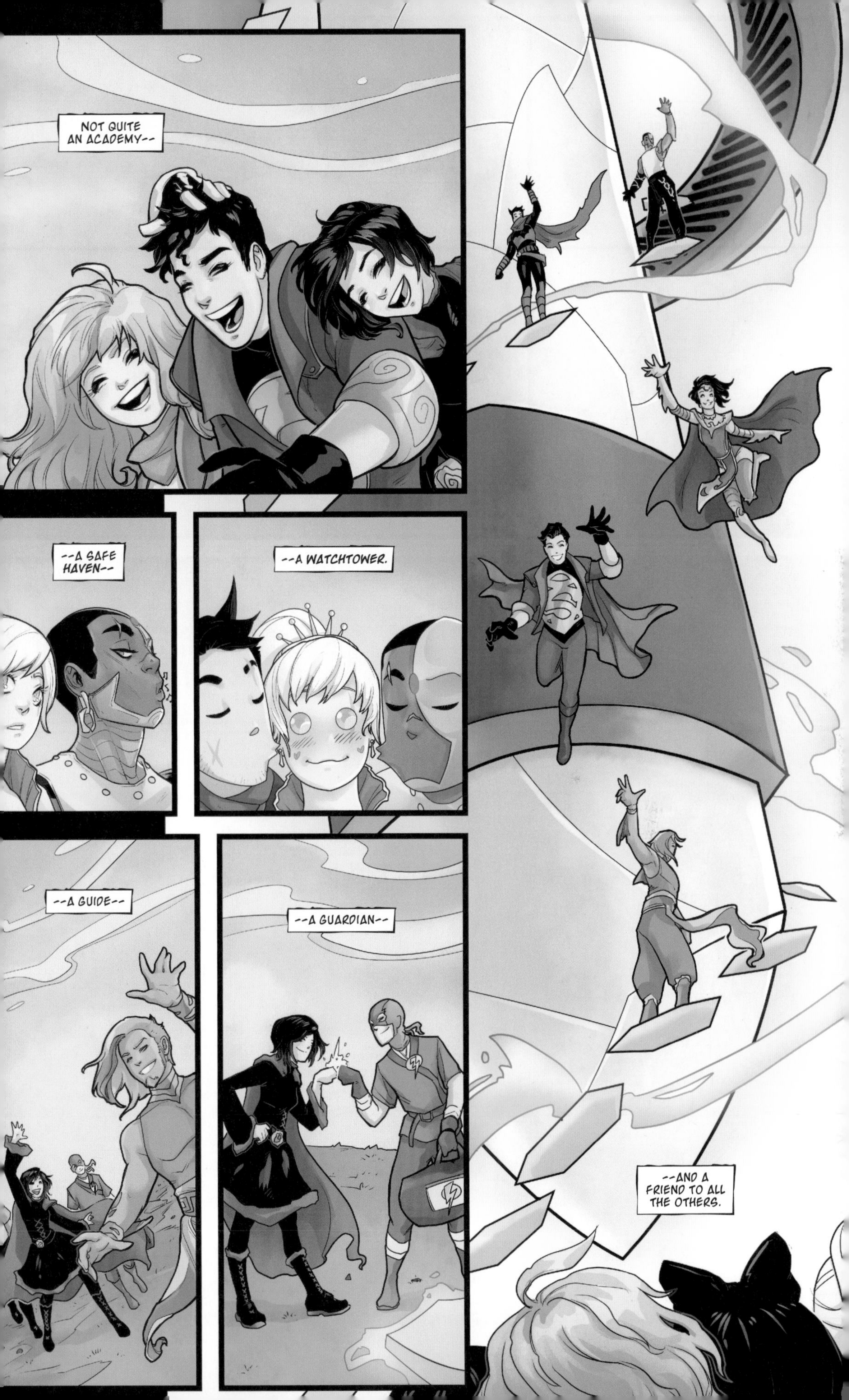
NOT QUITE
AN ACADEMY--
--A SAFE
HAVEN--
--A WATCHTOWER.
--A GUIDE--
--A GUARDIAN--
--AND A
FRIEND TO ALL
THE OTHERS.

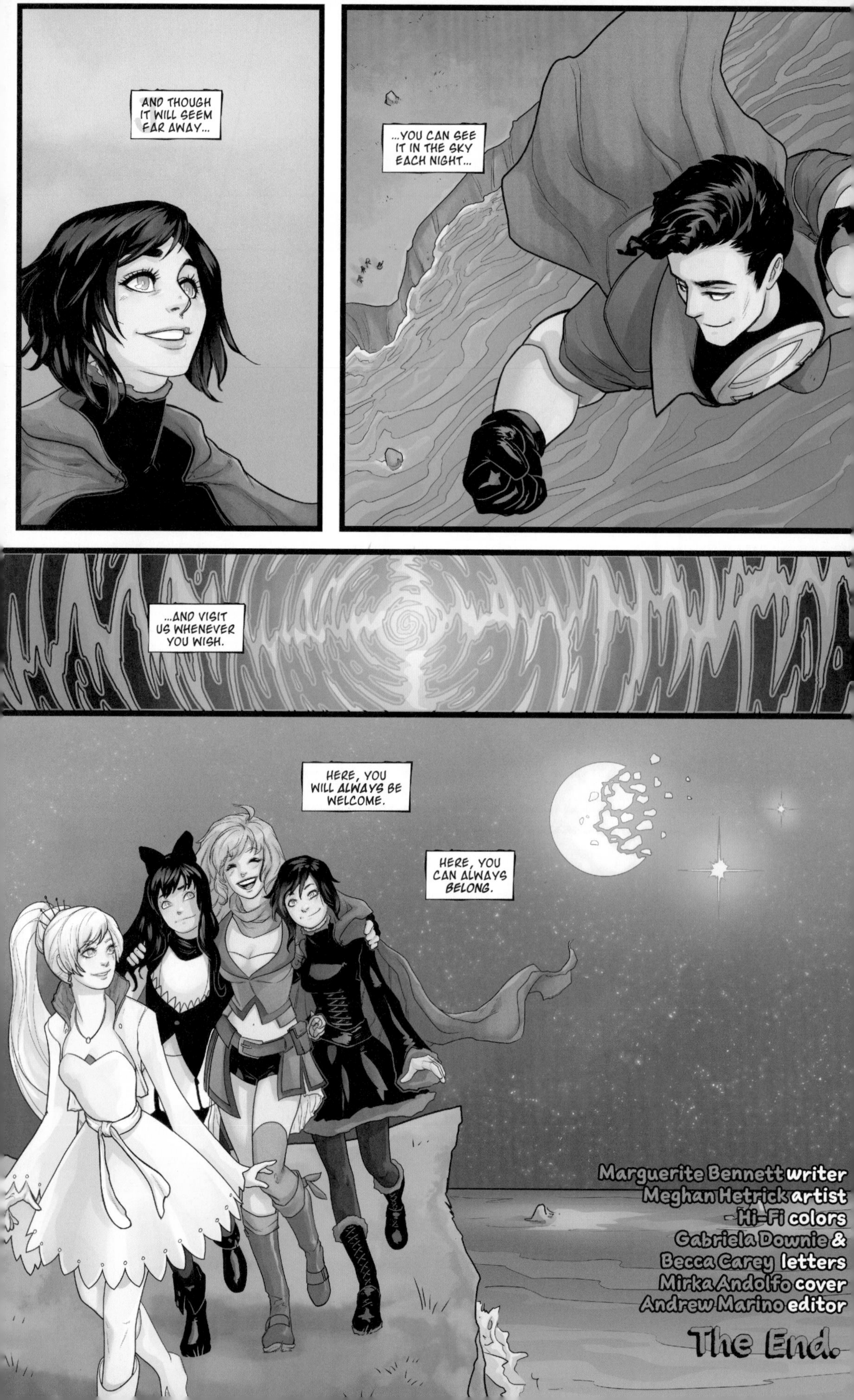
AND THOUGH IT WILL SEEM FAR AWAY...
...YOU CAN SEE IT IN THE SKY EACH NIGHT...
...AND VISIT US WHENEVER YOU WISH.
HERE, YOU WILL ALWAYS BE WELCOME.
HERE, YOU CAN ALWAYS BELONG.
Marguerite Bennett writer
Meghan Hetrick artist
Hi-Fi colors
Gabriela Downie & Becca Carey letters
Mirka Andolfo cover
Andrew Marino editor
The End.

RWBY
JUSTICE LEAGUE

The Design Sketchbook of **MIRKA ANDOLFO**

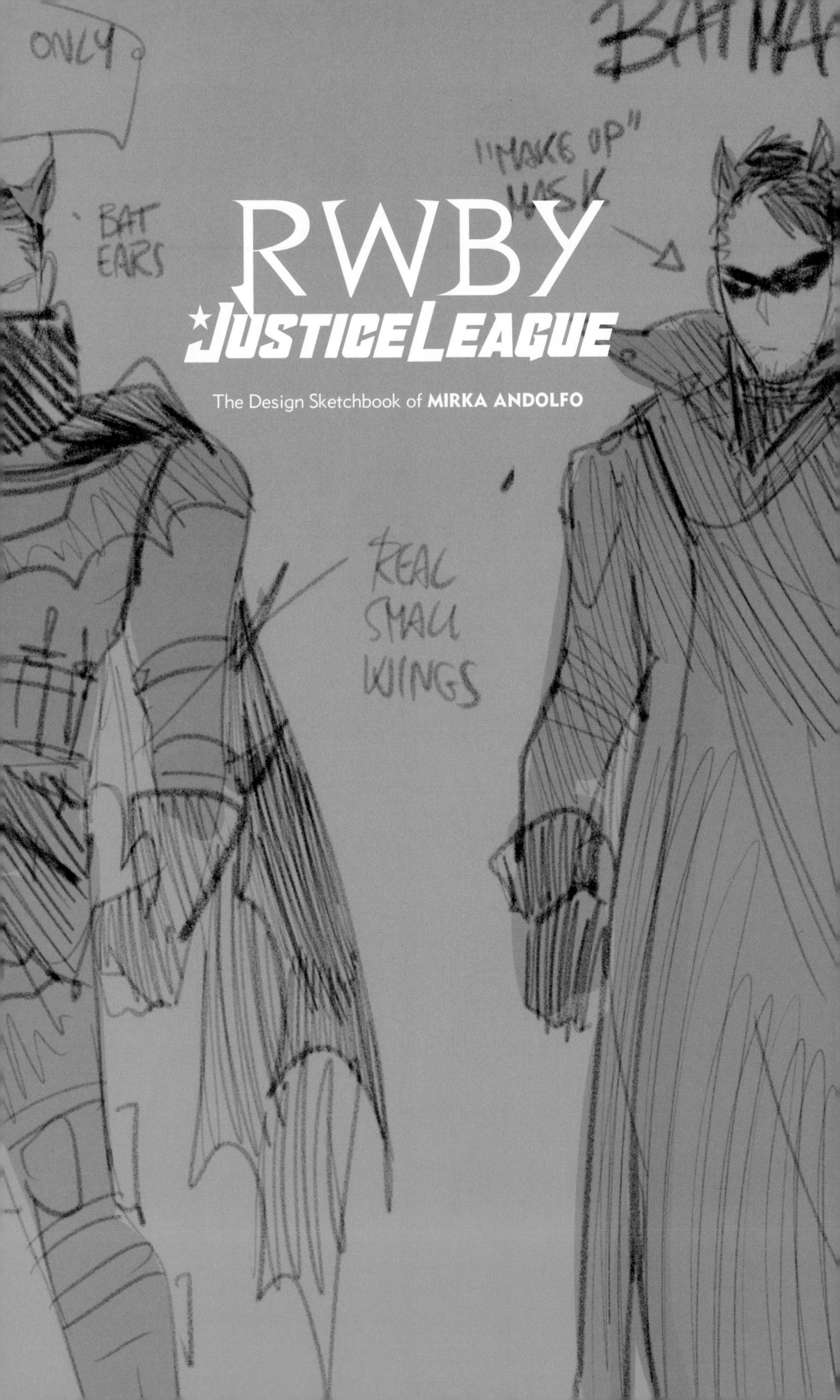
ONLY
BAT EARS
"MAKE UP" MASK
REAL SMALL WINGS

Wonder Woman design by **MIRKA ANDOLFO**

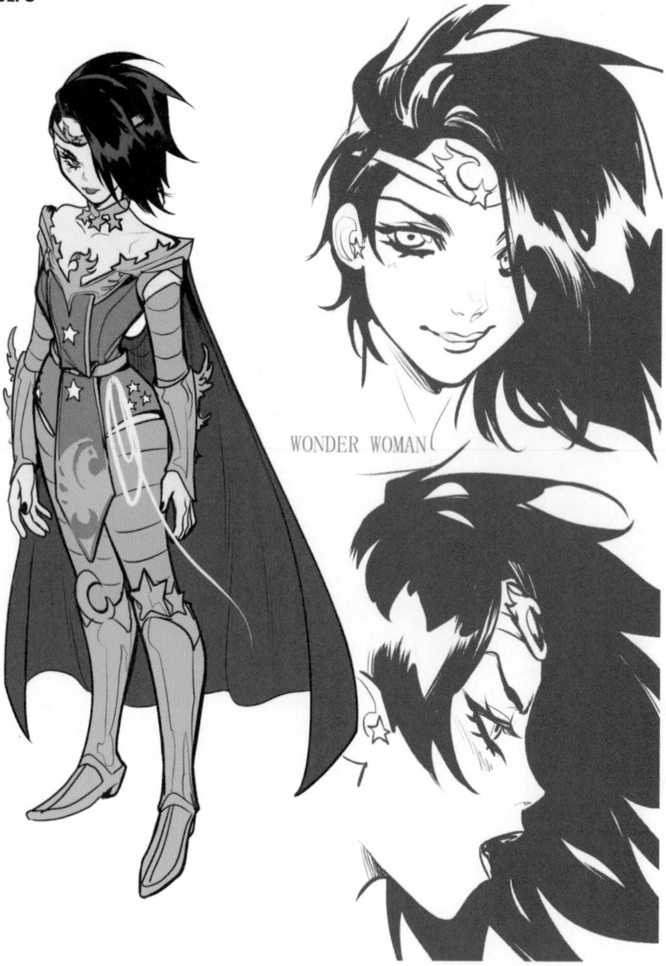
WONDER WOMAN

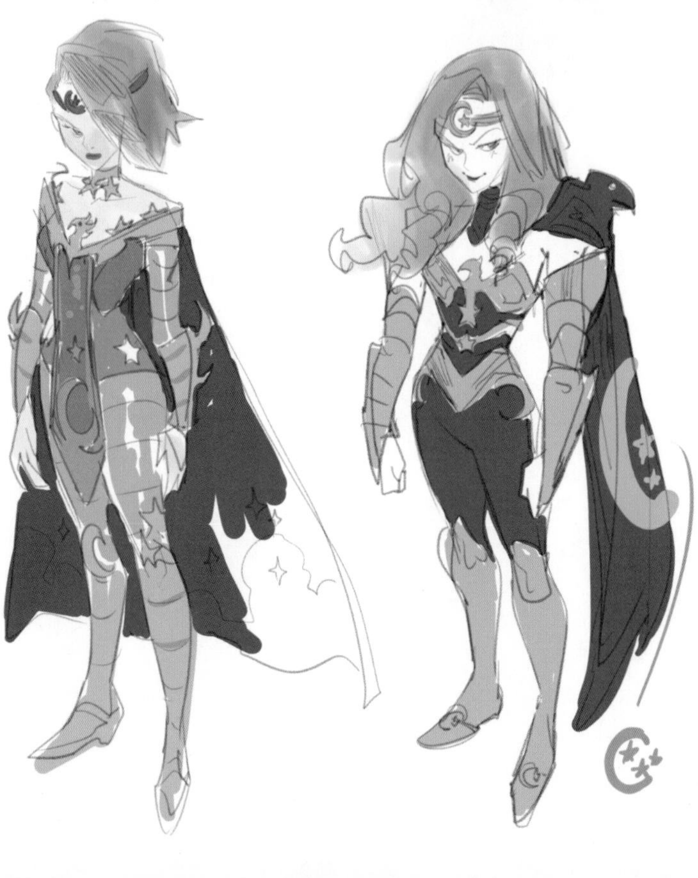

Superman design by **MIRKA ANDOLFO**

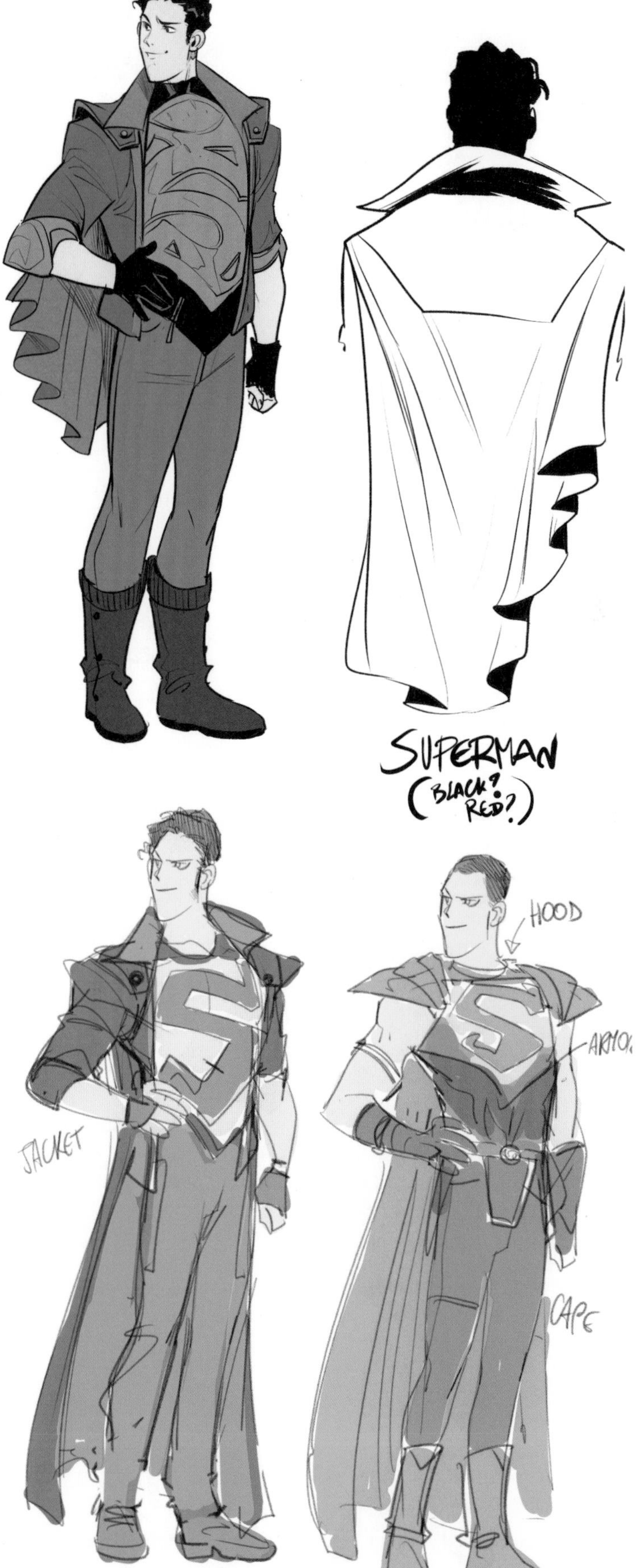
SUPERMAN
(BLACK? RED?)
HOOD
ARMO
JACKET
CAPE

Batman design by **MIRKA ANDOLFO**

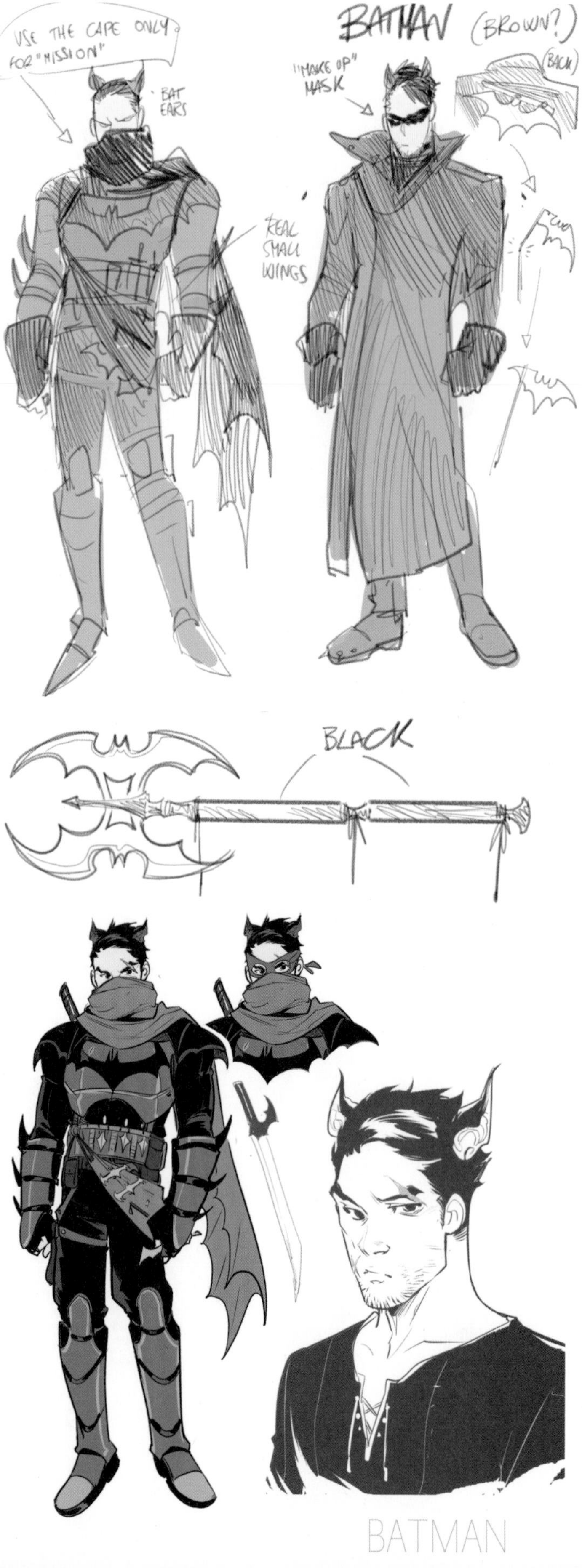
USE THE CAPE ONLY FOR "MISSION"
BAT EARS
REAL SMALL WINGS
BATMAN (BROWN?)
"MAKE UP" MASK
(BACK)
BLACK
BATMAN

Cyborg design by **MIRKA ANDOLFO**

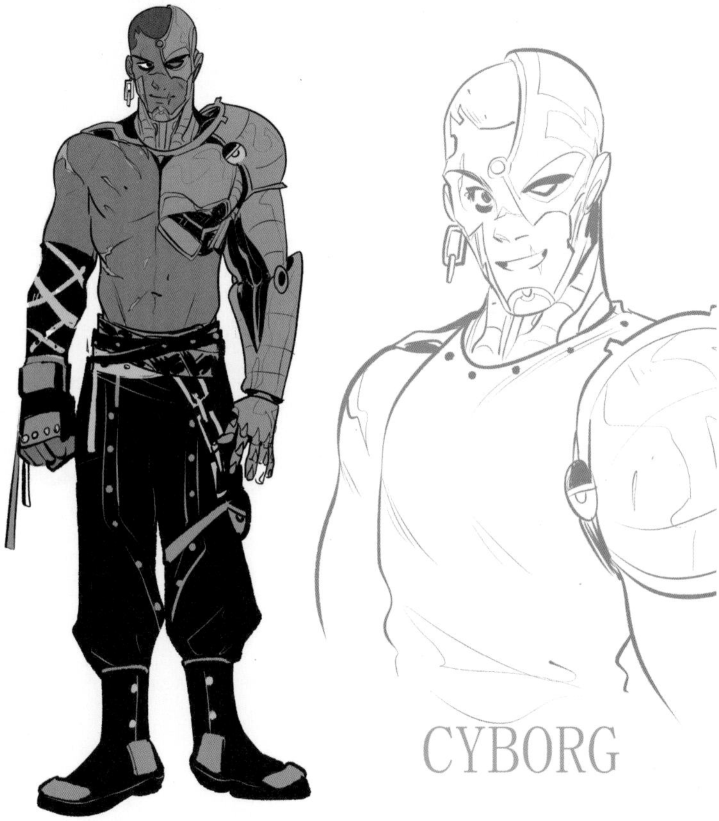
CYBORG

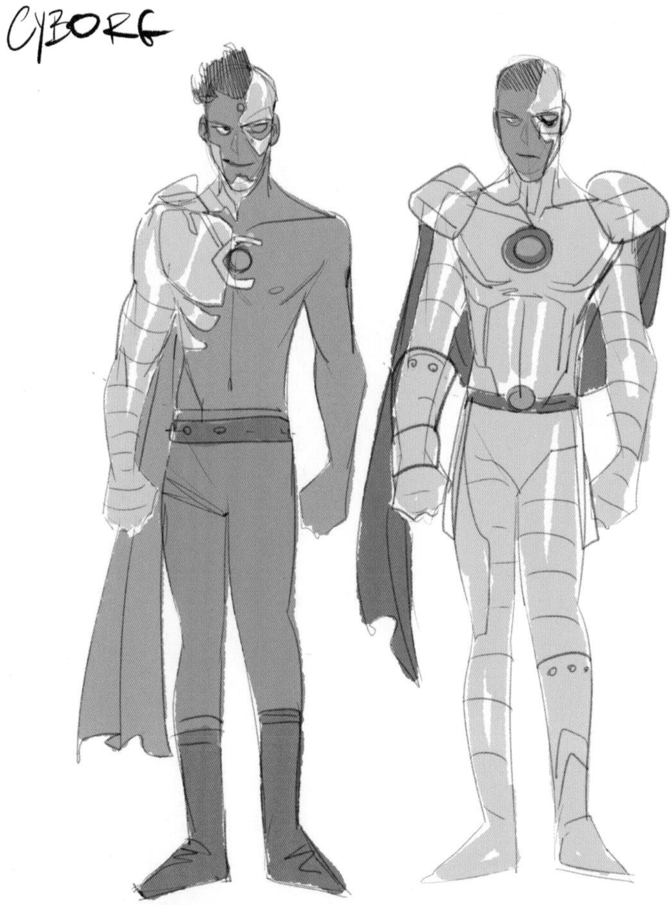
CYBORG

Flash design by **MIRKA ANDOLFO**

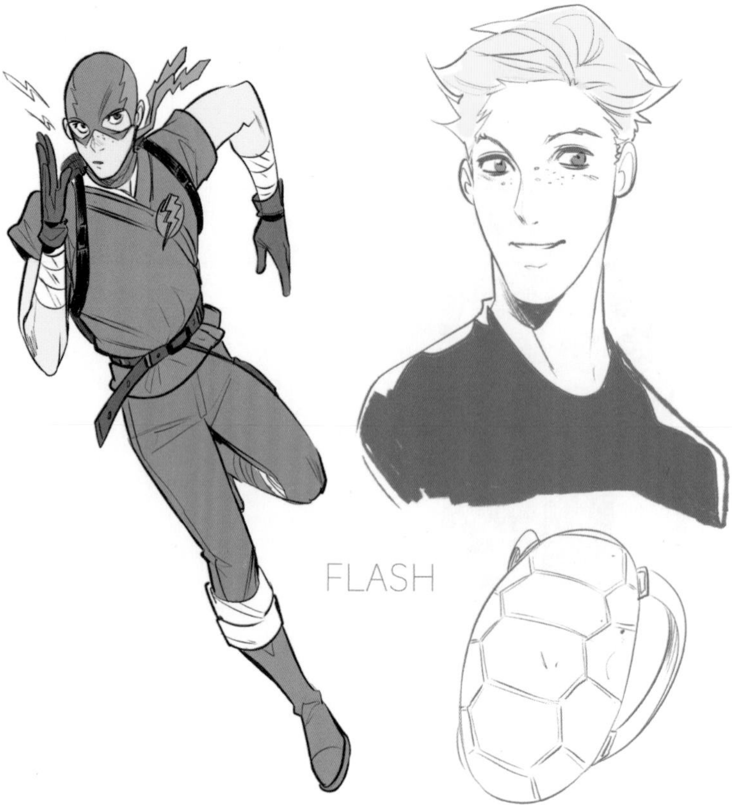
FLASH

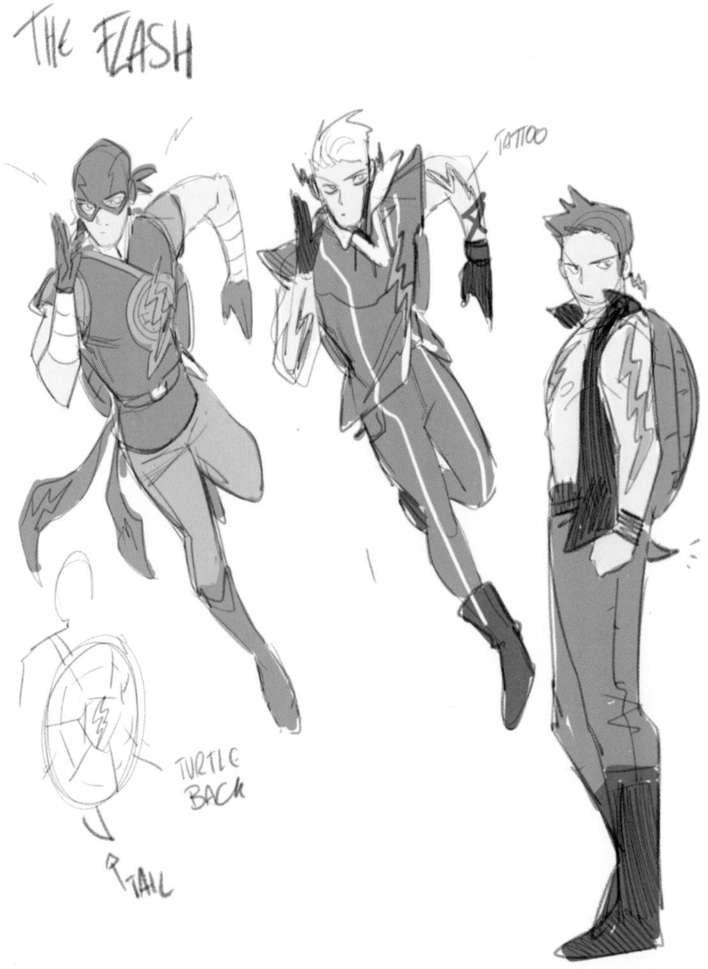
THE FLASH
TATTOO
TURTLE BACK
TAIL

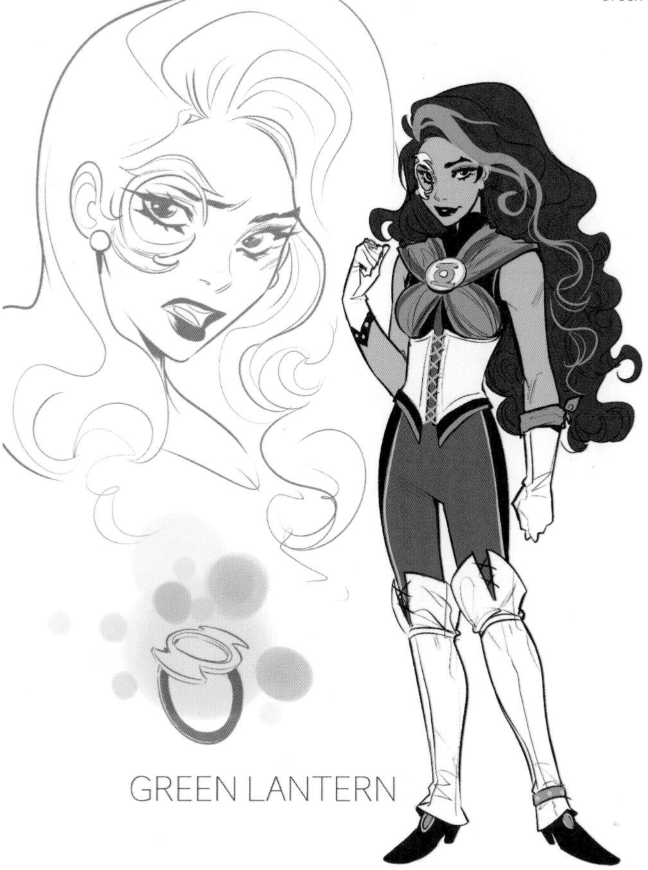
GREEN LANTERN

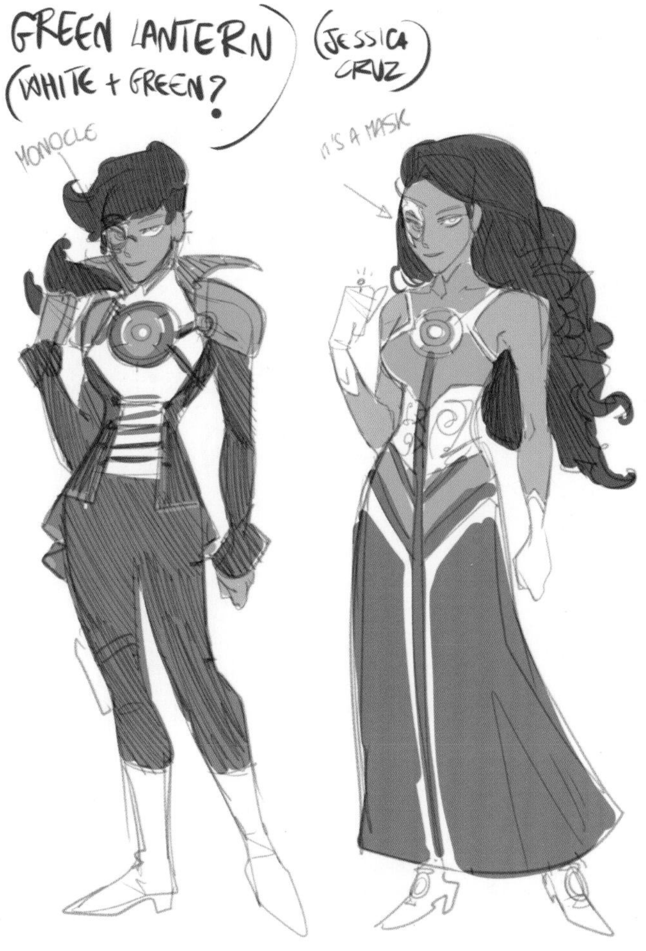
GREEN LANTERN
(WHITE + GREEN?
(JESSICA CRUZ)
MONOCLE
IT'S A MASK

Aquaman design by **MIRKA ANDOLFO**

AQUAMAN

AQUAMAN
(BLUE
PURPLE BLUE?)

Cover sketch and final cover by **MIRKA ANDOLFO**

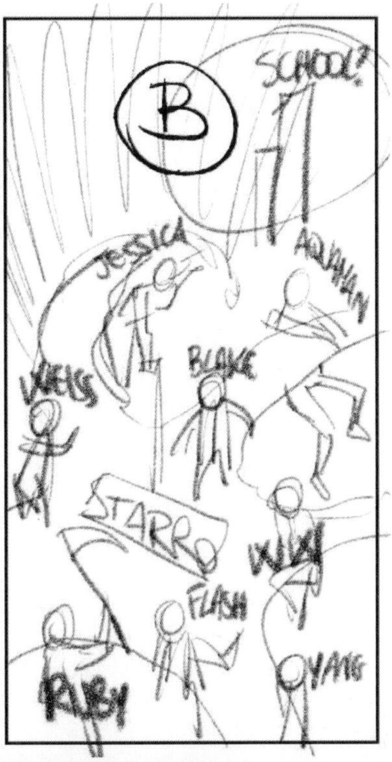
B
SCHOOL?
JESSICA
AQUAMAN
BLAKE
WEISS
STARRO
FLASH
RUBY
YANG

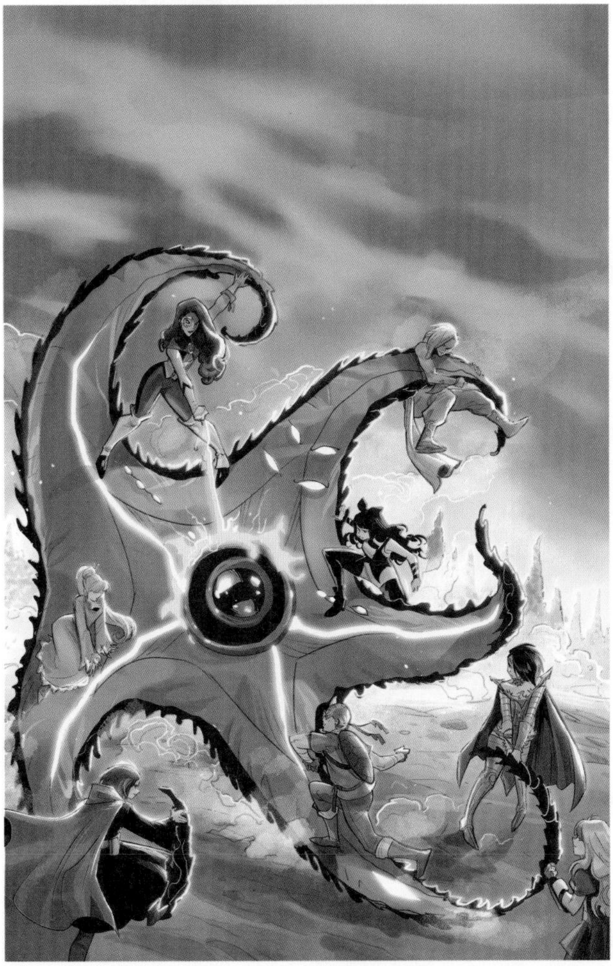

JUSTICE LEAGUE

VOL. 1: ORIGIN
GEOFF JOHNS and JIM LEE

THE NEW YORK TIMES BESTSELLER

THE NEW 52!

JUSTICE LEAGUE

VOLUME 1 ORIGIN

"WRITTEN BY GEOFF JOHNS WITH ART BY THE GODLY JIM LEE. JUSTICE LEAGUE IS A MUST READ."
— COMPLEX MAGAZINE

GEOFF **JOHNS** · JIM **LEE** · SCOTT **WILLIAMS**

JUSTICE LEAGUE
VOL. 2: THE VILLAIN'S JOURNEY

JUSTICE LEAGUE
VOL. 3: THRONE OF ATLANTIS

Get more DC graphic novels wherever comics and books are sold!